1991

Beethoven and the
Creative Process

Beethoven
and the
Creative Process

BARRY COOPER

CLARENDON PRESS · OXFORD

1990

Oxford University Press, Walton Street, Oxford OX2 6DP
Oxford New York Toronto
Delhi Bombay Calcutta Madras Karachi
Petaling Jaya Singapore Hong Kong Tokyo
Nairobi Dar es Salaam Cape Town
Melbourne Auckland
and associated companies in
Berlin Ibadan

Oxford is a trade mark of Oxford University Press

Published in the United States
by Oxford University Press, New York

© Barry Cooper 1990

British Library Cataloguing in Publication Data
Cooper, Barry
Beethoven and the creative process.
1. German music. Beethoven, Ludwig van. Critical studies.
I. Title
780'.92'4
ISBN 0–19–816163–8

Library of Congress Cataloging in Publication Data
Cooper, Barry (Barry A. R.)
Beethoven and the creative process/Barry Cooper.
Bibliography: p.
Includes indexes.
1. Beethoven, Ludwig van, 1770-1827—Sources. I. Title.
ML410.B4C74 1989 89-32325 780'.92—dc20
ISBN 0-19-816163-8:

Typeset by The Alden Press

Printed in Great Britain by
Biddles Ltd.
Guildford and King's Lynn

To
Susan Catherine

Acknowledgements

I WISH to record here my thanks to all those who have helped in any way towards the preparation and publication of this book. First I should like to thank Joseph Kerman and Alan Tyson, who originally introduced me to Beethoven's sketches in a series of graduate seminars at Oxford University in 1972–3 and who kindly continued to take an active interest in my work long after the course was finished. In particular I have continued to benefit from many valuable and fruitful discussions with Alan Tyson, whose own extensive work on Beethoven has set extremely high standards that cannot be matched here.

Other Beethoven scholars who are to be thanked for having been of assistance at some point include William Meredith, William Kinderman, Lewis Lockwood, William Drabkin, Nicholas Marston, and Sieghard Brandenburg. I am also indebted to the latter in his capacity as Director of the Beethoven-Archiv in Bonn, and to his predecessor Martin Staehelin and the rest of the staff there, for allowing me access to manuscripts in the archive and for providing me with excellent working conditions. Similarly to be thanked are the staff at other libraries including the Gesellschaft der Musikfreunde in Vienna, the Musikabteilung of the Staatsbibliothek Preussischer Kulturbesitz in Berlin, the British Library in London, and the Bibliothèque Nationale in Paris; and M. Camatte, Director of the Tours Conservatoire, who kindly supplied me with photocopies of the Beethoven sketches held there.

I am also grateful to Anthony Mulgan and Bruce Phillips of Oxford University Press for the helpful discussions about the shape and content of this book, and to three readers who read my typescript anonymously and made several valuable comments and suggestions that have been adopted. Particular thanks must also go to the Royal Society of Edinburgh, who funded a one-year research fellowship that enabled me to complete the work.

Finally I am especially grateful to my wife Susan, to whom the book is dedicated, for providing abstracts of several relevant publications, for her unfailing enthusiasm and encouragement, and for all her support throughout the project.

Contents

List of Facsimiles

Abbreviations

Abbreviations for titles of individual books appear in the Bibliography.

A-	Letter no. in Anderson, *Letters* (see Bibliography)
AcM	*Acta Musicologica*
BeJ	*Beethoven-Jahrbuch*
BS	*Beethoven Studies*
FAM	*Fontes artis musicae*
GdM	Gesellschaft der Musikfreunde in Wien
Hess	Item no. in Hess, *Verzeichnis* (see Bibliography)
JAMS	*Journal of the American Musicological Society*
JRMA	*Journal of the Royal Musical Association*
ML	*Music & Letters*
MQ	*The Musical Quarterly*
MR	*The Music Review*
MT	*The Musical Times*
NCM	*19th-Century Music*
ÖMz	*Österreichische Musikzeitschrift*
PRMA	*Proceedings of the Royal Musical Association*
SBH	Item no. in Schmidt, SBH (see Bibliography)
SPK	Staatsbibliothek Preussischer Kulturbesitz, Berlin
SV	Item no. in Schmidt, SV (see Bibliography)
WoO	Werk ohne Opuszahl (work without opus number) as listed in KH (see Bibliography)

Note on the Transcriptions

As explained in Chapter 7, many of Beethoven's sketches are difficult to decipher and in places it is impossible to be certain precisely what he intended. The accuracy of the transcriptions therefore cannot be guaranteed in all cases, although every effort has been made to reproduce faithfully what he appears to have intended. In places where there is great doubt, a question mark has sometimes been placed above the relevant note, but this should not be taken to imply that there is no doubt about adjacent notes. In certain cases a named pitch is placed editorially above a note: for example, if the note looks like a B in the sketch but a C was perhaps intended, then 'c?' is placed above a printed B. To aid in the reading of the sketches, certain other notes and signs have been added editorially, especially in places where Beethoven's intentions are clear to the author but might not be to the reader. These additions are all placed in square brackets or indicated by standard conventions—dotted barlines and crossed slurs and ties. In many cases, however, Beethoven's notation has been left incomplete or even inaccurate so that its ambiguities may be seen as they stand. Angle brackets ⟨ ⟩ are used to denote material deleted by Beethoven in the original. The extracts do not indicate whether they start at the beginning of a sketch or in the middle, but where a sketch continues beyond the passage quoted, '[etc.]' is placed at the end of the extract; it is not to be confused with 'etc' (without brackets or full stop), which is sometimes used by Beethoven at the end of a sketch.

PROLOGUE: Approaching Beethoven's Creative Process

THE creative process of any composer is always to a certain extent shrouded in mystery. Even the composer himself will not fully understand the psychological processes by which ideas occur to him, nor remember afterwards exactly how he put a piece of music together. The problems of understanding how Beethoven composed are even greater than those with a living composer, and any attempt to present a complete picture of his compositional activity must be doomed. Nevertheless more than enough relevant documents survive for us to be able to gain considerable insight on the subject. In fact there is so much source material that it will take years for it all to be thoroughly examined, and any conclusions reached here must be somewhat provisional; but it is still useful to bring together now what is currently known on the subject. Much has of course been written on it already, and a traditional picture of his compositional process (derived chiefly from nineteenth-century studies by Gustav Nottebohm) has existed for many years. But this picture, which portrays Beethoven as a slow and laborious worker who composed with great difficulty, has been modified in recent years by more detailed research. Hence one of the aims of the present study is to establish a more up-to-date but comprehensive view, based on a more wide-ranging and detailed assessment of the sources than was possible in Nottebohm's day. Another aim is to see what were Beethoven's chief compositional goals, and what difficulties he had to overcome in order to achieve them.

The sources that throw light on these and related questions come in a variety of forms, including letters written by (and to) Beethoven, other writings of his (diaries, memoranda, etc.), conversation books, memoirs and accounts by his contemporaries, and similar documents. The music itself can also, by its own structure, provide clues as to how it was put together. But by far the most informative sources are the numerous rough drafts and sketches that Beethoven made for his compositions. Around 8,000 pages of such sketches still survive,[1] in addition to all the preliminary, cancelled versions of passages which can be found in the surviving autograph scores and which could also be called sketches in the broadest sense. All these sketches show his works in the actual course of being created, and they are therefore central to any understanding of his creative process.

---

[1] See Schmidt, SV, p. 7; Schmidt's total of over 7,500 pages has been supplemented by various additional discoveries since 1968.

Perhaps the two most fundamental questions that can be asked about Beethoven's creative process are why he composed and how he composed. As Beethoven himself expressed it, in another context: 'Let us begin with the primary original causes of all things, how something came about, wherefore and why it came about in that particular way and became what it is.'[2] Both the 'why' and the 'how' questions can be asked either generally, about Beethoven as a composer, or specifically, about a particular piece. Thus it can be asked why he composed at all, and why he composed a particular work at a particular time and in a particular way. Such questions form the basis of Part I of the present book. Similarly it can be asked both how he composed in general, and how he composed certain works in particular. These questions form the basis of Parts II and III. Why and how are not altogether independent lines of enquiry. One can ask why, say, *Fidelio* was composed, and find musical, extramusical, and professional reasons why Beethoven wrote it. But when one asks more detailed questions about why it ends in C major, is scored for particular forces, or (at the most detailed level) why particular notes occur where they do, the answer lies in Beethoven's aesthetic sense; and this was brought into sharpest focus in the sketches, where he was constantly having to select between alternative versions and ideas, and where we can now see what other directions the music might have taken. Hence an understanding of how the work was composed helps to explain 'why it came about in that particular way and became what it is', to use Beethoven's words again. Some of the more general conclusions reached will hardly be unexpected, but it is at least reassuring to find out that Beethoven's masterpieces, like any documents of comparable complexity, reached their final form only after much planning, drafting, reworking, additions, excisions, and last-minute amendments.

First let us examine the different types of sources to establish what sorts of information each type can provide, and what are their limitations and pitfalls. Of nearly 1,600 known letters of Beethoven, about a quarter make some kind of reference to his compositional activity, and it is misleading to say that 'he wrote almost exclusively letters that concerned everyday affairs and the sale and publication of his works'.[3] But many of his references to composing are brief and superficial. Some simply indicate that a certain work has been completed, thus providing valuable dating evidence but little more; and even these dates must be treated with caution, since works were often not as advanced on paper as his letters imply.[4] His letters are, none the less, often the most reliable means of dating the composition of a work, and are

---

[2] A-1068.   [3] Unger, 'Workshop', p. 323; cf. also TF, p. 247.

[4] See e.g. A-1085, where he refers to a quartet as 'not quite finished' even before he had started sketching it; A-1106, where he describes a new Mass as 'not yet finished' although he only ever made a few sketches for it; and A-1159, where he says the Ninth Symphony will be finished in a fortnight, although other evidence indicates he had not at that time finished even the first movement and took nearly a year to complete the work.

a much better guide to chronology than opus numbers, which indicate only an approximate order of publication (rather than composition) and contain many anomalies.[5] The letters may equally refer to periods of inactivity in his composing—mostly caused by illness, but sometimes due to other distractions such as preparing concerts, legal action concerning his nephew, or demands by his patron Archduke Rudolph for frequent lessons.[6] Other interruptions were caused by such things as the French invasion of Vienna in 1809,[7] and even the effects of champagne or bad weather.[8]

The letters also include quite a few details about the final stages of composition (e.g. correction and amendment lists, metronome marks, and notational problems), and about works he was planning to write—these are often mentioned in response to a request from someone for a particular type of piece. In addition Beethoven made a number of statements about his artistic aims and the role of the artist (see Chapter 2), and occasionally made general comments about his creativity—for example, he mentioned that he often produced three or four works at the same time,[9] and that he had to 'scrawl' for money to support himself while he wrote a great work.[10] He rarely, however, wrote anything about the initial conception of new works. The letter about the canon 'O Tobias' (WoO 182), a piece which he said originally occurred to him in a dream while on a journey and which he elaborated and wrote out the following day,[11] is quite exceptional in the way it describes both the mental processes and the external circumstances surrounding the creation of the work.

Direct references to his sketches are so rare in his letters that each case is worth mentioning individually. In 1794 he wrote that he was planning to make a fair copy of a sonata (WoO 51) because the original draft was 'practically only a sketch' ('fast nur Skizze').[12] He used a similar phrase ('beinah nur Skizze') for the original score of some Scottish folksong settings, Op. 108.[13] In about March 1814, when he was working on the revision to *Fidelio*, he reported that before a recent concert on 27 February he had 'just made a few sketches here and there'.[14] And a few days before his death he reported that he had sketched a new symphony (the unfinished Tenth).[15]

More elliptical references to his sketches are only slightly commoner. When a collection of fifty-three folksong settings sent to the Edinburgh publisher George Thomson had apparently been lost in the post, Beethoven said that he had been forced to complete 'my first ideas which still remained in manuscript, and to make so to speak the same composition twice',[16] implying there was some kind of rough draft to work from. When he feared

---

[5] WoO numbers are of even less help: WoO 63 was probably his first piece and WoO 62 his last!   [6] A-1167.

[7] A-220.   [8] A-1427 and A-1303.   [9] A-51.   [10] A-903.

[11] A-1056.   [12] A-9; KH, p. 497.   [13] A-1063; KH, p. 310.

[14] A-479.   [15] A-1566.   [16] A-319.

that the Quartet Op. 132 had been lost, however, he observed that the ideas ('das Concept') were only jotted down on small scraps of paper and that he would not be able to compose the work the same again,[17] thus implying that the sketches were much more fragmentary on this occasion. Another reference to early drafting occurs in connection with the three piano sonatas Opp. 109–11. Of Op. 109 Beethoven says: 'On account of my ailing condition I had written down the draft more fully than usual.' But normally he would merely 'jot down certain ideas . . . and when I have completed the whole in my head, everything is written down, but only once.'[18] The latter part of this statement is actually rather misleading as it stands, since he clearly did not normally work everything out in his head before beginning to write out a final score; but he means that there was usually only one complete draft apart from all the sketches and rejected material. On another occasion he referred to his habit of writing down his first ideas at once, even if they came to nothing,[19] thereby indicating that amongst his sketches were many unused ideas. And in 1819 he mentioned that there were in his desk several compositions that he hoped to 'work out' later,[20] which again implies the existence of some kind of preliminary drafts or sketches.

One further reference to his working methods that appears in his letters comes in some instructions on composition sent to Archduke Rudolph in 1823. Assuming Beethoven practised what he preached—and there is considerable evidence that he did[21]—we have here quite a detailed account of certain aspects of his composing methods, and it is worth quoting at length.

Your Imperial Highness must now continue, in particular, your exercises in composition and when sitting at the pianoforte you should jot down your ideas in the form of sketches. For this purpose you should have a small table beside the pianoforte. In this way not only is one's imagination stimulated but one learns also to pin down immediately the most remote ideas. You should also compose without a pianoforte; and you should sometimes work out a simply melody, for instance, a chorale with simple and again with different harmonies according to the laws of counterpoint and even neglecting the latter. This will certainly not give Your Imperial Highness a headache; nay, rather, it will afford you real enjoyment when you thus find yourself in the very swim of artistic production.—Gradually there comes to us the power to express just what we desire and feel; and to the nobler type of human being this is such an essential need.[22]

Thus we can gather from Beethoven's letters that he certainly made sketches for many of his works. But we learn virtually nothing about the nature of those sketches—how many there were for each work, what types of sketches there were, the thought-processes that he went through as he planned a work, in what order he composed the various parts of a work, and similar questions. The same conclusions apply with his other non-musical writings. Many of them, including his memorandum book of 1792–4 (the

[17] A-1410; TDR, v. 542.   [19] A-558.   [21] JTW, pp. 4–6.
[18] A-1060.   [20] A-948.   [22] A-1203.

so-called *Jugendtagebuch*), make no references to his activity as a composer. His other *Tagebuch*, of 1812–18, is somewhat larger and much more diverse in content, but only a small proportion of it is concerned with composition. The only mention of his sketches is a reference to dividing up his musical manuscripts into various types including 'sketchbooks'.[23] In addition he made two other slightly puzzling references to his compositional process: 'Certainly one writes more beautifully as soon as one writes for the public, even when one writes rapidly'; and 'The best opening phrases in canons are built around harmonies';[24] but the former remark could refer to handwriting rather than musical style. However, the *Tagebuch* also contains several references to Beethoven's determination to sacrifice everything to his art, to study hard, and to leave Vienna in order to compose better,[25] and there are a few references to planned compositions—a hymn, an opera, a symphony, a choral cantata, and church music in general.[26] Since the *Tagebuch* was a private record, these ideas were certainly profound intentions and not just empty promises such as might be made to a demanding publisher, and they reveal what sort of music he really wanted to write. Thus the *Tagebuch* is of limited help in understanding his creative process, but it is by no means negligible.

The 140 surviving conversation books are likewise of limited use, but for rather different reasons. Their main drawback is that they normally only include one side of the conversations, for Beethoven would reply orally to the remarks written down by his friends. Moreover, most of the conversations are about such mundane matters as food and accommodation, and when music is mentioned it is often in connection with concerts or rehearsals rather than composition. Occasionally, however, the conversations contain clues about compositions—for example, indications that new works were being composed by a particular date, or (in one case) a reference to the otherwise unknown canon 'Hol euch der Teufel' (WoO 173).[27] Beethoven himself also made numerous entries in the books. A few times he wrote down his side of the conversation—presumably when he did not want to be overheard—but more often his entries are memoranda of various kinds; sometimes they are trivial matters such as shopping items or copies of newspaper advertisements, but a few are musical ideas and sketches for various works in progress. Thus the conversation books are often most revealing where they have been used in this way rather than for their proper purpose, while actual conversations imply quite a lot but allow frustratingly little to be deduced with certainty about his compositions.

After Beethoven's death several of his personal acquaintances wrote accounts and memoirs of their association with him, and many of them have something to say about his composing activity. Some, including Ferdinand

---

[23] Solomon, 'Tagebuch', no. 51.
[24] Ibid., nos. 16 (translation amended) and 37.
[25] Ibid., nos. 25, 40, 41, 48, 119, 169.
[26] Ibid., nos. 41, 84, 116, 119, 153, 162, 168.
[27] KH, pp. 678–9; TF, p. 744.

Ries, Carl Czerny, and Anton Schindler, knew him for an extended period of time, while others, such as J. R. Schulz, Louis Schlösser and Friedrich Rochlitz, wrote about their experiences of him after only a brief visit. Needless to say, some had more accurate memories than others; and while many attempted to report as accurately as they could, some were prone to deliberate distortion and fabrication. Most prominent in the latter category is Schindler, who not only made numerous errors and deliberate distortions, but even went to the trouble of inserting over 600 fake entries in Beethoven's conversation books after the composer's death—entries which were identified as spurious only quite recently.[28] Schindler's biography of Beethoven is therefore of very little use in understanding the composer's creative process.

Another writer with little regard for accuracy is Schlösser. His reminiscences include a supposedly verbatim report of what Beethoven said on one occasion about his creative process. This report has been widely quoted, yet it was almost certainly Schlösser's own invention, as has been demonstrated by Maynard Solomon.[29] Certain other writers, however, are much more reliable, for example Ries and Karl Holz. Occasionally they might make a mistake about a date (it is easier to recall what happened in an incident than precisely when it happened), but they seem never to have deliberately distorted, and many of their reminiscences are corroborated by independent evidence.

Clearly, then, it is often difficult to establish which writers and which accounts can be relied on; but where several witnesses have reported roughly the some observations we can be fairly sure that they are substantially accurate. And where there are differences it is sometimes possible to reconcile them. Consider three accounts of Beethoven's working day:

Beethoven rose every morning the year round at dawn and went directly to his desk. There he would work until two or three o'clock, his habitual dinner hour. In the course of the morning he would usually go out of doors once or twice, but would continue to work as he walked. These walks would seldom last more than an hour, and may be compared to a bee's excursions to gather honey. Beethoven would go out in every season, heeding neither cold nor heat. His afternoons were regularly spent in long walks. Late in the afternoon he would go to a favourite tavern to read the papers, unless he had already satisfied this need in a coffee-house.... Beethoven always spent his winter evenings at home reading serious works of literature. Only very rarely did he work with musical scores during the evening, for the strain on his eyes was too great. It may have been otherwise in his youth, but we know that he never composed at night. He would go to bed at ten o'clock at the latest.[30]

Thayer's account of Beethoven's life at his brother's estate in Gneixendorf in 1826, apparently derived direct from Beethoven's servant Michael Krenn, is similar in many ways:

[28] The identification was first made by Peter Stadlen; see also Beck and Herre, 'Schindler', where all the fake entries are transcribed.   [29] Solomon, 'Invention'.
[30] Schindler/MacArdle, *Beethoven*, pp. 385–6.

It was Beethoven's custom to get up at half-past 5 o'clock, seat himself at a table and write while he beat time with hands and feet and sang. . . . The family breakfast was eaten at half-past 7 o'clock, after which Beethoven hurried out into the open air, rambled across the fields shouting and waving his arms, sometimes walking very rapidly, sometimes very slowly and stopping at times to write in a sort of pocket-book. . . . At half-past 12 Beethoven would come home for dinner, after which he went to his room until about 3 o'clock; then he roamed over the fields until shortly before sunset, after which he never went out of doors. Supper was at half-past 7, and after eating he went to his room, wrote till 10 o'clock and then went to bed.[31]

Ignaz von Seyfried gives a slightly different version of the routine:

The whole forenoon, from the first ray of light till the meal hour, was devoted to mechanical labour, i.e. to transcribing; the rest of the day was given to thought and the ordering of ideas. Hardly had he put the last bit in his mouth before he began his customary promenade. . . that is to say, he hurried in double-quick time several times around the city, as if urged on by a goad; and this, let the weather be what it might.[32]

The three witnesses agree that Beethoven spent much of his time on long walks, regardless of the weather, but whether his periods indoors were before breakfast and after lunch (Krenn), during much of the morning (Schindler), or during the whole morning (Seyfried) is unclear. The differences in the accounts may have occurred because the authors were observing Beethoven at different stages of his life; but all three give the impression of a regular and well-ordered routine. Yet against these accounts must be balanced Czerny's report:

Beethoven had no fixed working hours. His active imagination was always at work, morning and afternoon, early and late. He would often get up at midnight, startling his neighbours with loud chords, thumping, singing, etc.[33]

It seems, than, that Beethoven had a sort of regular routine, but that it was often broken by particular circumstances and varied at different times of his life. Probably no two days were quite the same. There is general agreement, however, that much of his composing was done out of doors, particularly in later life; in addition to the accounts quoted above, several other witnesses refer to this habit, and to his habit of singing or humming while composing. Seyfried reports: 'He was never to be seen in the street without a small notebook, in which he jotted down whatever occurred to him at the moment.'[34] Similarly August von Klöber records: 'On my walks in Mödling I met Beethoven repeatedly, and it was most interesting to see how frequently he stopped, with a sheet of music-paper and a pencil-stump in his hands, as if listening, looked up and down and then scribbled notes on the

---

[31] TF, pp. 1007–8; cf. an entry of 1815 in Beethoven's *Tagebuch* (Solomon, 'Tagebuch', no. 48): 'Always study from half-past five until breakfast.'   [32] TF, p. 373.

[33] Czerny, *Performance*, p. 16.

[34] Quoted from Arnold and Fortune, *Companion*, p. 445; cf. TF, p. 372.

paper.'[35] Likewise Karl Braunthal: 'Now and then he took a second, sturdier notebook from his heart-pocket—I mean the left breast-pocket of a plain grey coat—and wrote with half-closed eyes.'[36] Ries refers to Beethoven's humming in an episode that happened in 1804: 'He had been all the time humming and sometimes howling, always up and down, without singing any definite notes. In answer to my question what it was he said: "A theme for the last movement of the sonata [Op. 57] has occurred to me."'[37] J. R. Schulz heard some similar humming in 1823: 'At other times he seemed quite lost in himself, and only hummed in an unintelligible manner. I understood, however, that this was the way he composed.'[38]

There is therefore quite a detailed picture of the external circumstances that surrounded Beethoven's composing acitivity; but it does derive almost exclusively from such eye-witness accounts. Beethoven hardly ever recorded the time of day at which he made a sketch, or the date or place: a note amongst some sketches of 1818 stating that they were 'written while walking in the evening between and on the mountains'[39] is most unusual. Thus we are forced to rely mainly on accounts and anecdotes of varying reliability when trying to establish where and when Beethoven did most of his composing.

As for his actual method of composing a piece, this could not be observed by his associates unless they either watched him very closely while he wrote sketches, or heard him composing at the piano. Nobody seems to have done the former, and although a few people heard him doing the latter, none of them recorded how he put a movement together. Treitschke, for example, referring to the composition of the aria 'Und spür' ich' in *Fidelio*, simply says that Beethoven 'seemed to conjure the motive of the aria' while sitting at the piano, and he gives no details.[40] And Beethoven himself made no explicit general statement on the subject (discounting the spurious statement reported by Schlösser).

The composer did, however, make something like a general statement about his creative process, but this comes in the form of a stylized representation in music.[41] The passage in question is, of course, the beginning of the finale of the Ninth Symphony, which is as specific and programmatic as anything he wrote. Three possible themes (from earlier movements) are in turn rejected by the bass instruments.[42] A fourth idea is then hit upon—a kind of preliminary version of the 'Freude' theme (bars 77–80)—and is then refined to form the 'Freude' theme itself. Finally after much progress all is rejected in favour of a movement with voices (bars 208–21). This sequence

[35] TF, p. 703.   [36] Quoted from Unger, 'Workshop', p. 326.   [37] TF, p. 356.
[38] *The Harmonicon*, ii (1824). p. 11; for identification of the author, see Tyson, 'Op. 70 No. 1', p. 2.   [39] TF, p. 715.   [40] TF, p. 573.
[41] He once stated that he had 'a greater impulse to reveal myself to the world by means of my compositions' than by writing about music; see A-1270.
[42] We know this is the meaning intended for this passage, because of some texts Beethoven planned for it at one stage; see N-II, pp. 189–91 (tr. in TF, pp. 892–4).

of events reflects what can be seen over and over again in Beethoven's sketchbooks—several ideas rejected, another taken up and refined, and an important new element incorporated at a relatively late stage.

The sketches themselves, despite being of such central importance for an understanding of Beethoven's creative process, present many difficulties. They are so hard to read that until the 1960s few scholars had attempted the task; and even when they have been deciphered, relating them to each other and to finished works is a slow and complicated process that calls for careful examination of every note. Many of the sketches have consequently not yet been thoroughly examined, and one of the aims of the present study has been to derive insights from sketches not previously assessed, as well as from those already well known. Another major drawback with the sketches is their fate since Beethoven's death. Although he himself had kept them reasonably well intact, many of them became scattered after the auction of his personal effects on 5 November 1827. Most were bought by publishers—chiefly Domenico Artaria—and during the next few decades most of the actual books of sketches had individual pages removed, these pages often being given away to friends of the owners as souvenirs of Beethoven. The loose leaves that had never belonged in a sketchbook became even more jumbled than they had been during Beethoven's lifetime, and one sketchbook was even dismembered completely, the individual leaves being sold off at a profit by the owner, Ignaz Sauer. The detailed history of Beethoven's sketches since 1827 is related in a recent monograph[43] and does not need repeating here. Suffice it to say that today the sketches are split up into over 400 sources (ranging from single leaves to complete sketchbooks), and scattered over many parts of the world.[44]

The first person to make a detailed and wide-ranging study of their musical contents was Gustav Nottebohm, who from the 1860s until his death in 1882 published many studies of them, including two monographs and a long series of articles that were later collected together and published in revised form as *Beethoveniana* and *Zweite Beethoveniana*.[45] Nottebohm's work was of such a high standard that not much work was done on the original sources of Beethoven's sketches for many years afterwards. Nottebohm said relatively little, however, about the musical significance of the numerous sketches he had transcribed, and considerable progress was made in this area in 1925 with the publication of a study of certain aspects of Beethoven's sketching process by Paul Mies, even though Mies relied on Nottebohm's transcriptions rather than making his own.[46] A later study of Beethoven's creative process was

---

[43] JTW; see esp. pp. 13–43.

[44] There is no complete inventory published at present, but almost all the sources are listed in SV and/or JTW.

[45] N-I and N-II; the two monographs are N-1803 and Nottebohm, *Skizzenbuch*.

[46] Mies, *Sketches*.

made by Kurt Westphal,[47] but it too was based on the sketch transcriptions of others—chiefly Nottebohm and Karl Lothar Mikulicz—and is limited in scope.[48]

Since the mid-1960s, however, much research has been done on the original sketches, going far beyond Nottebohm's work. The main thrust of this research, apart from greatly increasing the number of transcriptions and lists of contents of sketchbooks, was twofold. First there was the enormous task of trying to reconstruct Beethoven's sketchbooks as they were when he used them—that is, reversing conceptually the process of dismemberment that had taken place during the nineteenth century. The bibliographical techniques evolved for doing this have become quite sophisticated, involving among other things the watermarks in the paper, the minute examination of the stave-rulings (some of which show a single distinctive pattern throughout a sketchbook), the offsets produced by ink-blots, the stitch-holes made when the book was originally bound, any page numbers added to a leaf at any time, the matching profiles of leaves that were once conjunct but have since been cut or torn apart, descriptions by Nottebohm of the condition of a sketchbook when he examined it, and the musical continuity of the sketches themselves. The work has by and large now been accomplished, and has culminated in a book, *The Beethoven Sketchbooks*,[49] in which all Beethoven's seventy or so sketchbooks are reconstructed and described, and a detailed account is given there of the methods used in their reconstruction.

The other main area of research on Beethoven's sketches in recent years has been the investigation of his compositional methods in individual cases —usually a single work or movement and occasionally an even smaller compositional unit. Numerous works have now been studied in this way to a much greater depth than was achieved by Nottebohm, but many have not, and work of this sort is likely to continue for many years. Furthermore, although several authors have ranged over a number of works in separate studies, almost all individual studies have concentrated on only a very restricted group of sketches—those for a single work or opus. The one conspicuous exception, Douglas Johnson's survey of all Beethoven's early sketches,[50] treats the musical content of the sketches work by work but gives no general account of Beethoven's composing methods, and so the time is clearly ripe for such an overview.

Despite their enormous importance, however, the sketches do have limitations in what they can tell us. With most works some sketches are undoubtedly lost; and even if all of those for a work have survived, we can never know this for certain. Often it is also impossible to tell in what precise order they were written, even when the approximate order can be worked out. And

---

[47] Westphal, *Einfall*.
[48] Fuller surveys of the early history of the study of Beethoven's sketches can be found in Johnson, *Fischhof*, i. 1–12, and JTW, pp. 3–11.   [49] JTW.
[50] Johnson, *Fischhof*.

the sketches are only like a series of still photographs rather than a moving picture of how a work came into being. Beethoven's mental processes between his sketches have to be deduced by inference and extrapolation—an uncertain process at best. Yet the sketches do contain evidence that is strongly suggestive of the underlying thought, and taken as a whole they provide very great insights into the workings of Beethoven's mind and his creativity.

In addition to the sketches proper, early and superseded versions of certain passages are also generally to be found in autograph scores, in the form of cancellations of various sorts. Often these cancellations are very extensive, even though the fundamental shape of a work is rarely altered at this stage. Thus the investigation of the final stages of composition of a work cannot be restricted to the sketches, but must take account of the autograph score and any later material, such as corrected copies and early editions. Unfortunately many of Beethoven's autograph scores are lost; but most of the later ones survive, and in a few cases there are more than one, thus providing an extra layer for investigation. The autograph scores tend to be much more legible than the sketches; although they are still difficult to read, Beethoven did at least intend someone else to read them and so textual uncertainties are quite rare, whereas in the sketches, which he intended only for himself, notational ambiguities are common.

Beyond the autograph scores come the finished versions, as presented by the best modern editions after full textual criticism. Inevitably these finished versions contain much evidence about how they were composed; but this evidence must be treated with caution, and analysis of the finished work should not include the assumption that Beethoven composed a work in the way the analyst perceives it, unless there is good supporting evidence. Some analyses are too speculative to be relied on, while others can be demonstrably refuted by the sketches; but the better ones point out hidden features that Beethoven almost certainly planned and was aware of, even if the sketches provide no confirmation.

At the most elementary level, analysis can show, for example, that in the 'Waldstein' Sonata the second subject is immediately repeated with the harmony retained but the melody decorated by triplets. Several things can hence be inferred—namely that the theme was composed before the triplet decoration, that Beethoven must have decided on the structure of theme plus decoration before working out the details of the decoration, and that in composing the decorated repeat his main problem was to find suitable triplet figuration without altering the given harmonic progression. At a larger level, analysis shows that many movements are in sonata form. He must have been aware of this form (even though he never used a term to describe it), and therefore he must have been thinking of the overall form at an early stage of writing the movements in question.

With less obvious features in a work, it is more difficult to be certain how far they were consciously planned and how Beethoven went about creating them. For example, in the Ninth Symphony each movement contains an unexpected and abrupt modulation to the remote key of B major, followed by an equally abrupt modulation away from it (first movement, bars 108–15; second movement, bars 165–76; third movement, bars 91–8; finale, bars 833–41; in the second movement the music never settles properly in B major). This long-range key relationship is easily overlooked, yet Beethoven was presumably aware of it and, one imagines, planned it well before the symphony reached its final shape. Similarly, Charles Rosen has pointed out that all four movements of the 'Hammerklavier' Sonata are built around chains of descending thirds;[51] this happens so consistently that it is hardly likely to be accidental, even though this sort of planning, like the relationship between the B major sections of the Ninth Symphony, is not part of Beethoven's visible sketching process. With many less obvious features, however, there is considerable doubt as to whether they were consciously planned, emerged subconsciously through Beethoven's aesthetic instincts, or came about just through pure chance.[52]

Thus when all sources are taken together they provide a great variety of evidence about Beethoven's creative process; but they are bound to leave gaps in our knowledge. One important factor that cannot be observed directly is the role of improvisation in the creation of his works. As we have seen, he instructed Archduke Rudolph to compose both with and without a piano, jotting down ideas that were improvised; and on another occasion he composed the aria 'Und spür' ich' at the piano. According to Czerny, 'Beethoven was accustomed to composing everything with the aid of the piano, and would try out a given passage countless times.'[53] Czerny's report seems to have been no exaggeration, for Treitschke says that Beethoven improvised ideas for 'Und spür' ich' for several hours on end, forgoing supper in the process, and Ries gives an account of the finale of the 'Appassionata' Sonata being composed in a similar way 'for at least an hour'.[54] Such piano sketches were not made instead of written sketches, however, but were supplementary to them.

Improvisations of this type seem to have consisted of discontinuous fragments, but Beethoven was also outstandingly good at improvising whole pieces—often quite long ones. Almost everybody who has described these improvisations—including Ries, Czerny, Wegeler, Wurzer, Junker, Seyfried, Cramer, Amenda, Mähler, Starke, and Smart[55]—speaks of them with amazed admiration and delight. One might imagine that they were rambling, fantasia-like affairs with no particular structure or cohesion, but this does not seem to have been the case. Several writers speak of quite lengthy improvis-

---

[51] Rosen, *Classical*, pp. 407 ff.

[52] Some speculations on the role of the subconscious in Beethoven's creativity can be found in Graf, *Beethoven* (see esp. pp. 77–117), but many of the hypotheses are unsubstantiated.

[53] Czerny, *Performance*, p. 13.   [54] TF, pp. 573, 356.   [55] TF, *passim*.

ations unified by a single (often insignificant) motif, such as an eight-note decorative figure developed for twenty minutes, a fugue theme by Graun developed for half an hour, a few randomly chosen notes from the second violin part of a Pleyel quartet, and some equally random notes taken from the cello part of a Steibelt quintet after it had been placed upside-down on the music-stand![56] Czerny confirms that Beethoven often used only a few notes as a basis for a whole improvisation, citing as an example the three-note motif that forms the basis for the finale of the Piano Sonata Op. 10 no. 3.[57]

Czerny also discusses the overall form of Beethoven's improvisations, saying there were three types: (1) a movement in sonata form or rondo form, the sonata-form movements customarily having an extended development section in which the main theme was treated in all sorts of ways; (2) a free variation form similar to the Choral Fantasia (Op. 80) and the finale of the Ninth Symphony; and (3) a mixed or pot-pourri style, like the Piano Fantasia Op. 77.[58] According to Friedrich Starke, Beethoven also sometimes improvised fugues.[59] It appears, then, that Beethoven's improvisations give rise to the same sort of music as his written compositions, and that they reflect essentially the same creative process. His compositions, and in particular his lengthy sketching process, were apparently sometimes attempts to pin down and refine movements that he had already improvised complete at the piano. Thus when composing at the piano he did not just, in Czerny's phrase, 'try out a given passage countless times' before going on to the next fragment, but was capable of improvising, without interruption, a whole movement, which would differ from a later, written version of it only in matters of detail. This is confirmed by a few cases in which there is a known link between an improvised piece and a written one. Referring to a set of variations (WoO 40), Beethoven once wrote: 'I should never have written down this kind of piece, had I not already noticed fairly often how some people in Vienna after hearing me extemporize of an evening would note down on the following day several peculiarities of my style and palm them off with pride as their own.'[60] How much credence can be placed on this remark is uncertain, since the variations had in fact already been sketched extensively before Beethoven reached Vienna;[61] but it is significant that in his own mind extemporization and composition were clearly linked very closely. Similarly in 1808 his Choral Fantasia was performed at a concert on 22 December, but the piano introduction was improvised; it was not sketched and written down until well into the following year.[62] At the same concert he also improvised a piano fantasia, and this, too, may have given rise to a written composition the next year —the Fantasia Op. 77. Years later he apparently also improvised a complete movement for his unfinished Tenth Symphony, at a time when he had made

---

[56] TF, pp. 963, 367, 377, 257.
[57] Czerny, *Performance*, p. 15.
[58] Ibid.; TF, p. 368.
[59] TF, p. 526.
[60] A-9.
[61] Johnson, *Fischhof*, i. 415; ii. 119–23.
[62] JTW, p. 188.

only a few sketches for it.[63] The fact that he was capable of producing such on-the-spot compositions in the form of improvisations—and ones of very high quality—serves as a useful counterweight to the frequently held notion (derived from the laboured appearance of the sketches) that he found composition a slow and difficult process. He clearly found it all too easy to compose something, and the difficulty lay in trying to produce works that would surpass anything previously written.

Since Beethoven could evidently invent wonderful music at the piano without prior sketching, it must be asked whether when he was very pressed for time some of his works were actually composed without sketches, since in several cases virtually no sketches survive (conspicuous in this respect are the First and Fourth symphonies, the Septet, the Third and Fourth piano concertos, and numerous lesser works and individual movements). Certainly some works were written extremely fast: the Horn Sonata (Op. 17), a set of variations (WoO 70) and a sextet (Op. 71) are each said to have been written within a day;[64] *König Stephan* and *Die Ruinen von Athen*, which have a combined total of over 2,000 bars, were according to Beethoven written between late July and 13 September 1811;[65] and the overture and a chorus ('Wo sich die Pulse', WoO 98) for *Die Weihe des Hauses*, a combined total of almost 600 bars of full score, were conceived, composed, copied, rehearsed, and performed in the period 1 September to 3 October 1822.[66] Yet even when he was working to a strict deadline, as in the case of the last four works mentioned, he still made extensive sketches for every movement. Thus scholars are agreed that if there are no surviving sketches for a work, this is probably because they have been lost. A few very short, simple, or early works may have been written out without sketching, but for many such works sketches have survived where one might not have expected them to do so.

Aside from sources directly associated with Beethoven, there is the possibility that something may be learned about his creative process by examining the creative processes of other composers. Studies of these—particularly those of nineteenth-century composers—have proliferated in recent years, and there is today a substantial literature on the subject, covering such composers as Bach, Haydn, Mozart, Berlioz, Schumann, Liszt, Wagner, and Ravel. There have also been occasional discussions of the creative process of composers in general, perhaps the most prominent one being that by Julius Bahle.[67] Bahle asked a number of living composers a series of questions about their working methods, for both vocal and instrumental music, and after

[63] Cooper, 'Tenth Symphony', pp. 17–18.

[64] KH, p. 39; TF, p. 176; A-224; The claims come from Ries, Wegeler, and Beethoven respectively.   [65] A-325.

[66] A-1100; TF, p. 806.   [67] Bahle, *Schaffensprozess*; see also Graf, *Beethoven*.

incorporating some observations from accounts of past composers, he reached a number of conclusions about the musical creative process in general. He found that all composers had difficulty in choosing a suitable text for vocal music, and that a composer's own experiences, both musical and extramusical, played an important role in shaping his creative process. He noted that extramusical impulses of various sorts (e.g. other art forms, or a composer's own feelings) often generated music with programmatic content, whether vocal or instrumental in its realization; and there were purely musical impulses, such as a desire to imitate or follow the musical achievements of earlier composers, searching for new musical discoveries, attempting to write music of the highest quality, and wrestling with a particular musical problem. He also encountered an element of artistic compulsion —a hunger to compose, almost as a sacred duty—which some composers experience. Additional factors facilitating compositional activity included such things as a satisfactory environment in which to compose and a suitable frame of mind for doing so. Bahle observed, too, that artistic creation will start with the vaguest concept, followed by a skeletal framework from which everything will develop. All the above factors do indeed apply to Beethoven, as we shall see, but they are rather general conclusions and do not tell us how particular works were composed, nor how Beethoven differed from other composers in his approach.

On a more technical level, something can also be learnt about Beethoven's creative process by examining the nature of musical compositions—either those of all periods or more specifically those of his day. A number of kinds of broad problems that a composer is almost certain to face can be easily identified. These include, for example, deciding the form of a new work; reconciling the demands of linear motion with those of the vertical sound; creating an appropriate overall length for the material being used, and suitable lengths and proportions for each section; deciding which of several variants of melody or harmony is best (often the variants are all good in different ways); resolving the problem of needing particular notes that are unavailable or unplayable on the instrument being used; setting a poetic text in a way that balances the needs of the rhythm and meaning of the words with purely musical considerations; and overcoming obstacles when the music seems to be leading nowhere. Almost all composers will be familiar with these problems; in addition, in Beethoven's day there were problems peculiar to the musical language of the time, such as achieving satisfactory tonal balance and deciding whether to place a scherzo second or third in a quartet or symphony.

Anyone who has tried to write a work in Beethoven's style will quickly have become aware of these and other difficulties, which might not be illuminated purely by observing the sketches as they stand. Thus an understanding of the nature of composition can help us draw out the implications of Beethoven's sketches; but this approach, like Bahle's, only shows in what ways Beethoven is similar to other composers. It cannot demonstrate the uniqueness of his methods of composition, which emerge best through a comparison of his sketches with those of other composers. From such a comparison it becomes clear that his sketches, particularly those of his late works, are much more thorough and detailed than those of other composers. He often sketched a single passage very intensively, with sometimes as many as twenty or thirty variants, just like the 'countless times' he tried out variants at the piano, whereas in the case of most other composers, certainly before the present century, it is rare to find more than three or four such variants. Beethoven's sketches also tend to cover much more ground between the early and late versions of a passage, and he wrote down, or at least preserved, far more unused concepts and fragments than other composers. Moreover his habit of composing while wandering round the countryside or the streets of Vienna was sufficiently abnormal to be commented on by several witnesses.

Beethoven's creative process and compositional methods accordingly form a particularly worthwhile subject for study. Not only was he a very great composer, but he had very unusual (and often extremely complicated) composing habits, and he also left a great wealth of rough drafts and sketches —far more than any other composer of his day—that provide ample scope for investigation. And by watching a great composer at work through his sketches, we may learn something about the creative process and the art of composition *per se*, as well as increasing our historical knowledge about Beethoven himself and the music he created.

I

FACTORS AFFECTING
BEETHOVEN'S
CREATIVE PROCESS

2

Beethoven's Artistic Aims

WHAT was the underlying motivation for Beethoven's compositional activity? On one level he regarded composition as necessary for earning a living,[1] but the prime motivation lay much deeper. It seems that from an early age he felt an urge to compose, and this urge remained with him throughout his life. He did in fact expressly mention it at a remarkably early date (14 October 1783), in the dedicatory letter for one of his first compositions, the three 'Kurfürsten' sonatas (WoO 47): 'My Muse in hours of sacred inspiration has often whispered to me: "Make the attempt, just put down on paper the harmonies of your soul!"... My Muse insisted—I obeyed and I composed.'[2] In later life he occasionally repeated similar ideas, referring to his talent commanding him, or more poetically to sacrificing himself to art or to the heavenly Muses.[3] His desire to achieve greatness or even immortality through his compositions also played its part in stimulating his creative drive,[4] and in addition he felt a certain sense of mission to be accomplished.[5]

If the sense of compulsion to create was there, however, Beethoven also derived enormous pleasure from composing. This is referred to in a number of his letters, and occasionally he even mentioned a particular work as having given him delight: he dedicated the song 'Adelaide' (Op. 46) to the poet, Friedrich von Matthisson, informing him of 'the delight which the composition of your A[delaide] has afforded me'.[6] Beethoven also thanked a few other poets in a similar way on other occasions, according to Schindler,[7] and he even took pleasure in something as simple as providing accompaniments for Scottish folksongs sent to him by the Edinburgh publisher George Thomson.[8] 'To me there is no greater pleasure than to practise and exercise my art', he wrote on one occasion; and on another: 'I am entirely devoted to my Muses, as I have always been: and in this alone do I find the joy of my life.'[9]

This devotion, a direct counterpart to the delight that his art provided for him, underpinned all his compositional activity. His prime aim was to write great works rather than make money out of composition: 'I love my art too

[1] A-1143. [2] A-D.1 (Anderson, *Letters*, p. 1410).
[3] A-53; A-1306; Solomon, 'Tagebuch', nos. 25 and 169.
[4] A-143; A-85; Solomon, 'Tagebuch', no. 49.
[5] Solomon, *Beethoven*, p. 86; cf. the Heiligenstadt Testament (quoted ibid., p. 117): 'It seemed impossible to leave the world until I had brought forth all that was within me.'
[6] A-40. [7] Schindler/MacArdle, *Beethoven*, p. 337; see also A-506 and A-507.
[8] A-266. [9] A-54; A-1084.

dearly to be actuated solely by self-interest.'[10] And his single-minded dedication was conveyed to Goethe in 1823: 'My one aim has been to master the art of music', even if this did result in him becoming, as he admitted on another occasion, 'a bit crazy'.[11]

Music deserved such devotion in his view because it was a noble art—one that could 'raise men to the level of gods'.[12] and as it had such elevating powers it had to be treated with due respect in his compositions, and used for the benefit of noble listeners rather than merely for entertaining the masses. 'My supreme aim,' he wrote, 'is that my art should be welcomed by the noblest and most cultured people.'[13] Music for noble minds had to be rich, learned, elevated, and complex, and Beethoven's was conspicuously more so than that of any of his contemporaries—especially during the period 1800–20, when few composers aspired to such aims (Clementi and Cherubini are exceptions). Towards the end of his life he even wanted to write exclusively in the highest branches of composition—'operas, symphonies, church music, at most some more quartets', according to a letter of December 1822.[14] And his operas had to be on lofty subjects: those considered, apart from *Fidelio*, included Macbeth, Bradamante, Attila, Romulus and Remus, Brutus, and Melusine. Immoral or frivolous subjects such as Don Giovanni and Figaro were unacceptable[15] (although he did have great admiration for Mozart's operas on these subjects), as were magical subjects;[16] and he disdained such composers as Rossini who were only able to write frivolous music and pretty tunes.[17]

Beethoven's dedication to music was manifested initially as a performer, and resulted in long hours of practice in order to become a virtuoso pianist. Later, as he turned more to composition, it was reflected in the patience he showed in copying out large quantities of master-works by other composers—the traditional way of learning composition. Similarly he regarded it as his duty to read learned musical treatises to increase his understanding of his art, and he apparently read a great number: 'There is hardly any treatise which could be too learned for me.'[18] His devotion to his art and his determination to master it also produced a willingness to undergo rigorous instruction with Haydn and Albrechtsberger at the age of 22–4; and even at the age of 28–30, when he was already becoming well known as a composer, he undertook instruction from Salieri in order to perfect himself in the operatic style.

He considered that all aspects of composition had to be mastered, and he seems to have made a conscious effort to master each genre so as to become the complete composer. As early as 1801 he told Karl Amenda that he had composed 'all types of music, except operas and sacred works',[19] and these two deficiencies were soon remedied by *Christus am Oelberge* (1803) and the first version of *Fidelio* (1805). Beethoven showed a similar attitude late in life when applying for the post of Imperial and Royal Chamber Music Composer

---

[10] A-169.   [11] A-1136; A-894.   [12] A-376.   [13] A-1405.   [14] A-1111.
[15] TF, p. 947.   [16] A-175.   [17] TF, p. 804.   [18] A-228.   [19] A-53.

in 1822–3, boasting that he had composed 'works in all branches of music'.[20] And when he was planning to produce a complete edition of all his works he proposed to write a new work in each genre to add to those already written.[21] Indeed, few great composers of any period have been successful in such a wide range of genres.

It was his dedication to music and his desire to 'achieve the dignity of a true artist'[22] which led him also to sketching of unprecedented intensity when writing new works. Many earlier composers had, of course, made rough drafts for works they were writing, but as far as is known none had done so to nearly the same extent as Beethoven (a fact already observed by his contemporaries). In addition, when the composing was done, he often expended enormous energy on simply checking copies that were to be sent to publishers[23] or providing them with correction lists when inaccurate editions had been printed,[24] despite the fact that he found checking far less enjoyable than composing.[25] Even after completion and performance of a work, extensive labour was sometimes necessary for making revisions— notably in *Fidelio*, *Christus am Oelberge*, and the Second Piano Concerto; and his Quartet in F Op. 18 No. 1, completed in 1799, was substantially revised in 1800–1 because, as he put it, 'only now have I learnt how to write quartets'.[26] When revising *Fidelio* in 1814 he lamented the tiresomeness of the task, observing ruefully that composition in such circumstances was 'a very different thing from being able to indulge in free meditation or inspiration'.[27]

Beethoven's overriding desire was, therefore, not just to create music, but to create music of the highest artistic worth, and it was this which neces- sitated all the sketching and related labour. The sketches reveal a constant striving for perfection—a struggle to try and reach something unattainable; and the impossibility of complete success in his art, evidenced by the existence of imperfections in even his greatest works, was well recognized by him, being referred to in a letter written in 1812 to a girl of about nine years old: 'The true artist . . . has a vague awareness of how far he is from reaching his goal; and while others may perhaps be admiring him, he laments the fact that he has not yet reached the point whither his better genius only lights the way for him like a distant sun.'[28] As we shall see, one of the most prominent features of the sketches is the way they repeatedly show him grappling with 'problems' and difficulties', which could be overcome only with effort, if at all. And a sense of struggle is an idea that can be discerned in many of his finished works—a struggle that can lead to triumph (*Egmont*, Fifth Symphony), to joy (Ninth Symphony), to thanksgiving ('Pastoral' Symphony), to peace (Piano sonata Op. 111, the Agnus Dei of the *Missa solemnis*), or occasionally to despair ('Appassionata' sonata).

For Beethoven struggles and difficulties were obstacles not to be avoided

[20] A-1121.
[21] A-1028; A-1345.
[22] A-143.
[23] A-1325; A-1494.
[24] e.g. A-204 and A-1061.
[25] A-108.
[26] A-53.
[27] A-481.
[28] A-376.

but welcomed as a means of reaching the heights. Even in everyday life he found delight in tackling difficult challenges: in his letter to the 'Immortal Beloved' he expressed the pleasure he had derived from his journey from Prague to Teplitz, because the dreadful condition of the road and the dangers of a forest had provided difficulties that he had successfully overcome.[29] Similarly he considered technical difficulties for the performer to be a good feature in a piece of music: 'What is difficult is also beautiful, good, great and so forth... since what is difficult makes one sweat.'[30]

The artistic ideals he struggled for in his compositions, however, had a more specific focus: he sought to create something that was beautiful and artistic yet novel and surprising. This aesthetic goal emerges, rather unexpectedly, in an aside to his friend Ferdinand Ries, whom he asks to give his wife a surprise; he adds, 'Between ourselves the best thing of all is a combination of the surprising and the beautiful!'[31] This observation is not only the heart of Beethoven's aesthetic ideals, but also highlights a major deficiency of many lesser composers, of whom some have created works of great beauty which are nevertheless too predictable, while others have composed works which are highly original but too unpleasant and inartistic. Beethoven, by contrast, always managed to keep within the bounds of artistic sense and beauty, maintaining a certain inner proportion and logic even in his most original creations, and this ability to combine the surprising and the beautiful was an important element contributing to his greatness as a composer.

There are countless examples of this ability throughout his entire output, and they pervade his minor works almost as much as his major ones. Sometimes the surprise comes in the form of an unexpected chord, a well-known case being the opening of the First Symphony with its out-of-key dominant seventh. On other occasions there is an unexpected melodic turn, such as the C sharp in the opening theme of the 'Eroica' Symphony. Sometimes Beethoven combines chord progressions and melodic line to produce a surprising change of key—a fine example occurs in the slow movement of the Seventh Symphony (Ex. 2.1). Even in something as mundane as a harmonization of a Scottish folksong his capacity to produce something artistic but unexpected is quite remarkable, as in Ex. 2.2 (from 'O thou art the lad', Op. 108 No. 11), where the expected B flat chord at the cadence on the word 'see' is displaced from the first beat of the bar by a secondary dominant, and then displaced again by syncopation in the harmony.

Beethoven's love of surprise was sometimes turned to humorous ends. He reportedly took a certain mischievous delight in catching out unwary performers at an orchestral rehearsal by composing an unexpected rhythmic change and thereby 'unhorsing such excellent riders'.[32] Music's noble nature did not

[29] A-373.   [30] A-749.   [31] A-1209.   [32] TF, p. 371.

Ex. 2.1 Op. 92. ii

Ex. 2.2 Op. 108 No. 11

mean for him that all comedy should be excluded, and there are elements of wit and humour in many of his works (just as there are in his letters). It was he who established the scherzo ('joke') as the norm in symphonies in place of the more serious minuet, and the Allegretto scherzando in the Eighth Symphony, for example, is a movement full of subtle jokes and humour.[33]

His desire to surprise his listeners also went hand in hand with his belief that his art should always be moving forward: 'Art demands of us that we shall not stand still,' he is reported to have said to Karl Holz,[34] and his concern for the progress of art was expressed on other occasions too.[35]

---

[33] De la Motte, 'Scherzando'.   [34] TF, p. 982.   [35] See e.g. A-955.

Progress implied experiment for him and surprise for his listeners, and this suited him well since he was aware from quite an early age that his music contained certain 'peculiarities of style' which made it 'not entirely commonplace'.[36] He clung tenaciously to this independence of style, telling George Thomson on one occasion that he was prepared to write easy pieces only if this did not mean his abandoning the elevation and originality of style that had been so advantageous to him.[37] But originality was insufficient unless it was continually developing, and Beethoven on several occasions expressed concern for novelty in his music. He is said to have remarked, shortly before writing the piano sonatas Op. 31 of 1802, that he was dissatisfied with the works he had produced thus far and intended to follow a new path.[38] At times he even treated some of his earlier works with contempt, once referring to them as 'wretched old things of mine'.[39] Commentators have had little difficulty in discerning a profound stylistic change around 1802, and again around 1815, and these changes occurred partly because Beethoven felt it was not sufficient merely to go on producing more works in the same style.

But he did not undergo just two stylistic changes in the course of his output. Some writers have identified other approximate dates which seem to mark stylistic change, such as the years 1794, 1809, and 1820,[40] and in the last analysis each of his major works must be considered to represent artistic progress in some form. Often his works contain radically new departures, and he sometimes drew attention to new or unusual features in recently completed works. He described the two sets of piano variations in F and E flat, Opp. 34 and 35, as being written in 'a new manner'[41] and wanted to announce this fact in a preface to each set.[42] His Triple Concerto, Op. 56, was unusual in having a violin, cello, and piano as a concertino group, which he said was 'surely something new'.[43] In describing the Mass in C, he claimed to have set the text 'in a manner in which it has rarely been treated';[44] and he drew attention to 'a new type of partwriting' in the late quartets.[45] On other occasions he wrote in particular genres simply because they were unusual: he wrote the piano trios Op. 70 'since such trios are now rather scarce',[46] and similarly his two songs 'Opferlied' and 'Bundeslied' (Opp. 121b and 122) were scored with unusual combinations of accompanying instruments because 'so many songs have been composed with pianoforte accompaniment that for this reason I have made a change for once.'[47] About the same time he expressed the view that it was 'time to break away' from traditional methods of composition.[48]

Thus Beethoven's continual desire and effort to seek new effects formed an important creative impulse and arose from his devotion to his art and its progress. In addition to the comments quoted above, evidence for this desire

[36] A-9 and A-5 (both written in the early 1790s).   [37] A-136.

[38] Czerny, *Performance*, p. 13 (the precise date of this remark is uncertain).

[39] A-81.   [40] Solomon, 'Periods'.   [41] A-62.   [42] A-67.

[43] A-96.   [44] A-167.   [45] TDR, v. 318 (cf. TF, p. 982).

[46] A-169.   [47] A-1158.   [48] A-1170.

abounds in the music itself. In some works he almost seems to have begun by rejecting one of the standard principles of composition and exploring to find out what sort of piece could be written without it. In the Variations in F, Op. 34, he deliberately rejected two of the fundamental principles of classical sets of variations—that every variation should have the same tonic and that nearly all should have the same metre. Instead, each variation is in a different key and metre from the preceding one, and in strongly contrasting mood. Similarly in the Fantasia for Piano, Op. 77, he abandoned the notion that a piece should end in the same key as it begins, for this one begins in G minor but ends with a series of variations in the unlikely key of B major. In the Quartet Op. 131 his exploration proceeded in a different direction. Here the seven movements have the keys C sharp minor, D major, B minor, A major, E major, G sharp minor, and C sharp minor—a key scheme that would be more normal for the key centres within a single movement than for the main keys of consecutive movements.[49] And some of the movements themselves function effectively as links between other, longer movements, so that the distinction between movement and section begins to break down. Often the very odd features of such pieces occur at an early stage of the sketching process (as in the Variations Op. 34), thus reinforcing the view that they were a generating factor in the creation of the work in question. Such pieces could be described as experimental, but this would be a misleading term: the experiments were done during his sketching and his improvisations at the piano, and the works themselves are merely the results of experiments, or the solutions to the problems he had set up at the outset. Indeed, the sketches do sometimes contain even more far-fetched and unconventional ideas than the finished works, with experiments and surprises that were found too extreme to be able to be accommodated in a beautiful work of art. For example, in a draft for a sonata movement dating from about 1793 Beethoven planned to prepare the recapitulation in G major by using one of the most awkward keys possible—F major (Ex. 2.3); but the key change was evidently found to be too abrupt and the experiment was abandoned.[50]

But Beethoven does sometimes seem to have deliberately created composing difficulties along the lines of musical puzzles in order to try and solve them. This attitude is evident in the large number of short canons (over forty altogether) that he composed from about 1813 onwards, but it is perhaps most conspicuous in the late bagatelles, where the problems are more concentrated and focused than in larger works but more varied than in canons.[51] In the Bagatelle Op. 119 No. 7, the problem Beethoven creates is to write a piece where the main theme to be developed is just a trill and where the music is to be in the subdominant for most of the second half. In Op. 126

---

[49] See Winter, 'Plans', p. 135.
[50] SV 185, f. 47ʳ; see Kerman ed., *Miscellany*, ii. 198. For the dating of the sketch, see Johnson, *Fischhof*, i. 86–8. [51] See Cone, 'Bagatelles'.

Ex. 2.3 SV 185, fo. 47ʳ

No. 4 the problem is one of form: there is a scherzo and trio in which the trio section reappears complete as a coda, without the overall result sounding either like an ordinary ABAB form or in any way inconclusive (as it would in most other works after a return of the trio section).[52] In Op. 119 No. 10 the problems seem insuperable since the irregularities included almost defy the creation of an artistic whole: the piece begins out of key and lasts only about ten seconds, yet Beethoven creates a regular form (AAB) and a clear internal goal that is finally reached—the resolution of the initial tonal and rhythmic instability (Ex. 2.4). Other late bagatelles present less obvious but no less challenging problems, and the resulting novelties provided ideas that could be taken up again by Beethoven and developed in more important works.

Later in this book, where Beethoven's sketches are examined in detail, we shall see many more examples of how his artistic aims were fulfilled. His devotion to music, born out of a love of it that he developed at an early age, led to his desire to advance his art in any way he could; this in turn necessitated unprecedented intensity of sketching, in which improbable and fantastic ideas could be considered before being either rejected as too absurd or taken up as a means of extending the bounds of music beyond what was previously thought possible. His desire for novelty and surprise combined with order and beauty also could only be fulfilled with the aid of large numbers of sketches, which in turn are a great help today in drawing attention to his skill in combining these elements. Often the early sketches for a work show something that is musically adequate but insufficiently

[52] Ibid., pp. 97–8. Cone's view that the B section functions the first time as a trio and the second time as a coda is confirmed by the fact that Beethoven originally wrote a different coda; see Brandenburg ed., *Op. 126*, i. 23.

Ex. 2.4 Op. 119 No. 10

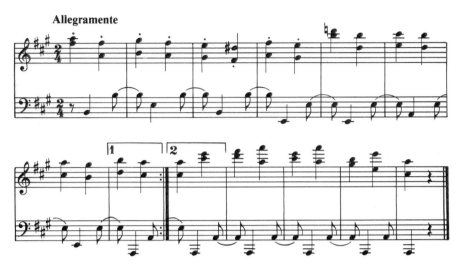

striking. The later sketches and the final version then reveal several aspects of the fulfilment of his aims: his perseverance and determination born of his devotion to art; the compositional difficulties that had to be, and were, overcome to create a great work; and the resulting artistic progress to new levels of originality combined with internal order—the surprising with the beautiful—which could be attained only by such intense sketching.

3

Professional Pressures

UNLIKE Haydn, who served the Esterházy family for many years, Beethoven was never employed in the direct service of a patron once he had left Bonn, and he tends to be regarded as the first example of the romantic ideal of an independent composer, working as a free artist, writing only what he wanted and when he wanted. To a certain extent this picture is correct, for although he had a number of patrons he was never in a situation in which he was obliged to compose what they asked, and when he was granted an annuity in 1809 by three patrons (Prince Kinsky, Prince Lobkowitz, and Archduke Rudolph) the sole condition they imposed was that he should continue to reside in Vienna. This annuity made him free of financial worry (in theory if not in practice) and enabled him to compose as much or as little as he liked for the rest of his life. One might imagine that from then on he wrote only what he considered to be in the best interests of his art, and the types of music he liked most. Yet even while he was negotiating the annuity contract he indicated that he would have preferred to enter the Imperial service as a composer with a regular salary and presumably corresponding obligations.[1] Similarly in 1807 he expressed a desire to become composer for the Royal Theatres in Vienna, even though he would have been obliged to write at least one opera a year plus other smaller stage works as required.[2] In fact he became a free-lance composer more by mischance than by design, and even so a surprisingly high proportion of his output was written because of particular combinations of circumstances that just happened to arise.

As a professional composer he frequently earned money by composing either what someone had specifically requested or what he felt would sell best in the music market. The professional influences from people around him, which as we shall see affected his output so substantially, came in a number of forms, including performances, commissions, publications, and combinations of these three. Works for a particular performance were sometimes written as a result of a specific commission—from a theatre director, for example; on other occasions the prospect of a performance, whether it was an orchestral concert or the arrival of a travelling virtuoso in Vienna, was a sufficient incentive for the creation of a new work. Commissions also sometimes came from publishers wanting a particular type of work, but more often he had to write a work and then try to find a publisher willing to pay him an appropriate fee for it. In addition commissions might come from

[1] A-F.4 (Anderson, *Letters*, p. 1421).   [2] A-I.1 (p. 1445).

private patrons who simply wanted to own a new work of his. (Close friends were sometimes able to request a work without paying a fee, and on occasion he even gave pieces away unsolicited.)

The different types of professional pressure that might generate a work could of course occur in combination. A work might be commissioned by one body, then performed by Beethoven at a benefit concert (where the composer took the profits) before being sold to a publisher, thereby raising three fees, as happened with the Ninth Symphony; but such a fortunate combination of circumstances did not often occur. Moreover, professional influences interacted with musical, artistic, personal, and extramusical influences in such a complex way that the relative weight of each factor cannot be precisely determined.

Let us now consider the professional pressures in more detail, beginning with Beethoven's stage works. Each of his large-scale stage works was written as a direct result of a specific commission, and was intended to be performed initially at a particular place on a particular occasion. This applies to the ballet *Die Geschöpfe des Prometheus* (1801), the version of *Fidelio* performed in 1805 (though it was Beethoven who insisted on rewriting the work for the revival of 1814), the incidental music to *Egmont* (1810) and the two works for the theatre at Pest—*Die Ruinen von Athen* and *König Stephan* (both 1811). *Die Ruinen von Athen* was later reused in 1822 for the opening of another theatre (the Josephstadt Theatre), and Beethoven was asked to collaborate in its adaptation: some of the libretto was altered and a new chorus was added, and he felt obliged to write a new overture because the old one would not have been suitable in its new setting.[3] Thus as with *Fidelio* a revival enabled him to make alterations which were not integral to the commission but which would nevertheless not have been made if the revival had not taken place. He also wrote several lesser stage works in the course of his life, and these were apparently also occasional pieces, written purely to suit the needs of particular circumstances.

It was difficult to have such stage works, large or small, published once they had been performed, simply because they were occasional pieces and not likely to be needed again; hence although he made efforts to find a publisher for some of them,[4] he managed to sell only a few overtures or piano reductions for publication. Even *Fidelio*, which had a more general appeal, was at first published only as a vocal score, the full score not becoming available until 1826.[5] The only professional reason for writing such works, therefore, was the original commission, and if the financial arrangements of this were inadequate for a new work it was simply not written. This is what happened with the opera *Romulus*. Beethoven wanted 200 ducats plus the takings from one performance, but the theatre directors were only prepared

[3] TF, p. 806; A-1103.
[4] See A-1153, in which Beethoven offers Simrock scores of *Die Ruinen von Athen* and *König Stephan*.
[5] KH, pp. 177–86.

to give him the takings without the 200 ducats,[6] and so the work was apparently never even begun.

Similar circumstances surrounded other large-scale choral pieces, few of which were written without a specific commission of some kind. The Mass in C was written in 1807 to a commission from Prince Nikolaus Esterházy, who had also commissioned Haydn's last six Masses a few years earlier.[7] Similarly the Choral Symphony was commissioned by the Philharmonic Society of London,[8] although the society did not specify a choral finale. The *Missa solemnis* was not strictly commissioned, but it was written in order to be performed on a particular occasion—the enthronement of Archduke Rudolph as Archbishop of Olmütz on 9 March 1820 (though in the end it was not ready in time). Whether or not the Archduke requested Beethoven to write the work for the occasion is not known, but Beethoven clearly felt it his duty, as well as a great honour, to do so,[9] and in a sense a commission fee had already been paid many times over by Rudolph, who had for years been Beethoven's most loyal patron and supporter.

The prospect of a performance of a large work, even if it had not been commissioned, was in fact quite often an important creative impulse for Beethoven. Many of his symphonies, for example, were written with a performance in mind—No. 1 for a concert that took place on 2 April 1800, No. 2 for 5 April 1803, Nos. 5 and 6 for 22 December 1808, and No. 9 for 7 May 1824. Even if it did not provide the initial impulse for the work, and the exact date was only fixed shortly before the event, the prospect of a concert in the near future provided a great incentive to complete these works; hence he sometimes worked very intensively at a symphony shortly before a proposed concert. The same could be said of several of the piano concertos: one of his main reasons for writing these (at least the earlier ones) was in order to play them himself at benefit concerts. This was often a good way of earning money, and one which Mozart had exploited a few years earlier. Some figures may be of interest here. In 1804 it was calculated that the annual cost of living in Vienna for an unmarried middle-class gentleman was 967 florins (or 1,200 florins including books and theatre tickets).[10] Beethoven's benefit concert of 1803, at which the Second Symphony, the Third Piano Concerto, and *Christus am Oelberge* were all performed for the first time, made a profit of 1,300 florins, and so the concert was clearly a very successful venture.

The prime example of a work composed as a direct response to a forth-coming concert is the Choral Fantasia, which was written shortly before Beethoven's concert of 22 December 1808. Czerny tells us: 'Shortly before the concert . . . Beethoven got the idea of writing a brilliant piece with which to conclude the programme. He chose a song fragment he had composed some years earlier, sketched the variations, the chorus, etc., and then the poet

---

[6] A-559.   [7] Knapp, 'Mass in C', p. 200.   [8] A-1110.   [9] A-948.
[10] Hanson, 'Incomes', p. 178; see also Biba, 'Concert Life', p. 82.

Kuffner quickly had to devise some words for it (following Beethoven's instructions). This is the way the Choral Fantasy Op. 80 was written. It was finished too late to be properly rehearsed.'[11] Certain other substantial works were written for specific events around 1813–14—notably *Wellingtons Sieg* (Op. 91) and the large-scale cantata *Der glorreiche Augenblick* (Op. 136), both of which are occasional works (though to such an extent that they have found little favour outside the context in which they were written).

If a concert could provide a stimulus to completion of a major work, lack of performance prospects was at times an inhibiting factor. In 1795 Beethoven began a symphony in C and may have intended to use it during a visit to Berlin the following year; but although the first movement was not far from completion in sketch form and some ideas were jotted down for the later movements, the work was finally abandoned. Perhaps it was simply not ready in time for Berlin, or some other factor prevented any chance of performance at that time.[12] At any rate, all he managed to salvage from this labour was a few bars which he incorporated into the finale of the First Symphony a few years later. Similarly in 1802 he began a concerto in D for violin, cello, and piano, at a time when there was the possibility of a benefit concert. The concert did not eventually materialize, and this is probably one reason why he lost interest in the work.[13] On this occasion he had made even less progress than he had with the symphony in C, and so when he returned to the idea of a triple concerto in 1804 he preferred to make a fresh start; the result is the work in C major, Op. 56. The Third Piano Concerto, however, fared better than the unfinished symphony and triple concerto. Its precise chronology is unclear, but it was apparently intended for the benefit concert in 1800. It was not ready in time, and a different concerto was played instead;[14] but it was sufficiently close to completion for Beethoven to be able to resurrect it three years later for the concert of 1803 (the published version clearly dates from this later time, as can be seen from the extended compass of the piano part). No piano concertos were completed after 1809, partly, no doubt, because Beethoven's deafness made him increasingly reluctant to perform in public, so that he was unable to repeat the success of his first three published concertos.

Unlike some composers, Beethoven rarely seems to have tailored music specifically to particular performers. The main exceptions are certain chamber works, some of which even date from his Bonn days: the Wind

---

[11] Czerny, *Performance*, p. 8.

[12] Johnson, *Fischhof*, i. 461–9. Alternatively Beethoven may simply have decided he was still not ready to write a fully fledged symphony, or that the musical ideas themselves were in some way inadequate.

[13] Kramer, 'Concertante', pp. 43–5.

[14] TF, pp. 255–6. Thayer suggests a later date (summer 1800) for the composition of the Third Piano Concerto; but more recent research seems to indicate that it was in the early part of the year (see JTW, pp. 96–9).

Octet, Op. 103 (together with its companion Rondo, WoO 25) was probably written for a group of musicians at the Electoral Court there, while the Trio for piano, flute, and bassoon (WoO 37) was written in Bonn for Count von Westerholt and two of his children.[15] In later life this pattern continued, and occasionally a major work was written for a particular performer—for example, the Violin Concerto (written for Franz Clement) and the 'Hammerklavier' Sonata (for Archduke Rudolph).[16] It is often difficult to be sure whether a work was written specifically for a performer or merely happened to be first played by him, but in a few cases a work was specially designed to suit a particular player. According to both Czerny and Ries, the Horn Sonata (Op. 17) was written extremely quickly for a travelling virtuoso named Johann Stich (alias Giovanni Punto) who had arrived in Vienna in 1800; Czerny says that Beethoven 'had to confine himself to devising melodies that would not cause that player any difficulty',[17] and indeed the melodies are peculiarly well adapted to the natural horn.

Beethoven's last violin sonata, Op. 96, was written for another travelling virtuoso, Pierre Rode, with the piano part intended for Archduke Rudolph, who played it at the first performance on 29 December 1812. In a letter to Rudolph shortly before the event Beethoven told him that the finale had taken longer to write than expected, because 'in view of Rode's playing I have had to give more thought to the composition of this movement. In our finales we like to have fairly noisy passages, but R does not care for them —and so I have been rather hampered.[18] Thus in at least one movement of the sonata the music was specially designed for a particular performer, and in fact the whole sonata has rather a gentle, lyrical character which was perhaps intended to suit Rode's style of playing. The 'Kreutzer' Sonata, Op. 47, was written in 1803 for a different violinist, George Bridgetower, but the finale of this work was certainly not written to suit the performer, for it had been composed a year earlier for a different sonata (Op. 30 No. 1) before being discarded. Bridgetower's appearance in Vienna simply gave Beethoven an incentive to compose a new work that could incorporate this spare movement.

Performances themselves could occasionally have an effect on Beethoven's output, too. A work might be revised as a result of him hearing a performance of it, a notable example being the Fifth and Sixth symphonies: Beethoven told his publishers, Breitkopf & Härtel, 'Tomorrow you will receive a notice about some small corrections which I made during the performance of the symphonies—When I gave these works to you, I had not yet heard either of them performed.'[19] The most conspicuous of these alterations is the insertion of bar 4 at the beginning of the Fifth Symphony (Ex. 3.1); this bar (and the coresponding bars later in the movement) is not in the earliest impression of the symphony to be printed.[20] The standard of

[15] TF, pp. 122–4.   [16] KH, p. 146; A-948.   [17] Czerny, *Performance*, p. 8.
[18] A-392.   [19] A-199.   [20] Brandenburg, 'Fifth Symphony', p. 177.

Ex. 3.1 Op. 67. i

performance could even have a profound effect on Beethoven's thinking. After hearing a particularly sensitive performance of one of his works by a young girl he expressed the intention of writing more piano music than he had done up to them;[21] conversely, a bad performance could have a very depressing effect: 'All desire to compose anything more ceases completely if I have to hear my work performed *like that*!' wrote Beethoven in 1806 after an under-rehearsed performance of *Leonore*.[22]

Works commissioned by publishers tended to be of a shorter, more popular type than those discussed above, although there are some notable exceptions. The longest-lasting of these publishers' commissions was the series of folksong harmonizations and variations that Beethoven supplied to George Thomson. Contact between Thomson and Beethoven was apparently first made in 1803 and was continued till at least 1819. During this period Beethoven supplied a large number of song harmonizations (WoO 152–7 and Op. 108) and some sets of variations (Opp. 105 and 107). Thomson asked for very much more, including sonatas with Scottish melodies as themes, trios, and quintets, but frequently a price could not be agreed and so these works were not written. Other publishers also sometimes asked Beethoven to write a work in a particular genre. Adolf Martin Schlesinger of Berlin asked him for three new piano sonatas in 1820, and although he was only prepared to offer 90 ducats rather than the 120 ducats that Beethoven initially asked for,[23] the works were duly written and published as Opp. 109–11. It was the composer–publisher Antonio Diabelli who provided the initial idea, and the theme, for Beethoven's gigantic set of variations Op. 120, although Diabelli had only asked him, like each of the other leading composers in Vienna, for one variation, rather than the thirty-three that Beethoven eventually provided. A different composer-publisher, Muzio Clementi, commissioned a fantasia and two sonatas for piano (Opp. 77–9) after meeting Beethoven in 1807, and even persuaded him to arrange the solo part of his Violin Concerto for the piano to turn the work into a piano concerto.[24] Another important arrangement that came about through the initiative of a publisher is the piano duet version of the *Grosse Fuge*: the publisher Matthias Artaria (with the aid of Karl Holz) persuaded Beethoven to make this arrangement and also to write a new finale for the B flat Quartet (Op. 130) to replace the *Grosse Fuge*, which was then published separately.[25]

More often, however, publishers took a less active role in Beethoven's

21 A-18.   23 A-1021, A-1024.   25 TDR, v. 298.
22 A-130.   24 TF, pp. 418–9.

creative process and were merely content to wait for him to offer them anything he had written. There was no system of royalties, and a publisher simply bought a work for a single payment at an agreed price, although it was sometimes possible for Beethoven to sell a work to two different firms, a British one and a Continental one, for simultaneous publication (and two fees), since they were selling to different markets.[26] Thus when deciding what to write he had to bear in mind what was likely to sell well. Large-scale choral works, for example, were often difficult to dispose of. The Mass in C had to be given away to Breitkopf & Härtel for no fee at all because, as they told him, 'there is no demand for church works'.[27] He was eager to have the Mass published since it was a work particularly dear to him, and publication would bring 'honour and glory', even if no profit;[28] but the experience meant that he was unlikely to write further works in this genre without very good reason, and it was more than ten years before he wrote his next Mass, the *Missa solemnis*. On this second occasion, however, he had the opposite problem. At least four publishers were prepared to buy it (Adolf Schlesinger of Berlin, Simrock of Bonn, Peters of Leipzig, and Artaria of Vienna),[29] and he eventually resolved to write at least two further Masses to satisfy them,[30] although this plan became crowded out by other works. In the end the *Missa solemnis* went to none of these publishers but to Schott's of Mainz.

Instrumental music was generally easier to dispose of than choral music, but even here the demand depended on the genre, and works for large numbers of instruments were less easy to sell than music for solo piano. Thus in 1801 Beethoven was charging the same price for a symphony, a septet, and a piano sonata. 'The reason is that I find that a septet or a symphony does not sell as well as a sonata,' he wrote.[31] It is hardly surprising, then, that he wrote far more sonatas than symphonies.

Towards the end of Beethoven's life there was a surge of interest in his compositions. As he told his brother in July 1822, 'There is a general scramble to secure my works.'[32] This scramble had already become evident by then in the competing demands for the *Missa solemnis*, and he tried to take advantage of the situation by digging out old works that had long lain unpublished. The plan met with only partial success for, as noted earlier, many stage works still did not represent a commercial proposition for publishers. Some old works—notably bagatelles and songs—needed revision or even completion before they could be published, and Beethoven soon found it was just as easy to write new pieces as to try and update old or incomplete ones; hence whereas some of the bagatelles of Op. 119 were reworkings of earlier material, those of Op. 126 were entirely new (see Chapter 16).

---

[26] This arrangement is referred to in several of Beethoven's letters; for a particularly clear statement about it, see A-1012.   [27] A-168.

[28] Ibid.   [29] A-1019, A-1074-5, A-1083, A-1093.

[30] A-1158.   [31] A-44.   [32] A-1086.

Meanwhile quartets had come into fashion again, and he received a commission for three from the Russian Prince Galitzin. As usual, Beethoven retained the right to sell these pieces to a publisher, and he found there was even more of a scramble for them than there had been for the *Missa solemnis*. Thus after disposing of the first (Op. 127) to Schott for 50 ducats he was able to raise the price to 80 ducats per quartet for the next two (Opp. 132 and 130). 80 ducats (or 360 florins) was a very considerable sum—more than a third of what he received for the *Missa solemnis* (1,000 florins), almost as much as he was paid for three piano sonatas (90 ducats), and not far short of the annual salary of such people as rank-and-file musicians at the Opera, school teachers, and junior lecturers at the university.[33] Even then demand outstripped supply, for Moritz Schlesinger wanted three quartets at 80 ducats each,[34] while Schott and Artaria were also prepared to pay the same price for at least one. Such a demand for what he had long regarded as one of his favourite genres greatly pleased Beethoven: 'It really seems that our age is taking a step forward,' he commented in 1826,[35] referring to the sudden demand for quartets. When he had completed the commission for Prince Galitzin he therefore had every incentive to write further quartets. Compared with a Mass they did not take long to write, so that he would receive some badly needed income fairly soon; and there was a ready market offering a good price that was more or less guaranteed before he started to compose a new work. Thus although the last two quartets (Opp. 131 and 135) were not exactly commissioned by the publishers, the distinction between a commissioned and an uncommissioned work is blurred in such cases.

Hence the role of the publishing world in the creation of a new work could range from a completely passive one (if the work was written without regard to publication prospects) to a direct and active request from a specific publisher. But often the market forces played some intermediate role in which the possibility of publication provided an additional incentive, and sometimes quite a strong one, to write a piece in a particular genre.

Commissions sometimes also came from private individuals wishing to possess a new work by Beethoven, as in the case of Prince Galitzin already mentioned. Again it is often difficult to distinguish between outright commissions, direct and indirect requests without offer of a definite fee, and cases in which Beethoven responded to a given situation by composing a work for someone on his own initiative. The Variations on Paisiello's 'Nel cor più non mi sento' (WoO 70), for example, were written for a lady who told Beethoven she had lost a set of variations (by another composer) on the same theme; Beethoven at once made good her loss by writing his own set,[36] but

---

[33] Hanson, 'Incomes', p. 180. These figures should, however, be treated with caution, as Hanson points out; e.g. orchestral musicians supplemented their salaries of about 480 florins by additional earnings elsewhere, and Beethoven's annuity of 1,360 florins dwarfed the fees he received for his quartets.   [34] A-1420.

[35] A-1481.   [36] TF, p. 176.

whether this was at her request or whether he simply sent them unannounced is not clear. He certainly did on occasion make unsolicited gifts of new pieces. Obvious though trivial examples are the various musical quips, phrases, and even complete canons that he sometimes included in his letters. More substantial gifts were also sometimes offered to friends—men, women, and even children—for example the *Gratulations-Menuett* (WoO 3) for Carl Friedrich Hensler in 1822, the song 'An die Hoffnung' (Op. 32) for Countess Josephine Deym-Brunsvik in 1805, and a trio in B flat (WoO 39) for the ten-year-old Maximiliane Brentano in 1812.[37]

A further problem concerning private commissions is that information is often lacking unless the relevant correspondence has happened to survive. Thus we know that Count Razumovsky commissioned three quartets (Op. 59);[38] that Prince Esterházy commissioned the Mass in C;[39] that the *Elegischer Gesang* was written at the request of Baron Pasqualati in 1814 to commemorate the third anniversary of the death of his wife;[40] that Count Oppersdorff paid Beethoven 500 florins for the Fourth Symphony and probably another 500 for the Fifth;[41] and that Beethoven set some texts by the poet Christian Ludwig Reissig at the latter's request (and without fee).[42] But we have little specific evidence about many of the other works commissioned, even though they were so numerous that Beethoven told Wegeler in 1801, 'I am offered more commissions than it is possible for me to carry out.'[43]

He worked out a regular method of dealing with these commissions, as explained by his brother Carl in a letter of 5 December 1802:

Finally I shall inform you touching the manner in which my brother [i.e. Ludwig] sells his works. We already have in print 34 works and about 18 [opus] numbers. These pieces were mostly commissioned by amateurs under the following agreement: he who wants a piece pays a fixed sum for its exclusive possession for a half or a whole year, or longer, and binds himself not to give the manuscript to *anybody*; at the conclusion of the period it is the privilege of the composer to do what he pleases with the work [i.e. he is free to publish it].[44]

This passage not only confirms that most of Beethoven's early works were written as a result of commissions rather than purely out of artistic enterprise, but also suggests clues to aid in the identification of works that were probably commissioned. A gap of more than six months between the time a work was completed and the date of publication implies a possible commission, and a longer gap makes the likelihood even stronger unless other reasons are known for the delay. An example is the String Quintet Op. 29, which was completed in 1801 but not published until December 1802:[45] other evidence confirms that this work was commissioned by Count Moritz von Fries.[46] The violin sonatas Opp. 23 and 24 were delayed for almost as long

---

[37] KH, pp. 431, 82, 482.   [41] TF, pp. 432–3.   [44] TF. p. 311.

[38] A-135.   [39] KH, p. 238.   [42] A-245, A-279.   [45] KH, p. 71.

[40] KH, pp. 341–2.   [43] A-51.   [46] TF, pp. 310–1.

and were probably also commissioned by Fries. Works were often dedicated to the person who commissioned them (as was Op. 29), but by no means always: sometimes dedications were just made out of friendship or in gratitude for past favours, and in some cases Beethoven changed the dedicatee at the last moment.[47] The three piano trios Op. 1 were dedicated to Prince Lichnowsky and were first performed at his house, at a time when Beethoven was actually living there; it seems very likely, therefore, that the prince actually commissioned the trios for performance at the weekly concerts held there, but this is by no means certain.

Another sign that a work may have been commissioned is if it shows no real artistic development over previous ones. The three marches for piano duet, Op. 45, have no great merit and are rarely performed today, and so it is no surprise to find that according to Ries they were written in response to a commission, from Count Browne.[48] Similarly the two short piano sonatas Op. 49 Nos. 1 and 2, written in 1796–7, seem elementary and retrogressive after the three sonatas Op. 2 of 1795 and are therefore likely to have been commissioned by a not very accomplished pianist—particularly as they were not published until several years later.

Beethoven's willingness to write in almost any genre for the sake of the commission fee, whether from a publisher, theatre director, or wealthy patron, might give the impression that he was a somewhat mercenary composer, concerned mainly with making as much money as he could; but he emphasized that this was not the case. The money he earned was not used for unnecessary luxuries but was actually badly needed simply in order to live independently or, in later life, to provide for himself and Karl.[49] After the adoption of his nephew in 1815, which had given him a major financial burden, he often felt the need to augment his income as much as possible from his compositions. His financial worries, and the need to earn more through his works, are expressed particularly often in his letters of the early 1820s when the problem of providing for Karl and himself, despite frequent ill health, was apparently at its greatest.[50] At this time his annuity was clearly insufficient, and as his only other income came from composition he was ready to grab almost any opportunity that came his way. A glance at the list of the principal works written during his last ten years, the period where there is most evidence and where the professional pressures are particularly apparent, shows that virtually every one of them was occasioned by professional factors of various kinds or by the immediate circumstances around him (see Table 1).

As can be seen from the table, in the early part of this period financial pressures were not particularly great: the 'Hammerklavier' Sonata was just a present to his most loyal patron in return for past favours and out of

[47] See e.g. Tyson, 'Razumovsky', p. 134.   [48] TF, p. 307.
[49] A-272, A-1083.   [50] See e.g. A-1059, A-1143, A-1237, A-1300, A-1321.

TABLE 1. *Principal Works, 1817–1826*

Date	Opus No.	Work	Probable initial stimulus
1817–19	106	'Hammerklavier' Sonata	For Archduke Rudolph in gratitude for loyal patronage
1819–22	123	*Missa solemnis*	Archduke Rudolph's enthronement in March 1820
1819–23	120	Diabelli Variations	Request from Antonio Diabelli
1820–1	119/7–11	Bagatelles	Request from Friedrich Starke
1820–2	109–11	Three piano sonatas	Commission from Adolf Schlesinger
1822	119/1–6	Bagatelles	Request from Carl Friedrich Peters for short piano pieces
1822	124 (+ WoO 98)	*Die Weihe des Hauses* overture and chorus	Commission from Carl Friedrich Hensler
1823–4	125	Ninth Symphony	Commission from Philharmonic Society
1824	126	Bagatelles	Hopes for quick sale to repay debt to brother Johann
1823–5	127 132 130	Quartets	Commission from Prince Galitzin
1825–6	131 135	Quartets	Requests (quasi-commissions) from Schott, Moritz Schlesinger, and perhaps other publishers
1826	134 130. vi	Arrangement of *Grosse Fuge* New finale for quartet	Request from Matthias Artaria Request from Matthias Artaria

friendship.[51] The *Missa solemnis* was a similar present but was written with a specific occasion in mind. And the Diabelli Variations were very much more substantial than what Diabelli had asked for. But most of the remaining works, those of the 1820s, took the form of commissions, with the fee being negotiated before composition began.

Commissions were clearly an integral part of Beethoven's composing career and rarely seem to have been refused outright. If he failed to respond to a commission it was usually because he had too many on offer, as he pointed out to Wegeler (see above). For example, although Count Apponyi apparently asked him for a quartet in 1795, his first one was not begun until the middle of 1798 (though this may have been because he felt unready in 1795 to write in the highest and most refined medium of the day). Similarly near the end of his life he undertook to write a quintet and a sonata for piano duet for Antonio Diabelli,[52] as well as an opera, an oratorio, and two Masses, but all these projects were crowded out by other works such as the late quartets. Occasionally, too, he did not fulfil a commission because the price he asked was too high, even after a bit of haggling. For instance, when in 1816 the London publisher Robert Birchall asked him for some variations he suggested a fee of £30; and although he later reduced this to £20 the publisher was unwilling to pay more than £12, and so the work was never written.[53]

Despite persistent financial pressures, however, Beethoven stressed on a number of occasions that he did not compose merely to earn money but that he always had artistic aims in view.[54] He was able to realize these aims by retaining firm control over the content of his compositions, so that although the choice of genre was often made by someone else the actual style and form used were decided by him alone; outside interference in this realm was tolerated only on a few exceptional occasions and was normally firmly rejected. When he was asked in 1802 for a sonata following a specified plan and tonal scheme he replied: 'The lady can have a sonata from me, and, moreover, from an *aesthetic* point of view I will in general adopt her plan —but without adopting—her keys.'[55] And except during a brief period around 1814, he was not prepared to compromise his style in order to give his works a more popular appeal. As already noted, he was willing to write easy pieces on occasion, but he refused to lower himself from 'that elevation and originality of style' that were so characteristic of his music.[56] Thus external factors affected only the choice of genre, not the style, and he was well aware of this:

[51] A-948.   [52] A-1304, A-1310, A-1313.
[53] A-662, A-680; for a draft of Birchall's reply to the first of these two letters, see Sotheby auction catalogue, 9 May 1985, item 6.
[54] A-1024, A-1080.
[55] A-57. Whether the lady received a sonata in the end is not known; it is not impossible, however, that one of the set Op. 31 was later sent to her.   [56] A-136.

My situation demands that my actions [i.e. in deciding what to write] be determined by what is likely to be more or less of advantage to me. Quite different considerations operate, of course, in the case of the work itself [i.e. the style]. There, thank God, I never think of the advantage to be reaped but only of how I am composing.[57]

His aim was to advance and develop his art in general, and this could be done in many different ways and in a variety of genres. There was insufficient time for him to explore all of them, and so some kind of selection had to be made. It was relatively unimportant which of the various avenues he explored, so that accepting a request for a particular genre in no way impeded his artistic progress but just turned that progress in a particular direction. It still allowed plenty of scope for experimentation and innovation in such features as form, harmony, rhythm, and other aspects of style.

Beethoven also made some effort to manipulate the commissions so that they coincided with what he wanted to write. He had been wanting to write a Ninth Symphony ever since completing the Eighth in 1812 and had even made a start on it in 1815–16, but for a long while he had no incentive to work at it intensively. Then in July 1822 he wrote to Ferdinand Ries in London: 'Have you any idea what fee the Harmony Society would offer me for a grand symphony?'[58] Ries took up the matter with the members of the Philharmonic Society and the result was a commission that Beethoven was pleased to accept in December 1822.[59] Similarly he was planning to write some more quartets even before he received the commission from Prince Galitzin in 1822.[60]

Nevertheless it was the commissions that were often the deciding factor in determining which of the works he had in mind were written. As he said himself: 'Although I certainly do not compose merely for the sake of the fee, yet my circumstances demand that I give some consideration to this matter.'[61] Thus he was forced to accept a situation in which the direction of his artistic progress was determined partly by outside factors. He found the situation tolerable but not ideal, and he felt that his artistic goals would have been better served if he had not had to bear in mind financial constraints. He complained of having to 'scrawl' and to write 'potboilers' in order to support himself while writing a great work;[62] and he noted in a conversation book of 1823 that because of his inadequate income he was not writing what he would most like to, and that he hoped one day to be able to write what would be the highest achievement for him and his art—music for Goethe's *Faust*.[63]

Thus professional pressures, from patrons, performers, and publishers, played very little part in shaping the actual content and style of any of Beethoven's music, but they certainly played a major and often decisive role, and a much bigger one than he would have ideally liked, in determining what

---

[57] A-1158.   [58] A-1084.
[59] A-1110; the fee was £50 (see TF, p. 913), i.e. 500 florins.   [60] TF, p. 815.
[61] A-1472.   [62] A-903, A-1059.   [63] TF, p. 834.

works were written at any paticular time. They probably account for the existence of well over half his major works and are the main reason why the distribution of his works throughout his career follows such an irregular, almost random pattern. Very little was written purely for art's sake or for an audience in an ideal world that he hoped lay somewhere in the future; in some ways he was very much a man of his time and place, and had he been surrounded by a different set of patrons his output would almost certainly have been very different. Although he wrote nine symphonies he might easily have written double that number if there had been sufficient incentive. If Prince Esterházy had liked the Mass in C, instead of finding it 'unbearably ridiculous and detestable',[64] Beethoven would no doubt have been willing to write more Masses for him. If the theatre directors in 1815 had been prepared to pay Beethoven another 200 ducats we should probably now have two operas by him instead of just the one. He would not, but for Adolf Schlesinger, have written his last three piano sonatas. And the romantic notion of the ageing master turning his back on the world of public music in 1824 in order to devote himself to the string quartet as the loftiest and most esoteric genre of the day, without concern for immediate profit but purely for art's sake and perhaps for a small circle of admirers in an increasingly hostile world, must be laid aside. Surprising as it may seem, the evidence indicates a much more mundane and opportunistic approach to the composition of these late quartets, at least as far as choice of genre is concerned, despite the extraordinary quality of the music itself.

[64] Knapp, 'Mass in C', p. 201.

4

Extramusical Factors

IT is difficult to assess how much extramusical influence there was on Beethoven's output, since any answer is bound to involve some speculation; but there is some firm evidence that can be brought to bear on the subject. It is a subject about which a great deal has been written already, but much of the literature has tended to confuse the issue rather than illuminate it. In some cases errors of dating have led to false conclusions about extramusical influence, and three other things have also been allowed to cloud the picture: hearsay evidence, pure speculation, and the notion that Beethoven's music is a close parallel to his life. It will be best to dispose of each of these ideas first.

Hearsay evidence comes from a number of Beethoven's acquaintances, who claimed after his death that he had told them something about the meaning of his music. Some of these accounts may be true, but where uncorroborated they should be treated with greatest caution: as mentioned in Chapter 1, some witnesses are known to have invented stories about Beethoven to suit their own purposes. In particular, Anton Schindler tried to give the world the impression that Beethoven had given him unique insights into the music; a number of his fake entries in Beethoven's conversation books were made for this purpose.[1] Since he went to such great lengths to fabricate evidence, any statement by Schindler purporting to give an authentic interpretation about the meaning of a particular piece is especially likely to be fraudulent, even though such statements have been widely quoted and accepted. One example is Schindler's report that when he asked Beethoven about the meaning of the piano sonatas in D minor and F minor, Op. 31 No. 2 and Op. 57, he was told, 'Read Shakespeare's *Tempest*!'[2] This supposed conversation has even resulted in the D minor Sonata sometimes being known as the 'Tempest' Sonata, and in some commentators suggesting which parts of it might represent Prospero and Miranda. Schindler did in fact claim that Beethoven planned to attach programmatic titles to all his compositions[3]—an idea that would have appealed to Beethoven's romantic successors but surely not to Beethoven himself. The most celebrated of all Beethoven's programmatic remarks, that the start of the Fifth Symphony represents Fate knocking at the door, also derives from Schindler[4] and must therefore be dismissed too.

Schindler was not the only one of Beethoven's acquantances to transmit

---

[1] See e.g. Beck and Herre, 'Schindler', Conversation Books 110 fo. 27^r and 129 fo. 6^r.
[2] Schindler/MacArdle, *Beethoven*, p. 406.   [3] Ibid., p. 400.   [4] Ibid., p. 147.

extramusical ideas about instrumental works. Czerny states that 'Beethoven got many of his ideas from chance occurrences and impressions'[5] and gives several examples—bird-song for motifs in the Fifth and Ninth symphonies, country musicians for the Mass in C and the Trio Op. 70 No. 2, and a galloping horse for the finale of Op. 31 No. 2, although in the latter case the sketches do not bear him out (see Chapter 12). Ferdinand Ries and Charles Neate also both claim that Beethoven 'often' (Ries) or 'always' (Neate) had something specific in mind when composing,[6] but there is rarely any trace of such things in the sketches except in overtly programmatic works like the 'Pastoral' Symphony. An exception, however, is the slow movement of the Quartet Op. 18 No. 1, which according to Karl Amenda represented the tomb scene from *Romeo and Juliet*.[7] Among the sketches for this movement are some otherwise puzzling remarks: 'il prend le tombeau', 'il se tue', and 'les derniers soupirs'.[8] There is no proof that these refer to *Romeo and Juliet*, but the comments certainly fit the situation in the play.

The slow movement of another quartet, Op. 59 No. 2, also has allegedly extramusical associations, for Czerny reports that Beethoven conceived the movement as he gazed at the stars.[9] This is indeed quite plausible, for Beethoven several times used E major, the key of the movement in question, for songs mentioning stars, as in 'Abendlied unterm gestirnten Himmel' (WoO 150), 'Sehnsucht' (WoO 146), and 'Komm, Hoffnung, lass den letzten Stern' in *Fidelio*. Thus there is evidence that Beethoven sometimes when composing had in mind an extramusical idea not expressed in the final score, but how often this happened is unclear, for he was 'not very communicative on this subject, except occasionally when in a confiding humour';[10] and in many cases the extramusical idea probably provided no more than an initial stimulus for one musical idea, rather than a definite programme for a whole work.

Nevertheless some later writers have speculated about pictorialism in his instrumental music, and have claimed to be able to interpret its meaning in extramusical terms. Such speculation has given rise to a number of popular nicknames, including 'Moonlight' Sonata and 'Ghost' Trio. In some cases the interpretation goes beyond mere titles, and individual passages are characterized, even to the extent of complete movements being analysed in largely extramusical terms. In some of these poetic interpretations, writers even claim that Beethoven himself thought along these lines. Perhaps the most notable example is the work of Arnold Schering, who attempted to uncover an underlying programme for many of Beethoven's instrumental works and associated each one with a well-known literary work such as Homer's *Iliad* or Goethe's *Faust*. Such ideas are extremely speculative and form no basis for a proper assessment of extramusical factors in Beethoven's

[5] Czerny, *Performance*, p. 12.   [6] TF, pp. 436 and 620.   [7] TF, p. 261.
[8] SV 46, pp. 8–9. Nottebohm (N-II, p. 485) mentions only the last of these remarks.
[9] Czerny, *Performance*, p. 60.   [10] Ibid.

music. In many cases, too, they would be undermined by an investigation of the sketches for the work in question.[11]

The third notion to be disposed of is the idea that Beethoven's music is an accurate reflection of his personal life and moods. Some people express amazement that Beethoven could write two such contrasted works as the Fifth and Sixth symphonies at almost the same time, but in fact such contrasts were a necessary and inevitable part of his creative process, and sometimes changes in the mood of the music were very rapid. For example, in the Piano Sonata Op. 28 Beethoven sketched three bars of the slow movement, a sad and delicate one in D minor, and then almost with the same stroke of the pen he moved on to a sketch for the exuberant finale (see Ex. 4.1). From their

Ex. 4.1 SV 163, fo. 1ᵛ

layout it is clear that these were written as a single draft. On the next two staves there is a further idea for each of these movements, after which appear some more for the slow movement followed by two for the finale. One cannot accept that Beethoven's moods kept altering suddenly in line with the changes of moods in these sketches.[12]

One must not, however, adopt the opposite standpoint, that Beethoven's artistic and personal lives were two entirely different worlds, with his internal world of composition aloof from outside influence. Such ideas have sometimes been expressed, and very often they derive from Thayer's observation that the Second Symphony, a strikingly cheerful work, was written at about the same time as the Heiligenstadt Testament.[13] In fact, Thayer was

---

[11] See e.g. Brandenburg, 'Dankgesang', p. 164.
[12] Cf. also Beethoven's own remark (A-351): 'The artist must often be able to assume all humours; and thus my good humour may have been feigned.'   [13] TF, p. 306.

inaccurate about the date of the symphony, which was completed in about April 1802,[14] well before the Heiligenstadt Testament of 6–10 October 1802 and at a time when Beethoven's moods alternated between optimism and pessimism; hence its cheerful nature should not surprise even those who expect the work to reflect some of Beethoven's innermost feelings.

With certain types of evidence thus excluded, what is left, and in what ways could extramusical influences be shown to affect the music? Basically there are two ways: changes in Beethoven's life could have brought about changes in his musical style and output almost subconsciously; and pieces with some programmatic content, such as vocal works, could have been chosen at a particular time because of their content, as a conscious attempt to express their ideas in music. These two types of influences are to a certain extent interrelated, but let us consider each in turn. To demonstrate the first it is necessary to show that changes in life-style were more or less contemporary with changes in musical output, and then it may be possible to deduce that the two changes are related rather than just coincident. With Bach this is not too difficult: when he was organist at Weimar he wrote much organ music; as court composer at Cöthen he wrote mainly instrumental and chamber music; and as Kapellmeister at Leipzig he began by writing a large number of cantatas. In the case of Beethoven, although professional pressures did exist (see Chapter 3), they were never as strong as they were for Bach, and he tended to write the same types of music throughout his life. Similarly, his life itself did not change very dramatically, in that, once he had left Bonn in 1792, he remained in Vienna as a free-lance musician almost all the time.

Nevertheless his life in Vienna can be divided into three phases, separated by two very dramatic turning-points or crises in his life. The first came in about 1800–2, with the gradual onset of his deafness. The first symptoms had actually appeared in about 1798 and the problem persisted throughout his life, but it was in about 1800–2 that he began to realize that the deafness was progressive and incurable. The crisis came to a head in the Heiligenstadt Testament of 6–10 October 1802, with its talk of suicide, despair, and yet determination to persevere. After this date the mental and emotional turmoil seems to have subsided somewhat as Beethoven came to accept his affliction and be reconciled to living with it. It seems clear, however, that the crisis had a marked effect on his musical output. His work has long been divided into three periods, and although scholars are not agreed as to exactly when the second period began, all accept a date somewhere around 1801–3; even those writers who have divided the music into different numbers of periods are agreed that a dramatic turning-point took place at about this time,[15] with heroic elements becoming prominent in many works.[16]

[14] See Brandenburg ed., *Kessler* vol. ii p. iv.   [15] See Solomon, 'Periods'.
[16] See Tyson, 'Heroic', for a discussion of Beethoven's 'heroic phase'.

Beethoven's deafness had two other noticeable effects on his output. Firstly there was a dramatic reduction in the amount of piano music being written; this was no doubt partly due to the termination of his career as a piano virtuoso necessitated by his deafness. Another effect was that, with less effort now being put into piano playing, he could devote more attention to composition, and there was a dramatic increase in his output at the beginning of the new century. (It has also been suggested that his increasing deafness, especially during his final ten years, was the cause of his harsh and eccentric harmony, but this seems doubtful.)

The event which changed Beethoven's whole way of life a second time was the death of his brother Caspar Carl on 15 November 1815. From then on Beethoven became the guardian of his brother's nine-year-old son Karl, and the composer's bachelor existence was disrupted by all the practical and psychological problems of caring for his nephew. The crisis was also complicated psychologically by the aftermath of an extremely intense love affair of some three or four years earlier with his so-called 'Immortal Beloved' (see below). Like the deafness crisis, this one too seems to have had a profound effect on Beethoven's music, and his 'third period' begins about this date. Again it cannot be agreed exactly when this period begins, but it is generally accepted that the change took place somewhere between 1812 and 1816. The music of the third period is characterized by, amongst other features, a serene quality almost unmatched by any other composer, an occasional childlike naïvety, and a marked drop in the number of works being completed. These features could be due to biographical influences: the serenity may be due to a feeling on Beethoven's part that he had weathered life's storms; the apparent naïvety may be due to the fact that he was sharing his life with a child; and the drop in the number of works, resulting in virtually nothing being completed in 1817, may be due partly to his long-running battles over Karl's guardianship, although after these ended in 1820 his productivity increased again. From around 1815–17 there also date several abandoned works and a great array of undeveloped concept sketches in the sketchbooks, suggesting a period of self-doubt and seeking after a new style not yet found. In any case, however, it is surely no coincidence that the three periods into which Beethoven's musical output is customarily divided match the major biographical changes almost exactly. Further changes, in such matters as his methods of sketching and his relationship to his patrons, also tend almost uncannily to reinforce, rather than cut across, those already discussed.[17] In both his biography and his musical output, too, an additional period could be added at the beginning, covering his period in Bonn up to 1792.

There is also the question of how far Beethoven's temperament in general is reflected in his music. Again it is difficult to be certain, but some connections seem reasonably clear. He was generally regarded as an irascible person, and he clearly had sudden bursts of anger more often than most people. His

[17] Solomon, 'Periods'.

music in places reflects this trait: it contains probably a higher proportion of violent off-beat sforzandos than that of any other major composer; it also contains some ferocious discords virtually unmatched by any of his contemporaries, such as a passage in the 'Eroica' Symphony (Ex. 4.2) and the seven-note discord (using all the notes of the D minor scale) near the start of the last movement of the Ninth Symphony (Ex. 4.3). Thus his music contains both rhythmic and harmonic violence to an unusual degree for its

Ex. 4.2 Op. 55. i

Ex. 4.3 Op. 125. iv

date. He was also generally considered eccentric, if not positively insane, by his contemporaries, and his eccentric behaviour tended to become more pronounced as he grew older. His music likewise is full of eccentricities, some of which go well beyond his desire for novelty and surprise (mentioned in Chapter 2). Finally his determination to succeed despite adversity, so evident in several areas of his life, seems to be reflected in many works, especially those of a heroic nature.

Let us turn now to Beethoven's works with overtly extramusical content. His two great crises might be expected to have been reflected in such works, and indeed each evidently gave rise to a specific piece—one which provided a kind of universal discussion of his problem without referring to it explicitly. In the earlier case, Beethoven tried various remedies for his deafness, without success; eventually, as a last desperate resort, he spent six months (April–October 1802) away from Vienna in the quiet village of Heiligenstadt. As this period drew to a close it became apparent that this treatment, too, had been unsuccessful; his last hope had gone and his deafness was going to persist permanently. This was the context in which the Heiligenstadt Testament was written. 'Yes, that fond hope—which I brought here with me, to be cured to a degree at least—this I must now wholly abandon.' He was 'compelled to face the prospect of a lasting malady'. The departure from Heiligenstadt thus marked a decisive turn in his life, and he recognized this: 'Heiligenstadt, October 10th, 1802, thus I bid thee farewell—and indeed sadly.'[18] His problem from then on was not how to cure his affliction but how to live with it, and his next work, indicating a resolution to overcome his misfortune, was therefore unusually significant.

Apart from the duet 'Nei giorni tuoi felici' (WoO 93), which was not so much a composition as an exercise in preparation for launching himself as an operatic composer, and which may anyway have been begun before 6–10 October, the first work Beethoven conceived after Heiligenstadt was the oratorio *Christus am Oelberge*, as is clear from the 'Wielhorsky' Sketchbook (SV 343). Exactly when it was begun is uncertain, but it seems to have been before the end of November 1802,[19] and the oratorio was first performed on 5 April 1803. The libretto, by Franz Xaver Huber, has much in common with the Heiligenstadt Testament: both contain ideas of extreme and undeserved suffering, expressions of terror, a sense of isolation, fear of imminent death, resignation to fate, fierce struggle, love of mankind in general, and the prospect of ultimate triumph over adversity.[20] It appears that Beethoven provided the ideas for the oratorio, adapting them from his recent experiences, and Huber simply put them into verse. Many of the ideas also recur in *Fidelio*, but the latter is not nearly so specifically concerned with a single subject, and there is less concentration on the idea of suffering. *Christus*, on the other hand, is a highly specific study in triumph over suffering through endurance and through universal love, and it would almost certainly not have been written but for the events in Beethoven's personal life immediately beforehand. Beethoven universalized his own misfortune by presenting it in

---

[18] Translations from Solomon, *Beethoven*, p. 118. 'Thee' refers to Heiligenstadt, not to some mysterious person (as has sometimes been conjectured).

[19] See Fishman, 'Wielhorsky'. A later date is suggested in JTW, but a letter from Beethoven's brother apparently referring to it is dated 23 Nov. 1802.

[20] For a detailed comparison of the two texts see Cooper, 'Oratorio'. See also Tyson, 'Heroic'.

the figure of Christ, and was thereby evidently able to overcome his emotional turmoil.

His second great crisis, that of 1812–15, was more complex since it comprised both the affair with the 'Immortal Beloved' and the question of the nephew, problems separated by about three years but closely related psychologically in that both concerned intense love and affection on Beethoven's part. The main evidence for the affair with the 'Immortal Beloved' is a passionate letter written by Beethoven that omits the name of the addressee and was evidently never sent.[21] Her identity was for a long time a mystery, but she has now been identified with a reasonable degree of certainty as Antonie Brentano.[22] She was of Viennese origin but had married in 1798 and moved to Frankfurt. She moved back temporarily in 1809 and met Beethoven in 1810. During 1811–12 their friendship deepened and he started presenting her with compositions, including a song significantly entitled 'An die Geliebte' (To the Beloved, WoO 140); this is his only song with accompaniment for guitar, an instrument on which Antonie was expert. Then on 6–7 July 1812, while he was in Teplitz and the Brentanos were in Karlsbad, he wrote the famous letter beginning 'My angel, my all, my very self'. A few months afterwards the Brentanos left Vienna for good and returned to Frankfurt, but Beethoven had been profoundly affected by the affair and for nearly a year composed very little. Even after this, although they never met again, he and Antonie continued to retain a high place in each other's affections.[23]

The death of his brother in 1815, and the adoption of Karl, altered Beethoven's attitude to women in general and to Antonie in particular. Up to that time he had needed her for two basic reasons—their deep love, and his need for a wife. Now he no longer felt the same need for a wife, as his desire for a family had been fulfilled and he could devote all his attentions to his nephew, who became the chief object of his love. Meanwhile his love for Antonie would always continue, but it could become a more pure, spiritual love; he became reconciled to the fact that they would probably never meet again and she could remain a 'distant beloved'. He could still, however, communicate with her at the deepest level and express his love for her—through his art. This, more than anything, was what enabled him to become reconciled to their permanent separation.

Thus it is not surprising that the first major work begun by Beethoven after his brother's death was the song cycle *An die ferne Geliebte*, which reflects his new attitude. The work was almost certainly begun and ended within a

[21] A-373.

[22] Solomon, *Beethoven*, pp. 158–77. Attempts to undermine Solomon's hypothesis, e.g. in Goldschmidt, *Unsterbliche*, have been unsuccessful. See my review of the latter in *ML*, lx (1979), 463–4.

[23] For a fuller account of Antonie Brentano and her relationship to Beethoven, see Solomon, *Beethoven*, pp. 158–89, on which the above paragraph is largely based.

short space of time, and the poems, by Alois Jeitteles, seem to have been written specially for Beethoven, since they are not known elsewhere.[24] Nothing is known of the relationship between the composer and the poet at this time, but both were living in Vienna and it seems very likely that the poems were written at Beethoven's instigation. He probably outlined the subject-matter in greater or lesser detail and Jeitteles put it into poetry. In other words, the situation was probably very similar to that arising thirteen years earlier, in the conception of *Christus am Oelberge*.

If the text of *An die ferne Geliebte* is compared with Beethoven's situation, there appear, as with *Christus*, remarkable similarities, which here concern his relationship to Antonie. The most obvious similarity is that the Beloved in the poems is distant, and Antonie was living in distant Frankfurt. Distant beloveds are by no means rare in poetry of that period, and they appear in about a dozen of Beethoven's other Lieder.[25] In many of these songs, however, the love for the absent one is not mutual, or at best there is some doubt about whether it is. In the remainder there is usually some anticipation of reunion. Sometimes, too, there is no great emphasis on distance. In contrast *An die ferne Geliebte* places great stress on the distance between the two lovers; secondly the love is mutual, as is evident from the final two lines; and thirdly there is no prospect of reunion, but instead the poems examine ways in which the separation can be made more bearable. These features distinguish this song cycle from Beethoven's other songs about distant beloveds, apart from 'Ruf vom Berge' (WoO 147); significantly this was also written in 1816, a few months after *An die ferne Geliebte*.

The other striking parallel between the song cycle and Beethoven's personal situation is that the lover feels he can reach his beloved through his songs—through his art:

Nimm sie hin denn, diese Lieder,	Then take these songs
Die ich dir, Geliebte, sang.	That I sang to you, Beloved.
Singe sie dann abends wieder	Sing them again in the evening
Zu der Laute süssem Klang...	To the lute's sweet sound...
Und du singst, was ich gesungen...	And you sing what I have sung...
Dann vor diesen Liedern weichet,	Then these songs overcome
Was geschieden uns so weit,	What has kept us so far apart,
Und ein liebend Herz erreichet,	And a loving heart is reached
Was ein liebend Herz geweiht.	By what a loving heart has dedicated.

These extracts from the final song mirror closely what Beethoven appears to have felt about Antonie, for he felt himself still able to reach her heart through his music and he dedicated to her, or sent her a copy of, several of his later works. There are also further similarities between the song cycle and Beethoven's personal life. The picture of domestic bliss portrayed in the fifth song recalls a desire for marriage that he had often expressed himself; and

---

[24] Kerman, 'Geliebte', p. 123.   [25] Ibid., p. 129.

even Antonie's guitar can perhaps be discerned in the last song, transformed into the more poetic lute.

The exact function of the song cycle in Beethoven's life is uncertain (a number of suggestions have been put forward),[26] but it is probably best seen as having performed two main functions for him. Firstly it was a means of communicating his love to Antonie, and the only means of doing so at the deepest level. Secondly it was a means of coming to terms with his plight by universalizing it, just as he had done in *Christus*. The song cycle is not just about Beethoven and Antonie Brentano, but about all separated lovers and how they can communicate by transforming, spiritualizing, and sublimating their passions. By expressing this out in the open in general terms Beethoven was apparently able to work out his emotional crisis and overcome it. Once again, as in 1802, he had been saved by his art, and once again his conflict had been expressed in vocal music.

Beethoven's songs are an obvious place to look for other evidence of the influence of his life on his output, and together they form a significant document on his emotional life. Sometimes he chose poetry simply because he liked it and thought it would go well in a musical setting,[27] but many poems were selected partly for their relevance to his personal life. It is difficult to relate many of his songs to particular stages of his relationships, but there does sometimes seem to be a connection. One example is 'An die Hoffnung' (To Hope, Op. 32), which he may have viewed in part as expressing a hope of a successful outcome to his relationship with Josephine

Ex. 4.4 *a* Op. 32

Die du so gern   in heil'gen Nächt - en   fei - erst

b WoO 132

Der Hoff-nung letz - ter Schim-mer sinkt da - hin

Deym; he sent her the score early in 1805,[28] and may well have written the song for her initially. By 1806 it was clear to Beethoven that she had rejected him,[29] and this is reflected in the song 'Als die Geliebte sich trennen wollte' (When the beloved wished to part, WoO 132) of May that year. The song includes the lines 'The last ray of hope is sinking' and 'Ah, lovely hope, return to me', which certainly stirred memories of 'An die Hoffnung': the

---

[26] Ibid., pp. 131–2; Solomon, *Beethoven*, pp. 297–8.
[27] See A-40, A-506, and A-1136—letters thanking poets for providing him with suitable texts.
[28] KH, p. 82.
[29] Solomon, *Beethoven*, p. 153.

first four notes of each song are identical in pitch and almost identical in rhythm (Ex. 4.4). And once again the poet, in this case Stephan von Breuning, was in close contact with Beethoven at the time.

His last two published songs, excluding revisions and reworkings, both appear to have been chosen because of the content of the text. The earlier one, 'Resignation', was finished in 1817, a very depressing year for him in which he completed virtually nothing of substance; the song expresses a seeking for death and a loss of hope in the world. The second song, 'Abendlied unterm gestirnten Himmel' (Evening Song under a Starry Sky, WoO 150), composed in 1820, similarly expresses a death-wish but is more optimistic. The poet muses on the stars and anticipates his homecoming to heaven; he has weathered life's storms and can no longer be troubled by earthly forces.

Many of the extramusical ideas mentioned so far occur in other works too —especially the question of suffering, which is often connected with the idea of heroism and may have political overtones (as indeed it does in *Christus*). An obvious example is *Egmont*, for which Beethoven provided incidental music in 1810. The play concerns Egmont's struggle against the Spanish oppressors, a subject particularly topical when Vienna had been overrun by the French; Egmont is eventually put to death, but not before predicting the eventual liberation of his country. Beethoven, who was strongly opposed to political repression, was greatly fired by the subject, and several of the ideas in the play (for example the ultimate victory) are implicit even in the overture.

Another work concerned with the death of a hero is the 'Eroica' Symphony (1803–4), with its funeral second movement and its statement, on the title-page of the first edition, that it was written 'to celebrate the memory of a great man'. Again there are strong political overtones for, as is well known, it was originally to have been dedicted to Napoleon as a champion of freedom, but Beethoven tore up the title-page of the manuscript when he heard that Napoleon had proclaimed himself Emperor.[30] The work then became regarded as an expression of heroism in general, of any and every hero, including, no doubt, Beethoven himself as well as the better side of Napoleon. Another hero represented by the symphony is Prometheus, for the finale borrows a theme from Beethoven's ballet *Die Geschöpfe des Prometheus*—a connection that would surely not have been missed by Viennese audiences after the great success of the ballet. The original playbill describes the ballet as 'A heroic, allegorical ballet' and refers to a 'heroic dance' for Bacchus (No. 12); the use in the 'Eroica' of a prominent theme from the work therefore carries with it overtones of the artist-hero who, like Prometheus, 'found the men of his day in a state of ignorance and civilised them', making them 'susceptible to all the passions of human life by the power of harmony'.[31] The symphony finale is probably more progammatic than is

[30] TF, pp. 348–9.   [31] Quoted from the original playbill as cited in TDR, ii. 219.

often realized: the ballet finale begins with the main tune, but in the symphony finale this main tune is preceded by some material that seems to refer to the earlier part of the plot of the ballet. The ballet begins with a storm and so does the symphony finale; Prometheus then encounters his two clay statues, and what could be more statuesque than the stiff, unharmonized bass-line that begins the main part of the symphony finale? This bass-line is then gradually brought to life by the counterpoints placed around it and eventually by the melody placed above it. (How far the rest of the movement is open to similar programmatic interpretation is more uncertain.)

A very different type of hero is Coriolanus, on the subject of whom Beethoven wrote an overture in 1807. The work was intended for a play by Heinrich von Collin, although no particular production seems to have been envisaged when the overture was written. Collin's play, unlike Shakespeare's, is not so much a personal tragedy as a philosophical debate about the freedom of the individual set against the laws and customs of society. The fact that the overture was not written for a particular occasion indicates that Beethoven was attracted by the subject itself, and the music reflects several ideas from the play (for example, the fragmentation of the theme near the end expresses the death of the hero).

The Funeral Cantata on the death of Joseph II (WoO 87), written in 1790, demonstrates that Beethoven's concern for political freedom stemmed from an early age, for Joseph had been an 'enlightened' ruler who had done much to ease political oppression. The work is one of Beethoven's finest from the Bonn period, far more moving and deeply felt than its companion piece, the Cantata on the elevation of Leopold II, written later the same year. That Beethoven himself regarded it highly is shown by the number of devices that he reused in later works,[32] and one complete section ('Da stiegen die Menschen') was actually borrowed for use in the second finale of *Fidelio*.

After the death of Joseph II many of his political reforms were reversed; heavy censorship returned, a strong secret police was active,[33] and there were intermittent threats of invasion. This is the background against which to see works such as the 'Eroica', *Egmont*, and (to a certain extent) the Ninth Symphony. The latter certainly has republican undertones and implied opposition to a ruling class, as in such phrases as 'All men become brothers'. There are clear affinities here with the ideas of *liberté*, *égalité*, and *fraternité* expressed in the French Revolution. But Schiller's text should not be thought of as anticipating a future, post-Revolutionary Utopia in which all men will be equal in a political sense: the sentiments are expressed in the present tense —and Beethoven was clearly aware of this, for the earlier version of the line quoted above, 'Beggars become brothers of princes', was once misquoted by him as 'Princes are beggars'.[34] This misquotation gives an insight into Beethoven's view of the aristocracy, and although he was not actually

---

[32] See Solomon, *Beethoven*, p. 49.   [33] Ibid., p. 91.
[34] SV 106, fo. 43ʳ; see N–I, p. 41.

directly opposed to the nobility (he regarded himself as a noble, though he was not), he strongly opposed the tyranny that princes so often exerted.

There are two other particularly significant features about the text of the Ninth Symphony. Firstly, Beethoven had a lifelong affection for Schiller's poem and was planning a setting of it about thirty years before the date of the Ninth Symphony. Secondly, only a fairly small proportion of the poem was actually included in the symphony. Beethoven, a careful chooser of his text (as ever), selected the passages about joy (recalling the end of the Heiligenstadt Testament—'grant me at last but one pure day of joy'), about the brotherhood of man, about a dear wife, and about a loving Father who dwells above the stars, but he omitted the sections on drinking and general merry-making.

There were, then, three ideas of particular concern to Beethoven that were often expressed in his music: suffering and heroic struggle; woman's love and the prospect of marital bliss; and liberty. All three came together in *Fidelio*. It was a work over which he laboured for an exceptionally long time, producing three versions with three different librettists over the period 1804–14, and perhaps this long labour reflects how deeply the subject touched him. Even the final version did not satisfy him, for he wrote to Treitschke only a few days before the first performance of it, 'let me add that this whole opera business is the most tiresome affair in the world, for I am dissatisfied with most of it.'[35] The fact that he pressed on with the necessary revisions, while partly a tribute to Treitschke's skill in revising the text in 1814, is also an indication of how much the work meant to him.

In some ways *Fidelio* continues the ideas of the Heiligenstadt Testament and *Christus*, as mentioned earlier. Florestan's plight is eloquently expressed in his recitative and aria: 'God, what darkness here...O harsh trial! Yet God's will is righteous. I'll not complain...In the springtime of life, happiness has fled from me...But I have done my duty.' This is not far removed from Christ's prayer at the beginning of *Christus*; indeed, Christ as portrayed in the oratorio has even been described as an 'Ur-Florestan'.[36] Meanwhile if the word 'darkness' is substituted by 'deafness' the sentiments begin to resemble those of the Heiligenstadt Testament.[37] It is perhaps significant that this section was one of the passages most heavily revised in both 1806 and 1814. Florestan is, of course, rescued from isolation and oblivion by his wife —something which Beethoven himself dearly longed for, especially during the period when he felt unable to mix with society because of his deafness. His feelings are reflected in his borrowing of two lines from Schiller's 'An die Freude' that were later reused in the Ninth Symphony:

Wer ein holdes Weib errungen,	Let him who has won a dear wife
Stimm' in unsern Jubel ein.	Join in our rejoicing.

---

[35] A-481.   [36] Tyson, 'Heroic', p. 141.   [37] Ibid.

The other main element that initially attracted Beethoven to the plot was the question of oppression. He had just written the 'Eroica', dedicated in part to the ideals of the French Revolution. Here now was an opportunity for a much more explicit comment on the subject of wrongful imprisonment (Florestan was in prison because he had 'dared to speak the truth'). Beethoven captures the feeling of oppression in a number of ways, not least by skilful choice of keys: from a basic norm of C major the music ascends to a peak of E major on the sharp side for Leonora's aria 'Komm, Hoffnung', before descending on the flat side to A flat major and F minor for Florestan's dungeon. This whole scheme is summarized at one point, on the word 'Leiden' (sufferings), which modulates from E to A flat in a single bar (see Ex. 4.5).

Ex. 4.5 Op. 72. xi

Among other extramusical influences on Beethoven's work, the most important is his love of nature. He expressed this love on numerous occasions, notably in a letter of 1810: 'No-one can love the country as much as I do.'[38] It found its musical expression in the 'Pastoral' Symphony of 1808, and scattered amongst the sketches for the work are various remarks which give some indication of Beethoven's intentions about the symphony:[39]

It is left to the listener to discover the situations for himself.

Sinfonia caracteristica—or recollections of country life.

All tone-painting, when pushed too far in instrumental music, loses its value.

Sinfonia pastorella. Anyone possessing an idea of country life can imagine the composer's intentions without the aid of titles.

The whole work can be perceived without description—it is feeling rather than tone-painting.

[38] A-258.　　[39] N-II, p. 375.

These comments reinforce the movement titles. There is no secret message in the 'Pastoral' Symphony waiting to be discovered by some ingenious cryptologist; the music can be understood by 'anyone possessing an idea of country life'. The music is of course full of pastoral elements and feelings —the cheerfulness evoked by almost incessant major keys (except in the 'Storm'), the feeling of ease and repose by subtle use of the subdominant, and the feeling of breadth and expansiveness portrayed by static harmony and repetitions of short motifs with very little forward movement—and so, again, not just the title but also the actual style of the music is profoundly influenced by extramusical factors.

One of these factors is a religious element. Whereas two of the birds represented in the second movement—the cuckoo and the nightingale—are common in pastoral poetry, the choice of the third—the quail—is surprising; its significance for Beethoven can be traced to his setting of a poem on the quail ('Der Wachtelschlag', WoO 129) in 1803, where the quail's call of three repeated notes is interpreted by the poet as representing calls to God: 'Fürchte Gott! Liebe Gott! Lobe Gott! Danke Gott! Bitte Gott! Traue Gott!' (Fear God, love God, praise God, thank God, pray to God, trust God). By incorporating the quail in the symphony Beethoven is recalling the words associated with its call and making this part of the symphony represent nature's song of praise and thanks to God, just as the last movement is mankind's. That he regarded nature as capable of praising God is apparent from some comments written about 1810: 'It seems as if in the country every tree said to me "Holy, Holy"—Who can give complete expression to the ecstasy of the woods?'[40]

A very different type of song of thanks is the 'Heiliger Dankgesang' in the A minor Quartet, Op. 132. The full heading in the autograph score reads: 'Holy Song of Thanksgiving to the Divinity by a Convalescent, in the Lydian Mode.'[41] The quartet had been begun in early 1825 but, with work on the first two movements more or less finished, progress was interrupted by a serious illness in April and May. The next movement Beethoven wrote after his rcovery was the 'Heiliger Dankgesang'; it was clearly a very personal movement and he was determined to communicate this fact. He therefore not only gave the movement an overall title but also marked the contrasting, dance-like second section 'Feeling new strength' and the coda 'With most intimate feeling'. In the first section, the use of one of the ancient modes is significant. Beethoven had encountered the modes during his early composition exercises, and in later life he increasingly came to regard them as the most appropriate medium for sacred music. In 1818 he wrote: 'In order to write true church music, go through all the plainchants of the monks etc.'[42]

Religious elements, then, appear in several of Beethoven's works; but they found their highest expression in the *Missa solemnis*. The work took four

[40] TF, p. 501.   [41] KH, p. 401.
[42] Solomon, 'Tagebuch', no. 168 (translation amended).

years to complete (1819–23), requiring more sketching than any other work, and Beethoven came to regard it as his greatest composition. Despite the specific nature of the occasion for which it was intended (see Chapter 3), he was attempting in the Mass to demonstrate supreme mastery of one of the most traditional musical forms, and clearly there were also strong religious impulses behind the work. Thus like several of his other works the Mass owes its existence to three different types of stimulus: the practical need to write a work for a specific occasion; the musical impulse to write in a particular genre; and the extramusical impulse to give expression to his deepest religious feelings. Beethoven seems to have felt that he could, through his art, communicate more directly with God than could most of his fellow men, and then in turn use his art to reach them. In 1824 he wrote, concerning the *Missa solemnis*: 'My chief aim...was to awaken and permanently instil religious feelings not only into the singers but also into the listeners.'[43] Thus he used in his setting every means of musical imagery to enhance the meaning of the text and make it more intelligible to the listener.[44]

Various other influences from Beethoven's life and times make themselves felt occasionally in his music, though mostly in such minor works as his canons. Perhaps the most significant of these influences is the element of patriotism that pervades some of his works, mostly dating from 1813–15, around the time of the overthrow of Napoleon. The significance lies partly in the fact that, although these works earned Beethoven considerable popular acclaim for a time, they are among his least successful from an artistic point of view. This suggests that he did not have his heart in them and was not greatly stimulated by ideas of patriotism *per se*, unless it was connected with the question of liberty. As noted earlier, this distinction was already apparent in the two patriotic cantatas he had written in Bonn. The best example is *Wellingtons Sieg* (Wellington's Victory, or The Battle of Vittoria, Op. 91), a work that reflects Beethoven's oft-expressed admiration for the English nation. Although it is of relatively little artistic value it is the purest piece of programme music that Beethoven ever wrote. The French army is represented by the key of C major and the tune 'Marlborough' (or 'Malbrouk'), the English by E flat major and 'Rule Britannia': the outcome of the battle becomes clear when a motif appears successively in the keys of A flat, A, B flat, B and then unexpectedly E flat (the 'English' key) rather than C, and the work concludes with a victory symphony.[45]

Many books on Beethoven are primarily biographical, with little attention being given to his music. Other writers have concentrated on the music and largely ignored his personal life. Even authors who have considered both life

[43] A-1307.

[44] See Kirkendale, 'Missa'; for a fuller discussion of Beethoven's religious attitudes see Solomon, 'Faith'.

[45] On the work's origins, and Maelzel's contribution, see Küthen, 'Wellington'.

and music in something like equal amounts have in many cases placed the two subjects in different parts of their books, so that connections between his life and works are often omitted or at least not given as much prominence as they might have been. Hence the impression may be given that, as with Handel or Haydn, little of Beethoven's personal life is reflected in his music. It is now clear, however, that these extramusical factors are actually quite significant. One notable conclusion is that, although the majority of his major works have no explicit extramusical associations, many of those that do were written as a direct response to events in his life or to his attitudes towards his surroundings. His only opera, oratorio, and song cycle, three of his nine symphonies, and numerous other works were all generated, at least in part, by various aspects of his life that had profoundly affected him. Even his whole musical style seems to have undergone major changes partly as a result of external forces in his personal life. But specific extramusical elements are confined mainly to the vocal works and a few instrumental pieces with programmatic titles, such as the 'Pastoral' Symphony and the Sonata 'Les Adieux' (or, more correctly, 'Das Lebewohl', written to reflect the departure, absence, and return to Vienna of Archduke Rudolph in 1809–10). There may also have been a few instrumental pieces sparked off by such things as a galloping horse, a starry sky, or twittering birds.

Although the rest of Beethoven's music seems to have had no specific programmatic ideas, however, it is inappropriate to draw too rigid a distinction between programmatic and absolute music: even a simple tempo mark like 'vivace' already carries with it certain extramusical associations, and some of his tempo marks went much further. Such marks as 'scherzando' and 'dolce' are commonplace, and in his later works there appear such directions as 'slow and full of longing' and 'fast but not too fast, and with determination' (both in Op. 101), and 'exhausted, lamenting' and 'little by little reviving again' (both in Op. 110). It is only a small step from these indications, which are little more than hints at the character of the music, to actual titles expressing emotions, such as *Sonate pathétique* (Op. 13) and 'La Malinconia' (Melancholy, in Op. 18 No. 6), and thence to more explicit titles like 'Das Lebewohl' and the headings in the 'Pastoral', where an idea derived from Beethoven's personal life is the starting-point for the music. And in borderline cases such as 'La Malinconia' it is impossible to be certain whether the movement is just a melancholy one with an illustrative title, or an objective attempt to portray the state of melancholy, or a subjective expression of Beethoven's feelings at the time.[46] Thus although his personal life undoubtedly played a vital role in his creative process, there are limits to how far one can now identify that role.

[46] See Dahlhaus, 'Malinconia'.

5

Recurring Ideas

BEETHOVEN'S musical style was inevitably founded in the musical language of the time and shaped by the influences of a great variety of music from Bach and even Gregorian chant to works by such contemporaries as Clementi and Cherubini. But from these influences and within this language he created his own highly personal style, easily recognizable because many of his most original and characteristic musical ideas recur in several works. As he grew older and built up an increasingly large fund of original ideas that could be reused, his distinctive style became even more pronounced. The term 'musical idea' in this context is very broad, ranging from short motifs to overall structures; it can encompass harmonic progressions, individual chords, key relationships, methods of development, rhythms, textures, types of contrast, and combinations of these or other elements. The idea may be reused in a quite different way and in a different context, and it may be modified so much that it is almost unrecognizable, so that it is difficult to tell in borderline cases whether there is any real relationship or not. And some ideas are so basic and commonplace that their reuse is not confined mainly to Beethoven; here too there are borderline cases. With these few caveats in mind, let us examine the various ways in which ideas from his earlier works reappeared in later ones, and how far back in his output such ideas can be traced.

Beethoven's reuse of his earlier ideas is extremely widespread, and even purely motivic reuse is more common than is often realized, as has been shown by Leilani Lutes.[1] According to her calculations, 37 per cent of Beethoven's works contain motifs used elsewhere by him; and although the exact figure depends on what constitutes reuse and how one defines a work (the Gellert songs, for example, could count as one work or six, and Lutes considers two versions of certain pieces as two separate works), the total number is clearly quite substantial. The reuses can be grouped into three basic types:[2] revision or 'amelioration'; arrangement, that is, transcription for a different medium; and adaptation of the whole or any portion of a movement for use in a different context. There is occasionally a slight overlap between the categories.

The first two need little comment. Revisions to completed works are merely an extension of the compositional processes already present in Beet-

[1] Lutes, 'Re-uses'; see esp. pp. 389–90.
[2] Lutes (ibid., p. 391) gives four categories, but two of them are essentially different aspects of the same principle.

hoven's sketches and working autographs. Whether more than one version of a work actually survives in any given case is relatively fortuitous, and depends mainly on external factors surrounding the composition (for example, if it was performed before the finishing touches had been added there would be two versions—the one performed and the one published), and on whether manuscript material relating to an early version has happened to survive (as in the case of the early version of the Quartet Op. 18 No. 1) or has been lost (as in the case of *Christus am Oelberge*).[3]

Transcriptions were a very common phenomenon in Beethoven's day, and a large number of his works were arranged for other media in order to make them more widely available. Beethoven had relatively little interest in most of these transcriptions and often left the task of transcribing to such pupils as Ries and Czerny,[4] merely checking their work and making minor alterations himself. Even when he did do the work, however, one cannot describe the two versions as separate works; they are two forms of the same work (even though they may have different opus numbers, as with the Septet Op. 20 and its arrangment as a piano trio, Op. 38), and every bar in the arrangement corresponds to one in the original version. Table 1 is a list of the principal transcriptions in which Beethoven is known or thought to have had a major role.

In some cases not listed here, Beethoven made substantial alterations during the course of arrangement, and this brings us to the third category of reuse, in which something less than a whole work reappears in a different form or context. This third category covers a very broad spectrum, ranging from cases where almost the whole of one work was reused (i.e. the second work was little more than an arrangement with revisions) to cases where only a very small musical idea was borrowed. A good example from the former end of the spectrum is the Wind Octet, Op. 103 (completed *c.* 1793), much of which was reused in the String Quintet Op. 4 (*c.* 1795). In Thayer's view the quintet, 'though it employs the same *motivi* as the Octet, is an entirely new work';[5] but it could equally be regarded as a transcription of the octet, combined with a substantial revision of the structure and texture—a revision comparable to that in the two versions of the Quartet Op. 18 No. 1.[6] That Beethoven regarded Op. 4 as having superseded its octet version is perhaps implicit in the fact that he never attempted to publish the octet in later years —it was first printed posthumously in 1830.

A less well-known instance of almost the whole of one work reappearing in a different context is the aria 'Mailied' (Op. 52 No. 4), which was probably first composed in the early 1790s. It was then reused with certain modifi-

---

[3] The early version of the latter can be partly reconstructed; see Tyson, 'Christus'.
[4] See TF, p. 302.   [5] TF, p. 196.
[6] See Johnson, 'Decisive', pp. 2–13, for a brief comparison of Op. 4 with Op. 103; see Levy, *Choices*, for a more extended comparison of the two versions of Op. 18 No. 1.

TABLE 1. *Beethoven's Principal Transcriptions*

Source work	Arrangement
Piano Trio, Op. 1 No. 3	String Quintet, Op. 104 (arranged by someone else but thoroughly revised by Beethoven)[a]
Piano Sonata in E, Op. 14 No. 1	String Quartet in F
Piano Quintet, Op. 16	Piano Quartet
Septet, Op. 20	Piano Trio, Op. 38
Symphony No. 2, Op. 36	Piano Trio
Die Geschöpfe des Prometheus	Piano arrangement[b]
Violin Concerto, Op. 61	Piano concerto
Wellingtons Sieg, Op. 91	Piano arrangement of orchestral version (the original version was for Mälzel's panharmonicon)[c]
Grosse Fuge, Op. 133	Piano Duet, Op. 134
Ritterballett, WoO 1	Piano arrangement
March for Wind, WoO 29	Piano arrangement (two versions; there is also a version for musical clock)[d]
'Hochzeitslied' in C, WoO 105	Arrangement in A, for different group of voices[e]

[a] See Tyson, 'Op. 104'.
[b] The piano arrangement was made by Beethoven himself according to Czerny. See KH, p. 102.
[c] Lutes, 'Reuses', pp. 362–3; KH, pp. 251–5.   [d] Lutes, ibid., pp. 313–8; KH, pp. 468–9.
[e] Lutes, ibid., pp. 370–8.

cations for an aria (WoO 91 No. 1) in a performance in 1796 of a Singspiel originally written by Ignaz Umlauf; the words and accompaniment of 'Mailied' were altered for this purpose but otherwise the two songs are quite close.[7] Several others of Beethoven's stage works contain movements based on earlier compositions, including *Die Ruinen von Athen*, which includes a Turkish march arranged from the Piano Variations Op. 76; the music for *Leonore Prohaska* (WoO 96), which includes an arrangement of the funeral march in the Piano Sonata Op. 26; the music for *Die Weihe des Hauses*, which apart from the overture and one new chorus was derived with very little alteration from *Die Ruinen von Athen*; and the finale of *Fidelio*, which incorporates a theme from the Funeral Cantata (WoO 87). In each of the remaining examples showing clear cases of extensive borrowing, a melody (with its harmony) is reworked in a different context. They are listed in Table 2.[8]

As well as these clear-cut melodic borrowings, there are numerous cases of melodic similarity between two or more of Beethoven's works. Some are probably conscious borrowings of a melodic phrase; in others a more or less

[7] Lutes, 'Re-uses', pp. 17–23.

[8] Lutes, 'Re-uses', *passim*. According to Lutes and many earlier authorities, the *Contredanses* WoO 14 Nos. 7 and 11 probably preceded the versions in the finale of *Prometheus*; but early, relatively primitive versions of both themes are found amongst early sketches for the ballet finale (SV 61, pp. 139 and 143), proving beyond reasonable doubt that they originated in the ballet.

TABLE 2. *Other Melodic Borrowings*

Source Work	Later borrowing
Piano Quartet, WoO 36 No. 3.i	Piano Sonata in C, Op. 2 No. 3.i
Piano Quartet, WoO 36 No. 3.ii	Piano Sonata in F minor, Op. 2 No. 1.ii
Allemande in A, WoO 81	German Dance, WoO 13 No. 11, and String Quartet, Op. 132.ii
'Gegenliebe', WoO 118.ii	Choral Fantasia, Op. 80
Piano Sonata in G, Op. 49 No. 2.ii	Septet, Op. 20.iii
Prometheus, Op. 43.xvi, 1st theme	Contredanse, WoO 14 No. 7; 'Prometheus' Variations, Op. 35; 'Eroica' Symphony, Op. 55.iv
Prometheus, Op. 43.xvi, 2nd theme	Contredanse, WoO 14 No. 11
Canon 'Es muss sein', WoO 196	String Quartet, Op. 135.iv

Ex. 5.1

a WoO 146

b Op. 109. iii

commonplace figuration or progression occurs more than once; and in yet others the connection may be only very tenuous and perhaps subconscious. For example, the theme of the song 'Sehnsucht' (WoO 146, Ex. 5.1a) is similar to that of the finale of the Sonata Op. 109 (Ex. 5.1b); and there are a number of thematic interconnections among the late quartets, one of the most conspicuous being the beginning of Op. 132 (Ex. 5.2a), which resembles the main theme of the *Grosse Fuge* (Ex. 5.2b).[9] Occasionally there is an extra-

Ex. 5.2

a Op. 132. i

b Op. 133

[9] Many others are listed in Cooke, 'Unity', although some of the relationships that Cooke claims to have discovered are too remote to be convincing.

Ex. 5.3

a Op. 123. iii   *b* WoO 188

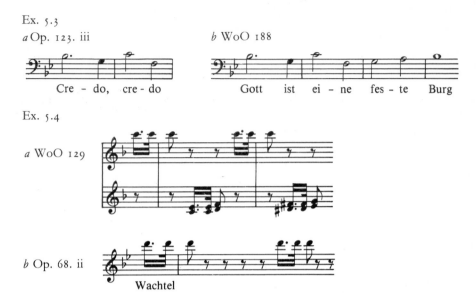

Cre - do, cre - do   Gott ist ei – ne fes - te Burg

Ex. 5.4

a WoO 129

b Op. 68. ii

Wachtel

musical connection reinforcing the melodic similarity between two works, as in the Credo theme of the *Missa solemnis* (Ex. 5.3*a*), which reappears in a canon (Ex. 5.3*b*), and the quail theme that appears in 'Der Wachtelschlag' (WoO 129, Ex. 5.4*a*) and the 'Pastoral' Symphony (E. 5.4*b*).[10]

Similarity or influence of this kind is not confined to melodic contours, but can be found just as much in other aspects of the music. As regards rhythm, Beethoven was particularly fond of the motif ♪♪♪|♩ , as has often been pointed out. Some form of it is used conspicuously not only in the Fifth Symphony but also in several other works, among them the Sonata in C minor Op. 10 No. 1 (third movement), the 'Appassionata' Sonata Op. 57 (first movement), the *Egmont* Overture, and the Fourth Piano Concerto Op. 58 (first movement). Other types of rhythmic devices common in Beethoven's music include off-beat sforzandos—which are far more frequent in his music than in that of any other major composer—and various types of rhythmic disruption, such as a clash between phrase structure and underlying pulse, or a shift of the natural accent of a melody by one beat.

Sometimes the cross-fertilization consists of a characteristic harmonic progression. The dominant seventh on C, used so successfully at the start of the First Symphony of 1799–1800, reappeared a year later in the same place in the *Prometheus* Overture, which is also in C major. The harmonic scheme at the start of the 'Waldstein' Sonata, with its distinctive turn to the flattened leading-note, is almost identical to that in a slightly earlier sonata, Op. 31 No. 1 in G. The influence of one work on another can even be confined to a single chord: the very striking F major chord on the word 'Gott' in the finale of

[10] A number of other supposed borrowings, with varying degrees of similarity between the source work and the borrowing, are given in Lutes, 'Re-uses', but many more could be found.

Ex. 5.5

a Op. 113. viii

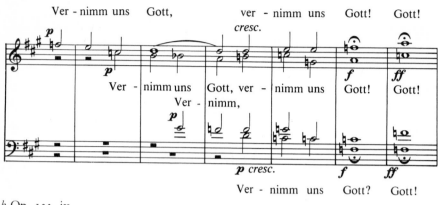

b Op. 125. iv

the Ninth Symphony (Ex. 5.5*a*) is identical (apart from slight differences in scoring) to a chord for the same word in *Die Ruinen von Athen* (Ex. 5.5*b*); and the dominant minor ninth on A later in the symphony, at the words 'über Sternen muss er wohnen', is clearly influenced by the same chord, also played tremolando but in its first inversion, at bars 30–3 of the Sanctus in the *Missa solemnis*.

In the field of tonality, Beethoven used certain keys (notably C minor) very frequently while using others no more remote (such as B minor) hardly at all. Certain key relationships were also used repeatedly: a number of works in C major make prominent use of E major (the piano sonatas Op. 2 No. 3 and Op. 53, the Mass in C, and *Leonore* overtures Nos. 2 and 3); works in C minor often have a conclusion in C major—an idea which even found its way into such an improbable context as Beethoven's setting of the folksong 'The Miller of Dee' (WoO 157 No. 5).

Unusual formal devices were sometimes used more than once, too. The idea of running the penultimate movement of a work into the finale without a break, rarely used by earlier composers, became so common in Beethoven's music of around 1804–10 that it is almost the norm rather than the exception. He also frequently uses abnormally long development sections or codas in his

Ex. 5.6

a Op. 35. viii

b Op. 53. iii

sonata-form movements, for example the 'Eroica', where the development occupies 244 bars out of 691, and the Sonata 'Das Lebewohl', where the coda of the first movement occupies ninety-six bars out of 255. On a smaller structural level, certain other formal devices are reused: there is a particularly distinctive pattern of matching phrases in which the first four bars of a movement are transposed up a fourth to make an answering phrase—a pattern used on three occasions (in Op. 26. ii, Op. 27 No. 2. ii, and Op. 119 No. 10).[11] Even the texture of a piece can function as an element for reuse: a striking example is the eighth of the *Prometheus* Variations, Op. 35 (Ex. 5.6*a*), the texture of which foreshadows that at the beginning of the finale of the 'Waldstein' Sonata (Ex. 5.6*b*).

Sometimes there is a less tangible connection between two works, with several commonplace ideas being reused in the same combination, rather than a single distinctive idea providing the connection. The trio section of the sonata Op. 27 No. 1 (Ex. 5.7*a*) has several features in common with the bagatelle Op. 33 No. 7, which was completed only a little later (Ex. 5.7*b*): both are in A flat major, in a fast triple time, with repeated left-hand chords and the texture spreading into the treble clef only towards the end of the phrase. None of these factors on its own would be sufficient to draw a valid connection between the two works, but in combination they make the relationship between the two unmistakable. Similarly the Choral Fantasia has often been regarded as a foreshadowing of the finale of the Ninth Symphony —not because of any single factor but because there are so many similarities of form, procedure, texture, and melodic style.[12]

---

[11] Cone, 'Bagatelles', p. 86.

[12] Lutes ('Re-uses', p. 85) identifies 12 similarities between the two works.

Ex. 5.7

a Op. 27 No. 1.ii

b Op. 33 No. 7

Complex interrelationships of this type are particularly likely to occur if the two works are in the same key, especially if they are approximately contemporary. There are a number of similarities, for example, between the *Coriolan* Overture and the Fifth Symphony, beyond the fact that both are in C minor and both date mainly from 1807; it is as if Beethoven was so full of C minor ideas of a passionate character that some spilt over from the symphony to form a new work, the overture. Similarly the so-called 'Pastoral' Sonata (Op. 28) and the Second Symphony, both in D and both dating partly from 1801, have a number of features in common,[13] and the finale of the Sonata Op. 111 has several features (including key, melodic shape, and certain patterns of figuration) in common with the Diabelli Variations, especially the final variation.[14]

The same sort of pattern of reuse of earlier ideas can be found when the sketch material is considered—whether it be preliminary sketches for completed works or sketches for abandoned projects. Sometimes a complete melody is used in one work after being rejected in an earlier one; in fact a melody is much more likely to be borrowed from a discarded sketch than

[13] See Coren, 'Op. 28'.   [14] See Kinderman, *Diabelli*, pp. 115–18, 126–30.

TABLE 3. *Some Borrowings from Abandoned Sketches*

Work and movement	Original source of melody
Piano Sonata in D, Op. 10 No. 3.iii (trio section)	Theme in A flat, probably intended for Piano Sonata in E flat, Op. 7
First Symphony, Op. 21.iv	Unfinished symphony in C.i
String Quartet, Op. 59 No. 3.iii	Unfinished keyboard fantasia in C minor
Seventh Symphony, Op. 92.ii	Amongst sketches for Op. 59 No. 3
Piano Sonata in C minor, Op. 111.i	Theme in F sharp minor (SV 263, fo. 37^v), amongst sketches for Violin Sonata Op. 30 No. 1
String Quartet, Op. 130.iv	String Quartet, Op. 132.iv
String Quartet, Op. 132.v	Ninth Symphony, instrumental finale
String Quartet, Op. 135.iii	Coda to string quartet, Op. 131

from a finished work, as can be seen from the selection of examples shown in Table 3, which is by no means a complete list.[15]

Often, however, the borrowing from discarded sketch material is much less substantial and conspicuous, and consists merely of the reuse of some musical idea or device such as a key scheme or figuration, just as happens so often with borrowings from finished works.[16] Again such cross-fertilization is particularly common in works that are nearly contemporaneous and/or in the same key. For example, the early sketches for the Piano Sonata in E flat Op. 27 No. 1 are found amongst sketches for *Prometheus*, and in a few cases it is hard to tell which of the two works a particular sketch was intended for; sometimes a sketch clearly intended for one work was eventually used in the other instead.[17]

Sketches for abandoned works often contain ideas that were later used in completed works, so it sometimes becomes questionable whether they can be described as sketches for the abandoned work or for the completed one. In the 'Kafka' and 'Fischhof' sketch miscellanies there is an extended sketch for a sonata movement in C minor, probably dating from early 1798 (see Ex. 5.8);[18] it does not closely resemble any finished work, yet it contains several ideas that were incorporated into the 'Pathétique' Sonata of 1799 (such as a slow chordal introduction characterized by dramatic rests and diminished sevenths, and a tremolando on C at the start of the Allegro section), and also some ideas used in the C minor Quartet, Op. 18 No. 4, of around 1800.[19] The sketch could therefore be regarded as an early idea for the 'Pathétique' Sonata

[15] For details of these borrowings, see Johnson, *Fischhof*, i. 335 (Op. 10 No. 3); ibid., i. 464 (Op. 21); Kramer, 'Op. 30', p. 169 (Op. 59); N-II, p. 107 (Op. 92); Nottebohm, *Skizzenbuch*, pp. 19–20 (Op. 111); N-I, p. 53 (Op. 130); N-II, p. 180 (Op. 132); Winter, 'Plans', p. 125 (Op. 135).

[16] Several cases of borrowings from sketches for the Sonata in D minor Op. 31 No. 2 are mentioned in Ch. 12.

[17] See SV 61, p. 103 staves 5–6, p. 129 staves 2–3, p. 130 stave 1, p. 138 stave 1.

[18] SV 185, fo. 117^r; SV 31, fo. 20^v; see Kerman ed., *Miscellany*, ii. 156, and Johnson, *Fischhof*, i. 443–5 and ii. 150.

[19] Johnson, *Fischhof*, i. 445.

Ex. 5.8 SV 185, fo. 117^r

or as an abandoned work, and unfortunately there are no known sketches for the 'Pathétique' that clarify the issue (in fact hardly any survive at all).

Several more examples may be given to illustrate the types of ideas, originating in unfinished works, that might be taken up in a different context. A sketch for a symphony in C minor (Hess 298; shown in Ex. 5.9*a*) dating back to Beethoven's Bonn days anticipates the key and something of the mood of the Fifth Symphony, and the theme vaguely resembles that of the third movement (Ex. 5.9*b*). In the case of an abandoned triple concerto of 1802 it was the unusual scoring that was preserved, in the Triple Concerto Op. 56. Similar cases arose in later years: during the composition of the *Missa solemnis* he was planning to write another Mass, in the key of C sharp minor; in this case the unusual key remained in his mind, emerging in the Quartet Op. 131, which, with its fugal opening and suggestions of the Phrygian mode, betrays the ecclesiastical influence on its conception. And a plan to write a B–A–C–H overture in the early 1820s was eventually absorbed into the *Grosse Fuge* in 1825 (extensive sketches for the overture suddenly cease after the date of the *Grosse Fuge*); here it was the monumental character and the fugal texture, as well as the key, that were transferred from the one work to the other.

Thus Beethoven's reuse of material from both his sketches and finished works can be divided into two distinct categories (excluding revisions and arrangements), with very little overlap between them: borrowings of whole melodies, and reuse of individual ideas. Quite different criteria governed the two types. In the case of complete melodies or sections of music, he seems to have set himself very strict rules about what could be reused. Virtually all of his borrowed melodies were from abandoned sketches or early, immature works that he probably did not intend to publish (see Table 2 above), the

Ex. 5.9

a SV 185, fo. 70[r]

b Op. 67. iii

exceptions being those in the *Prometheus* Variations (where a pre-existing melody of his own is used as a basis for variations) and a few minor ballroom dances, and those that were reused because of some extramusical significance (as in the borrowings from Op. 43 to Op. 55, from Op. 26 to WoO 96, from Op. 76 to Op. 113, and from WoO 196 to Op. 135). Occasionally shortage of time was a contributory factor in persuading him to make use of earlier compositions, as in the Choral Fantasia theme and the Turkish march in *Die Ruinen von Athen*, but even here the usual criteria still applied: the Choral Fantasia theme was taken from an early unpublished song, while the Turkish march had relevant extramusical associations. The Sonata Op. 49 No. 2 appears to be something of an exception, since it was published not long after the Septet that had borrowed a melody from it; but Beethoven may not have intended to publish the sonata when he borrowed the melody from it, and it may have been his brother Carl who was responsible for persuading him to do so (or possibly even for publishing it without his consent), since he was closely involved in Beethoven's affairs at the time.

The early unpublished works that provided substantial material for later published ones were therefore effectively relegated by Beethoven to the status of sketches. Like the discarded melodies found amongst his sketches in general, the melodies of these works were often of excellent quality, whatever the defects of the work from which they came, and they had often been worked on at some length before reaching their final form. Hence in the borrowings from both them and discarded sketches Beethoven was consciously trying to salvage something good which he had created and which would otherwise be wasted. He once even noted down in a sketchbook his desire to operate in this way: 'Also one of many ideas, which cannot be used where found, is good to save up'.[20] In fact this attitude was probably one of the main reasons why he preserved so carefully his sketches and juvenilia. It was precisely because the melodies had been effectively abandoned that they could be resurrected in a different context. So if, for example, the early piano quartets had been published, or the Third 'Razumovsky' Quartet had contained the theme now found in the Seventh Symphony, it would be difficult to believe that Beethoven would have felt able to reuse these themes in a different context as well.

Where more limited ideas or devices were being reused, however, Beethoven seems to have had no restrictions and to have been quite happy to adapt them from earlier works, published or unpublished, complete or unfinished. Whether or not an idea had been discarded in an earlier work was immaterial. If it had been, this did not render the idea unfit for use in a later work, for in a different context it might be entirely suitable. On the other hand, if it had already appeared in one work, this did not prevent its reuse in a later one. Such devices, unlike complete melodies or musical sections, frequently occur in two or even several works.

There is, then, as with most composers, a certain unity of style that pervades almost all Beethoven's works, including unfinished ones and rejected fragments. This unity can be pinned down to numerous individual musical ideas and devices or combinations of devices that are used over and over again in various ways. Either a very distinctive idea is reused, or a distinctive combination of relatively ordinary devices is created (as in the relationship between the Choral Fantasia and the Choral Symphony), or, in some cases, a very ordinary device (for example, the key of C minor with its associated mood of pathos) is simply used unduly often. It is these types of reuse of material that make Beethoven's style as a whole so distinctive. Often some device recurs in more than one movement of a single work, a celebrated case being the opening rhythm of the Fifth Symphony, which appears in different forms in the later movements. Some analysts have regarded such recurrences as unifying features and have even gone to considerable lengths to try and demonstrate these unifying relationships within multi-movement works.[21] Some of these relationships were undoubtedly intended by Beethoven as unifying devices; but others were probably not, and one must beware of attaching too much importance to them in view of the fact that they occur between works that are totally independent almost as much as

---

[20] Unger, 'Workshop', p. 325.   [21] e.g. Réti, *Sonatas*.

they occur between different movements of the same work. Ideas sketched for one movement are sometimes transferred to a different one within a work,[22] but they may just as easily be transferred to another work altogether.

This stylistic unity spans the whole of Beethoven's output, so that despite his stylistic development and his distinct creative periods, many of the most characteristic features of his early music persist right through to the end, and conversely many features common mainly in his later works can be traced back to remarkably early in his output. The idea of a C major piece modulating into E major can be found in an early Viennese sketch of about 1793,[23] and certain other ideas can be traced back even earlier, to his Bonn period. The idea of a funeral piece in C minor bursting into a triumphant conclusion in C major dates back to what is probably his earliest extant composition —the Dressler Variations, WoO 63. Another Bonn work (also in his characteristic key of C minor) that displays many signs of the mature Beethoven style is the Funeral Cantata (WoO 87); in addition to containing an actual melody later borrowed in *Fidelio* (see above), the cantata contains a number of smaller ideas that influenced later works.[24] Indeed the similarity between the start of the cantata and the opening of the dungeon scene in *Fidelio* is so close that it can almost be regarded as a full-scale borrowing of four bars of music, rather than just a reuse of a single musical idea.[25] The Righini Variations (WoO 65) of 1791 are still more remarkable for their use of characteristics typical of Bethoven, for they contain a veritable gold-mine of ideas that were to influence a whole range of later compositions (see Table 4).

The question must be raised as to why a composer with such a fertile imagination so often resorted to reuse of earlier ideas, especially when one of his major goals was novelty and artistic progress. Several comments may be put forward in reply. Some of the relationships discussed earlier may possibly have been unconscious and have resulted merely from the tendency of Beethoven's mind to work repeatedly along certain lines. But on other occasions he was well aware of the connections and at times even alluded to them: as he was finishing the Ninth Symphony he offered it to at least three publishers and in each case mentioned that the finale was similar to his Choral Fantasia but on a far grander scale.[26] He was also aware of relationships between the Ninth Symphony and *Die Ruinen von Athen*: in August 1823, when he was working exclusively on the Ninth Symphony, he wrote to his brother Johann asking for the score of *Die Ruinen von Athen*, adding: 'As I happen to be composing something else of this kind I badly need my manuscripts.'[27] In such cases he was using a step-by-step approach to artistic progress. A novel idea in one work could be used in several other ways on

---

[22] Klimowitzki, 'Autograph', p. 160; see also Winter, *Op. 131*, p. 128.

[23] SV 185, fo. 40ᵛ–41ʳ.   [24] Solomon, *Beethoven*, p. 49.

[25] Lutes, 'Re-uses', pp. 24–6.   [26] A-1267, A-1269, A-1270.

[27] A-1231.

TABLE 4. *Characteristic Devices in the Righini Variations, WoO 65*

Variation in WoO 65	Device
1, 6, 7, 10, 12, 14, 16, 21, 24, Coda	Off-beat accent or sforzando (one of Beethoven's most characteristic traits)
4	Trill used motivically, not just decoratively (cf. Bagatelle in C Op. 119 No. 7, and Sonata Op. 106, finale)
4, 6, 14, 20	Use of register as a means of development (a device used in several later works, e.g. Op. 119 No. 7, Op. 35)[a]
4, 6, 20, 23	Very widely spaced chords (also used e.g. at end of 'Abendlied', WoO 150)
6 (2nd half)	Tonic and dominant harmony superimposed (Ex. 5.10; cf. Sonata 'Das Lebewohl', Op. 81a.i, coda)
5, 13, 15, 19	High level of virtuosity (a feature found in many of his later piano works)
6, 7, 16, 19, 21	Chord progression V–Ic–I at a cadence (cf. Ex. 5.10; a common device in Beethoven but almost unknown in other composers)
7, 19, 21	Use of canonic or fugal elements (contrapuntal devices are particularly common in his late works)
14	Use of fast and slow sections within a variation (cf. Diabelli Variations, Var. 21)
14	Crescendo leading to piano (one of Beethoven's principal thumb-prints)
21 (bars 13 and 15)	Suspension and resolution sounded simultaneously (a common mistake in his counterpoint exercises of 1793; also found in later works—see Ex. 17.9a)
23 (bars 22 and 30)	Unexpected turn to the subdominant key (experiments with subdominant harmonies are found in several later works, e.g. the end of the Gloria in the *Missa solemnis*)[b]
Coda	Very long coda, with unexpected modulations to remote keys (both features are common in Beethoven)

[a] See Reynolds, 'Op. 35', pp. 53–5.
[b] Cf. Cone, 'Bagatelles', p. 97, where there are several further examples of Beethoven's 'strong interest in taming the subdominant'.

later occasions, and if the idea was good enough it was worth developing some of the possibilities. In this way he could build on his earlier experiments to create new and perhaps greater works that nevertheless owe something to his earlier ones.

The Choral Fantasia and Ninth Symphony in fact provide a good example of this process. The former is remarkable for its high degree of originality in structure and overall concept. The finale of the latter, though unquestionably greater and more advanced, is perhaps less highly original in that it borrows so many ideas from its predecessor; but it might well have been inconceivable without the precedent of the Choral Fantasia. Similarly the late

Ex. 5.10 WoO 65. vi

bagatelles contain compositional experiments that gave rise to more developed forms of the same ideas in later and more major works.[28]

One of Beethoven's most persistent ideas was to develop ways of linking consecutive movements in a multi-movement work—something his predecessors had done only rarely but which he did quite often. The aim seems to have been to find various middle ways between the multi-sectional fantasia, in which no section was self-contained, and the multi-movement sonata structure, in which each movement was independent. An early exercise along this line of exploration was the Sonata 'quasi una fantasia' Op. 27 No. 1, where all the movements are joined and material from the slow movement returns near the end of the finale. Then from 1804 it became very common for his finales to follow the preceding movement without a break. From here it was only a short step to the song cycle *An die ferne Geliebte*, where each song is linked to the next by a modulatory passage (except Nos. 3 and 4, which are in the same key and so flow continuously anyway), and ultimately to the extraordinary relationships in the Quartet Op. 131—relationships that were able to be created only through a lifetime's experience in developing composition along these lines.

Beethoven's repeated use of certain ideas may also owe something to his customary economy in employing material. This economy is apparent in his tendency to improvise at great length on a single theme rather than on several different ones in turn, and also in his habit of writing very long development sections and codas; in each case there is the underlying notion that more can be done with the material being used, and he was particularly good at finding different and unexpected ways of developing such material. It was not a

[28] Cone, 'Bagatelles'.

matter of trying to exhaust all the possibilities of using a motif (this could never be done) but simply of exploring some of the potentialities of an interesting idea, whether by development within a work or by reuse in different ways in several works. The *Prometheus*–'Eroica' theme provides a good illustration. After developing the theme motivically within the *Prometheus* finale Beethoven explored other ways of developing it—first as a dance tune for use at a ball, then as the basis for a set of variations, where further development of the theme took place, and later still as a symphonic theme, where still more of its possibilities were revealed. Even then the theme's potentialities were not exhausted: shortly after the 'Eroica' was completed, Beethoven played the finale on the piano to some friends, and then without a break continued improvising for a further two hours![29] Thus his reuse of earlier ideas, far from being a sign of a limited imagination, is an indication of his extraordinary ability to discover hidden possibilities in them.

[29] TF, p. 337.

II

BEETHOVEN'S
COMPOSITIONAL
METHODS

6

The Sketchbooks and their Use

It is not known precisely at what age Beethoven started making sketches for compositions, but it was probably almost as soon as he started composing; he once referred to 'the bad habit I formed in childhood of feeling obliged to write down my first ideas immediately'.[1] No actual sketches for finished works have survived from before about 1787,[2] but certainly by the time he left Bonn for Vienna in November 1792 he was sketching extensively, for no fewer than twenty-one leaves devoted exclusively to sketches are known to date from his Bonn period,[3] as well as a number of leaves which contain other material but which have sketches in the empty spaces. When he left for Vienna in 1792 he took with him a portfolio of manuscripts that included both finished works and also these sketches, and the fact that so much early material survives indicates how central the sketching process was to his creativity even at an early age, and how highly he regarded his sketches throughout his life.

Up to about 1798 he continued to make sketches on loose leaves of manuscript paper rather than in books, and for the most part the amount of sketching for each work was fairly small compared with that carried out in later years. It is of course possible that there were originally many more leaves from this period, containing large quantities of sketches for some of these works, but the evidence suggests otherwise. Sketches survive for surprisingly many early works, including nearly all of those published in the 1790s with opus numbers (exceptions are Op. 12 No. 1, Op. 14 No. 2, and possibly Op. 2 No. 3), as well as many of those without opus numbers and those written at that time but published only later. Yet it is quite rare to find more than about four sides of sketches devoted to a single work from this period. The Second Piano Concerto is an exception, but this has a long and complex history involving several revisions (see Chapter 17). Another exception is the E major Piano Sonata Op. 14 No. 1: there are extended drafts for all three movements and nearly all the sketches seem to have survived, allowing a continuous thread to be traced from the earliest ideas to the latest draft, yet even here, sketches for the three movements combined occupy less than eight sides.

Usually Beethoven made sketches for more than one work on a single page during this early period. This is a further indication of the rapidity with which he switched from one work to another, and of the relatively small number of sketches for each work. Pages devoted entirely to sketches for a

---

[1] A-558.   [2] Johnson, *Fischhof*, i. 27.   [3] Ibid., p. 219.

single work, such as are frequently found in later material, were rare at this time. The appearance of several different works on a single page is also an indication of Beethoven's attempts to save paper—he could not afford to waste expensive manuscript paper at this stage of his life. The density of sketching on some pages is in fact quite remarkable, as can be seen for example on Fo. 50ᵛ of the 'Kafka' Sketch Miscellany (SV 185; see Facsimile 1), where there are more than a dozen unrelated sketches, some for known works (Contredanses for Orchestra, WoO 14) but many not connected to any known work. Such density is by no means unique in the early sketches.

By 1798 Beethoven had a substantial pile of sketches, miscellaneous jottings, and rough drafts of unpublished scores, including some that dated back to his Bonn days, and at about this time he seems to have gathered them together into a single portfolio. He probably also sewed them together into bundles about this time, for most of the leaves have stitch-holes, representing at least three different patterns of stitching, although each pattern appears on sketch leaves that are unrelated chronologically. In addition he may have systematically discarded a number of pages at this time, keeping only those that interested him; it has been suggested that leaves filled entirely with sketches for works that had been published by then may have been thrown out, since there are very few such leaves extant today. But it is not necessary to accept this hypothesis, since there are not many leaves with even a single

Facsimile 1. 'Kafka' Sketch Miscellany (British Library, London, MS Add. 29801), fo. 50ᵛ

side devoted entirely to sketches for works published by them. It is equally possible that pages were discarded in a much more haphazard way over a perid of several years before 1798. This collection of loose leaves assembled in 1798 has survived substantially intact to the present day, along with two leaves added later (both dating from about 1799). During the rest of his life Beethoven no doubt occasionally removed a sheet from the portfolio— perhaps a song or bagatelle that he planned to publish—but otherwise it was intact at his death. Since then a number of further leaves have been removed and the collection has been split into two parts, known as the 'Fischhof' and 'Kafka' miscellanies (SV 31 and SV 185) respectively.[4]

During Beethoven's early years in Vienna his sketching became gradually more and more elaborate, and by 1798 it had become so substantial that he began to find it convenient to have complete manuscript books specifically devoted to this activity. The first such book is Grasnick 1 (SV 45), which dates from about late summer 1798 to early 1799. This coincides with the period when he started writing his first string quartets (Op. 18)—a genre for which he had a particularly high regard and one which he had previously deliberately avoided.[5] Thus the change to sketchbooks may have been a conscious policy to help him cope with the peculiar compositional problems of the genre; this supposition is supported by the fact that the first pages of the sketchbook as it now stands are devoted largely to work on the first of the quartets to be written (No. 3 in D major). On the other hand, there are nine leaves now missing from the beginning of the book, some of which survive elsewhere; although three of them (SV 111, 112, and 241) also contain work on the same quartet, another leaf, possibly the first in the book but now in several fragments, does not.[6]

From this time onwards most of Beethoven's sketching was done in books rather than on loose leaves. Single sheets or bifolios continued to be used from time to time, however. Most of them date from short periods when no sketchbook was in use. The usual pattern was that Beethoven would finish one sketchbook before he had acquired another, and so for a short time he had to resort to loose leaves. In the course of writing out scores he inevitably acquired more manuscript paper than he needed, and so there was never a shortage of loose leaves of various sizes for making sketches on if no sketchbook were in use at the time. Sometimes the number of left-over papers became so great that instead of buying a new sketchbook he simply stitched together the various scraps, some of which might even have been partially filled already, to form a home-made sketchbook. As a result of this we find that some of his sketchbooks consist of several different paper types with different stave rulings, yet with the content of the leaves fairly con-

[4] The 'Fischhof' Miscellany is transcribed in Johnson, *Fischhof*, vol. ii. The 'Kafka' Miscellany is published in fac. and transcription in Kerman ed., *Miscellany*.

[5] Kerman, 'Early', p. 522; Webster, 'Quartets', p. 97.

[6] For a description of the fragmented leaf see Johnson, *Fischhof*, i. 206–10.

tinuous. A third type of sketchbook was sometimes made by buying a uniform batch of loose manuscript paper and then sewing it together before use. Of about thirty-two standard-format sketchbooks that have been identified, nearly three-quarters are of the home-made type (with either newly acquired or left-over paper), including all those dating from after 1808.[7]

Once a sketchbook had been either bought or stitched together it generally superseded loose leaves as a repository for Beethoven's latest ideas, and loose leaves were then probably only used when they were for some reason nearer to hand than a sketchbook. After he had started a sketchbook he continued using it until it was full, and there is rarely any overlap between the end of one sketchbook and the beginning of the next. Occasionally odd pages might be left blank, but he never left any large gaps in a book. The exception that proves the rule is SV 27 part 2: this consists of forty-eight sides, of which only the first twelve have been filled, and it was the sketchbook in use when he died.

Beethoven's second sketchbook, Grasnick 2 (SV 46), dates from 1799; after filling it he appears to have used one now lost, for there are hardly any sketches for some very substantial works from late 1799 and early 1800, including the Quartet Op. 18 No. 4, the Septet Op. 20, the First Symphony, and the Third Piano Concerto. A similar situation arises with the period 1806–7, from which time there are very few sketches for such major works as the Fourth Piano Concerto, the Fourth Symphony, the Violin Concerto, and the Overture to *Coriolan*. It is impossible to believe that no other sketches were made for such complex works; and it is more likely that a single book has been lost in each case than that a lot of loose leaves are all missing.

From 1800 to 1805 there survives a series of sketchbooks, mostly still more or less intact, that provide a detailed calendar of Beethoven's compositional activity. The picture of his work between 1805 and 1808 is more confused, partly because of the disappearance of the large quantity of sketches mentioned above, and partly because most of those sketches that do survive are not in proper sketchbooks. There are, however, a group of leaves from 1806 devoted to the quartets Op. 59 (part of SV 265),[8] a small home made sketchbook from the summer of 1807 (SV 213) devoted to the Mass in C, and another group of leaves once forming a home-made sketchbook but since dismembered, devoted chiefly to the Fifth Symphony, the Cello Sonata Op. 69, and *Leonore* Overture No. 1.[9] In 1808 Beethoven returned to using proper sketchbooks for work on the 'Pastoral' Symphony, and he continued using sketchbooks of various types after this for most of the rest of his life. The main gaps in later years occurred around 1813 and 1817–18, from which periods there are no large sketchbooks. There was actually a pause in his productivity at both these times, but one major work was begun in 1817 —the 'Hammerklavier' Sonata, Op. 106. This is sketched in pocket-sketch-

---

[7] See JTW, esp. pp. 48–9.   [8] JTW, pp. 524–6.
[9] See Tyson, 'First Leonore', and JTW, pp. 160–5.

books (see below) and on a large number of loose leaves, but apparently not in any standard-format sketchbooks.

During the course of his life Beethoven's sketching process was continually tending to become more complex. Whereas in his early years a complete work would be sketched on only a few pages, by the end of his life a work of similar length and complexity might well fill the equivalent of an entire book. And the later works themselves, of course, tended to be more complex and have much larger dimensions than the early ones, extending still further the need for detailed sketching. Coupled with this trend was an increasing tendency (referred to in Chapter 1) for him to do much of his composing out of doors. It was obviously impracticable to carry large sketchbooks, quills, and ink around with him, and as there was a danger that he would forget some of his ideas, he took to making outdoor sketches in pencil, which could then either be copied into the main desk-sketchbooks, developed, inked in, or simply rejected when he returned home. Full-sized sheets of manuscript paper would have been too unwieldy for this purpose, but if a standard-size leaf of oblong paper (about $9'' \times 12''$) was folded once down the middle it became a suitable size for carrying around in one of Beethoven's rather voluminous pockets.

Thus arose what might be referred to as sketches for sketches—mostly fairly short ideas jotted down in pencil on paper which still today bears a clear fold down the middle. Often a whole sheaf of single leaves in oblong format was simply folded down the middle to form a rough-and-ready sketchbook consisting of a single gathering in which each page was in upright format and half the width of a normal page. The change to this type of sketching was a very gradual one. Possibly the earliest specimen of outdoor sketching is SV 185, fo. 96, a Bonn leaf that has been folded at least twice and contains unidentified pencil sketches (in early handwriting) on the verso. Another relatively early example of a pocket-sketch is pages 13–14 of SV 265, a leaf partly written in pencil and folded rather oddly, which was apparently carried around by Beethoven before being returned to its proper place.[10] But although, according to Ries, Beethoven always carried manuscript paper around with him as early as 1805,[11] very few other pocket-sketches survive from such an early date. By 1810, however, he was doing a fair amount of sketching in pencil, often on loose leaves outside his main sketchbook, and several of these leaves are folded down the middle, suggesting possible outdoor use. For example, of the two main sources of sketches for the *Egmont* Overture of 1810, one (SV 273) is written partly in pencil, partly in ink, and partly in pencil that has been inked in (with minor modifications), but it has no fold down the middle; the other (SV 272) is written almost entirely in ink, with only a few pencil additions, but the pages have all been folded down the middle. It seems likely that both manuscripts were used partly at Beethoven's

---

[10] See N-II, p. 87; Kramer, 'Op. 30', p. 62; Tyson, 'Razumovsky', pp. 117–19 (includes fac.).   [11] TF, p. 367.

desk and partly outside (SV 273 could have been rolled up instead of being folded).

The earliest sheaf of pages clearly used as a pocket-sketchbook is a group of ten leaves in Artaria 205 (SV 17) which were used in 1811 for *Die Ruinen von Athen*;[12] but apart from these, the earliest proper pocket-sketchbook known, Mendelssohn 1 (SV 70), dates from 1815. And it is perhaps significant that there is a noticeable increase in the amount of pencil in the standard-format sketchbooks dating from about 1815 onwards,[13] although this trend had already begun a few years earlier. In Beethoven's final decade such pocket-books became quite numerous—much more numerous than the ordinary desk-sketchbooks (though not usually so big). Three devoted largely or entirely to the *Missa solemnis* have been published in facsimile and transcription,[14] and there are several more for the Ninth Symphony and the late quartets. The pocket-sketchbooks did not replace the need for full-size desk-books written mainly in ink, but were used in conjunction with them as a supplementary source of sketches, so that the interrelationships are often very complex. Moreover, as a pocket-book did not normally last nearly as long as a desk-book, a single desk-book was often contemporary with several pocket-books.

Beethoven progressed a stage further during the period of the late quartets, when there was a sudden increase in the use of loose bifolios for the purpose of making 'score sketches' (see Chapter 8). This type of sketch material, which could legitimately be regarded as a separate class from loose leaves, desk-books and pocket-books, has until recently received little attention in the Beethoven literature, but Robert Winter has drawn attention to the fact that there are over 200 such bifolios in existence containing score sketches related to the late quartets.[15] This type of sketch complicates the relationships between the sources still further, for although the tendency was for Beethoven to work from pocket-book to desk-book to score sketch, all three types were liable to be used at any stage of the composition of a particular work.

Thus at first Beethoven sketched just on single leaves or bifolios; from 1798 he used sketchbooks too, and from 1815 pocket-sketchbooks offered a third possibility. It is noteworthy how closely these three periods of sketching match the three periods into which his music is customarily divided. This may be more than just coincidence, even though the date of 1798 is earlier than that generally given for the start of his second period, and even though the change to pocket-sketchbooks was a rather gradual one. What happened in each case was that as his compositions became more complex he took positive action over his compositional methods to allow for this change; and

[12] JTW, pp. 337–9.   [13] See Winter, *Op. 131*, p. 10.
[14] SV 81–3; see Schmidt-Görg ed., *Missa solemnis i*, *Missa solemnis ii*, and *Missa solemnis iii*.
[15] Winter, 'Symphonie', p. 544, and 'Plans', p. 107. For a fuller survey see JTW, pp. 463–508.

having taken this action, he soon found that the extra 'elbow-room' thereby created enabled him to expand his style considerably. It would have been difficult for him to compose works like the 'Eroica' on the one hand, and the *Missa solemnis* on the other, if he had been hampered by the limitations of his sketching methods of a few years earlier. The same applies to the expansion into score sketches in 1824, for the complex polyphony of the late quartets frequently demanded sketching in open score.

Apart from grouping it in the four broad categories described above, there is no easy way to classify the sketch material. Even to define what constitutes a sketchbook (or for that matter a sketch) is no easy task. On the one hand there are proper books with a completely uniform structure; then there are books with a nearly uniform structure, such as the 'Petter' Sketchbook of 1811–12 (SV 106), the first nine leaves of which are of different paper from the rest; and then there are bundles of paper, often a variety of different types and apparently stitched together by Beethoven, which could be classed as books. Sometimes the stitching of the latter was done only after some or all the sketches had been entered: an example is SV 184 (the first part of the 'Kafka' Miscellany), which is uniform in paper type and content (all the sketches are from summer 1811) but which has the pages hopelessly jumbled, so that in a sense this is not a true sketchbook. Still less so are the groups of miscellaneous leaves in SV 185 referred to above, and yet when Beethoven had them stitched together each group would have appeared outwardly similar to his true sketchbooks. The situation is further confused by artificial sketchbooks put together after Beethoven's death by owners of loose leaves, such as Artaria. These contain music from a wide range of dates—in fact, sometimes it seems that pages were deliberately chosen to represent several different periods of the composer's life. An example is Landsberg 12 (SV 66), which contains thirty-eight leaves of various shapes and sizes, including material from the Second, Fourth, Fifth, Sixth, and Ninth symphonies plus a wide range of other works; a few of the leaves originated in genuine sketchbooks but most were probably separate initially.

The pocket-sketchbooks are in many cases just a small sheaf of pages folded together—in fact they may consist of any number of leaves from two (forming eight pages) upwards. How many loose leaves need to be put together before they can count as a true sketchbook is a matter of opinion.[16] In some cases several pocket-books have been put together since Beethoven's death to form something more substantial. Artaria 205 (SV 17), for example, consists of 116 half-leaves, made up out of seven sheaves of pocket-sketches from different periods. Meanwhile Artaria 180 and 200 (SV 13) together include a large jumble of pocket-leaves, and it is still unclear precisely how many pocket-sketchbooks they represent.

If classification by format is difficult, classification by content is certainly no easier. Some sketchbooks may have been allotted to specific projects while

---

[16] In JTW the authors have discounted most of the unstitched gatherings of four leaves or less, relegating them to the status of loose leaves.

others were more in the nature of calendars or chronicles of compositional activity into which Beethoven entered a variety of sketches in the order they occurred to him;[17] but this distinction works at best only up to a certain point. In almost every sketchbook that may initially have been intended for a particular project—for example, Grasnick 1 for the quartets Op. 18, Mendelssohn 15 for *Leonore*, and the 'Pastoral' Sketchbook for the 'Pastoral' Symphony—other works were intruding before long (the home-made sketchbook for the Mass in C, SV 213, is an exception). Only if a sketchbook is very small or the work very big do we find only one work in it, and in such cases the work will spill over into another book. What is not found in general is a pair of exactly contemporary books allotted to two different works. The sketchbook for *Meeresstille und glückliche Fahrt*, which contains several entries from 1813, may have continued in use until late 1814 or even early 1815, outlasting both Landsberg 9 (SV 63) and the 'Dessauer' Sketchbook (SV 270) of 1814; but this now seems unlikely (see Chapter 14), and normally the only situation in which two books are contemporary is where one is a desk-book and the other a pocket-book; in such cases any work with substantial sketches in one book will also appear in the other.

What is true of complete books is also true for parts of a book—Beethoven does not on the whole seem to have allotted different parts of a book to different works. Where a number of consecutive pages are devoted to a single work it can generally be concluded that he was working intensively on that one work for some time. The situation is not always clear, however, and the whole question of the order in which he filled a sketchbook is a very complicated one. Often it is impossible to be certain which of several pages, or which of several staves on a page, was written first. But the order of the entries is clear sufficiently often, either from their layout or from their content, for certain generalizations to be made. These generalizations are useful in that they provide a working hypothesis for assessing places where the order of the entries is uncertain—in fact, it is only by making such hypotheses that one can make much progress in interpreting the sketches.

Generally speaking, Beethoven used the pages of a sketchbook in the right order. But there are exceptions. The last two sides of the 'Petter' Sketchbook, for example, were apparently filled earlier than the rest of the book, although the pages may have been rearranged. Sometimes, where progress on a work was temporarily impeded, he left space (often not enough) and went on to something else. When he returned to fill in the space this sometimes necessitated a complicated series of cross-references marks to connect the various bits of a single draft. If he left too much space instead of too little, some pages might remain blank or might be filled in only later. In the 'Wielhorsky' Sketchbook (SV 343), pages 46–85 are taken up with a duet ('Ne' giorni tuoi felici', WoO 93) while the oratorio *Christus am Oelberge* appears from page 90 onwards. On the four pages between these two works is a lot of miscel-

[17] Kramer, 'Op. 30', p. 56.

laneous material. It may well be that Beethoven began the oratorio before he had finished sketching the duet, and left blank four more pages than the number eventually necessary to complete the duet. This is certainly a possible explanation for why four consecutive pages have such a mixed bag of ideas.

Sometimes Beethoven was working intensively on one work when he thought of some unrelated fragment; this 'concept' might then appear in the middle of the drafts for the main work, but often he turned forward to a blank page and wrote down the idea at the top of that. Hence one very often finds the top two lines (or more) of a page filled with material unrelated to the rest of the sketches on the page. This material might then be used in some other work or a later movement of the same work (for example, in SV 263 the top of fo. 44^r contains early ideas for the second movement of Op. 30 No. 1 which are worked out in detail a few pages later, after the sketches for the first movement); but most often it just remained as an isolated fragment. In some cases the lower part of a page containing such 'concept sketches' would be left blank; Beethoven might then return to this blank space when the rest of the book was full, as happened with the main surviving sketch for the Piano Sonata Op. 31 No. 2 (see Chapter 12). One other situation in which he did not always use pages in the right order was when working on a pair of facing pages. He seems to have regarded such a pair as a single unit, and so sometimes the right-hand page, or at least part of it, was used before the left-hand one was finished.

The entries on an individual page were normally written down in the right order, from top to bottom. If two separate ideas were included in a single line, the one on the left was usually put down first. There were exceptions once again, however. The first few entries on a page were often well spaced out: there might be several short ideas, each occupying less than a whole stave, placed underneath each other, with the right-hand side of the page left largely blank; or there might be a complete stave left blank between two sketches. Beethoven then sometimes decided to fill in these blank spaces rather than turn over to a new page, especially if what he wanted to put down was related to the sketches already present.

Did Beethoven ever keep quantities of manuscript paper unused for several years, thereby confounding our attempts at chronology? Or did he ever make alterations or additions to early sketch leaves in later years? On the whole it seems he did not, but exceptions can as usual be identified. When he was planning a set of bagatelles in 1822 he annotated several early sketches of piano pieces, either simply allotting them a number in the proposed series or (in most cases) making actual alterations to the notes as well (see Chapter 16). Similarly an autograph of the song 'Der freie Mann' (WoO 117) written about 1794 (SV 185, fo. 62^r) was headed 'No 4' only later, possibly in 1803–4 when he was planning to publish the song as part of a set. A different situation occurred on a loose leaf (SV 77) containing counterpoint studies from about 1794; it was reused about 1809 for sketches for the song 'Mignon'

(Op. 75 No. 1) and a movement from *Egmont*.[18] Another *Egmont* sketch which turns up in a surprising place is a short passage from the final part of the overture; this appears (in pencil) on an otherwise blank page of Landsberg 7 (SV 61, p. 78), a sketchbook used mainly in 1800–1. And yet another peculiarity appears in a leaf (SV 187, fo. 31) of which the paper itself apparently dates from about 1808 and yet the two pieces sketched, *Der glorreiche Augenblick* (Op. 136) and the song 'Resignation' (WoO 149), were written much later, in 1814 and 1817 respectively.[19] But such cases are rare; normally all the paper of a single type was used within a fairly short space of time, and the sketches made on it were not then added to significantly later.

Thus there is a surprising amount of orderliness underlying the apparent chaos of the sketches. Despite the confused state in which they now survive, with their original complications exacerbated by the destructive tendencies of some later owners, the sketches show that Beethoven's compositional methods underwent no really fundamental changes during his life, but gradually evolved from fairly simple sketches in his early youth to extremely complex one with numerous interrelationships between different manuscripts in his final years. Once he had begun his series of desk-sketchbooks in 1798 they remained, except in a few brief periods, a constant feature of his compositional methods right up to his last significant completed work—the finale of the Quartet Op. 130, finished in November 1826; and had he lived a little longer he would probably have begun a new desk-sketchbook for his unfinished Quintet in C, for which substantial sketches can be found on loose leaves and in a pocket-sketchbook but only very few appear at the end of his last desk-sketchbook (SV 30). A single sketchbook of this type lasted on average about six to nine months, depending on its size and the intensity with which it was used. As for a single side of a sketch-leaf, it can be worked out that, allowing for what has been lost, Beethoven used very approximately one side per day on average for most of his life. Obviously there were many days when he made virtually no sketches—for example, when he was fully occupied with making scores or when he was ill or had other business to attend to—and there must have been many other days when he filled several pages of sketches. Estimates suggest that a single full-size page would have been filled in about half an hour to an hour and a half if Beethoven was working at it without interruption. Thus he could quite well have sketched ten sides or more in a single day on occasion, and there are times when he apparently did this. *Christus am Oelberge* was according to Beethoven written in only a fortnight, and yet the sketches occupy nearly a hundred sides. *Die Ruinen von Athen* and *König Stephan* were together apparently written within a space of about three weeks, and there are over a hundred pages of sketches

---

[18] See Johnson, *Fischhof*, i. 85–7.

[19] Tyson, 'First Leonore', p. 316. There is, however, another sketch for 'Resignation' dating from *c.* 1814: see JTW, p. 239.

a hundred pages of sketches for these two works combined. Even when allowance is made for possible exaggeration by Beethoven about the time-span involved, it is clear that a lot of sketching was done in a very short space of time in these cases.

These figures are of some significance when the question of dating the sketches is considered. Often the dates allotted to a sketchbook are based on very slender evidence—the date of a letter offering a work to a publisher, for example; and dating sketches by means of letters about the works has the added hazard that works were often not as far advanced as the letters imply. But there is usually just sufficient evidence available for reasonably accurate dates—which are unlikely to be wrong by more than a few months at the most—to be offered for the beginning and end of a sketchbook, even if these dates are based on that of a work from somewhere in the middle of the book. Dating loose leaves of sketches is more difficult, particularly if they contain unfamiliar material. Nevertheless much progress has been made in recent years in establishing which leaves originally belonged in sketchbooks, allowing their relative positions to be fixed exactly; most of the remaining loose leaves have been dated approximately by means of their content and its relationship to other sketches, or by means of similarities of paper type or handwriting characteristics to other known sketches or autograph scores.[20] Thus from the vast array of over 400 sketch sources now known, a relatively compact table of the principal ones can be produced (see Table 1). Such a table is very far from being a complete inventory, but it does provide an overview of Beethoven's entire output and represents virtually all his major works, in chronological order, as well as all his main sketchbooks.

[20] Johnson's dating of early works by this means has been particularly useful (see Johnson, *Fischhof*, vol. i. esp. pp. 25–64).

TABLE 1. Beethoven's Principal Sketch Sources[a]

SV[b]	Name of source[c]	Main works[d]	Approximate date[e]
31 185	'Fischhof' 'Kafka' } miscellanies	Opp. 1–16	Up to 1798
45	Grasnick 1	Op. 18/1, 3: quartets	Aug. 1798 – early 1799
46	Grasnick 2, fos. 1–40	Op. 18/1, 2, 5: quartets	Early 1799 – Aug. 1799
—	(lost)	Op. 18/4: quartet Op. 20: septet Op. 21: Symphony No. 1 Op. 37: Piano Concerto No. 3	Aug. 1799 – Apr. 1800
29	Autograph 19e, fos. 75–94	Op. 18/1, 2, 6: quartets Op. 22: piano sonata Op. 23: violin sonata	May – Aug. 1800
61	Landsberg 7	Op. 23: violin sonata Op. 24: violin sonata Op. 26: piano sonata Op. 27/1: piano sonata Op. 36: Symphony No. 2 Op. 43: Prometheus	Aug. 1800 – early 1801
—	'Sauer' (dispersed)	Op. 27/2: piano sonata Op. 28: piano sonata Op. 29: quintet	Spring – summer 1801
263	'Kessler'	Op. 30: violin sonatas Op. 31/1: piano sonata Op. 35: piano variations Op. 36: Symphony No. 2 Op. 47: violin sonata	Late 1801 – June 1802

343	'Wielhorsky'	Op. 31/3: piano sonata Op. 34: piano variations Op. 35: piano variations Op. 47: violin sonata Op. 85: *Christus am Oelberge*	Aug. 1802 – Apr. 1803
60	Landsberg 6	Op. 53: piano sonata Op. 55: Symphony No. 3 Op. 72: *Leonore* Op. 85: *Christus am Oelberge*	May 1803 – Mar. 1804
67	Mendelssohn 15	Op. 54: piano sonata Op. 56: Triple Concerto Op. 57: piano sonata Op. 72: *Leonore*	Mid-1804 – autumn 1805
265	A36 (miscellany)	Op. 59: quartets	1806
–	(lost)	Op. 58: Piano Concerto No. 4 Op. 60: Symphony No. 4 Op. 61: Violin Concerto Op. 62: *Coriolan* Overture	Late 1805 – early 1807
213	'Mass in C' Sketchbook	Op. 86: Mass in C	Summer 1807
289	1807–8 Sketchbook (largely dispersed)	Op. 67: Symphony No. 5 Op. 69: cello sonata Op. 138: *Leonore* Overture No. 1	Sept. 1807 – early 1808
188	'Pastoral'	Op. 68: Symphony No. 6 Op. 70: piano trios	Feb. – Sept. 1808
47	Grasnick 3	Op. 73: Piano Concerto No. 5 Op. 80: Choral Fantasia	Late 1808 – early 1809
226	'Meinert'	Op. 73: Piano Concerto No. 5	Early 1809

Table 1. *Continued*

SV[b]	Name of source[c]	Main works[d]	Approximate date[e]
59	Landsberg 5	Op. 73: Piano Concerto No. 5 Op. 74: quartet Op. 76: piano variations Op. 81a: piano sonata Op. 115: *Namensfeier* Overture	March – Oct. 1809
65	Landsberg 11	Op. 83: 3 Goethe songs Op. 84: *Egmont* Op. 95: quartet Op. 97: piano trio	Jan. – Sept. 1810
173 358 390 etc.	1810–11 Sketchbook (dispersed)	Op. 95: quartet Op. 97: piano trio Op. 117: *König Stephan*	Late 1810 – summer 1811
184	Add. 29801, fos. 2–37	Op. 113: *Die Ruinen von Athen*	Aug. – Sept. 1811
106	'Petter'	Op. 92: Symphony No. 7 Op. 93: Symphony No. 8 Op. 96: violin sonata Op. 113: *Die Ruinen von Athen*	Sept. 1811 – Dec. 1812
138	'Meeresstille'	Op. 94: 'An die Hoffnung' Op. 112: *Meeresstille*	Mar. 1813 – early 1814
–	Loose leaves (many lost)	Op. 91: *Wellingtons Sieg* Op. 94: 'An die Hoffnung'	1813
63	Landsberg 9, pp. 17–68	Op. 72: *Fidelio*	Early 1814
270	'Dessauer'	Op. 72: *Fidelio* Op. 90: piano sonata Op. 115: *Namensfeier* Overture	Mar. – Sept. 1814

69	Mendelssohn 6	Op. 89: polonaise Op. 136: *Der glorreiche Augenblick*	Sept. 1814 – early 1815
364	'Scheide'	Op. 98: *An die ferne Geliebte* Op. 101: piano sonata Op. 102/2: cello sonata	Mar. 1815 – May 1816
28/1	Autograph 11/1	Op. 101: piano sonata	Summer – autumn 1816
–	Loose leaves and pocket-sketchbooks	Op. 106: piano sonata	1817–18
154	'Wittgenstein'	Op. 109: piano sonata Op. 120: Diabelli Variations Op. 123: *Missa solemnis*	Spring 1819 – Apr. 1820
11	Artaria 195	Op. 109: piano sonata Op. 123: *Missa solemnis*	Apr. 1820 – late 1820
12	Artaria 197	Op. 110: piano sonata Op. 123: *Missa solemnis*	Late 1820 – late 1821
14	Artaria 201	Op. 111: piano sonata Op. 123: *Missa solemnis* Op. 124: *Die Weihe des Hauses* Op. 125: Symphony No. 9	Late 1821 – late 1822
107	'Engelmann'	Op. 120: Diabelli Variations Op. 125: Symphony No. 9	Jan. – Mar. 1823
62/1	Landsberg 8/1[f]	Op. 125: Symphony No. 9	Spring 1823
62/2	Landsberg 8/2	Op. 125: Symphony No. 9	Spring 1823 – late 1823
280	A50[g]	Op. 125: Symphony No. 9 Op. 126: bagatelles	Late 1823 – June 1824
28/2	Autograph 11/2	Op. 127: quartet Op. 132: quartet	Autumn 1824 – early 1825

TABLE 1. *Continued*

SV[b]	Name of source[c]	Main works[d]	Approximate date[c]
104	'De Roda'	Op. 130: quartet Op. 132: quartet Op. 133: *Grosse Fuge*	May – Sept. 1825
30	'Kullak'	Op. 130: quartet Op. 131: quartet Op. 133: *Grosse Fuge* Op. 135: quartet	Oct. 1825 – Nov. 1826

[a] The pocket-sketchbooks and score-sketch bifolios have been omitted (for details, see JTW). But sketch-leaves used as a substantial group between one sketchbook and the next (e.g. SV 184 and SV 265) have been included, in order to fill in gaps in the chronology.

[b] The SV number refers to the principal part of the MS; in many cases additional leaves have been removed and can be found elsewhere. For details of these, see JTW.

[c] The name given is either the nickname (usually that of a former owner of the MS) or the MS number, and is usually the same as that used in JTW. Not all the pages in a MS as it now stands necessarily belong to the book as it was when Beethoven used it, and it has not always been practicable to indicate which ones do not.

[d] Works are normally listed only if there is a substantial amount of sketching for them and they have an opus number. Most of the sketchbooks also contain brief sketches for many more works than are listed here.

[e] The dates have been derived from a variety of sources of information and in most cases are only very approximate. Each refers to the main period when a sketchbook was in use. There are sometimes odd pages from outside the main period—e.g. fos. 152 and 162 of SV 185 were probably used in 1799, and p. 49 of SV 61 was probably begun in 1798.

[f] Continuation of SV 107?   [g] Continuation of SV 62/2?

7

The Visual Appearance of the Sketches

THE sheer visual appearance of Beethoven's sketches has deterred many a scholar from making full use of them. Quite apart from the fact that related sketches are now often in widely separated locations and have presented formidable difficulties for reconstructing the sketchbooks as Beethoven used them, there are considerable problems in simply deciphering what he has written. It therefore seems desirable here to discuss first the nature and appearance of the sketches, and the problems of deciphering and transcribing them into ordinary notation, before examining their contents in detail; for an understanding of what they signify and in what ways they may be ambiguous is greatly helped by a knowledge of their peculiar notational features and Beethoven's idiosyncratic handwriting. Moreover there has hitherto been no detailed discussion of what are the principal difficulties of reading the sketches, and how these difficulties may be overcome.

For decades after Beethoven's death his sketches were treated mainly as souvenirs of his handwriting rather than as material to be transcribed, studied, and understood. This attitude is well illustrated by a remark made by Vincent Novello on a sketch (SV 183) which he presented to the British Museum on 27 July 1843; 'I have the pleasure of presenting this rare and curious specimen of Beethoven's singular mode of making hasty memoranda and indicative sketches (which no one could understand but himself) of his musical thoughts,—for preservation in the Library of the British Museum.' In the following decades, however, Gustav Nottebohm (amongst others) demonstrated that it was possible to make some sense of the sketches, and his work was so skilfully done and so wide-ranging that many subsequent scholars have been content to rely on his transcriptions rather than face the problems of making their own. Only relatively recently has this situation changed significantly, as scholars have come to realize the limitations of Nottebohm's work and become aware what a fruitful field of investigation sketch study is; but even today one's initial reaction on seeing a Beethoven sketch after never having seen one before is likely to be one of bewilderment akin to that of Vincent Novello.

The difficulties involved in making sense of the sketches lie partly in their fragmentary and somewhat jumbled nature, but also in their near-illegibility. Although the autograph scores are usually extremely untidy compared with those of many composers and can be transcribed accurately only by a skilled and experienced copyist, Beethoven did at least try to make them legible, and there are surprisingly few genuinely doubtful readings. But the sketches were never intended to be copied by anyone but himself, and so there was no necessity for him to aim for complete clarity. Several factors contribute to the difficulties of deciphering the sketches; most of these factors are also present in the autograph scores, but not nearly to the same extent. Some sketches are deleted so heavily that it is impossible to be certain what lies beneath the deletions; others are altered so many times that it becomes difficult to decide either which version of the sketch is the final one or the order of the preceding versions that lie under it. Some sketches are very cramped and minute; others have large blank bars or are very blotchy. Large ink-blots are quite common, although they often do not obscure any music.[1] A common type of sketch in Beethoven's later years is one made in pencil which was then inked in at his desk; during the inking in he usually modified his concept, so that the ink version is slightly different from the pencil one underneath, which is usually very hard to decipher. Pencil sketches in general, in fact, pose their own peculiar problems; pencil does not show up well on a microfilm, and the writing is sometimes very badly faded—almost to the point of disappearance—particularly if the page in question was the outer page of a gathering or sheaf.

Even if the sketch is clearly visible, transcription is rarely easy, and it requires practice before it can be done efficiently. The exact position of a note-head on the stave is often unclear, sometimes suggesting three or four possible pitches since Beethoven took little care to place note-heads accurately. In the case of crotchets the problem is sometimes compounded by uncertainty·about which end of a stem the note-head is meant to be, since note-heads are often so tiny as to be almost non-existent. With minims and semibreves the pitch is usually clearer than with smaller note values, but sometimes a note-head is so large that it spans two or three lines on the stave. Often the pitch of a passage is clearest where Beethoven is using leger lines, which are usually clearly drawn and which restrict the pitch of an individual note to a maximum of two possibilities. Occasionally the pitch of a note is so unclear that Beethoven has actually written in the name of the note (using a small italic letter), which makes the pitch absolutely certain, as in Ex. 7.1

Ex. 7.1 SV 189, fo. 10ᵛ

---

[1] The blots must have been an inconvenience to Beethoven, but they sometimes help today in reconstructing his sketchbooks (see JTW, pp. 62–3), and he was not averse to joking about them, as in a heavily blotted letter to Zmeskall (A-340) in which he offered the recipient 'a present of a few ink-blots'.

(SV 189, fo. 10ᵛ staves 1–5). Where this has been done, the name of a note often bears little relationship to the apparent position of it on the stave. Some notes and other signs are situated between two staves in such a way that it is impossible to be certain whether they belong to the upper or lower stave, and Beethoven never draws a line between two staves to separate material for one from material belonging to the other.

If one wants to make any sense of the sketches there is little point in transcribing the notes absolutely literally, for the numerous imprecisions will tend to obscure the conceptual evolution of a work between different sketches. The only sensible course (and therefore the one adopted in the present volume except Ex. 7.1) is to transcribe what are thought to be the notes Beethoven intended when he made the particular marks on the manuscript paper. This will inevitably involve a certain amount of interpretation and guesswork, and the transcriber needs to take into account not only what he sees in front of him but also corresponding bars in different sketches, later in the same sketch, and in the final version of the work. The transcription must also make some sort of musical sense, since Beethoven never composed musical nonsense. The futility of a 'diplomatic', that is, literal, transcription of a sketch has become increasingly apparent in recent years and has been commented on by several writers.[2]

Another hazard for the potential transcriber is Beethoven's idiosyncratic style of notation. Ex. 7.2 shows some of the most common musical symbols as they appeared in his hand from about 1800 onwards.[3] As can be seen, many of them are very different in appearance from the common forms of the symbols today, and the quaver rest can easily be mistaken for a crotchet note in some cases. Notice that the treble clef somewhat resembles a back-to-front S, while the bass clef normally resembles a rather crooked S and almost invariably has the two dots present. The tenor clef (not shown) is roughly the same as the alto clef, which looks a little like a capital B, but the soprano clef is quite differently formed. The natural is formed by a zigzag stroke (♮) and a nearly horizontal line across it, while the flat sometimes has a little hook on the right-hand end but more often turns the other way and can resemble a figure 6.

Ex. 7.2 Crotchet, quaver, and semiquaver rests. Clefs and accidentals

[2] See e.g. Gossett, 'Sixth Symphony', p. 249.

[3] Before 1800 many of them were undergoing rapid change; a detailed study of these changes can be found in Johnson, *Fischhof*, i. 25–64.

Most of Beethoven's sketches use only one stave at a time, with the main melodic thread represented but with little indication of harmony. In a few of them, chiefly for piano pieces and vocal works, two staves are used, and in a few others as many as four (or even more) staves are used at a time (though some may be left largely or completely blank). These four-stave sketches appear mostly in connection with the late quartets, for which Beethoven resorted to making 'score sketches' as well as single-line drafts to provide more space to work out the part-writing (see Chapter 8). Clefs, key signatures, and time signatures are rarely written in. Where they do occur they are most often in an initial concept, written down before he had decided much about the piece apart from the key and the opening idea, or else in a late draft that was initially intended as a final score but which broke down into sketches as he ran into difficulties.

The absence of a time signature poses no great inconvenience, since it can nearly always be guessed, even for a very short idea which never evolved into a finished work. The lack of a key signature can be much more of a problem, particularly if the sketch is a very short or unfamiliar one. Sometimes it is impossible to be certain what key signature is intended—for example, whether a theme is intended to be in the major or the minor. Ex. 7.3 shows a concept sketch for a 'second symphony' to go with No. 7, which had been sketched earlier in the same sketchbook; the clefs and time signature can be inferred, but what is the key—C major, E flat major, or even C minor? Another problem is that accidentals are often omitted, especially if a certain accidental is to apply to several bars in a row, in which case a single accidental at the beginning of the passage often suffices. Anyone reading the sketches must be constantly aware of the possibility of missing accidentals and be prepared to supply them where necessary; and there are occasional places where nobody can be sure whether or not an accidental has been omitted (this is true even of finished works—the question of whether there are missing naturals in bars 225–6 of the first movement of the 'Hammerklavier' Sonata has never been settled conclusively). But if the accidental is very important or unexpected and has not been used just before, Beethoven nearly always includes it. Particularly notable are the accidentals for the leading-notes of minor keys, which he normally remembers to insert; in fact such accidentals are sometimes the only way of confirming the key and clef of an unidentified sketch.

Clefs can generally be deduced when a sketch is on two or more staves,

Ex. 7.3 SV 106, fo. 35ʳ

but when it is on a single stave there may be some doubt. Sometimes the bass
and treble parts are even squashed on to a single stave, with both clefs
implied at the same time—one for one note and another for a note directly
above it on the same stave. Usually the clef of a single-stave draft can be
deduced by reference to the final version of the work but sometimes the
sketch is too short, unclear, or unfamiliar for this to be done. The problem
is compounded in material such as the sketches for the duet 'So ruhe dann'
in *Christus am Oelberge*, which use not just treble and bass but soprano and
tenor clefs too, without usually indicating which is intended.[4] No doubt there
were times when even Beethoven had to think twice about what clef he had
intended in an earlier sketch. At any rate he appears to have made a musical
joke about the problem, in Variation 15 of the Diabelli Variations. Towards
the end of this variation there appears to be a treble clef sign missing in the
left-hand part (Ex. 7.4), and some editors have even inserted one, followed
by a bass clef about four bars later. Another interpretation of this passage is
that Beethoven 'partly imagined a treble clef, and he partly imagined a bass
clef. And therefore it escaped him that he'd forgotten to write a little passage
getting the left hand from the roughly middle C register down to the bass.'[5]
But it seems more plausible to assume that the clefs have been omitted
deliberately as a kind of private joke—a trap for the unwary pianist (or
editor), and a musical pun (his letters are full of puns) on the ambiguity of
a stave without a clef. The variation is, after all, marked 'scherzando'.

In addition to purely musical symbols, the sketches frequently contain
other symbols or ordinary words, which are generally no less difficult to
decipher than the notes. The words, though usually in German, may also be

Ex. 7.4 Op. 120. xv

---

[4] See SV 343, p. 137 (Fishman ed., *Wielhorsky*, transcription, p. 143).
[5] Alan Tyson, in Winter and Carr, *Detroit*, p. 143. See also Czesla, 'Skizzen', and literature
cited there.

in any of three other main languages (Italian, French, and Latin) and occasionally in others too, depending on the context. Beethoven also used two quite different types of script—Gothic for German and italic for Romance languages; thus including capitals each letter could appear in any of four different forms.[6] Several letters are similar in appearance, and this, coupled with Beethoven's habitually bad handwriting, has led to a number of errors of transcription, even by experienced scholars.[7] Words are quite often abbreviated, too, and not always in standard abbreviations.

Some types of verbal text found in the sketchbooks can be quickly passed over. These include texts of vocal works, where the text is usually included with the sketches although in individual sketches it may be missing. Tempo marks usually appear in the same sorts of context as key signatures and time signatures, that is, in early concepts for movements still uncomposed; dynamic marks and indications of instrumentation may also occur. If a work is for the stage, there may be occasional stage directions, as in some of the sketches for the ballet *Prometheus*.[8] Sometimes sketch-leaves were treated as simply the nearest bit of paper to hand, and were used for personal memoranda, drafts for letters to publishers or friends, copies of newspaper advertisements, and similar material.[9]

More interesting are words which are directly connected with the creative process. These may be general comments about the nature of the work in hand—the most famous examples are the remarks found amongst the early sketches for the 'Pastoral' Symphony, including 'It is left to the listener to discover the situations for himself' and 'Sinfonia caracteristica—or recollection of country life'.[10] Often such words consist merely of the title of some new work, such as 'Sinfonie' (SV 106, fo. 42ᵛ), perhaps with a key indication ('Sinfonie in C moll': SV 106, fo. 61ᵛ) and/or a number ('2te Sinf. d moll': SV 106, fo. 29ᵛ). Where there is a number, this only relates to a group of works being written at the time, as in the sketch shown in Ex. 7.3, which was labelled '2te Sinfonie' but was planned as a companion to No. 7.

Words can also occur where Beethoven is planning the formal scheme of a work or movement. Such plans usually contain a mixture of musical notes and words. A good example is the first sketch for the finale of the 'Eroica' Symphony (Ex. 7.5),[11] where there are remarks concerning form ('principio', 'Var.'), texture ('Fuge'), key ('dope in Es'), tempo ('un poco adagio'), and instrumentation ('Clarinetto solo', 'Corno solo'), interspersed with

---

[6] See Unger, *Handschrift*, Tables I–III, for all these letter forms and also the arabic numerals.

[7] e.g. the phrase 'beyde ohne Widerholung' (both without repeat) in SV 335 has been deciphered by Abraham Klimowitzki (Klimowitzki, 'Autograph', p. 162) as 'bringen zur Durchführung' (bring to the development): only the first letter and the last three are correct.

[8] See Mikulicz ed., *Notierungsbuch*, pp. 65–7.   [9] See e.g. N-II, p. 353.

[10] Ibid., p. 375; SV 188, fo. 2ʳ. See also Ch. 4 for remarks on the nature of the slow movement of Op. 18 No. 1, found amongst the sketches.   [11] See N-1803, p. 50.

Ex. 7.5 SV 60, p. 70

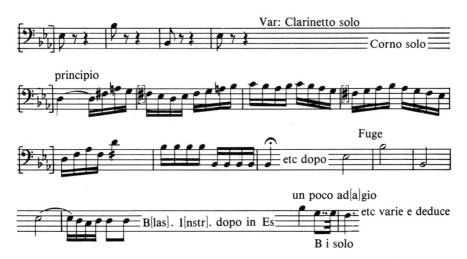

fragments of thematic material; meanwhile the main theme, though already decided on, does not appear at all in this sketch. Sometimes such plans consist mainly of words, as in the first sketch for the Piano Variations Op. 34 (SV 263, fo. 88ᵛ), where two bars of theme are followed by this remark: 'Jede V[ariation] in einer andern Taktart—oder abwechselnd einmal in der l[inken] H[and] passagen und dann fast die nemlichen oder andere in der rechten Hand ausgeführt' (Each variation in a different metre—or passages played alternately once in the left hand and then almost the same passages or others in the right hand). At other times the sketch will be mainly notes, with only one or two words connecting or labelling them. A number of individual words are frequently found in this context, some of them referring to instruments but many of a quasi-analytical character. These include 'Thema', written beside the main theme of a movement; 'Ende', 'Schluss' or occasionally 'finis', usually denoting part of the coda; 'erster Theil' (first part) and '2ter Theil' (second part), denoting the sections before and after the middle double bar of a sonata-form or binary-form movement;[12] 'm.g.' (*mitte Gedanke*, i.e. middle idea,[13] sometimes used to label a subsidiary theme such as the second subject in a sonata); 'Cadenza', often referring to a written-out cadenza-like passage not in a concerto; 'dann' or 'dopo' (then), usually used to connect short thematic fragments, often with the implication that there is still some linking passage to be composed; 'd.c.', which is used much more extensively in sketches than in finished works and indicates any kind of reprise of the main theme; and 'Ritornel' or more often simply 'R', which indicates an instrumental passsage in a primarily vocal work. Less common

---

[12] The terms 'erster Theil' and 'zweiter Theil' are derived from Koch, *Versuch.*

[13] Occasionally the term is written out in full, e.g. in SV 189, fo. 13ᵛ.

terms include 'Zwischensatz' (transition; see SV 185, fo. 88^v), 'Haupt-gedanke' (main idea; see SV 185, fo. 154^v), and simply 'Gedanke'.

The frequent use of so many words of this type serves to emphasize how much Beethoven was concerned with such matters as shape, design, and structure rather than just thematic patterns and successions of pitches. Similarly the common appearance of the name of a key, sometimes without any melodic idea alongisde, shows that the principal keys of a movement or work were to be considered before the problem of how these keys should be reached, and even before the problem of what motif should be used when they were reached.

Other words and signs found in the sketchbooks are concerned with the sketching process itself rather than the musical content of the sketches. Most common of these is the Latin word 'Vide' (see), which is used to connect the end of one sketch fragment to the beginning of another, where Beethoven had run out of space; 'Vi=' is written at the end of the first fragment, and the music continues elsewhere at a place marked '=de'. 'Vi=' is sometimes also found in the middle of a sketch, with the following bars deleted, in which case the passage marked '=de' is a substitute for them. The two syllables are usually found on the same page or else on adjoining ones, but sometimes they have been written on two completely separate pieces of paper, in which case one or other piece may now be lost, leaving a completely disconnected join. In a few cases there is evidence that, although only one syllable is present, the other was never actually written down; but nearly always the presence of one half of 'Vide' demands a search for the other half. Spotting either syllable can be difficult since they are often little more than a scrawl; but they can usually be recognized by means of the double hyphen which is invariably present and usually fairly clear.

Since Beethoven so frequently needed to make such cross-references between two sketch fragments there was a danger that several 'Vide' signs might become confused, and so he evolved a variety of other symbols for connecting sketches together. These include crosses and circles such as the following: ✕ ⊠ ⊗ . Numbers are also often used; these sometimes take the form of 'No' without any figures, but usually 'No' is followed by a figure of several digits, such as 100, 500, 1000, or even 20000, and sometimes the 'No' itself is missing. According to Schindler the size of the figure indicated to Beethoven the worth of the sketch,[14] but as this is precisely the sort of information that Schindler was most inclined to fabricate, this idea must be dismissed. Different numbers were occasionally used, however, to denote successive passages in a sketch: a good example of this appears in SV 189, fo. 7^v–8^r, where a short sketch concludes with the number 10, which connects up to a sketch beginning with a 10; this sketch is in turn connected

---

[14] TF, p. 250.

to another by means of the number 60, thence to a fourth by means of 70 and on to a fifth by means of 80 (see Ex. 13.8).

Several other words and abbreviations were used in connection with the actual process of sketching, including 'etc', 'oder', 'gut' and 'le meilleur'. The first of these generally occurs at the end of a short sketch which has been deliberately left uncontinued—perhaps if Beethoven had already sketched the rest previously, or if he had not decided how to continue but was not immediately concerned with this problem. The word 'oder' (or) is often found beside a short sketch that is an alternative to a passage in a longer draft nearby; sometimes there are several alternatives in quick succession, each labelled 'oder'. If a deleted passage was to be restored, this was indicated by the word 'gut' (good, meaning 'stet'), and a wavy line above the passage in question; or sometimes the wavy line was just used on its own for the same purpose. (A wavy line could also be used to prolong an '8va' sign, but this use can be distinguished from its use as 'stet' since the material beneath is not deleted.) Beethoven sometimes made several alternative drafts without at first deciding which was the best. When he eventually made this decision, the chosen passage might be marked 'le meilleur', and this phrase is common in sketches from his later years—particularly, it seems, in those from around 1815–16. Other abbreviations found amongst the sketches are concerned with various types of performance indication, such as 'B.I.' (*Blasinstrumente*, i.e. wind instruments), 'r.h.' (*rechte Hand*, i.e. right hand), and '8tel' (quavers). It is important, therefore, to remember that an undeciphered remark may serve any one of a number of functions.

Good examples of many of the foregoing features can be found in the 'Kessler' Sketchbook (SV 263), on f. 94^r (see Facsimile 2). This page consists entirely of sketches for the development section of the first movement of the Piano Sonata in G Op. 31 No. 1, except for the last two staves, which are for the exposition. Stave 1 begins with a prominent '=de' and then a bar later has the sign ⊗ . This first bar was intended to connect the beginning and middle of the development, which appear on staves 2–4, with the retransition on stave 1; thus the '=de' continues from the 'Vi=' at the end of stave 4. The retransition sketch was then replaced by one on stave 5, and so the first bar on stave 1 is linked to this by means of the sign ⊗ . The picture is somewhat confused by the appearance of another crossed circle, at the end of stave 2, which connects to an almost obscured corresponding mark in the middle of stave 3 (immediately after the deleted bars). The first bar on stave 1 has the figure 4 (altered from 2) and a curved line above it: this indicates that the bar is to be played four times (cf. Op. 31 No. 1, bars 158–61). A similar sign is found above two bars on stave 7 and the second bar of stave 14. Most of stave 1 is in the bass clef (indicated at the beginning), but in the last bar the upper note (g″) is to be read in the treble clef and the lower (GG) in the bass; the bass clef is placed in front of the latter note, though not on the correct part of the stave. Above the middle of stave 4 appears 'Vi=',

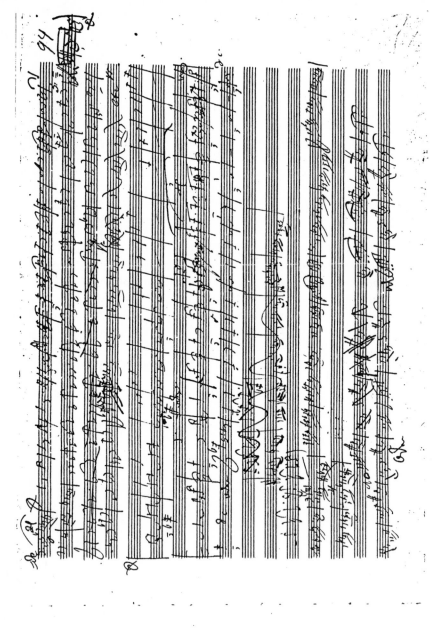

Facsimile 2. 'Kessler' Sketchbook (Vienna, GdM, A 34), fo. 94ʳ

which connects to the '=de' on stave 13; harmonically these two passages do not quite join up (cf. bars 136 and 140 of the sonata), but the gap is represented by the 'etc' near the end of stave 4 between two deleted bars and the 'Vi=' that connects to stave 1.

Staves 5–6 and 7–8 are sketched in score (with treble and bass clefs) rather than on a single line, but the continuation is on a single stave (stave 9, first note). The passage is for the retransition, so that when the recapitulation was reached Beethoven simply wrote 'd c' (stave 9, first bar). He also considered an alternative to the sketch on staves 7–8, writing 'oder' on stave 7, bar 3, which connects to the 'oder' beside the alternative on stave 9. The latter sketch again leads right up to the recapitulation, and so there is another 'd.c.' at the end of the stave. In the first bar of stave 6 there is a low D, while in the first bar of stave 7 there is an e‴♭; there is so little space between the staves that these two notes are virtually side by side, with the note belonging to stave 6 actually slightly lower on the page than that belonging to stave 7, and with the flat sign lower than it should be; but any doubts about Beethoven's intentions here are dispelled by a comparison with the final version of the piece (bars 170 and 182). On stave 15 there is a sketch marked 'No', which connects from another 'No' at the end of stave 5 of the opposite page, as an alternative to the beginning of stave 6 on that page. On the bottom stave of fo. 94ʳ are two further alternatives for these bars, each marked 'oder'.

Thus the main draft on the page can be traced as follows. It begins with the whole of stave 2 and continues in the middle of stave 3 and as far as the middle of stave 4. Next there was to have been an unsketched passage represented by the 'etc' and connecting via a 'Vide' to stave 1, bar 1, and thence to stave 5; but most of the details of this passage are worked out in the other 'Vide', on staves 13–14, which joins up by implication to the beginning of stave 5. The draft then runs through to stave 9 without further interruption apart from one alternative ('oder') added on stave 9 as a variant of part of staves 7–8.

This page therefore illustrates many of the difficulties of deciphering and understanding Beethoven's sketches, but the problems are not nearly as great as is sometimes imagined. Most of the notes and other signs on the page are reasonably legible when one knows what to expect, and the same applies in general to other pages (apart from a few that are heavily deleted or very faded). And the layout of the material on the page, though apparently very jumbled, has a certain orderliness about it and is by no means haphazard. Nearly all the loose ends join up, either explicitly or by implication, and form a coherent picture of a gradually evolving piece of music in which certain details had not quite been fixed. With a little practice and some sound musical sense, such sketches can be deciphered and interpreted by most musicians who are prepared to take the trouble to overcome the initial barriers that the visual appearance of the material presents.

8

Types and Relationships of Sketches

NOT all of Beethoven's sketchbook entries have precisely the same function in the compositional process, and it is convenient to classify them into a number of different types. Certain broad types keep recurring throughout his work in almost all the sketchbooks, regardless of the pieces being composed, and the relationships between the different types are also fairly consistent. It is therefore possible to give an account of the various types and how they relate to each other; this account will be valid with only minor modifications for nearly all the works he wrote. Altogether there are about eight main types, several of which were mentioned in the previous chapter. They include concept sketches, continuity drafts, variants, synopsis sketches, score sketches, brouillons, piano exercises, and random notations. Nearly all Beethoven's sketches fall into one of these types, although occasionally there are borderline cases or irregular types.

A concept sketch is a short new idea for a movement about to be written. It is defined by Alan Tyson, who evidently invented the term, as 'the germ of an idea for a number: nothing detailed, only a suggestion for the scoring, or a brief hint as to the treatment'.[1] It often occurs at the top of a page, suggesting that it may have been written down several pages further on than the part of the sketchbook Beethoven was principally using at the time. By definition it is no more than a few bars long; it is best to restrict the term for the most part to ideas for a movement Beethoven was on the point of writing or was at least thinking of possibly writing, but it can by extension also be applied to new ideas for later parts of a movement, such as a second subject, an episode, or indeed any new ideas. Very often such sketches come complete with key signature and even time signature, since key and time were among the first things that had to be decided on. Quite often they are on two staves, giving not just the melody but also some indication of the harmony, and sometimes they include a few words as well as notes, such as an indication of key or theme.

The ideas found in concept sketches were not always developed into finished movements. Often they were promptly abandoned and are unrelated to any known work; at other times Beethoven wrote several alternative concepts for the same movement on different pages, perhaps eventually abandoning them all for something quite different. A good example is the finale of the Quartet Op. 130: in the course of sketching the earlier movements he wrote down over a dozen different concept sketches for a

[1] Tyson, 'Christus', pp. 570–1.

finale, all of which were eventually supplanted by the *Grosse Fuge* and later by its replacement finale.

In contrast to a concept sketch, a continuity draft is by definition a fairly long sketch and tends to represent a relatively late stage of composition.[2] It consists of a single-stave (occasionally two-stave) draft for an extended portion of a composiiton: a typical length might be an exposition of a sonata-form movement, but a draft may be shorter or longer, and sometimes covers an entire movement. In these drafts Beethoven can be seen fitting together the more fragmentary ideas made earlier into a coherent whole. Features such as key signatures were not necessary since they had been decided on much earlier, and so they are rarely present. The drafts enabled him to judge the proportions of the different parts of a movement or section and the sense of continuity from one part to the next. The term 'continuity draft' does not necessarily imply a continuous burst of compositional activity; in some cases a draft begun on one page has been suddenly broken off and then resumed elsewhere, possibly not until some time afterwards. Parts of the draft may also be modified by 'Vide' marks, so that tracing its continuity can mean jumping from stave to stave, as was seen in Chapter 7 in the draft for the development section of Op. 31 No. 1.

A continuity draft could form the basis from which the autograph score was made, and in many cases an autograph score shows very few conceptual differences from the latest continuity draft but is just an amplification of it. Occasionally such a draft actually appears in an autograph score on a separate stave, as a kind of 'cue-staff' or guide for Beethoven as he wrote out the score[3]—a particularly convenient device to use in a large orchestral score with a complex texture. Continuity drafts are particularly common amongst the sketches for his early works, and are often more or less all that survives in the form of sketches for a work; this is especially noticeable in the 'Kafka' and 'Fischhof' miscellanies, where lengthy drafts are the rule rather than the exception. As the sketching process grew more complicated over the years, short fragmentary sketches became increasingly common; and since the continuity drafts were meant to be the immediate predecessors of the autograph scores, the shorter sketches could be regarded as sketches for the continuity drafts rather than as direct preparations for the autographs. Needless to say, although the continuity drafts were intended to precede the autographs directly, Beethoven often found them unsatisfactory in some way. This meant that a draft was either amended until it was satisfactory or was replaced by another draft. Thus in the case of the 'Eroica' there are four continuity drafts for the first part of the first movement:[4] the first two have the wrong proportions and are too short, so they were replaced by the third;

---

[2] The term 'continuity draft' was coined by Joshua Rifkin and used by Lewis Lockwood in 1970 (Lockwood, 'Definition', p. 42), since when it has become the standard term for such sketches.

[3] Lockwood, 'Definition', p. 45.   [4] N-1803, pp. 6–14.

this has roughly the right proportions, but it still has details which needed to be altered and so is heavily amended, almost to the point of illegibility in places; in the end Beethoven was therefore forced to make a fourth draft to make everything clearer. For later works there are sometimes even more than four drafts, which do not necessarily appear to supersede each other in order. *Meeresstille und glückliche Fahrt*, for example, has at least nine for its first movement, and it was not the last one that was selected as the basis for the autograph but one of the earlier ones (see Chapter 14).

The sketches referred to above as 'variants' are those which are alternatives to or modifications of other sketches. Unlike the very short concept sketches and the very long continuity drafts, variant sketches can be of more or less any length, although if they are sufficiently long they can be considered as continuity drafts in their own right; it is therefore preferable to consider a variant sketch as being by definition no longer than about half of the nearest continuity draft. This type of sketch is in the majority in the sketches as a whole, and can take on a wide variety of characters; in fact one can regard any sketch which is neither a concept sketch, a continuity draft, nor any of the other distinctive types listed above as being a variant sketch. As was seen earlier, some are labelled 'oder' (or), or if they are intended to replace the middle of a longer draft they may be marked '=de' (corresponding with a 'Vi=' in the middle of the longer draft); but most often they have no label and are simply further ideas related to the movement being sketched. They are in some way variants or extensions of sketches already made. Generally they are quite short; sketches of intermediate length between short variants and longer drafts (i.e. of about fifteen to twenty bars) are relatively unusual. Variant sketches for the early works are not quite so common, but in material from later years they proliferate, so that the relationship between each of the numerous ideas and alternatives becomes very complex. Sometimes a variant is sufficiently different from any previous sketch for it to be legitimately regarded as an independent concept, and there are therefore inevitable borderline cases between variants and concept sketches, just as there are between variants and continuity drafts.

Another type of sketch sometimes found is one which gives a kind of synopsis or précis of an entire movement (or even an entire work). At no time were such sketches common, but they were made in all periods; they seem to have been most frequent around 1800–4[5] whereas before 1800 they were rare. An example of such a sketch for a single movement is the initial sketch for the finale of the 'Eroica', already quoted (see Ex. 7.5), while other good examples are the two main sketches surviving for the first movement of the sonata Op. 31 No. 2 (see Exx. 12.3 and 12.7). Sometimes synopsis sketches spread over several movements—for instance the earliest sketches for the 'Eroica' (SV 343, pp. 44–5), which include a series of ideas for the first three movements. There are several such sketches for the Quartet Op. 131,

[5] Lockwood, 'Earliest'.

each covering practically the whole work.[6] Recent literature has not yet produced a standard term for this type of sketch, though several have been suggested, including 'large-scale plan', 'work plan', 'movement plan', 'telescoped draft', and 'tonal overview'. The term adopted here, 'synopsis sketch', emphasizes that Beethoven was in such a sketch looking simultaneously at a large portion of a work, whether it was a substantial section of a movement, a whole movement, several movements, or an entire work, in order to see the overall shape. He drafted the main corner-stones of the movement or work—principal themes, key centres, and perhaps tempo markings or formal devices—but omittted the transitional material. As was seen earlier, such a synopsis often consists partly or even mainly of words rather than notes, thereby demonstrating clearly that Beethoven was initially more interested in key centres and formal shapes than in melodic patterns, which tended to be altered much more than the basic ground-plans found in synopsis sketches. It can be regarded as an extension of the principle of the concept sketch: the latter gives an idea for the beginning of the movement whereas a synopsis sketch gives a more extended idea of the shape of the whole. Again, there are some borderline cases between the two types. And if Beethoven drafted concept sketches for each movement of a work side by side, the group as a whole would effectively amount to a synopsis sketch for the entire work.

Although most of Beethoven's sketches are on single staves, a few— mainly for the late quartets—are in open score. Since at first sight these quartet sketches look like discarded fragments of autograph scores left unfinished, and the interrelationships between different sketches in the late quartets are already very complex, score sketches have only recently been identified as a separate category. In them Beethoven was trying to combine some sense of horizontal continuity with the problem of sketching vertical harmony and texture. No longer would a single melodic line suffice to represent the flow of the music, and several parallel lines became necessary, although often not all the voices were filled in. Another advantage of a score sketch was that if it was particularly successful it could simply be amplified and incorporated into the autograph score without having to be copied out again, though whether Beethoven ever did this is doubtful (he normally seems to have regarded writing out the autograph as a separate and more advanced phase than making the score sketches). But the relationship sometimes worked the other way round, with pages intended for the autograph score eventually degenerating into score sketches.[7] Of course the term 'score sketch' refers as much to layout as to function; thus a concept sketch or a continuity draft could equally well be written in open score to allow sketching of texture as well as melody. In fact score sketches largely fulfil the role of continuity drafts in the late quartets, so that extended single-stave

---

[6] See Winter, 'Plans'; Winter, *Op. 131*, Ch. 6.

[7] Winter, *Op. 131*, pp. 70, 194.

continuity drafts written in pocket- or desk-sketchbooks became relatively infrequent, while most score sketches are quite lengthy drafts.[8]

Score sketches are not exclusive to the late quartets. There is one from as early as around 1790 for the Second Piano Concerto (see Chapter 17), one from 1799 for the F major Quartet Op. 18 No. 1,[9] and others from the early and middle periods (for example a six-stave sketch on fo. 87ʳ of the 'Kessler' Sketchbook dating from 1802). But there is strong evidence that at this time, even in quartets, Beethoven generally worked straight from single-line drafts to the final score,[10] making only occasional brief sketches in score for awkward passages. Score sketches became slightly more common later on —there are several for the Diabelli Variations of 1819–23[11]—but they apparently became part of his standard sketching process only in 1824. Whether they would have been used to any extent after that date had he been writing a symphony, or whether they were designed only for chamber music, cannot be determined. One might expect them to function as an intermediate stage between continuity draft and autograph score, but actually they were used almost from the initial stages of creation, for some of them bear very little relation to the final version. Ex. 8.1, for instance, shows part of an early score sketch for the fourth movement of the Quartet Op. 131: although it is clearly part of a variation of the main theme (cf. bars 15–21) this variation was not used in the final version.

A slightly more advanced type of sketch is that referred to by Nottebohm as a 'brouillon', that is, something between a sketch and a final score. Though not very common, brouillons function as early drafts for autographs, with all the essential shape of a piece present but without all the details necessary in a polished score. If the complete piece is present, but only very roughly, the score is often referred to as an *Urschrift* (original draft of an autograph score) as distinct from a *Reinschrift* (fair copy); the distinctions between score sketch and brouillon and between brouillon and *Urschrift* are often very fine, and the term 'brouillon' is therefore not much used in recent sketch literature. The difficulty of classifying such scores is well illustrated by the fact that, of early drafts for three of the bagatelles in Op. 126 preserved in Paris, those for Nos. 1 and 6 have been counted as sketches while No. 2 counts as an autograph;[12] but in fact the latter is a very rough *Urschrift* of the whole piece, while the other two are discarded fragments of the final score—incomplete in terms of bars but fuller and neater notationally.[13]

In addition to such discarded pages from the middle of autograph scores, there are other types of incomplete score which are not true sketches but are

[8] Ibid., pp. 68, 113.
[9] SV 29, fos. 92–4; see Kramer, 'Op. 30', pp. 125–31 and App. III.
[10] Tyson, 'Razumovsky', p. 128.   [11] Kinderman, *Diabelli*, pp. 25, 48.
[12] KH, p. 381; SV 222 and 233.
[13] Brandenburg ed., *Op. 126*, ii. 65–6; facs. in i. 37–50.

Ex. 8.1 SV 186, fo. 2^r

[etc.]

worth mentioning here. Sometimes Beethoven began an autograph but left off after a few bars for no apparent reason: the only manuscript material surviving for the Piano Sonata Op. 49 No. 1 is a neat score, complete with title ('Sonatine'), of just the first seven bars.[14] On other occasions a score was abandoned as Beethoven ran into difficulties, leaving a sketch that looks like a brouillon; an example is the abandoned score for the Piano Concerto in D of 1815.[15] There are, too, fragments of scores where the remainder has simply been lost.

Beethoven's sketch-leaves also contain a great number of miscellaneous themes and motifs of various kinds which are not closely related to any known work, finished or unfinished. Their function is not certain; different ones probably served different functions. One type that stands out among the

---

[14] SV 185, fo. 66^r.   [15] Hess 15; see Lockwood, 'Unfinished'.

earlier sketches consists of passages of piano figuration of a somewhat virtuosic character on two staves. In the days before Clementi's *Gradus ad Parnassum* and the studies of Czerny, Chopin, and others, the amount of published material for improving the advanced player's technique was fairly limited. Consequently at the stage when Beethoven regarded himself as a pianist as much as a composer, that is, in the early Viennese years, he would have found it helpful to invent his own piano exercises for improving his technique. These exercises are usually only a few bars long but sufficiently developed to have some kind of musical, as opposed to merely mechanical, shape.[16]

Most of the miscellaneous ideas, however, are not obviously piano exercises, and some are clearly not intended for piano at all. Not surprisingly, they have received very little critical attention from scholars, though they are discussed briefly by Joseph Kerman in the introduction to his edition of the 'Kafka' Miscellany.[17] Kerman mentions two types in particular—those concerned with piano figuration or texture, and those that resemble tunes that Beethoven sometimes wrote for ballroom dances in Vienna. He suggests they may sometimes be memoranda that formed the basis for Beethoven's improvisations; or that they may have been intended as ideas for possible later use in actual compositions. But many may never have been intended for actual compositions, and Kerman suggests that these were what he calls 'improvisations on paper'—abstract compositional studies without any context in mind, and a means of keeping ideas flowing even if they did not belong to works in progress. It is along these lines that the nature of these jottings is probably best understood. Many people when equipped with paper and pencil habitually make artistic doodles, in the form of either abstract patterns or concrete images, sometimes as an aid to thought. Beethoven rarely did this (see, however, SV 185, fos. 50ʳ and 88ᵛ), but his musical 'doodles' may be somewhat analogous: ideas would flow out of his fertile mind automatically, as a kind of mental improvisation and possible stimulus to actual composition.

Many of these fragments in fact probably originated in actual improvisations done in private. Beethoven was apparently in the habit of improvising on the piano with a small table beside him, so that he could jot down on paper any noteworthy ideas; and he found such activity a stimulus to his imagination, as he once explained to Archduke Rudolph.[18] These ideas might equally be opening or transitional material, and probably the more remote they were, the more likely he was to want to write them down. Hence one would actually expect to find precisely the kind of jottings that do appear: a mixture of initial ideas and transitions, many of which are strikingly original and unconventional.

[16] Some examples are given in N-II, pp. 356–63.

[17] Kerman ed., *Miscellany*, vol. i pp. xviii–xix.

[18] A-1203; see also Ch. 1 above.

Ex. 8.2 SV 88, p. 1

Ex. 8.3 Op. 7. i

At other times Beethoven may have been consciously trying to think up short but interesting motifs away from the piano, even though they had no immediate context. In this case they would function as a counterpart to work on a more extended composition, where the context already existed but motifs and transitions still had to be invented for it. Some of the 'doodles' are clearly experimental, making use of improbable modulations, textures, or melodic shapes, but most of them would look quite plausible as parts of longer works. Mnay of them do indeed have some element in common with a work written later, and the relationship is occasionally even quite close. For example, one such jotting written in about 1793 begins as in Ex. 8.2 (SV 88, p. 1 stave 5); something very similar turned up in a different key a few years later, in 1796–7, as the second subject in the first movement of the Piano Sonata Op. 7 (Ex. 8.3).

Transitional fragments such as Ex. 8.2 became much less common after Beethoven's early years,[19] but opening motifs—concept sketches for unfinished works—were made throughout his life. They were particularly plentiful during the period 1813–16, as well as in his early years. He was clearly capable of composing far more works than he had time for, as he never seems to have been short of ideas; many sketches belong to works that might have been written but which were not, and in most cases he was probably aware at the time that they were not going to be. The very act of writing down a brief concept sketch for a work may even paradoxically have served as a way of confirming that he did not intend to write that work.

[19] Kerman ed., *Miscellany*, vol. i p. xix.

Often many unused concepts appear together or in quick succession in a sketchbook, and it must be doubted whether he ever intended to use them as the basis for actual pieces. Amongst his sketches altogether there are more unfinished works represented than finished ones.

One function implied by some of the jottings is that of clearing the mind for fresh ideas after he had become stuck in a mental rut. This is well illustrated amongst the sketches for the Eighth Symphony (SV 106). This symphony was begun immediately after the Seventh, but it started life as a piano concerto: the earliest sketches (SV 106, fos. 35–40) indicate an orchestral exposition in F major, using motifs now associated with the Eighth Symphony, followed by pianistic figuration.[20] Perhaps Beethoven then began to have doubts about writing a piano concerto—doubts associated with his abandonment of his career as a pianist, and ones which re-emerged in his attemnpt at a Sixth Piano Concerto in 1815. At any rate he seems to have worked himself into a rut from which no further progress could be made, and so on the following pages of the sketchbook (fos. 41–2, 44–5; fo. 43 belongs later in the sketchbook) he tried to clear his mind by shaking out a great variety of ideas of the most diverse types: concertos in other keys, a polonaise, an adagio for horns, an overture that incorporated a setting of Schiller's 'An die Freude', ideas for four symphonies, and a note of the tune played by the posthorn at Karlsbad.[21] Fo. 44ʳ is a particularly densely filled page, in an unusually uniform hand and ink despite the diversity of material; this indicates that Beethoven did not simply reserve this page for random jottings written at various times but actually wrote them all together, probably at a single sitting. Having thus shaken himself very thoroughly out of his rut, he was then able to return to his 'piano concerto' in F with fresh ideas, and on the following pages (fos. 45ᵛ–50ᵛ) the first movement is worked on with great intensitiy, now as part of a symphony.

Having seen how the abandoned sketches relate to Beethoven's compositional methods, we shall now examine how the sketches for finished works relate to them and to each other. The relationships vary slightly from piece to piece, but not as much as has sometimes been assumed. The apparently great differences between sketches for different works can be accounted for largely by the postulation of missing sketches: in some cases only a small proportion of the sketches survives, whereas in others nearly all do; sometimes only the earliest ones survive, whereas sometimes it is only the late ones; in some cases all the sketches are compressed into a single book, while in others they are scattered on loose leaves. Once missing sketches are taken into account the main difference in compositional procedure between different works is the gradually increasing sophistication of the sketches in later works, as already mentioned. Thus in general a certain pattern of compositional procedure almost always prevails, and once this pattern is

[20] Brandenburg, 'Petter', pp. 135–9.
[21] Ibid., pp. 139–40; N-I, p. 41; N-II, p. 289.

established it becomes possible to make sense of the more difficult cases, such as those where only a few sketches survive or where the work was left unfinished. This general pattern has been described by several writers, but not always with complete accuracy, many having relied too heavily on a rather unbalanced impression of Nottebohm's writings. For example, Thayer's description of Beethoven's working methods,[22] though still widely read, stands in need of modification in the light of more recent research. The following passage is particularly misleading:

One readily sees that, when the general plan of a work is clear and distinct before the mind, it is quite indifferent in what order the various parts are studied; and that Beethoven simply adopted the method of many a dramatic and other author, who sketches his scenes or chapters not in course but as mood, fancy or opportunity dictates. It is equally evident that the composer could have half a dozen works upon his hands at the same time, not merely without disadvantage to any one of them, but to the gain of all, since he could turn to one or another as the spirit of compositions impelled . . .[23]

The first part of this quotation suggests that Beethoven wrote the different parts of a work in no particular order, whereas in fact he normally worked through from beginning to end in more or less the right order. The second part suggests that several works might be begun and ended about the same time, and that the sketches for this period would show a complete jumble of ideas relating to each of these works; as we shall see, this was also not the case.

Sketches for a typical movement might begin with a few concepts, or perhaps a single concept sketch. Sometimes these initial ideas were very ill-defined—a key centre, a rhythm, or a figuration, but not much more; in other cases there was a clear thematic motif which was not greatly altered in the course of further sketching. Sometimes the initial sketch was on a larger scale and more in the nature of a synopsis of the whole movement; this was particularly likely to occur if the movement was to have an unusual shape, as in the finale of the 'Eroica' Symphony or the first movement of Op. 31 No. 2. After this the first section of the movement would be sketched more intensively, with the opening idea extended as far as possible and other ideas added. The early ideas tended to be rather primitive and skeletal, but were gradually decorated, elaborated, intensified, and made more interesting and less straightforward. After a certain amount of sketching Beethoven would attempt a continuity draft for the whole of the first section of the movement; this might be the whole of the exposition, or the whole of the first group of themes up to the transition, or, in a vocal work, the whole of the first section of text. The draft might even cover the whole movement. Such a draft would then be altered and amended; alternatives would either be superimposed, obscuring the notes underneath, or written further down the

[22] TF, pp. 249–52.   [23] Ibid., pp. 250–1.

page or on an adjacent page. Beethoven generally left the bottom few staves of a page blank at first to accommodate such variants, and quite often at least the bottom stave remained blank. Thus continuity drafts tend to proceed from about the twelfth stave (out of sixteen) on a page to the first stave on the next page. Sometimes the top of a page had already been used for variants or other concepts, however, in which case the draft would resume further down. Usually a single continuity draft would be insufficient and would be replaced by one or more revised drafts. Even though Beethoven sometimes eventually adopted features found in early drafts but omitted in later ones, successive drafts tend to increase in sophistication and also in length, as well as becoming more and more similar to the final version; thus it is generally possible to determine which of several drafts on different pages is the latest, even if the pages have now become widely separated.

In the course of sketching one section of a movement Beethoven would tend to look ahead from time to time, and so one often finds ideas for later sections of a movement mixed up amongst the main activity for an earlier section. When one section was nearly finished, he started jotting down ideas for the next with increasing frequency, but not until one section was extensively sketched did he normally proceed to detailed work on the next. During work on later sections of a movement there are often further ideas for an earlier section (possibly even a new continuity draft) but this is far less common than the reverse. Thus where the external structure of a sketchbook has not been disturbed or where it can be reconstructed, one tends to find a series of drafts for the first section of a work, together with associated variants, followed by drafts for the second section, the third section, and so on. The precise scheme depended on the work in question: there was a certain amount of backtracking, and the length of a draft was very variable. Nevertheless the most intensive sketches for the various sections of a movement generally appear in roughly the right order.

Not only were the different sections sketched in the right order, but as far as can be established the different movements were also almost invariably sketched in the same order as they appear in the finished work. Early ideas for later movements sometimes appear, albeit only sporadically, amongst sketches for a first movement, and this demonstrates that Beethoven did not simply allot different parts of a sketchbook to different movements or sections and then work on all of them more or less concurrently, but that he actually had only a vague idea of the later movements while working on the first. Thus each movement in turn was sketched in detail until he had a clear picture of its overall shape, and then he moved on to the next one.

This procedure has been demonstrated in a large number of sketch studies for various different types of work and is confirmed paradoxically by the cases where the movements are demonstrably not sketched in the right order, for such cases almost all fall into certain special categories. One such category is overtures: if Beethoven was composing a stage work the overture was always written last, after all the vocal numbers; clearly he felt it had to be related in character and sometimes even in theme to the rest of the work, and so it could not be written until that character and those themes had been composed. Indeed in both *Egmont* (1810) and *Fidelio* (1814) the overture was left so late that it was not ready for the first performance. In such stage works, where the numbers are discontinuous and often separated by spoken dialogue, the order of composition of later movements occasionally seems to have been disrupted too; one sketchbook (SV 65) contains sketches for most of the movements of *Egmont* in the order 7, 1, 8, 9, 2, 3, 6,[24] while in *Die Ruinen von Athen* Nos. 4 and 5 appear to have been composed last, since they are not found amongst the main sketches (SV 184) but are represented at the beginning of a later sketchbook (SV 106, fo. 9ʳ).[25]

In other cases sketches appear in the 'wrong' order because the movements are based on material originally intended for other works. The finale of the 'Kreutzer' Sonata (Op. 47) was originally designed for an earlier violin sonata, Op. 30 No. 1, and so its sketches are found with the latter, somewhat earlier than those for the first two movements of the 'Kreutzer'. Likewise the main theme of the second movement of the Seventh Symphony was originally sketched in 1806 for the Quartet Op. 59 No. 3;[26] and the fourth movement of the Quartet Op. 130 had initially been sketched in the middle of the previous quartet, Op. 132. A similar situation occurred if a movement was replaced: the middle movment of the 'Waldstein' Sonata must have been sketched after the finale (although the sketches are lost), since it replaced the original slow movement (published as an 'Andante favori', WoO 57), the sketches for which occur in the expected place between those for the first and third movements of the sonata (SV 60, chiefly pp. 131–7).

The other common situation where Beethoven might sketch the parts of a work in an order different from that of the final version was when composing a set of variations. Here he tended to sketch a variety of variation patterns (often just the first few bars) and then to try to decide in what order the variations should come. This sometimes resulted in a sketch for a single variation containing ideas that were later developed in more than one variation, and in variations being numbered and renumbered in various orders, which might be quite different from the final order, as is very clear in the *Prometheus* Variations.[27] In the Diabelli Variations Beethoven decided on the order in a relatively early draft in 1819, but when he came to complete the work in 1823 he inserted additional variations at various points in the cycle.[28] There are also one or two exceptional cases where movements in a

[24] N-II, p. 276. More recent research (Fecker, *Egmont*) has produced evidence that the *Egmont* entr'actes (Nos. 2, 3, 5, and 6) were probably sketched before the main work on the overture but after that on the other numbers. This would be a logical way for Beethoven to have proceeded and it is more or less corroborated by Nottebohm's account of SV 65, although the sources are too incomplete to provide a firm chronology.

[25] Fo. 9 originally preceded fos. 1–8 of SV 106; see Brandenburg, 'Petter', p. 126.

[26] N-II, p. 86.   [27] Reynolds, 'Op. 35' (see esp. pp. 61–3).

[28] See Kinderman, *Diabelli*.

work were sketched out of order for no obvious reason—for example the Mass in C (sketched in SV 213), the Credo of which appears to have been left till last.

It is sometimes assumed that all or almost all of the sketching for a work was finished before Beethoven began writing out the autograph score, but this was certainly not always the case; indeed in works of any great length or complexity it was probably the exception rather than the rule, and he may in some works have alternated fairly frequently between sketchbook and score. The evidence of the few works that he abandoned after making substantial progress tends to confirm that he often began writing out the autograph score at a surprisingly early stage of composition. Fragmentary scores, with some of the texture not filled in, survive for part of both the unfinished triple concerto in D of 1802 and the unfinished Sixth Piano Concerto of 1815, yet in neither case are there any significant sketches beyond the first movement (though the piano concerto progressed considerably further than the triple concerto).[29] In both cases Beethoven may even have begun writing out the score precisely because he was having difficulty making headway with the sketches. Presumably these two scores would have been filled up and completed as final versions had Beethoven finished the works in question, but it is possible that they would have remained as incomplete scores and been superseded by proper autograph scores. A few works, as mentioned earlier, survive in both an *Urschrift* and a *Reinschrift*, and many more preliminary scores, either complete or incomplete, may have been made and then thrown away; but the evidence suggests this was not what normally happened (see Chapter 1).

Another unfinished work for which Beethoven apparently began some kind of score is the string quintet he was composing when he died (WoO 62). Diabelli published a keyboard arrangement of the only movement which was more or less finished, although he apparently destroyed the score from which his arrangement was made. This score was probably complete in most of its principal details, even though the second movement had not advanced very far in the sketches,[30] but it may have been just a score sketch, or at best an *Urschrift* with several details missing.

Sketches are also sometimes found within an autograph score—indeed if one defines a sketch as any version of part of a work that precedes the final version, then the autographs are full of sketches, for most of them contain numerous indications of changes of plan such as deletions, alterations, additions, discarded leaves, and inserted leaves. Even if a narrower definition is adopted, in which the term 'sketch' is restricted to musical ideas that are intended from the outset to be preliminary jottings, whereas 'autograph score' denotes a manuscript intended to be a complete and final draft (however much it may later be altered), the distinction between sketch and

---

[29] Kramer, 'Concertante'; Lockwood, 'Unfinished'.
[30] Details in Staehelin, 'Quintet'.

autograph is a narrow one at times, as has been demonstrated at some length by Lewis Lockwood.[31] In some works, for example, a score that begins clearly gradually undergoes more and more alterations further on until it degenerates into sketches. In other cases short variant sketches can be found at the foot of the score or on a blank page; and the cue-staff mentioned earlier is really a type of sketch. Functioning as a continuity draft but located in the autograph rather than a sketchbook, it was no doubt an invaluable guide to Beethoven when he was planning the layout of the score.[32] Conversely certain score fragments which were written on odd leaves to replace cancelled passages look more like sketches because of their incompleteness; a few are even found in actual sketchbooks,[33] thus blurring the distinction between sketch and autograph still further. In general, however, once Beethoven had produced a satisfactory draft in a sketchbook he either wrote out the autograph score direct, using this draft as a basis, or else copied the draft into the foot of the score as a cue-staff sketch and completed the score from this.

What about the relationship between sketches for different works being composed about the same time? Beethoven himself provided some information on this in an oft-quoted remark to Wegeler in 1801: 'Hardly have I completed one composition when I have already begun another. At my present rate of composing, I often produce three or four works at the same time.'[34] This statement gives the impression that he worked on several compositions concurrently, hopping from one to another with great frequency, 'like the author of a profound literary work, who relieves and recreates his mind by varying his labours, and executes his grand task all the more satisfactorily, because he, from time to time, refreshes himself by turning his attention to other and lighter topics'.[35] If this were indeed the case one might expect to find one page of a sketchbook devoted to a sonata, the next to a quartet, the next to a song, then back to the sonata, and so on. In actual fact the sketches are not nearly as jumbled as this, and it can be fairly firmly stated that Beethoven hardly ever worked intensively on two works, or even two movements, at the same time in alternation. What he did sometimes do was start working on one piece before the autograph of the previous one had been fully written out, in which case both might be completed about the same time, resulting in several new works being offered to a publisher in a single letter.[36] Sometimes there are a few very late sketches for a work or movement situated in the middle of intensive sketching of a slightly later one; those for the earlier one can then be interpreted as being

---

[31] Lockwood, 'Definition'.

[32] Examples of cue-staffs can be seen in the scores of the Violin Concerto and the Kyrie of the *Missa solemnis* (both available in fac.), as well as the unfinished Sixth Piano Concerto (see Lockwood, 'Unfinished', pp. 632–3).

[33] Lockwood, 'Definition', p. 41; Lockwood, 'Op. 69', pp. 26, 42.

[34] A-51.   [35] TF, p. 251.

[36] e.g. A-41, which offers the Second Piano Concerto, the Septet, the First Symphony, and the Sonata Op. 22—three new works and one newly revised.

associated with the writing out of the autograph—in other words, the autograph of one work or movement was still being written out during intensive activity on another. In the case of the 'Razumovsky' Quartets, for example, there is some external evidence, in the form of water-staining, indicating that Beethoven had sketched the first movement of No. 3 before writing out the score of the last two movements of No. 2.[37] Thus there was usually some overlap, but this is not quite the same as concurrent work on two different pieces.

On other occasions a work was begun but then interrupted by other ones and held over for a while before being resumed later. This was, of course, particularly likely to happen to long works. Thus *Leonore* (1804–5) was interrupted by two piano sonatas (Opp. 54 and 57), the Triple Concerto, and the song 'An die Hoffnung' (Op. 32), all of which were begun after the opera but probably finished before it; at any rate sketches for all of them appear before work on the later part of the opera (see SV 67). Other works which were held over for a time include the sets of variations Opp. 34 and 35, begun before the sonatas Op. 31 but not finished until after them, and also the Ninth Symphony, *Missa solemnis*, and Diabelli Variations, all of which were begun before 1820 but which were held up by each other and by the composition of the last three piano sonatas (and other works) and were only completed in 1823 and 1824.

In a few cases a work was not simply begun and then held over but was sketched intermittently over a period of time. In a sense this is true of the Ninth Symphony, for Beethoven had ideas for setting Schiller's 'An die Freude' sporadically for about thirty years; but none of his early ideas for this were developed, and he worked on the symphony intensively only for a short period in about 1817 and a longer one in 1823–4.[38] Intermittent work can, however, be seen on a small scale in the sketches for the scherzo of the Quartet in G, Op. 18 No. 2, which 'give the impression that Beethoven did not work continuously on the movement but turned to it from time to time during the composition of the Largo and the finale'.[39] A similar procedure can be seen on a much larger scale with the Fifth Symphony and the *Namensfeier* Overture. The earliest sketches for the former date from about the beginning of 1804 (SV 60, pp. 155–7), while later ones were made sporadically perhaps from about 1805–7, though the exact chronology is difficult to establish, and the main sketching was evidently done in 1807.[40] The *Namensfeier* Overture was begun in 1809 and resumed about 1811, when Beethoven began writing out a full score, pages of which were then discarded and used for sketches for *Die Ruinen von Athen* (SV 184, fos. 3, 9–12, 17, 20);

[37] Tyson, 'Razumovsky', p. 130. For other examples see Kerman, 'British Museum', pp. 80–1; Winter, *Op. 131*, p. 38.
[38] See Brandenburg, 'Op. 125', for details.
[39] Brandenburg, 'Op. 18 No. 2', p. 148.
[40] See Tyson, 'First Leonore'; JTW, pp. 160–4.

the work was eventually completed in 1815, although the final score had been begun in October 1814 and been interrupted yet again.[41]

Cases such as these throw light on Beethoven's creative process in relation to such unfinished works as those mentioned earlier. It is inadequate to assume, as has sometimes been suggested,[42] that works were abandoned because the ideas in them were not sufficiently promising. Beethoven, of all composers, was outstanding for his ability to make a great work of art out of unpromising materials: he once improvised at great length on some completely insignificant notes from a second violin part of a Pleyel quartet, to the astonishment and delight of all;[43] and his monumental Diabelli Variations, on a trivial waltz theme, still astonish us today. If the initial material was unsatisfactory in some way he was quite capable of overhauling it completely without destroying the essence of the original idea, as is clear from the sketches for the Sonata Op. 31 No. 2 (see Chapter 12). Conversely, some of the works he did complete are distinctly second-rate, at least by his standards, and one is almost tempted to ask why he bothered to finish them. Thus if the unfinished works had been completed they would probably have turned out just as good as some of the finished ones, and except in cases where he was dealing with an unsatisfactory text (as in the unfinished opera *Vestas Feuer*)[44] there was no inherent reason why they should not have been completed. If works were left unfinished, it was therefore usually either because he became distracted by others which were for him more interesting or because there was not sufficient external pressure requiring them to be completed.

Moreover, as was seen in Chapter 5, ideas in abandoned sketches were often taken up and developed later in finished works. Such sketches demonstrate that the distinction between sketches for an unfinished work and those for a finished one is not nearly as clear-cut as might be imagined. Just as there are several clearly defined types of sketch and yet also some sketches which fall between two of the types, there are also sketches which fall between the two basic categories of those that belong to finished works and those that were abandoned. Such sketches could themselves be classified into various types, such as those intended for one work but containing ideas developed in another, those intended for one work but containing nothing actually used in the final version, and those containing ideas developed in more than one work. Thus it is best to think of the types of sketch as forming a continuum or spectrum of sketching methods, with each type merging into another. And similarly sketch relationships exist over the entire range of possibilities from those that are almost completely unrelated to any work, through those that are to a greater or lesser extent related to one, to those that coincide exactly with an autograph score.

[41] KH, p. 332.
[42] Kramer, 'Concertante', pp. 48–9; Lockwood, 'Unfinished', p. 628.
[43] Czerny, *Performance*, p. 15.   [44] See A-87a.

9

The Sketching of Form and Key

WHEN Beethoven began composing a new work he generally began not with melody but with decisions on the type of work and the key. This is not to say that he did not sometimes sketch isolated melodic ideas which might later form the basis for finished works, but this was not his normal starting-point. He normally began by deciding whether the next work would be, say, a sonata, a quartet, or a symphony, and by deciding on its key and character. For this reason we shall examine here how he sketched key and form, before proceeding in the next chapter to the question of melodic sketching.

Initially he was confronted with a very basic question—not what melodic ideas to use nor even what form the work should be in, but which of several possible works should he compose. As we have seen, he was capable of inventing far more works than he had time to write down, and so the decision as to which of these possible works was the most worthy of exploration and development was at times a considerable problem in itself. The large number of concept sketches for works that were never written has already been mentioned in the previous chapter; in some cases these probably represent a choice of alternative beginnings for different works, just as variant sketches represent alternative passages within a work. This suggestion is strengthened by the fact that the number of concept sketches for unfulfilled works tends to be particularly large in the sketch-leaves that fall between the main work on one composition and the beginning of the next. Some good examples of this process of creating possible works occur in the 'Petter' Sketchbook (SV 106). This is the only sketchbook in which Beethoven sketched two symphonies at length (Nos. 7 and 8), but it also contains ideas for no fewer than eight other symphonies (fos. 23^r, 29^v, 35^v, 42^v staves 5 and 13, 44^r, 45^r, and 61^v), and there are at least two further contemporary sketches for symphonies elsewhere, in SV 93 (formerly part of the 'Petter' Sketchbook)[1] and SV 134 (which also contains sketches for the finale of the Eighth Symphony). It is known that he was planning to write three symphonies at that time,[2] and so the obvious conclusion is that these ten symphony sketches represent various ideas for the third symphony in the group. Some writers have seen it as significant that three of the sketches are in D minor, the key of the Ninth Symphony; but on the other hand there were plenty of other keys under consideration in this material, which

---

[1] See Schmidt, SBH 702; JTW, p. 218.   [2] A-370.

includes concepts in C major, G minor with B flat major, C minor, E flat major, and E minor. Thus Beethoven had the capacity to write any of these ten symphonies, but in the end wrote none of them, although all would indirectly affect the way he thought about his next symphony when he eventually did start to write it.

Yet it is curious that although each of these ten ideas is clearly marked as a symphony, neither of the two real symphonies in the sketchbook—Nos. 7 and 8—is anywhere labelled as such. It is as if, by writing down the labelled concepts, Beethoven were noting down the symphonies he was not going to write; at the very least, he seems to have had no intention of developing them at that stage, and they would·have served merely as ideas that might be taken up at some later date. The two actual symphonies in the sketchbook began quite differently from these ten labelled symphony concepts. No. 8 began as a piano concerto, although it is not labelled as such and was converted to a symphony only after several pages of sketching.[3] No. 7 began with a cluster of ideas in A major, but no clear theme. As Nottebohm reported,[4] before the first sketches with clear resemblance to the symphony there are several ideas in various rhythms, some of which gradually come to resemble motifs from the final version of the symphony.

In choosing a key for a new work, Beethoven apparently took several factors into consideration. One of the most important was the key of previous works in the same genre. He tended to think of each genre as a separate category, as is evident from the fact that, when he was considering the publication of a complete edition of his works, he proposed to the publisher Peters that for each genre published he would compose one new work.[5] Thus any composition would normally be not only in a different key from the one immediately preceding, but also in a different key from the previous work in the same genre. Eleven of the first twelve piano sonatas published were in different keys; the first seven symphonies were all in different keys, and the first to reuse a key, the Eighth, had begun as a piano concerto (in a different key from each of the five previous piano concertos). In no genre, however, did Beethoven methodically use up each of the common keys in turn, and certain keys (particularly C minor) tended to appear far more frequently than others. Thus in 1826 Karl Holz reproached Beethoven for writing a new quartet (Op. 135) in F major—the third in that key—while he had still not written one in D minor.[6] Presumably Beethoven felt that the other two (Op. 18 No. 1 and Op. 59 No. 1) were so much earlier that they were no longer relevant; he would have been more concerned with the immediate neighbours of the quartet, and certainly each of the late quartets is in a different key from the others.

Beethoven frequently produced instrumental works in a group of three, all in the same genre. In these cases not only did he customarily compose the

---

[3] See Brandenburg, 'Petter', pp. 135–40, for further details.
[4] N-II, p. 101.   [5] A1079.   [6] TF, p. 1009.

three in different keys, but he also tried to maximise the contrast between the keys: no two pieces in the group should have either the same keynote or the same key signature; there should be at least one flat key and at least one sharp key; and one of the three should be in a minor key. The latter condition is disregarded in Op. 12, and two of the Op. 1 trios share the same key signature, but otherwise these principles are followed consistently in Opp. 1, 2, 9, 10, 12, 30, 31, and 59; they also apply in the three sonatas of Opp. 13–14, in Op. 27 if it is grouped with either Op. 26 or Op. 28, and in the last three sonatas, Opp. 109–11, which were written as a set of three, even though they have three different opus numbers. None of the three quartets written for Prince Galitzin, Opp. 127, 130, and 132, is in a sharp key, but they include several individual movements in sharp keys (Op. 130.iv, Op. 132.ii and iv), and the lack of a sharp-key quartet was soon remedied in the next one to be composed—Op. 131 in C sharp minor.

Other factors affecting Beethoven's choice of key were more mundane. In general he avoided keys with large numbers of accidentals except for special effects; although his music often passed through unusual keys, particularly in his later works, and key signatures of up to seven flats can be found even at the beginning of a middle movement (e.g. Op. 26.ii), complete works rarely begin with a key signature of more than four accidentals. (The main exceptions are the Piano Sonata in F sharp major, Op. 78, and *Christus am Oelberge*, which beings in E flat minor.) Instrumental compass could also influence the decision. In the 'Kafka' Miscellany there is a sketch in G major (fo. 86ᵛ stave 1), with an additional comment written above: 'F major is better for this because of the top F'. The highest note available on most pianos at the time was f‴, and so he would be denied the use of a high tonic if the work were written in G major. (The sketch did not in the end come to fruition.) Similarly the availability of a‴ on the flute was probably a factor which helped to persuade Beethoven to set *Meeresstille und glückliche Fahrt* in D rather than E flat, which would have necessitated a b‴♭—a note too unreliable for him to use in flute parts elsewhere.

It is quite common to find amongst the earliest sketches for an instrumental work a conglomeration of ideas in a key without a clear theme, as in the material for the Seventh Symphony mentioned above. Themes would then gradually emerge while the key remained unchanged. On other occasions the theme would be fairly clear right from the outset—or at least from the earliest surviving sketches. More rarely a theme was tried in more than one key in the early stages of a work. For a while, for example, Beethoven was uncertain whether to write the second sonata of Op. 31 in the key of A minor or D minor (see Chapter 12), although at this stage the theme had not properly evolved either. And in the case of the Sonata Op. 79, the theme was first sketched in C major, with the heading 'Sonata facile', before being transposed to G major, with some modification, in later sketches.[7] In both

[7] N-II, p. 269.

these cases it is significant that the two alternative keys are closely related.

Vacillation over choice of key seems to have been more common in vocal music, however. Whereas in instrumental music the key was one of the main generating factors for the whole work, in vocal music the starting-point was not the key but the text to be set. Beethoven apparently had very definite, albeit rather indefinable, feelings about each key, regarding each as having a completely independent character made up of a number of different elements, so that the twenty-four resulting key characters were almost as distinctive as the characters of twenty-four different people. According to Schindler, Beethoven's sense of key was so acute that he could tell the key of a piece regardless of the actual pitch being used, and that he even regarded C sharp major and D flat major as two quite different keys, suited to different purposes.[8] 'To deny without reason the special character of the different keys was to Beethoven like denying the effect of the sun and the moon on the ebb ebb and flow of the tides.'[9] While one must be wary of placing too much credence on Schindler's statements of this type, the evidence of the music certainly seems to confirm that Beethoven chose his keys with extreme care. The difficulty about vocal music, however, was that the character of a text did not always exactly match any of the characters of the keys; hence just as the producer of a play might find that none of his actors was entirely suited to a particular role, so Beethoven might find difficulty in 'casting' his text to an appropriate key. This sometimes led to changes of mind about which key to use, even at a surprisingly late stage of composition. Thus amongst the numerous E major sketches for the song 'Sehnsucht' (WoO 146) there are a few in E flat major;[10] and the duet 'So ruhe dann' in *Christus am Oelberge* was sketched in A major at one point, with the remark 'or E major', before he finally settled on his original choice of A flat.[11] Another example is *Meeresstille und glückliche Fahrt*, in D major; the second movement was originally planned in B flat, and even at a very late stage he had still not decided whether to set the first movement in E flat or D (see Chapter 14).

The keys of themes for middle movements in instrumental music were apparently altered rather more often than those for the first movements. One reason was that Beethoven thought of subsidiary keys in terms of the work as a whole, and so the keys of middle movements were liable to be interchanged with each other or with subsidiary keys in the first movement. Thus in the sonata in D minor, Op. 31 No. 2, B flat was originally considered as a key for the second subject of the first movement, but was eventually used for the slow movement instead. In the case of the 'Waldstein' Sonata the situation was reversed. The theme for the original slow movement (later published as the 'Andante favori', WoO 57) was sketched briefly in E major[12] but was then tranposed to F, while E was retained for the second subject of

[8] Schindler/MacArdle, *Beethoven*, p. 368.   [9] Ibid., p. 369.

[10] Lockwood, 'Sehnsucht'; see also N-II, p. 333.

[11] SV 343, p. 134.   [12] SV 60, p. 121.

the first movement. Similarly, amongst the early sketches for the Sonata Op. 31 No. 1 in G major, there is a concept sketch in B major (the key of the start of the second subject) which clearly seems to be intended as an idea for the slow movement of the sonata (SV 263, fo. 92ʳ staves 3–4). The finale theme of the C sharp minor Quartet was originally sketched in F sharp minor as the scherzo.[13] One of the reasons for its transposition to C sharp minor for the finale, with a scherzo in E major substituted in its place, must have been that the quartet had several movements in relatively flat key areas already, and in particular it also had a heavy emphasis on F sharp minor in the first movement. A slightly different situation regarding transposition occurred with the previous quartet, Op. 130. The theme of the D flat slow movement was first sketched in G, while the Cavatina in E flat was initially sketched in D flat; thus the original keys, G and D flat, were retained in the final version for the fourth and third movements respectively, while the thematic material was transferred elsewhere. The unusual key scheme of the work, in which B flat provides a frame for keys as far apart as D flat and G, was a fundamental feature from an early stage, despite all the apparent changes of direction during the sketching.

Tranposition of a theme was also liable to occur if the theme was transferred from one work to another. A good example is provided by the same quartet, of which the G major Danza tedesca was originally sketched in A major for the previous quartet, Op. 132, and the theme of the *Grosse Fuge* appeared first in E flat in connection with sketches for Op. 127. Similarly the second subject of the first movement of the Sonata in E flat Op. 7 originally appeared in A, not B flat, in an isolated sketch apparently associated with no particular work (see Exx. 8.2 and 8.3). Another theme transposed in the course of transfer is in the trio section of the Sonata Op. 10 No. 3; this theme was first sketched in A flat instead of G and was intended for another work —probably Op. 7.[14] One fairly advanced sketch for the finale of the Sonata in B flat Op. 22 (more well-developed than some of those in the right key, and lasting over fifty bars) shows the movement in A major (Ex. 9.1); perhaps in this case Beethoven was considering transferring the theme to another work but then decided against it.

It is clear, then, that as soon as Beethoven had decided on a work's main key, the first and most fundamental feature of any instrumental composition at that time, the question of subsidiary keys—both those in the first movement and the main keys of middle movements—began to raise itself. (Works such as *An die ferne Geliebte* and the C sharp minor Quartet, in which the movements are run together, show clearly how the distinction between subsidiary key areas and the keys of middle movements began to break down in his later period.) For him the character of a work was determined as much by its combination of keys as by any thematic features; and for classical music

---

[13] Winter, *Op. 131*, pp. 126–31.   [14] Johnson, *Fischhof*, i. 335.

Ex. 9.1 SV 224

in general the form of a movement was determined largely by its key sequence. Beethoven seems to have considered certain key combinations particularly effective in producing well-rounded characters for works, for they were used on several different occasions. An obvious example is the number of C major works using E as a subsidiary key (see Chapter 5). F major works tend to go to D major surprisingly often (Op. 10 No. 2, Op. 33 No. 3, Op. 68.iii, Op. 93.i), and E major works to E minor and vice versa (Op. 2 No. 3.ii, Op. 14 No. 1, Op. 59 No. 2, Op. 90, Op. 109); for a short while in the 1790s Beethoven was also interested in exploring the relationship between E flat and E major.[15]

If both the key scheme and the overall form of a work or movement were fairly conventional there would be relatively little need for any synopsis at an early stage of sketching; but the more unconventional the form or key scheme, the more likely there was to be some kind of initial large-scale planning. Thus in composing the Quartet Op. 131, where the overall scheme is highly unusual, Beethoven made several early attempts at sketching a synopsis of the entire work, and his chief concern initially was to define the overall tonal outlines;[16] an attempt at an overall plan even predates the idea of having a subdominant answer in the opening fugue. Similarly in the 'Eroica' Symphony his decision to have a new theme in E minor in the middle of the development section was apparently made at a very early stage. His concern with key centres also helps to explain why some of his early thematic ideas for a work are so undistinguished: they are simply a means of providing a visual realization of a key centre, rather than being real themes for the work. On other occasions the thematic element is reduced still further, and he resorted simply to words to describe the key scheme in mind: the bare names of keys, sometimes with some indication of their place in the work (e.g. 'erster Theil in B' in SV 263, fo. 90ᵛ, indicating that the exposition should end in B flat), are common throughout the sketches.

At the same time as Beethoven was planning the key scheme of a work he would also be thinking about other aspects of its overall shape, such as the

[15] Ibid., p. 324.   [16] Winter, 'Plans'.

metre and tempo of later movements, and this mental activity sometimes surfaced in the form of a synopsis sketch (or a group of concept sketches) showing formal and structural ideas as well as tonal ones. When the sketch concerned the form of a movement, Beethoven was somewhat hampered by a rather restricted vocabulary of analytical terms. As has been seen, he had words for first subject ('Thema'), second subject ('m.g.'), orchestral interlude ('R'), exposition ('erster Theil'), and coda ('Schluss'), and formal-generic names like 'rondo' and 'minuet'; but he lacked terms for such concepts as binary, ternary, sonata, and sonata-rondo forms, development section, recapitulation ('d.c.' had to suffice), and retransition. These had to be expressed by means of keys, themes, or the terms that he did have available. When combined they produced a synopsis sketch, and such synopses came in several varieties, as we have seen. Some represent a whole work, but more often they represent part of a work (such as the earliest 'Eroica' sketch, representing the first three movements), a single movement, or part of a movement. Sometimes they appear as the first idea for a work; on other occasions, however, they only represent a later part of a work of which the earlier part is already sketched, and so they may represent Beethoven looking ahead from a point where he is still uncertain where his ideas are leading him —they are an 'outgrowth of uncertainty' rather than positive creation.[17]

But these overviews and large-scale plans represent only one side of the coin. It was a very common situation for Beethoven to be composing one movement with very little idea of what was coming later in the work or even sometimes in the same movement. In extreme cases he might even begin with an opening idea and just work forward to see where it led—in fact his improvisations must by their very nature have tended to require such an approach. Thus at the most fundamental level he had to confront the basic compositional problem of whether to approach a new work as an entity, working on all the different ideas more or less at the same time and possibly juggling with their order from time to time, or whether to adopt the improviser's approach and just work forward from the beginning. The choice lay between a 'structural' and an 'improvisatory' approach. Benjamin Britten once remarked to the present writer (and no doubt did so to others too) that composing a piece is rather like approaching a house in a fog: first the general outline is seen, and then on closer approach more and more of the detail becomes apparent. But this was not Beethoven's method: he struck a fine balance between this approach and that of the improviser. For him the 'house' would have been more like a long wall, with only the near end clear initially and the far end lost in the mist. But if his approach was therefore not as 'structural' as Britten's, equally it was not as 'improvisatory' as that of, say, Handel, the composer he most admired. In fact there seems to have been a gradual tendency over recent centuries for composition to change from an 'improvisatory' to a 'structural' method, at least in instrumental music (in

[17] Ibid., p. 129.

vocal music the structure has always to a certain extent been predetermined by the text). If such a change has taken place, Beethoven would have felt his approach to be more 'structural' than that of his predecessors, and it seems that he did, for he once remarked that his custom was 'always to keep the whole in view', even in instrumental music (and by implication still more so in vocal music, where there was a text to provide overall shape).[18] A similar notion appears in a remark by J. R. Schulz, who reported after meeting Beethoven in 1823 that he learnt that Beethoven 'never writes one note down, till he has formed a clear design for the whole piece'.[19] In both cases there is an implication that Beethoven's method of keeping the whole in view from the start was relatively uncommon and therefore worth remarking on.

The synopsis sketches, which reflect the structural approach, contrast with certain continuity drafts, which reflect a more improvisatory approach. Sometimes such drafts seem from their visual appearance to have flowed from Beethoven's pen with great rapidity and without too much concern for exactitude of shape or proportion, which could be determined later. Sometimes there are several continuity drafts for the same section, each beginning in more or less the same way, as in the four main drafts for the opening of the 'Eroica';[20] these can be viewed as an attempt to gain a quasi-improvisatory flow from a more or less fixed section to a more indeterminate one. Such groups of drafts also gave Beethoven the chance to judge the relative size and proportion of each section in successive versions after they had been written out, and this was probably one of their main functions. The occasional appearance of completely blank bars, sometimes even several in succession, within a larger draft reinforces this view.

The planning of size and proportion has received relatively little attention in most of the literature on Beethoven's sketches, since it is much less immediately apparent than melodic modifications; but it was of considerable importance to Beethoven. By and large, successive drafts tend to be of increasing size, so that the piece represented by the first main sketch is usually smaller—often much smaller—than the final version. Sometimes one suspects that the work eventually grew to a size much larger than intended originally: examples include the 'Eroica' Symphony, the 'Waldstein' Sonata, and the *Grosse Fuge*. On the other hand Beethoven must have realized that such growth tended to occur and so must have made some allowance for it in his initial plans. In fact some sketches show what can only be interpreted as deliberate and conscious compression, with expansion intended as a later phase of composition. One example is the main extant sketch for the Sonata in D minor, Op. 31 No. 2 (See Ex. 12.7), where the entire second part of the movement is compressed into a mere fifty-six bars (in the final version there are 136), even though there are no visible gaps in this part of the sketch.

---

[18] A-479.

[19] *The Harmonicon*, ii (1824), 11; quoted in Tyson, 'Op. 70 No. 1', p. 3.

[20] N-1803, pp. 6–14.

Another example is a sketch of about thirty bars for Op. 131 that includes no fewer than five major modulations.[21]

Expansion generally took place through the insertion of extra phrases or paragraphs into the overall form and tonal plan. These insertions might be needed to provide a suitable link between passages or alternatively a contrast to them; and they were also sometimes needed to adjust the proportions between larger sections—for example, to increase the length of the second subject group in relation to the first in an exposition. Ideally the insertions fulfilled all three functions and perhaps several others too. Often they are only a few bars of relatively insignificant material, but sometimes they are much more substantial. An outstanding example is the second subject of the first movement of the 'Appasionata' Sonata, Op. 57. The first continuity draft for the exposition[22] shows a forty-nine-bar (instead of sixty-five-bar) exposition, of which thirty-eight bars precede the second subject group—far too high a proportion. Missing is the whole of the section in A flat major containing the warm, melodious theme that gives the movement in its final version so much of its character (bars 35–50). A second continuity draft[23] shows fairly similar proportions, with the second subject group still beginning with the semiquaver theme in A flat minor (Ex. 9.2; cf. bars 30–33, 51–54). The A flat major theme was later inserted in a darker ink by means of a 'Vi=de' sign[24]—perhaps only after the theme had evolved in the development section, which is where it is first found in the sketchbook in the lighter ink. This insertion and a slightly revised continuation bring the length of the exposition up to fifty-eight bars, with the proportions more or less correct and with a necessary contrast in mood for the start of the second subject group.

Another method of expansion was by what might be termed 'local development': a theme or motif which originally occupied only one or two bars could be expanded by means of repetition and variation. Again the first

Ex. 9.2 SV 67, p. 192

[etc.]

[21] Winter, *Op. 131*, pp. 142–4.

[22] SV 67, p. 182; quoted in N-II, pp. 437–8.

[23] SV 67, p. 192; partly quoted in N-II, p. 439 (first ex.).

[24] Ibid.; partly quoted in N-II, p. 439 (second ex.).

movement of the 'Appassionata' provides a good example. Bars 51–54 are represented by only two bars in the earlier sketches (see Ex. 9.2). In a later sketch[25] the second bar is doubled in length through certain notes being repeated or sustained; and in the final version the first bar is also doubled in length through the repetition of each half.

Although expansion of material during successive sketches was the norm, contraction could also occur before the final length was established. Indeed in some cases Beethoven, after sketching several versions of a section that all looked too short, appears to have deliberately made an excessively long-winded version, in order to establish what would be too long. A good example of such a draft of excess is a score sketch for the finale of the Quartet Op. 131.[26] After several earlier and shorter drafts, this one is in places much longer than in the final version. Although the first subject group is only thirty-seven bars long as opposed to fifty-two in the final version, the transition to the relative major is twice as long in the sketch—eight bars instead of four. The second subject is eighteen bars long, as in the final version, but the codetta and link to the development section are over twenty bars in the sketch, with much of the second subject material being repeated, whereas in the final version this passage is reduced to a mere four bars. A similar picture can be seen in the sketches for the retransition in the first movement of the 'Waldstein' Sonata:[27] the first complete sketch resembling the final version is eleven bars, and the next is only ten bars, but the third is a rambling one of twenty-four bars. The length in the final version is fourteen bars (bars 142–55).

It will be noticed that most of these adjustments of proportion were made in the transitional passages, and indeed the joins were often the most problematical passages to compose, generating more sketches than the thematic sections. Nottebohm observed that in the material for the exposition of the 'Eroica' Symphony the sketches become more and more numerous towards the close.[28] Tyson has made a similar observation about the 'Ghost' Trio: 'The end of the exposition, however, evidently caused Beethoven difficulties'.[29] In the first movement of the 'Pastoral' Symphony, 'so much of the movement is born without struggle that the number of retransition sketches is imposing'.[30] The earliest sketches for both the 'Waldstein' Sonata and the Third 'Razumovsky' Quartet are concerned not only with the main theme but also with how to lead into it.[31] The *Egmont* Overture presents a good example of the joins between sections in different metre creating major problems; they are discussed in detail in Chapter 15.

It has often been pointed out that one characteristic of Beethoven's style

[25] SV 67, p. 190; N-II, p. 439 (third ex.).

[26] SV 20, pp. 209 ff.; see Winter, *Op. 131*, p. 191 and Ex. 47.

[27] Cooper, 'Waldstein', p. 181.   [28] N-1803, p. 19.

[29] Tyson, 'Op. 70 No. 1', p. 8.   [30] Gossett, 'Sixth Symphony', p. 252.

[31] Cooper, 'Waldstein', p. 171; Tyson, 'Razumovsky', p. 122.

is its emphasis on transition and development—a sense of growth that is sometimes described as the symphonic ideal; compared with his predecessors he tends to place less emphasis on the juxtaposition of areas of stability and far more on elements of transition, which helps to give his music its characteristic forward thrust and momentum. This stylistic feature and the emphasis on transition that is commonly found among the sketches go hand in hand: because he wanted forward thrust he had to work particularly hard at the transitions, and because he did so the music acquired this sense of thrust. Another reason why transitional sketches are so common is that it was much easier to adjust the proportions in a movement by altering the joins than by changing the more thematic sections, whose length tended to become more or less fixed at a relatively early stage. Thirdly, the nature of the dramatic relationship between the main themes depended very much on what came between them,[32] and so this transitional material was capable of modifying the whole character of the movement, even if it was in itself relatively uninteresting.

Finally, the question of overall form and proportion was considerably affected by whether or not there was to be a repeat. As with other aspects of a work, Beethoven was generally very attentive to this problem—far more so than the many modern performers who disregard his repeat signs. But although his concern for repeats often led him to decide early on in the sketches whether or not there were to be any, he sometimes changed his mind about them later, even at a very late stage. Examples of early decisions about repeats occur in the first sketch for the Sonata Op. 31 No. 2 ('2da parte colla repetizione e la prima senza');[33] in the first sketch for the Sonata Op. 79 ('2da parte anche due volte');[34] in an early sketch for the finale of the Seventh Symphony ('2ter Theil in d moll beyde ohne Widerholung');[35] and in an early sketch for a scherzo in the Quartet Op. 131 ('mit Trio in Dur 2 mal widerhohlt . . .').[36] Only in the last of these cases was the early decision upheld in the final version, and even here it was a very different scherzo from the original one. Such changes of mind are hardly surprising, however, when one considers how often a repeat was removed even after an autograph score had been completed. In the first movement of the Quartet Op. 18 No. 1, Beethoven originally planned both halves to be repeated, as is clear from the early version he sent to Karl Amenda; but when he undertook a thorough revision of the quartet the second repeat was cancelled. In the autograph score of the First 'Razumovsky' Quartet (Op. 59 No. 1) no fewer than three movements have a repeat which was then cancelled,[37] and the first movement of the 'Waldstein' Sonata is another with a cancelled repeat sign in the autograph. The first movement of the 'Eroica' Symphony also nearly lost its

[32] Winter, *Op. 131*, p. 176.   [33] SV 263, fo. 90ᵛ.   [34] N-II, p. 269.
[35] SV 335.   [36] Winter, *Op. 131*, pp. 126, 128.
[37] Tyson, 'Razumovsky', pp. 132–3; see also the fac. ed. (London, 1980).

repeat, according to Beethoven's brother Carl, who reported that Beethoven finally made up his mind only after he had heard several performances of the work.[38] And in the third movement of the Fifth Symphony his intentions were never made entirely clear. Most modern editors have assumed an ABA' form for the movement, but there is a strong evidence to indicate that Beethoven intended the first two sections to be repeated *en bloc*, creating an ABABA' form.[39] Thus even after a work was ostensibly finished, questions of form and proportion could still remain to be resolved.

In sketching the form and key scheme of a work or movement as a whole, then, Beethoven generally struck a balance between working within a preconceived mould and simply following the internal logic of the opening ideas. If there was to be a preconceived mould it was generally represented by an early synopsis sketch that showed both form and key scheme, unless the mould was a well-tried formula like sonata form. The sections of the mould were then developed and modified by means of internal expansion, with the final adjustments to the size, shape, and proportions being made mainly in the transitional passages between the main themes, and also in the coda, which are the places where there was always most scope for such amendments.

[38] TDR, ii. 625 f.   [39] Brandenburg, 'Fifth Symphony'.

10

The Sketching of Melody

SINCE most of Beethoven's sketches consist of single-line drafts, it is inevitable that they should appear at first sight to be concerned mainly with melodic shape. This impression is reinforced by the way successive sketches for a work nearly always display conspicuous melodic alterations; and such refinements tend to be highlighted when only short extracts from sketches are published. But melodic refinement was only one part of the sketching process and is intimately bound up with other aspects of the music; the sketches were frequently concerned with such things as formal shape, phrase structure, and tonal scheme rather than melodic detail, even if melodic alterations were being made at the same time, and the melodic changes themselves were often dependent on these other aspects.

A common misconception about Beethoven's melodic sketching—it applies to his sketching in general but is particularly relevant to the sketching of melody—is that the sketches represent a slow and painful struggle towards an ideal solution, which is eventually reached in the finished version after he has groped his way through unsatisfactory variants. When we see in a sketch a 'wrong' version of an all-too-familiar melody it is easy to lapse into this way of thinking, and the fabricated statement attributed to Beethoven about his compositional process—'since I am conscious of what I want, the basic idea never leaves me'[1]—tends to reinforce this view since it implies that he had some clear notion of the totality embodied in the final version even before he had reached it. The evidence of the sketches indicates, on the contrary, that his ultimate aim during the sketching of melody was often anything but clearly perceived. It is better, in fact, to think of the final version of a melody as one possible realization, and the best Beethoven could think of at the time, of the ideas contained in the sketches, rather than as the only possible outcome, which his sketches had gradually revealed to him. This conclusion is probably best appreciated by studying sketches for melodies that never reached a final version, or by examining the sketches of a work before one has encountered the final version.

Similarly, when one has the advantage through hindsight of having seen the final version of a tune, the early sketches often seem dull, four-square, and generally uninteresting, so that one is apt to ask how Beethoven could have considered such ideas in the first place and why he took so long to think up

[1] Solomon, 'Invention', pp. 273–4.

what now seems a simple and predictable melody. The answer is twofold: firstly, as already seen, in many early sketches the motifs represent not so much finished tunes as a realization of a key area and an indication of the type of rhythmic or melodic shape planned; and secondly, the 'simple and predictable' melodies of the final version are usually anything but straightforward, and it is only familiarity with them that makes them seem so. Again, studying the sketches of a work one knows well can give a rather distorted impression of them, since everything that is familiar from the final version will automatically seem better than what is unfamiliar in the sketches, and Beethoven's struggles will seem unduly laboured. Undoubtedly the final version of a passage is normally the best; but to imagine that one can tell it is, when it is really just the most familiar, is self-deception.

It is important when examining melodic sketching to distinguish between vocal and instrumental music. Some of the problems of melodic sketching are more apparent in vocal music, especially Lieder, partly because the texture of the music necessarily contains clear melodic lines, whereas in instrumental music this is not always the case; and partly because one can adduce some relatively objective criteria, such as word-painting and verbal rhythms, when judging a vocal melody, whereas assessment of an instrumental melody tends to rest on more subjective and elusive criteria. We shall therefore begin by considering Beethoven's procedures in sketching vocal melody, and then turn to instrumental music. He evidently had considerable problems in writing satisfactory song melodies, for he once stated that one of the most difficult undertakings for composers was to write 'an original good air'.[2]

Is there always a best version of a melody? Perhaps not. Sometimes there may be two or three variants all equally good, or each good in different ways. And sometimes the best melodic shape is not the most appropriate in the context of the piece as a whole. Thus it is possible to find amongst the sketches some wonderful melodies that never found their way into finished pieces. For example, the melody shown in Ex. 10.1 occurs among the sketches for *Christus am Oelberge*. Most composers would have been more

Ex. 10.1 SV 343, p. 93

(Father, deeply bowed and lamenting, thy Son implores up to Thee)

[2] A-529.

than satisfied to have invented such a fine theme, which when filled out with accompaniment and a little decoration might have looked in its final version something like Ex. 10.2. In addition to its very graceful shape, with a falling phrase answered by a rising one that reaches its climax with a large leap, the tune also admirably suits the meaning of the words. The idea of a pleading mood as the Father is addressed is conveyed by the avoidance of the temporary tonic (E flat) on the word 'Vater' and the use instead of the submediant, a much less affirmative degree of the scale; the phrase 'tief gebeugt und kläglich' is appropriately expressed by a gradually descending line, with 'kläglich' being set to a sighing appoggiatura; and the answering phrase has a rising shape that vividly illustrates the words 'hinauf zu dir'. The final version of the passage is almost completely different (Ex. 10.3) and in some ways less striking; yet it is more suitable in context since it stresses the note E♭ instead of C, which being the key of the aria as a whole ought not to be emphasized at the beginning of the second subject as well. The final version is also slightly more varied and complex, and the emotion is intensified by the repetition of the words 'zu dir' on very high notes.

Another example of different melodic ideas being good in different ways occurs in the Mass in C at the words 'Gratias agimus tibi'. After sketching

Ex. 10.2

Ex. 10.3 Op. 85. i

Va - ter! tief ge - beugt und kläg - lich, fleht dein

Sohn hin - auf zu dir, zu dir!

the bold opening section of the Gloria in C major, Beethoven planned to have a gentler, more lyrical passage for the 'Gratias', and he sketched a number of possible themes (Ex. 10.4). All four examples quoted are attractive melodies with an elegant and interesting shape, and they might have sounded very effective either as a second subject in some sonata, where they could later be developed, or at the beginning of a strophic song, where they could be heard several times. But in a subsidiary section of a Gloria, where the words cannot suitably be heard again later, these tunes all carry far too much weight, and the listener would feel cheated if he heard such a fine melody only once. Thus on the next page of the sketchbook Beethoven stripped the melody down to its bare esssentials; the subdominant tonality is retained, with a strong emphasis on Bb, but the melody is reduced to a virtual monotone so as not to carry too much weight (Ex. 10.5). From this totally bare line he could then begin to add a little decoration and interest, so that the final version (Ex. 10.6) has sufficient interest, unlike Ex. 10.5, without being too elaborate like those in Ex. 10.4. Few people would claim that the final version is best from the point of view of being an attractive melody, since there are too many repetitions of the Bb, but it is the most suitable in context, and it also suits the rhythm of the words better than some of the earlier sketches in that it places less emphasis on the unimportant preposition 'propter'.

The examples from *Christus* and the Mass in C show that Beethoven was not concerned with just refining a melody during the course of melodic sketching; instead he often thought up several quite different melodies and wrote them all down as alternatives before trying to refine one of them. His aim was, therefore, not to obtain just the best version of a suitable melody but to find the most suitable melody first and then work towards the best version of it. That this was his customary procedure is also illustrated by an apparently whimsical remark that he wrote on the score of his settings of Goethe's 'Sehnsucht' (WoO 134). He had, perhaps, been asked by someone to set this text, but instead of making just one setting he made four, adding the following comment on the manuscript: 'NB: I did not have enough time to produce a good one, so here are several attempts'.[3] On the face of it the

---

[3] KH, p. 598. See also the autograph fac. published by the Beethovenhaus (Bonn, 1970).

Ex. 10.4

a SV 213, fo. 3^r

gra - ti - as   a - gi-mus   ti - bi   pro - pter   mag - nam

glo - ri - am   tu - am.

b SV 213, fo. 3^r

[a?]

gra   -   ti - as   a - gi - mus   ti   -   bi   pro   -   pter

mag-nam   glo - ri - am   tu - am.

c SV 213, fo. 3^r

[f?]

[orch.]   gra   -   ti - as

a _____ gi-mus   ti - bi   pro - pter   [mag-nam]

d SV 213, fo. 4^r

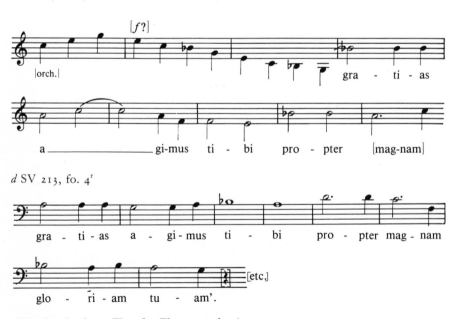

gra - ti - as   a - gi-mus   ti - bi   pro - pter mag - nam

[etc.]

glo - ri - am   tu - am'.

(We give thanks to Thee for Thy great glory)

Ex. 10.5 SV 213, fo. 4ᵛ

Ex. 10.6 Op. 86. ii

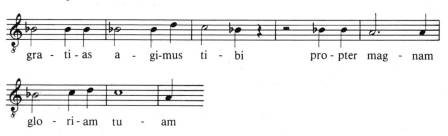

comment seems an absurd paradox: he did not have time to produce one setting so he made four instead. He evidently did have sufficient time to make sketches for at least two of the four settings,[4] so that one might easily assume that he simply produced four settings as a kind of experiment. Yet this remark does bear out what was seen in the two previous cases. He had no difficulty in thinking up several quite different melodies for the same text; the real problem lay in deciding which of them was the best and then refining that one, and this is what he apparently did not have time for in the case of 'Sehnsucht'. This twofold care with melodic composition—care over obtaining the right melody as well as the right form of it—immediately places his work on a higher level than that of most contemporaries, just like his twofold care over form, seen in Chapter 9—selecting the best of several possible works before proceeding with shaping its form.

What happened when Beethoven did have time to produce a good song melody instead of four possible ones is well illustrated in the sketches for 'An die Hoffnung', Op. 32. These sketches were described only briefly by Nottebohm: 'For the song *An die Hoffnung* there are (pp. 151–7) five large, mainly complete sketches and a fairly large number of smaller, fragmentary ones . . . They match the printed form only in certain particular places. We regard these sketches as preliminary work. Some time must have elapsed before the final version was established.'[5] There are actually six (not five) more or less

---

⁴ Sketches for No. 2 are in SV 66, 122, and 123; sketches for Nos. 2 and 4 appear on a leaf sold by Sotheby's (9 May 1985) and now in the Beethoven Center, San Jose.

⁵ N-II, pp. 436–7.

Ex. 10.7 SV 67, p. 151

Die   du   so gern   in heil-gen Näch-ten fei - erst und sanft   und

weich den Gram ver - schlei-erst der ei - ne zar - te See - le   quält,

(You who so gladly celebrate in holy nights, And softly and gently dispel the grief
 Which torments a tender soul)

complete drafts of the first verse of the song (the only verse sketched since
the setting is strophic), and the first (Ex. 10.7) is almost completely different
from the final version. The second draft, on the next page, is slightly
incomplete, but it is modified and expanded to form quite a clear third draft
(Ex. 10.8). This version bears very little resemblance to the first and should
be seen as an alternative to it rather than a modification of it. The key is the
same but the metre and rhythm are different, the shape of the melody has
been completely altered, and the key of the cadence at 'quält', which was B
flat in Ex. 10.7, is changed to G minor, or more probably a half close in C
minor, in Ex. 10.8. There are comparable differences in the second half of the
verse too, with the first sketch returning to E flat straight away while the
other modulates to C major before the return to the tonic. Here then, we have
two attempts at a tune, analogous to the four attempts at 'Sehnsucht', and
both are fine melodies in their own right. The choice for Beethoven then lay
between making another attempt or modifying one of these two, and he did
the latter. The remaining three drafts in the sketchbook, while developing
Ex. 10.8, show substantial differences from it without coming very close to
the final version (Ex. 10.9) except, as Nottebohm observed, in a few places.
Even this final version does not represent Beethoven's last thoughts for this
text, for he made a very different, non-strophic setting about ten years later
(Ex. 10.10), published in 1816 as Op. 94.

Ex. 10.8 SV 67, p. 153

die du   so [gern in   heil' gen Näch-ten fei - erst,   und sanft   und

weich den Gram ver - schlei-erst, der ei - ne zar-te See - le quält,]

Ex. 10.9 Op. 32

Die du so gern in heil'gen Näch - ten fei - erst und sanft und

weich den Gram ver-schlei-erst, der ei - ne zar - te See - le quält,

Ex. 10.10 Op. 94

Die du so gern in heil'- gen Näch - ten fei - erst, und

sanft und weich den Gram ver-schlei-erst, der ei-ne zar -te See- le quält,

Another type of procedure sometimes adopted in the creation of vocal melody was for Beethoven to write out numerous similar tunes, all conceived as possible variants. The idea was presumably that he could later select the best one, or that the great variety of ideas thus created could point the way to a new and original synthesis that would not normally have occurred to a composer. A celebrated example of this approach is his setting of another song called 'Sehnsucht' ('Die stille Nacht umdunkelt', WoO 146), to a text by Reissig, not to be confused with the setting of Goethe's 'Sehnsucht' discussed above. From the sketches for this, Nottebohm published transcriptions of sixteen alternative beginnings,[6] and more recently Lewis Lockwood has listed thirty-one sketch entries for the song, the great majority of them for the opening passage.[7] One might easily gain the impression from these sketches that for Beethoven the composition of this song was a laborious process, in which he worked his way only very slowly towards a finished version. But as Lockwood observed, this great flood of alternatives seems to represent 'not long and tedious labour, but the rapid tumbling out of ideas, one after another'.[8] A somewhat similar picture can be seen in the sketches for the 'Freude' tune in the Ninth Symphony.[9] Again, there are numerous rather similar variants, most probably sketched very quickly, and there are particularly many for the fifth and sixth lines of the tune. At this point some

[6] N-II, pp. 332–3.   [8] Ibid., pp. 113–4.
[7] Lockwood, 'Sehnsucht'.   [9] Winter, 'Ode'.

of the sketches show a modulation to A major while others go to B minor; between them they pointed the way to a fusion of these ideas, so that the final version actually modulates to both B minor and A major.

When it came to refining vocal melodies, two of Beethoven's main concerns were to obtain correct declamation of the text with the best possible verbal rhythms, and to intensify any pictorial effects. Both these concerns are evident in the sketches for 'An die Hoffnung' discussed above: Ex. 10.7 has a very four-square, singsong style, but the final version is much more declamatory with more subtle verbal rhythm, as well as illustrating the word 'quält' more vividly. But Beethoven's concern for verbal rhythm and pictorialism was especially relevant in recitative, where such features are more important than well balanced forms, and so it is in recitative that we find some of the best examples. Although he wrote only a few recitatives he did study some theoretical writings on recitative composition in about 1802,[10] and his concern with rhythm and word-painting is very apparent. A striking example is found in the three versions of the phrase 'Gott! welch Dunkel hier' from *Fidelio* (Ex. 10.11). In the version of 1805 the word 'Gott' is given intensity by being placed on the most expressive degree of the scale, the flattened sixth, while a falling diminished fifth is used to express the anguish of Florestan's situation. The version of 1806 prolongs the word 'Gott' (allowing for the notational change from 1805) to give it more pathos, but in the final version (1814) the force of the word is greatly increased again, by the use of a much higher and even longer note, so that the sound is more of a cry of anguish than just a word. The diminished-fifth leap has gone, but Beethoven more than compensates in other ways: there is now the melodic dissonance of a major seventh between 'Gott' and 'Dunkel'; the diminished fifth has been preserved in the accompaniment in the form of the chord E–G–B♭ accompanying the word 'Gott'; and the loneliness associated with Florestan's darkness is conveyed by leaving the words 'welch Dunkel hier' completely unaccompanied, in contrast to the two earlier settings.

Ex. 10.11 Op. 72

a (1805)

Gott!   welch Dun-kel hier!

b (1806)

Gott!   welch Dunkel hier!

c (1814)

Gott!   welch Dunkel   hier!

(God!   What darkness here!)

[10] Kramer, 'Graun'.

Another recitative, and one which has the advantage that its final version will be unfamiliar to most readers, occurs in *Die Ruinen von Athen*. This work was written very quickly in 1811 in response to a commission, and so one would not expect to find many sketches for it, particularly not for something as straightforward as a recitative; yet there are actually quite a number, including four complete drafts for the one recitative in the work. All four occur in SV 184 along with most of the remaining sketches for the work; the pages in this sketchbook are in a very jumbled order but the chronological order of the recitative drafts can be determined on internal evidence (for example, a short orchestral ritornello added as an afterthought in the third draft is integrated with the main text in the fourth). The four appear, in order of development, on fos. 17^v, 24^{r-v}, 20^r, and 20^v. The first draft begins as in Ex. 10.12. It is not very far removed from the final version, but certain details need putting right. The heavy emphasis on the initial 'Mit' is removed in draft 3 by replacing the crotchet with a quaver preceded by a quaver rest, thereby throwing the emphasis on to the important word 'Freude'. In draft 3 also, the second syllable of 'Freude' is changed from D to G—a very tiny alteration, but one which helps to separate the first two phrases of the text; had this been done instead by a rest, it would have interrupted the flow of the sentence as a whole. Even when pushed for time Beethoven had concern for the minutest detail such as this. In the second phrase of the music the word 'holde' is given no emphasis in the first two drafts, and so in draft 3 the word is lengthened and raised a third above 'empfangt das' (Ex. 10.13). This causes a certain rhythmic confusion, represented by two barlines separated by only one beat; hence in the last draft, as in the final version, 'holde Schwesterpaar' is prolonged still more, for greater emphasis and for better rhythmic balance (Ex. 10.14). It will be noticed that the key of this cadence has also been changed. This is because the next section of the recitative was also to end in C, and so to create greater tonal variety the first section would have to end in a different key; and since the whole of this section is really concerned with only one idea, Beethoven found it best to end where it began, in G major.

Ex. 10.12 SV 184, fo. 17^v

Mit   re-ger Freu-de die nie er-kal-tet emp-fangt das hol-de Schwes-ter-paar

(With lively joy that never cools, receive the gracious pair of sisters)

Ex. 10.13 SV 184, fo. 20^r

emp-fangt das hol - de Schwest - er-paar

Ex. 10.14 SV 184, fo. 20ᵛ

emp-fangt das   hol - de Schwester-paar.

Later in the same recitative appear the words 'Was, mit dem Schicksal kämpfend, grosse Seelen litten' (That which great souls suffered, struggling against fate). The phrase doubtless had an immediate appeal for Beethoven in view of his own struggles with fate, and not surprisingly there are more sketches for this passage than any other in the recitative. He decided at once that the text called for a diminished seventh chord in the harmony and he never wavered from this idea, but the melodic shape was difficult to achieve, partly because there were so many important words. Which should have the highest note—'Schicksal' (fate), 'kämpfend' (struggling), or 'grosse' (great)? How could all three words be given due emphasis? The original sketch is hard to decipher, for it is in pencil and has been crossed out, but Ex. 10.15 shows a tentative transcription. Here the word 'Schicksal' is given appropriate expression through the leap up to the B♭, and 'grosse' is also well portrayed by a high note, but 'kämpfend' does not convey any sense of struggle. In the ink draft that replaced this sketch and was carried into draft 2, 'Schicksal' stands out an augmented fourth above the rest of the line, which is surprisingly plain (Ex. 10.16). In draft 3 the earlier version is restored with only very minor alterations. In the two versions of the passage that are found in draft 4, however, the word 'kämpfend' is at last given prominence, and the idea of using large leaps (falling diminished seventh and rising minor tenth) to intensify the melody is introduced (Ex. 10.17). Two further sketches at the foot of the page suggest further possiblities along similar lines (Ex. 10.18), although in his haste Beethoven managed to omit the word 'kämpfend' altogether at this stage. The phrase as a whole is one of the few places where draft 4 differs significantly from the final version, and although the differences are not very great it would be a brave reader who tried to predict on the basis of these sketches what the final version would

Ex. 10.15 SV 184, fo. 17ᵛ

[Was, mit dem Schick - sal   kämp-fend, gro - sse See-len   li -tten]

Ex. 10.16 SV 184, fo. 17ᵛ

Was mit dem Schick-sal kämp-fend   gro-sse See-len li - tten

Ex. 10.17 SV 184, fo. 20ᵛ

Was   mit   dem Schick - sal   kämp-fend gro - sse See - len   li - tten

Ex. 10.18 SV 184, fo. 20ᵛ

Was [mit dem Schicksal gro - sse See - len li - tten]   Was   mit dem

Schick-sal gro - sse See - len   li - tten

be, and only a very exceptional one who would succeed in doing so. The final version, of course, manages to reconcile the competing claims of all the important words (see Ex. 10.19): 'Schicksal' is given the dramatic falling diminished seventh; 'kämpfend' is given the upward leap of a minor tenth to a very high note (two whole octaves above the lowest note in the recitative); and 'grosse', though losing something of its previous prominence, still suggests greatness, by means of falling through an augmented fourth after starting on a very high note and by being rhythmically stressed compared with the previous word.

Always, then, even when in a great hurry and writing a fairly insignificant piece of recitative for an occasional work, Beethoven took great care over his vocal lines. Each word had to be given the correct rhythmic emphasis and due weight, the high points in the melodic line had to occur on the most suitable word, and the use of large leaps, small leaps, steps, repeated notes, and upward or downward motion had to be accurately judged to give the maximum expression to the text being set. Any words with pictorial possibilities had to be illustrated as vividly as possible, and the sketches for the words 'Schicksal' 'kämpfend' and 'grosse' clearly show Beethoven stretching the bounds of convention in order to achieve this effect. He would not tolerate any important word, such as 'holde', being passed over too quickly, or melodic lines that did not match the sense and structure of the text, unless there were overriding considerations of musical structure and shape (as there might be in a strophic song, for example, where each verse has the same tune even though the structure and meaning vary from verse to verse). In recitative more than anywhere else, musical considerations are subordinate to the text, and this is why recitatives provide such clear examples of this branch of Beethoven's compositional art.

Ex. 10.19 Op. 113. vi

Was,   mit dem Schick - sal kämp - fend, gro-   sse See - len   li - tten

Further examples of the problem of declamation can of course easily be found outside the realm of recitative. The numerous sketches for 'Sehnsucht' (WoO 146) mentioned above include about sixteen different rhythms for the opening two lines of text;[11] and one need only look at Ex. 10.7, 10.8, and 10.9 to see an example of how a change in verbal emphasis is gradually made between successive versions of a melody. In Ex. 10.7 the first important stress comes on the relatively unimportant word 'Die'; in Ex. 10.8 it is transferred to 'du', but in Ex. 10.9 the rhythm is further improved, with the first three words all subordinate to 'gern'. Another example of declamation problems in a lyrical song occurs in Marzelline's aria in *Fidelio*. The sketches have been discussed in an article by Philip Gossett, who examined in some detail the problems of verbal rhythm; one of his examples also highlights the problem inherent in all strophic songs—slight differences of verbal rhythm in consecutive verses.[12] Beethoven had discovered a suitable and interesting rhythm for the opening phrase, 'O wär ich schon mit dir vereint' (Ex. 10.20), but the rhythm does not fit the second stanza, 'In Ruhe stiller Häuslichkeit', as he soon found out when he moved on to sketch this part of the text to the same tune. He was therefore forced to adopt a more commonplace rhythm because it fits both stanzas reasonably well.

In later life Beethoven frequently adopted a varied strophic form in order to avoid this problem and bring out the meaning and rhythm of each stanza. An outstanding example is his song 'Abendlied unter'm gestirnten Himmel' (WoO 150), where each stanza has subtle differences of rhythmic or melodic shape to accommodate particular words; there are also a few examples in the song cycle *An die ferne Geliebte*. Given that Beethoven took such care over details of word-setting, one can easily imagine how frustrated he became when trying to set Scottish folksongs without knowing their texts. More than once he asked George Thomson in Edinburgh, who was supplying him

Ex. 10.20 SV 60, p. 152

O   wär   ich schon mit dir ver - eint

(O were I already united with you)

---

[11] Listed in Lockwood, 'Sehnsucht', p. 116.   [12] Gossett, 'Marzelline', pp. 160, 161.

with the tunes, to send him the texts too;[13] he was willing to arrange for German translations to be made and eventually threatened to stop setting them altogether if texts were not supplied.

Apart from questions of verbal declamation and pictorialism, the problems associated with the creation of vocal melody—problems such as the creation of variety of pitch and rhythm, the positioning of climaxes, and the use of appropriate phrase lengths—apply equally to instrumental music, to which we shall now turn. How Beethoven set about sketching instrumental melody has been discussed from various angles by a number of writers, particularly Paul Mies and Kurt Westphal,[14] and although most of them have tended to rely mainly on Nottebohm for their musical examples, their observations are none the less valid and often very perceptive. Mies discusses such aspects of melodic composition as repeated notes, suspensions, positioning of the apex, elimination of caesuras, use of upbeats, and use (or avoidance) of sequence, while Westphal concentrates on differences between successive sketches in the form of such features as note substitution, inversion of melodic direction, and enlivening of rhythm.

Few general rules can be derived from these studies. For example, suspensions, repeated notes, caesuras, and phrase repetition may be either added or eliminated in a later draft, depending on a combination of factors that applies only to that individual context. But there is generally an underlying aim that can be discerned: the later sketches of a melody tend to make it less regular and predictable, more original, more varied within itself, and more highly decorated. This much could actually be guessed from a study of the finished works. It is remarkable, for example, how frequently Beethoven's sequences in his mature works are not quite exact. A case in point is the beginning of the 'Waldstein' Sonata, where the first four bars are immediately repeated a tone lower but with the introduction of an unexpected A♭ in bar 8. It comes as no surprise to learn that in the early sketches this was an exact sequence, with the A♭ only being introduced in a ninth bar, after the strict sequence was finished.[15] A similar pattern can be seen in Beethoven's use of repeated phrases: in sketches these are often indicated just by repeat signs, whereas in a final version there may well be some modification to the repeat. An early sketch of bars 109–16 of the first movement of the 'Eroica'[16] shows a simple repeat (Ex. 10.21a) while the final version contains rhythmic modifications the second time, as well as being more complex than the sketch even in the first four bars (see Ex. 10.21b).

There are several reasons why the early versions of melodies tend to be simpler and more conventional than the final versions. In some cases, as mentioned in the previous chapter, early melodic ideas were intended primarily just to fix the tonal area and give visual reality to it and to give some impression of the melodic and rhythmic style or direction of the music, rather

[13] See A-266, A-319, A-352.   [14] Mies, *Sketches*; Westphal, *Einfall*.
[15] Cooper, 'Waldstein', p. 174; SV 60, p. 122.   [16] N-1803, p. 24.

Ex. 10.21

a SV 60, p. 18

b Op. 55. i

than being regarded as fully fledged melodies; in such cases complexity was unnecessary and might even obscure the overall intention. 'Beethoven was not so much drafting themes—the popular assumption concerning his sketching process—as groping towards something more elusive: overall tonal direction.'[17] In the earliest sketch for the second subject of the first movement of the 'Waldstein' Sonata (Ex. 10.22), Beethoven sketches a bald sequence with virtually no melodic interest; its main function is to fix the key area, E major (unusual at that date after a C major start), and the melodic direction—descending, to contrast with the ascending motion of the first subject. Nevertheless the final version of the theme is not as far removed from this initial sketch as might appear at first sight, and the sketches show clearly the transformation: the middle voice of the implied three-part harmony of Ex. 10.22 is isolated and given rhythmic interest in the next sketch (Ex. 10.23*a*); next the melodic direction is varied by having the theme turn back on itself (Ex. 10.23*b*), and finally the cadences in the fourth and eighth bars are made to contrast (Ex. 10.23*c*).

Ex. 10.22 SV 60, p. 120

<hr />

[17] Winter, *Op. 131*, p. 120.

Ex. 10.23 SV 60, p. 122

a SV 60, p. 123

b SV 60, p. 123

c Op. 53.i

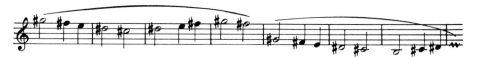

Early sketches may also appear dull because they were written as a kind of shorthand, with such elements as surface detail deliberately omitted to save time, even though they were intended from the start. There will then be the appearance of a melody gradually gaining in complexity, whereas conceptually it did not necessarily do so. Dots, for example, are often omitted where a succession of dotted figures is intended, giving the impression of a series of equal quavers or semiquavers. This also sometimes applies to upbeats. Mies has noted that 'there are a large number of instances in which melodies, originally without upbeat, are given one later on',[18] but in some cases this upbeat was deliberately omitted in sketches. This certainly seems to be the case, for example, in the *Prometheus* Variations, Op. 35, where an upbeat in the pre-existing theme is omitted in some of the sketches for variations[19] only to be reinstated in the final versions of them.

Another reason why the early versions of melodies generally seem rather bland is that if Beethoven was wanting an unusual, surprising, or highly decorated tune it was easier to achieve this in two stages; it was a much better procedure to write a simple version which could then be altered rhythmically or melodically in later sketches as the surrounding material evolved, rather than attempt to write a complex melody from the outset before the context had been properly established. At a time when melody tended to consist of

[18] Mies, *Sketches*, p. 5.
[19] e.g. SV 343, p. 25 staves 1 and 7, p. 26 stave 1.

two separate elements—structural notes and decorative ones—the structural notes could be composed first and the decorative ones added later, just as they had been added by improvisation in an earlier era; and although Beethoven's sketching procedure was normally not as simple as this, this was undoubtedly an underlying factor in his method of composing melody.

Rhythmic alterations could be made in a similar way. Beethoven had a quite extraordinary sensitivity to rhythm in general, and many of his rhythms are extremely subtle; in fact it could be argued that it is the rhythmic element in his music that most often makes an initial impact on the imagination of the untutored listener. But his complex and subtle rhythms were often only achieved, like his melodic shapes, in two basic stages—an initial sketch that outlined the sort of rhythmic pattern and phrase structure desired, and a series of modifications to make the rhythm less obvious and facile. Thus the first stage consisted in sketching a simple rhythm—perhaps a series of quavers, to contrast with a phrase of crotchets or semiquavers in an adjacent part of the work—and the second stage was to create an interesting pattern out of the rhythm. That Beethoven was aware that some of his initial melodic sketches were only provisional and destined to be altered cannot be doubted, considering the simplicity and even banality that some of them display. Again the 'Waldstein' Sonata provides a good example, and this time from a melody that is essentially non-thematic—the lead-in to the second subject. A tune as such was not wanted at this point in the movement, but whatever was to be used had to be more interesting than Beethoven's first sketch for this section (Ex. 10.24), and he surely knew it. Rhythmically it is naïve, while melodically it is basically just a long scale. By comparison the final version is a marvel of subtlety and ingenuity, with interesting cross-rhythms between the hands in a pattern that is no longer quite predictable and regular (Ex. 10.25), even though it is still closely based on the original sketch.

Ex. 10.24 SV 60, p. 122

Ex. 10.25 Op. 53. i

A further reason why the final version of a melody tends to be more complex than those in the sketches is that even if Beethoven had found what seemed to be a satisfactory version that needed no further reworking, he sometimes had second thoughts about it later on and realized that it could be made even better either by the addition of extra material, in parentheses (as it were), or simply by making the existing melody slightly less straightforward. That such changes were often unplanned afterthoughts rather than planned growth can be deduced from the sketchbooks (for example, if a melody is altered after remaining unchanged in several preceding sketches), and it is still more clearly demonstrable in cases where the autograph score is itself amended, or where there are two versions of the same piece.

The addition of new melodic ideas often involved the insertion of extra bars, but it could also occur without any alteration of the phrase structure. The change might be something as simple as the insertion of appoggiaturas to heighten the expression, as in bars 43–5 of Op. 18 No. 1; here the modification of the earlier version (Ex. 10.26*a*) by adding two appoggiaturas (see Ex. 10.26*b*) also has the effect of relating this passage more closely to a previous one (bars 31–3).[20] Similarly in the autograph score of the 'Waldstein' Sonata a crotchet B in bar 25 of the first movement (Ex. 10.27*a*) is altered to a group of semiquavers (Ex. 10.27*b*) to increase the decoration and the sense of continuity (and also, once again, to avoid exact repetition—of bar 23 in this case). On other occasions the revision could be much more substantial and even involve a brief modulation to another key, as in bars 136–43 of the first movement of the 'Eroica' Symphony. In one of the last sketches for this passage,[21] these bars are still rather bland, consisting simply

Ex. 10.26

a Op. 18 No. 1. i, earlier version

b Op. 18 No. 1. i, later version

Ex. 10.27 Op. 53. i

a   *b*

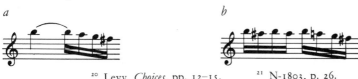

[20] Levy, *Choices*, pp. 12–15.   [21] N-1803, p. 26.

Ex. 10.28

a SV 60, p. 26 (after N-1803, p. 26)

b Op. 55. i, tune and bass only

of a prolonged 6-4–5-3 cadential pattern (Ex. 10.28*a*). In the final version the music modulates briefly and unexpectedly to A flat major (Ex. 10.28*b*); and although the number of bars is exactly the same as before the passage seems much longer because so much more happens within it.

Subtle refinement of melody could equally well be of rhythm rather than pitch. A sketch for the finale of the Second Piano Concerto shows the rhythm of the main theme as in Ex. 10.29*a*, whereas the final version is much more unorthodox (Ex. 10.29*b*). Yet in this case the situation is not quite as striaghtforward as it seems, for an earlier sketch than that shown in Ex. 10.29*a* shows the rhythm already as in the final version (SV 185, fo. 97ʳ)

Ex. 10.29

a SV 185, fo. 64ᵛ   *b* Op. 19. iii

—a clear demonstration that Beethoven's work on a movement did not always progress in a straight line and that he sometimes reverted to an earlier idea. Another minute rhythmic alteration, coupled this time with a pitch change, was made at a cadence in the Bagatelle Op. 126 No. 2. The first sketch (Ex. 10.30*a*) shows a very conventional, almost baroque cadence pattern, but later sketches and the final version introduce syncopation, unexpected leaps and shorter note values (Ex. 10.30*b*). Rhythmic alterations are often on a slightly broader scale than this, however. They may consist of adjustments to phrase lengths or of additions of short links to fill in the rests between phrases and provide greater overall continuity. Beethoven was particularly concerned with the problem of the latter in his later works, and the Bagatelles Op. 119, many of which are reworkings of earlier drafts, provide several examples of links being added to join phrases together or to fill in a first-time bar before a repeat (see Chapter 16).

Not all of Beethoven's melodies took a long time to reach their final form; some seem to have been invented without difficulty and remained unchanged from the earliest sketch to the final version. The second subject of the finale of the Quartet Op. 131, despite its dramatic and unconventional leaps, 'shows every appearance of having experienced a painless birth'.[22] The first subject of the first movement of the 'Eroica', with its curious descent to a C♯, also appears in its final form in its earliest sketches (SV 60). But one must beware of assuming that the earliest sketches known necessarily represent Beethoven's first thoughts on a tune, for he probably did quite a lot of 'mental sketching' or piano improvisation beforehand in many cases, and there may always be some early sketches that are now missing. In the case of the 'Eroica' it is clear that he had been thinking about the work for some time before making the main sketches in SV 60, for in the previous sketch-book, the 'Wielhorsky', there is an outline of the first three movements of an 'Eroica'-like work (SV 343, pp. 44–5); although the themes here are in general quite didfferent from that of the 'Eroica' itself, the main theme of the latter could have evolved gradually from this material during the following months. And there are also apparently some sketches missing from this period, for Czerny states that the main theme of the 'Eroica' was originally as in Ex. 10.31, roughly as in the coda of the final version (bars 631–62).[23]

Ex. 10.30

a SV 280, p. 14

b Op. 126 No. 2

---

[22] Winter, *Op. 131*, p. 176.   [23] Czerny, *Performance*, p. 13.

Ex. 10.31 (from Czerny)

Some of Beethoven's melodies were actually intended to sound simple and slightly naïve; these often required relatively little sketching (though there are exceptions, as in the finale of the Ninth Symphony). The second theme in the finale of Op. 131, though rather extreme and almost absurd in shape, is not actually very complex, which is probably why it was conceived so easily. But if a melody was intended to be a very refined, complex, or intensely emotional one then much sketching was almost invariably necessary. The most extreme example of a long, lyrical but totally unorthodox melody is surely the Cavatina in the Quartet Op. 130. Even a superficial analysis demonstrates its irregularities: the phrase structure of the first section, in terms of bars, is 8 + 6 + 5, + 6 + 6; the sequences are never quite regular, with the first subphrase, for example, being answered by a second one that begins the same (a degree lower) but is then prolonged and proceeds quite differently; the climaxes are in unusual places, the first eight-bar phrase having its apex much earlier than might be expected; and the phrases sometimes terminate on unexpected notes—for instance, the third phrase ends on the subdominant, over a dominant seventh. In his efforts to achieve this unconventional result and avoid the obvious, Beethoven's progress on this movement was unusually slow, as is documented in the sketches. Whereas the sketches for the third movement of the quartet seem to have been made in a fairly concentrated burst, and those for the fourth movement are fairly few in number, those for the fifth (the Cavatina), a much shorter movement in terms of pages or bars, are relatively numerous and protracted, beginning before most of those for the third movement and undergoing several changes of key or metre before being finished off only after the early sketches for the *Grosse Fuge* finale. The phrase structure and the melodic and rhythmic details all took a long time to clarify in Beethoven's mind, mainly because he wanted such a highly charged and extreme example of this particular style.

In his sketching of melody in general, then, Beethoven's overall strategy was not unlike that employed in his sketching of form or other aspects of the music. He would often begin with several quite different ideas and write them down before selecting the best and working on them. These initial ideas would be relatively basic, though by no means facile and often already quite unorthodox. Those chosen would then evolve by a kind of growth, with the themes tending to acquire more notes (particularly purely decorative ones and connecting notes between phrases) and less regular rhythms, moving away from the obvious and predictable towards something more original and unexpected. Sometimes Beethoven would overstep the mark in this direction, perhaps deliberately, and write a more elaborate and complex melody than was desirable before arriving at a happy medium. And occasionally, as in the 'Gratias' from the Mass in C, the whole process was reversed, with an elaborate melody being pared down too far before the right balance was found. The same basic procedures applied whether he was sketching a main theme or merely some linking passage or cadential formula, and all aspects of the melody had to be adjusted until they were right, with sufficient variety of pitches and rhythms, well-judged phrase lengths, suitably placed climaxes, appropriate relationships, and contrasts between different sections of the melody, and, in the case of vocal music, correct declamation and imaginative word-painting, before the sketching was finished.

11

The Vertical Dimension
and the Finishing Touches

THE sketches discussed so far concentrate on the horizontal dimensions of Beethoven's music—the form, lengths, and proportions of different sections, tonal relationships, rhythm, and melodic outline. But Beethoven also had to work out the vertical dimension, including such matters as harmony, texture, orchestration, and dynamics; each of these was tackled in a slightly different way from the others and in a very different way from the horizontal elements. Little has been written about this aspect of his compositional process except incidentally during discussions of other aspects, but such elements obviously play a vital role in the finished work and so it is important to understand how they were approached.

Let us begin with harmony. As has been seen, most of Beethoven's output can be, and in the sketches usually was, reduced to a single-stave outline with no indication of harmony. Does this mean that no harmony had been conceived in the initial stages and that it was only added later on? Or was the harmony conceived first, before the melodic detail on the surface? It is impossible to reach absolutely definite conclusions from a study of the sketches, but it seems that there was more than one way in which the harmony of a particular passage might be created. If the initial concept sketch was purely melodic, such a melody none the less carried strong harmonic implications (for example, it might be built largely around tonic and dominant chords, or have an arpeggiated outline that delineated the accompanying harmony). With a good knowledge of Beethoven's style it is possible to guess approximately what harmony was intended in such cases. For instance, on fo. 1^r of the 'Kessler' Sketchbook (SV 263) there is an unfinished minuet in which only the melody is written down, yet the harmonic implications are so clear that we can be sure he had in mind some definite harmony similar to that shown in Ex. 11.1. If he had regarded harmonization of a melody as a separate compositional task, to be approached in the same way as other compositional problems, we should expect to find sketches showing a clearly defined melody at the top of the page and a series of alternative harmonizations underneath. Such a layout occurs only in exceptional circumstances (see below).

On the rare occasions where there is a series of variant sketches fully harmonized, the melody and rhythm are likely to be altered on each occasion

Ex. 11.1 SV 263, fo 1ʳ

[etc.]

along with any changes in harmony. A good example is a group of eight variant sketches quoted by Nottebohm for the words 'judicare vivos' in the *Missa solemnis*.[1] Many of these show slight differences of harmony, but they also show differences of rhythm and melodic outline that are equally conspicuous; Beethoven was clearly experimenting with variants of the phrase as a whole rather than concentrating on the harmony. There are, however, occasional examples where the only change made to a sketch was in the harmony—for example by the insertion or deletion of an accidental. Thus in general it seems that a melody and its harmony were initially conceived as a unit (if the idea were improvised at the piano Beethoven would no doubt have included harmony), but either or both elements were liable to alteration later on. The single-line sketch that usually emerged was simply a mnemonic for the unit, rather than the first stage in the creation of it.

The first idea or concept sketch for a new work or movement was very often not a single-line melody but one that was partially or fully harmonized. Concept sketches are among the commonest places for sketches of harmony: since such a sketch was an entirely new one Beethoven was more likely to forget the intended harmony unless this was jotted down too, whereas when he had been working on a piece for some time a single-line melody would generally suffice as a reminder. Examples of such harmonized concept sketches have been given earlier.[2]

Synopsis sketches, which have a somewhat similar function to concept sketches in that they provide a preliminary indication of the character of a movement or work, are also quite often provided with a certain amount of harmony. The 'tonal overviews' for the Quartet Op. 131, discussed in detail by Robert Winter,[3] provide good examples, as does the synopsis for the first movement of Op. 31 No. 2 quoted in Chapter 12. Parts of these sketches have a bass-line or even complete chords, whereas other sections have just the melodic outline. As such sketches are concerned largely with tonal areas and the general character of the music, the vertical dimension of each section is sometimes more important than the rather plain and uninteresting melodic outline that is so often found at this stage of sketching.

In longer sketches, that is, continuity drafts, where Beethoven's main

[1] N-II, p. 155 (transcribed from SV 210). Another variant, hitherto unidentified, appears in SV 294, fo. 1ᵛ.
[2] See Exx. 7.3 and 8.2.   [3] Winter, 'Plans'.

concern was to establish correct proportions, overall form, and sense of continuity—basically horizontal elements—there is also occasionally an indication of the vertical dimension. For instance, if a passage of music contains two simultaneous melodies of roughly equal importance, both might be included in the sketch. Alternatively Beethoven might incorporate both the treble and bass in a single draft, either on two staves or on a single stave that confusingly requires the reader to imagine two different clefs at the same time. And in some sketches he drafts the bass instead of the treble for a few bars, especially if the treble has some complicated figuration and he is simply wanting to write down the harmonic progression. In such cases the bass is a kind of shorthand for the harmonic outline, and the implicit harmonies are often made explicit by means of figured-bass notation, as in Ex. 11.2. Certain sections of a continuity draft can, then, be intended for establishing a harmonic progression in which the surface detail is only incidental. But in these and other sketches, the harmony was a fundamental part of the concept rather than just a supplement to the melody, and it was unlikely to be altered unless the whole passage was amended.

The one exception to this rule is, of course, the type of sketch in which Beethoven was working with a pre-existing melody. Here a number of harmonizations were possible but the melody itself could not be changed. An early example appears in his setting of the Lamentations of Jeremiah (SV 185, fo. 96ʳ), where the plainsong melody is provided with a variety of different harmonizations (many of them very chromatic), although these are not alternative sketches but varying harmonies to be used to accompany successive verses of the text. Beethoven's folksong settings also make use of independently composed melodies that had to be harmonized. Again a variety of harmonies was possible for each melody, as he explained to the publisher George Thomson: 'In No. 2 one quite quickly finds some harmonies to harmonize such songs, but [because of] the simplicity, the character and nature of the song, to do so successfully is not always as easy for me as you might believe: one can find an infinite number of harmonies, but only one of them conforms to the type and character of the melody.'[4] In this song (Op. 108 No. 2) Beethoven seems to have tried out several harmonizations before establishing the best one, and was thus treating harmony in much the same way that he often treated a melodic outline. Actual sketches for folksong settings, which might illustrate this process, are rare—the 'infinite number of harmonies' were probably normally tried out on the piano rather than being written down; but there are one or two good examples. In a

Ex. 11.2 SV 343, p. 125

[etc.]

____
[4] A-892.

setting made in 1810 of the Scottish tune 'Faithfu' Johnie' (Hess 203) Beethoven's original ink draft of bars 9–10 was as in Ex. 11.3*a*, but the left-hand part was later altered in pencil to Ex. 11.3*b*, although the tune had to remain unchanged (and the necessary revision to the right-hand part was not written out). The final version was slightly different again, and in addition he later made a completely different setting of the melody (as Op. 108 No. 20), with yet another harmonization of the passage.[5] Such variant harmonizations give a clear indication of his approach to composing harmony for a pre-existing melody. But it must be emphasized that this was not his normal approach to composing harmony.

The working out of the texture of a piece, including such matters as register, chord spacing, and type of accompaniment figuration, was done in a different way from the composition of the harmony and tended to occur at a much later stage in the compositional process. Although even at the outset Beethoven generally had a rough idea of the type of texture he wanted, the exact details could be worked out only when he was fairly well advanced with the horizontal layout of the piece.

If the texture he wanted was mainly homophonic no major problems arose, and sketches for such passages always concentrate on the horizontal dimension, with little or no indication of the texture. Early sketches could indicate the register and possibly the type of accompaniment figuration, just as they

Ex. 11.3 SV 276, p. 1

a

b

[5] The sketch for Hess 203 is in SV 276 (though SV refers to it as Op. 108 No. 20); the final version of Hess 203 is published in Hess ed., *SGA*, xiv. 136–8.

might indicate the harmony, but no further sketching of the texture was necessary. As soon as a more complex sound was required, however, the sketches were likely to include some work on the texture, so that in the case of a fugue, for example, the exact details of the part-writing were often worked out in considerable detail in the sketches, although this might not be done until long after the main thematic ideas had fallen into place. The fugue in the *Prometheus* Variations (Op. 35), arguably his first great fugue, shows this procedure clearly. As in all fugues, the texture begins to be complicated as soon as the third voice enters, and so it is illuminating to see how Beethoven sketched this section. In the first sketch for the exposition (SV 343, p. 25) each voice is sketched only up to the entry of the next voice, so that the result is a single-line melody with changes of register to indicate the separate voices but with no countersubjects or other counterpoint. The horizontal dimension was as usual being worked out before the vertical. In the second sketch (SV 343, p. 35) Beethoven used two staves instead of only one, and attempted to fill in the counterpoint. The countersubject was entered without difficulty and is very close to the final version, but problems arose as soon as the third voice entered, and the sketch at this point contains several additions, deletions, and alterations. It is difficult to make out exactly what is underneath all the alterations, but at least three separate stages of sketching can be identified. In the first only the outer parts were present (Ex. 11.4*a*), with a slight alteration apparently being made to the top part. This top part was then recomposed with a middle voice added, and the first suspension was transferred from the top to the middle voice (Ex. 11.4*b*). The top part was then drafted in a new version on a supplementary stave (Ex. 11.4*c*), with the lower parts being implicitly left unchanged. The final version (Ex. 11.4*d*) was different again, but the running semiquavers of Ex. 11.4*c* were retained in a different section of the fugue, being transferred to the exposition of the inversion of the subject. Thus although Beethoven knew roughly what texture he wanted and was very sure of the main harmonic and melodic outline, it took him some time to find the right figuration for the countermelodies.

The sketch quoted in Ex. 11.4 occurs near the beginning of a continuity draft for the entire fugue. The draft continues with a fairly full texture for about a page, but after that it degenerates into only two parts and eventually just one (though still using two staves). In one place even the one remaining voice disappears (p. 36 staves 1–2), leaving just a series of blank bars; further blank bars also occur in a later sketch for the middle of the fugue (p. 40 staves 1–5). Sketches of this sort demonstrate yet again that Beethoven was initially more concerned with continuity and tonal direction than with textural details, and in some cases, as we shall see, such details were determined only when he came to write out the final score.

In music for more than one instrument, problems of texture could be very much more complex than in solo piano music, so that it was often not until Beethoven was writing out the final score that some of the problems even

Ex. 11.4
a SV 343, p. 35

b SV 343, p. 35

c SV 343, p. 35

d Op. 35 Finale

*The two parts are apparently alternatives, the lower probably later.

became apparent. Hence what tended to happen was that the beginning of the score, which had usually been fairly well prepared beforehand, suffered relatively few alterations, but as he progressed further the score became increasingly messy with corrections. These corrections were mostly not broad ones of tonal direction or overall form—such matters had by and large been worked out in the sketches—but minor ones concerning details of figuration and texture which had been left unresolved in his mind. Individual notes in the score could of course be altered without too much mess, but if the musical material needed to be reallotted to different instruments, whole bars often had to be cancelled and rewritten even if the harmonic and tonal direction remained unchanged.

Such alterations are very apparent in the autograph score of the first movement of the Cello Sonata Op. 69, where, with only one more instrumental part than in the *Prometheus* Variations, revisions to the texture are very numerous, especially in the development section. The score has in places become so messy that it is quite hard to make out the final version and even harder to decipher all the earlier versions that have been crossed out. A detailed study of the score has been made by Lewis Lockwood,[6] who discusses many of the changes of register, instrumentation, figuration, and other elements that were made during the writing out of the score. Two examples will suffice here; neither is discussed by Lockwood in great detail, but he does provide transcriptions of the changing versions (his transcriptions differ in minor details from those presented here, illustrating how hard it is to decipher the exact nature and chronology of deleted material).

The first section of the movement to suffer from heavy deletions begins at bar 65—the start of the second main theme within the second group. Bar 65 itself will serve to illustrate the changes made in this and the following bars. Beethoven began by writing out some of the cello part, but with a wrong turn of harmony on the second beat (Ex. 11.5*a*), and so this was immediately deleted. The replacement retained triplets in the cello part, with the main melody allotted to the piano right hand and a simple harmonic outline to the left, both instruments being marked 'f:' (Ex. 11.5*b*). He even added articulation marks to the cello part. Some time later he decided to delete the 'f:' and to reverse the roles of the cello and the piano left hand in this and the succeeding bars: at first he seems to have considered a slightly different type of figuration for the piano, with the cello sustaining the bass E on the second and third beats (Ex. 11.5*c*); but eventually he gave the piano some triplet figuration (similar to what the cello had had, only more pianistic), while the bass E in the cello was cancelled and a pizzicato mark added on the fourth beat to lighten the texture still further (Ex. 11.5*d*). The result looks bewildering on paper (see Facsimile 3) but when one sees the stages separated out as in Ex. 11.5, each step seems perfectly logical. In the corresponding place in the recapitulation (bar 202) there are comparable (though by no means identical) alterations, indicating that the final version of bar 65 as shown in Ex. 11.5*d* was not reached until after the early version of bar 202 had been fully written out. By extension this implies that Beethoven wrote out the whole of the movement in its initial form before making his main revisions to these sections, and that on a later occasion he revised the passages that include bars 65 and 202.

The second place to be discussed is bars 101–5, part of the development section that gave so much trouble and in which the revisions 'represent a wholesale conversion of this entire area of the movement from one means of instrumental realization to another'.[7] In the earlier version (Ex. 11.6*a*) a motif is played first on the piano and then repeated a fifth lower on the cello (with piano left-hand accompaniment). Although there are a few omissions in the

---

[6] Lockwood, 'Op. 69'.   [7] Ibid., p. 62.

Ex. 11.5 Op. 69. i

Facsimile 3. Cello Sonata Op. 69, autograph score, first movement, fo. 3^r (bar 65) (private collection; reproduced from a facsimile published by Columbia University Press, 1970—used by permission)

Ex. 11.6 Op. 69. i

a

b

score—the piano trills in bar 102, the legato mark for the cello in bars 103–5, and certain of the rests—the notation is fairly full, including dynamics, some slurs, and two 'espressivo' markings. After progressing only a few bars further, however,[8] Beethoven returned to this passage (and the following bars) and rescored it completely (Ex. 11.6*b*): the first phrase was placed an octave lower and allotted to the cello (the piano left hand was also put down an octave), while the second phrase was transposed up an octave and transferred to the piano (though the accompaniment in these two bars remained unchanged). At the same time he filled out the texture in bars 103–5 by adding a series of syncopated Es to the cello; the third pair of Es seems to have been altered to Gs a little later, but eventually the whole series of syncopations was cancelled altogether and replaced by rests for the cello (not shown in Ex. 11.6). Thus the main changes in this passage were of register and instrumentation rather than simply of texture; but the horizontal features of the passage were effectively unchanged, and all the variants in the score, in both this passage and the previous example, could have been modelled on the same continuity draft.

Examples such as these—and there are numerous others—show clearly that a typical single-stave continuity draft was not a fully adequate preparation for writing out a full score, and so it was more or less inevitable that Beethoven would eventually take to sketching in score as a regular procedure. The only surprising thing is that it took him so long to start doing so and that this form of sketching occurred regularly only from 1824 onwards. By this date he was showing even more awareness than before of the problems of part-writing and texture, as is evident from his reported reference to 'a new kind of part-writing' in the late quartets,[9] whereas previously it was mainly just in fugal passages that he had felt it necessary to work out the details of the part-writing in the sketches.

These score sketches for the late quartets show similar types of textural alteration to those in the score of Op. 69. Sometimes the alterations can be seen by comparing one score sketch with a later one for the same passage or with the final version. On other occasions the score sketch itself was altered —perhaps as thoroughly and repeatedly as the score of Op. 69. In the earlier score sketches for a particular movement, three of the four staves were often left completely blank in places, producing little more than a single-stave draft (usually of the Violin 1 part) with occasional suggestions of countermelodies or underlying texture.[10] Thus Beethoven was at this stage still concentrating on horizontal elements such as correct length; the bar numbers in such sketches often do not correspond to those in the final version (there are generally fewer bars), and the harmonic direction may be different in places, just as in an ordinary continuity draft. In later score sketches, however, the horizontal elements were already more or less fixed, and often many bars in

[8] See ibid., p. 64. [9] TDR, v. 318 (cf. TF, p. 982).
[10] See e.g. the score sketch quoted in Winter, *Op. 131*, pp. 260–3.

succession have a direct counterpart in the final version; yet there are still gaps in the accompanying instruments, and also many slight differences from the final version—chiefly in voice-leading, chord inversion, spacing, figuration, register, timbre, octave doublings, and other textural details. With this new dimension of sketching, Beethoven ought to have been able to write out the autograph scores of his late quartets with very little alteration, but as usual things did not work out that way, and the scores of these quartets are liable to have just as many alterations as those of earlier works, if not more. In Op. 131, for example, the variation movement was so extensively altered that one or more complete leaves had to be removed from the score in every variation except one, while what began as the final score of the finale gradually degenerated to the status of a sketch.[11]

When he was composing an orchestral work Beethoven was faced with the additional question of instrumental timbre and orchestration. This too could only be worked out in detail when he came to write out the music in full score, but he seems to have always had some idea of instrumentation from an early stage in the conception of a work, and references to particular instruments or sections of the orchestra are fairly common amongst the sketches. References to instruments are particularly likely to occur in early sketches, for instrumentation, like harmony, was an integral part of an initial concept and needed to be written down before it was forgotten. Hence some ideas that remained little more than disembodied concepts were given quite detailed and sometimes highly unusual instrumentation, as for instance in Ex. 11.7 (SV 185). And when Beethoven was mapping out the main elements of an extended orchestral work he would frequently refer to instruments. Thus in the course of a few pages of sketches for his unfinished Tenth Symphony he mentions stringed instruments, horns, timpani, and (full?) orchestra.[12]

The major part of orchestrating the music, however, had to be done during the course of writing out the full score. When he was ready to write this out his first step was to acquire a sizeable amount of uniform paper —the orchestral scores do not normally display the great variety of paper types found in some of the sketchbooks, in which left-over sheets were used.

Ex. 11.7 SV 185, fo. 83ᵛ

Basso fagot corni fagot corn fagot corni Basso

[11] Winter, *Op. 131*, pp. 213 and 194.
[12] Cooper, 'Tenth Symphony', p. 11.

Once any headings, lists of instruments, and so on had been written in the score, the elements normally entered next were the barlines, as is clear from a number of loose leaves, later used for sketches, that contain a row of disregarded barlines left over from some orchestral score. These preliminary barlines were normally well spaced out—often giving only three bars to a page—to allow room for corrections and the insertion of additional bars. Rather than filling up each bar in turn, Beethoven (once again) preferred to give precedence to horizontal rather than vertical elements, and so he customarily wrote out a single-stave version of a section of the piece before returning to fill in other staves. This single-stave version was the equivalent of a continuity draft in the sketchbook, and was generally closely modelled on one of his sketch drafts. Sometimes it took the form of a cue-staff at the foot of the score, but more often it was simply the main melodic part—in most cases Violin 1. Again it is abandoned scores that illustrate this best. A score of an early version of the *Namensfeier* Overture (Op. 115) was begun probably in 1811 but then abandoned, and many pages of it were subsequently used in August to September that year for sketches for *Die Ruinen von Athen* (SV 184, fos. 3, 9–12, 17, and 20). The music in this abandoned score is entirely confined to single staves (almost invariably for Violin 1, though there are a few bars for the cello/bass), with the remaining staves left blank, but the extant portion of the draft extends to 100 bars. Thus Beethoven clearly sometimes wrote quite a substantial portion of a work in this form before returning to fill in the other instruments. Once such a portion had been completed, however, he would normally fill in the principal accompanying instruments and any countermelodies, and eventually the whole texture would be completed. A good example of a score where some but not all the instruments had been filled in is the one of the unfinished triple concerto in D of 1802.[13]

Like other autograph scores, orchestral scores were liable to be very substantially altered—sometimes by the addition or excision of whole bars, but most often by alterations to the texture and orchestration. An example of this type of alteration is provided by bars 21–6 of the Kyrie of the *Missa solemnis* (see Facsimiles 4 and 5);[14] these bars are particularly convenient to study because the earlier version was cancelled only lightly and the revision written on a separate page rather than being superimposed on the earlier version as happened so often. In the earlier version the top eight staves are occupied by parts for double woodwind, four horns, two trumpets, and timpani; staves 9–12 are for strings, 13–16 for chorus, and 17–20 for solo voices. On stave 20 there are traces of the cue-staff (apparently from a very early version), mostly crossed out.[15] The order of the instruments is the same in the revision except that for some reason the parts for chorus are on staves

[13] See Kramer, 'Concertante'.

[14] A fac. edn. of the whole Kyrie appeared in 1965 with commentary by Wilhelm Virneisel.

[15] See Lester, 'Missa', pp. 429 and 435–6.

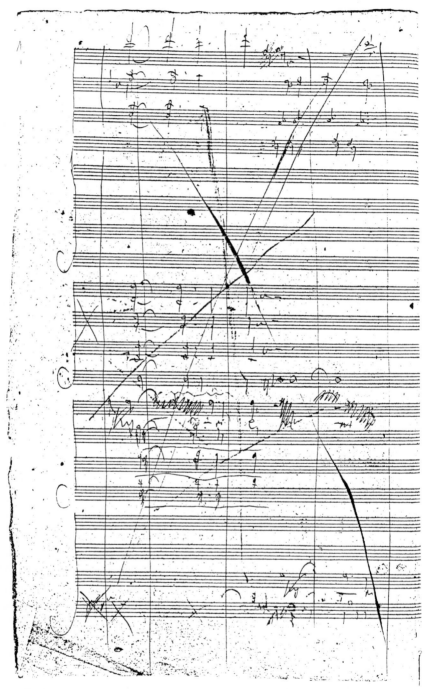

Facsimile 4. *Missa solemnis*, Kyrie, autograph score (Berlin, SPK, Musikabteilung, Beethoven aut. 1), fo. 2ᵛ (bars 21–4)

Facsimile 5. *Missa solemnis*, Kyrie, autograph score (Berlin, SPK, Musikabteilung, Beethoven aut. 1), fo. 3ʳ (bars 21–6)

9–12 and those for strings on staves 13–16. The first version was replaced before Beethoven had filled in all the instruments or the dynamics, and by the time he came to write the second version he realized that there were sufficiently few notes for him to be able to fit six bars on to the page rather than just the four he had originally included.

It will be noticed that the spacings of the woodwind chords are different in the two versions, particularly in bars 23–4, where the oboes are withdrawn in the revised version. The strings have also been rescored, with a much fuller sound, the top note an octave higher, and less emphasis on the tonic. The chorus was originally to have had a unison D, but this idea was almost at once replaced, still within the first version, by a closely spaced chord; in the second version the basses were given the lower octave again, with the tenors and altos also adjusted slightly. The overall effect of all these changes in scoring was to produce a more solid, stable, and massive sound, and therefore one more suited to the concept of an almighty 'Kyrie' (Lord); the difference in effect is caused especially by the revisions to the viola and chorus bass notes, and to a lesser extent by the higher first violin part and the increased contrast resulting from the reduced scoring in bars 23–4. These changes, however, although quite numerous, are all concerned with small details—the sorts of details that could not really be fixed until the full score was being written out. Needless to say, Beethoven also made much more substantial changes elsewhere in the Kyrie, including the addition of whole bars on the very first page.

The example above also illustrates something about Beethoven's notation of dynamics. Although they were eventually written in fairly fully, they were not normally inserted until after the notes—sometimes immediately after but often not till a little while later, as can be seen from their complete absence in the earlier version quoted. He also sometimes omitted dynamics that ought to have been included—for example the trumpets, timpani, and strings are not marked *f* at the beginning of the revised version of the passage quoted (in the chorus parts the *p* is omitted in bar 23, but this may have been deliberate). It was also not unknown for him to alter dynamic marks in an autograph score (usually when other changes were being made to the same passage), as was seen in the case of Op. 69 (see Ex. 11.5).

Dynamic marks can occasionally be found in the sketches, and they played a role even in the initial stages of a composition. But although Beethoven no doubt had some particular dynamic level in mind when he was making a sketch, it was rarely notated unless some special effect was intended. One sketch where dynamics are unusually prevalent is an Adagio in D for an unfinished concerto in the 'Kafka' Miscellany (SV 185, fo. 154ᵛ):[16] *p* or *pp* appears in ten places while one place is marked *ff*. In a note at the end of the draft, Beethoven writes: 'in diesem adagio muss alles durchaus piano gespielt werden, nur ein einziges forte darf vorkommen.' (In this Adagio

---

[16] Transcription in Kerman ed., *Miscellany*, ii. 128.

everything must be played piano throughout; only a single forte may occur.) A similar remark is written beside the one *ff*. Thus the dynamics were inserted more fully than normal because of the very unusual effect desired.

Many of Beethoven's autographs—perhaps most of them—were written out not in a single phase of activity but in several stages over a period of time. Sometimes this is clear from the fact that an exposition and a recapitulation both have matching alterations, indicating that Beethoven must have reached at least as far as the latter before returning to revise the former. Sometimes there are replacement leaves, perhaps of a different paper type, which suggest a later stage of composition. Or it may be evident simply from the number of revisions that a considerable amount of time probably elapsed between the earliest version in the score and the latest. Some scores contain more than one type of ink—for example, in both the Second and the Third piano concertos three different shades of ink can be distinguished,[17] implying at least three stages, and in both cases the three stages were apparently spread over a period of about three years (1798–1801 and 1800–3 respectively). In the autograph of the Violin Concerto there are at least two different shades of ink, as well as some pencil (mostly in sketches) and some red crayon— Beethoven's famous *Rötel*, which he used for adding the finishing touches to a number of scores, including those of his copyists. The *Missa solemnis* was another score that took a long time to complete. A version of it was practically ready by September 1820, but he became bogged down in composing the Agnus and Dona, then held up by checking the huge score; then there were delays over producing manuscript copies and eventually a printed edition, and during all this time he was making minor amendments to the work. A score and copied parts were in existence by May 1822 at the latest,[18] and probably some while earlier; but the official presentation copy was not handed over to Archduke Rudolph until 19 March 1823, and some changes were still made even later.[19] In certain other cases there was even a gap of many years between the beginning of a score and its final completion, as we shall see in some of the bagatelles associated with Op. 119 (see Chapter 16).

It seems to have been Beethoven's normal practice to write out an autograph score making changes along the way as he wrote it, and then to go through the entire work at least once more, correcting any errors such as missing accidentals and making further improvements—mainly, as we have seen, in the texture and figuration, but also sometimes by adding or cancelling bars. Often it was not until this stage that he added what might be called the finishing touches, such as fuller and more precise dynamics, slurs, accents, and other articulation marks. (Like dynamics, articulation marks do occasionally appear in the sketches, but only very infrequently and erratically

---

[17] Block, 'Gray Areas', p. 111; Küthen, *Klavierkonzerte I*, pp. 39–40.
[18] A-1076.   [19] TF, p. 819.

—one sketch of a work might indicate a few slurs or staccatos, but a revised sketch might omit them to save time.)

Usually the full score was written out only once by Beethoven, as he himself observed: 'I merely jot down certain ideas . . . and when I have completed the whole in my head, everything is written down, but only once'.[20] When only the one score existed he was naturally very concerned for its safety, and on one occasion he began to panic when, after lending part of the score of the Quartet Op. 132 to Holz, he started worrying that Holz might have lost it. He wrote to his nephew Karl: 'I am in a mortal fright about the quartet. For Holz has taken away the third, fourth, fifth and sixth movements. . . . What a terrible misfortune if he has lost the manuscript. . . . The ideas for it are only jotted down on small scraps of paper; and I shall never be able to compose the whole quartet again in the same way.'[21] This shows clearly not only that there was only one written score at the time but also that he had no complete recollection of the work in his head. His reference in the previous quotation to completing a work in his head therefore cannot mean that he knew every note from memory, but just that he had a rough idea of the outline of the whole work before he wrote out the score.

In some cases, however, more than one autograph score survives for at least part of a piece. This may simply be because one or two pages of the original score became so messy with corrections, or so far from his final intentions, that they had to be replaced; on other occasions, however, whole movements and even complete works were written out a second time by the composer, either because he wanted very extensive revisions or because he wanted a clean copy but for some reason was unable to enlist the help of a copyist. If the changes were extensive, scholars distinguish between a first and a second version, as in the Quartet Op. 18 No. 1, where significant alterations were made to the harmony, melodic lines, phrase structure, and especially texture in the later version;[22] but if the differences are fairly insignificant one usually refers just to a composing score (or *Urschrift*) and a fair copy (or *Reinschrift*). On occasion there were even more than two scores, as in the case of the Second Piano Concerto (see Chapter 17). But once the final score was completed—whether this was the only score, a score with replacement leaves, or even a complete *Reinschrift*—Beethoven's activity in composing the work should normally have come to an end, his only remaining tasks being to arrange for publication and perhaps performances.

The practical steps he had to take in connection with publication, including supervising and correcting manuscript copies, negotiating with publishers, and later proof-reading an engraved copy, have been described in detail by Alan Tyson,[23] but they have little to do with the creative process.

---

[20] A-1060.　　　[21] A-1410.　　　[22] See Levy, *Choices*.

[23] In Arnold and Fortune, *Companion*, pp. 459–89; see also Tyson, 'Copyists'.

What concerns us here is how much compositional activity sometimes continued after one might expect it to have stopped, with Beethoven continuing to add finishing touches as if never fully satisfied with what he had written. He knew that perfection was something to be aimed for but never achieved, and so it was theoretically possible for him to go on indefinitely finding ways of making improvements.

Reference has already been made to his correction of copyists' manuscripts. Some of his works were engraved by the printers direct from his autograph scores,[24] but often a copyist's score was used as the *Stichvorlage* (printer's copy). Before this score was sent to the printers Beethoven used to look through it checking for mistakes, and some of these *überprüfte Abschriften* (corrected copies) have numerous alterations by him, for example those of 'Ah! perfido' (Op. 65), the Fifth Symphony, the cello sonatas Op. 102, and *Opferlied* (Op. 121b).[25] Unlike the autograph scores and sketchbooks, no *überprüfte Abschriften* have yet been published in facsimile (despite their obvious value as aids to establishing authentic texts), and little study has been made of the alterations Beethoven made to them. But as well as correcting copying errors he sometimes made minor improvements such as amplifying the notation by inserting extra slurs and dynamics.[26] Thus although there is rarely any change of substance in such cases, compositional activity clearly persisted well beyond the autograph score.

One type of alteration made surprisingly often at a very late stage was the addition of trombones in certain passages of orchestral works. These were added almost as an afterthought on at least three occasions—in *Christus am Oelberge*, the *Missa solemnis*, and the Ninth Symphony. In the case of *Christus*, the evidence comes not only from copyists' scores but from Ferdinand Ries, who visited Beethoven at five o'clock in the morning on the day of the first performance and found him in bed writing out trombone parts that were actually used later that day.[27] In the second movement of the Ninth Symphony the trombone parts were also written out on separate sheets after the rest of the score, while in the *Missa* they were added in certain places only after Archduke Rudolph's copy had been written out and presented.[28]

Occasionally the last-minute changes were much more sweeping, with whole movements being swept away even after the first performance (though before publication), as in the case of the slow movement of the 'Waldstein' Sonata and the finale of the Quartet Op. 130; in each of these the movement replaced was later published separately—as the 'Andante favori' (WoO 57) and the *Grosse Fuge* (Op. 133) respectively. And it was only after several trial runs of the 'Eroica' that Beethoven decided to retain the repeat in the first movement.[29] One of the most remarkable late alterations was the insertion

[24] See Arnold and Fortune, *Companion*, p. 468.   [27] Tyson, 'Christus', p. 559.

[25] KH, pp. 154, 158–9, 283, 355.   [28] TF, pp. 329, 819.

[26] Tyson, 'Op. 104', pp. 162–3.   [29] TDR, ii. 625.

of the first bar of the slow movement of the 'Hammerklavier' Sonata. Again Ferdinand Ries was a witness: Beethoven sent the manuscript copy of the score to Ries in London in January 1819 indicating he wanted it published in England (as well as Vienna) within three months, and he sent a long list of corrections in March; but then on 16 April he sent a further letter including the additional bar and saying that this had 'still to be inserted'.[30] Fortunately the music had still not been printed, and so the original editions all include the extra bar.

On certain other occasions, however, the music had already been engraved by the time the change reached the printer, and Beethoven had to try and arrange for the plates to be altered before the music went into circulation. This seems to have happened regarding bar 105 of the first movement of the 'Waldstein' Sonata, where an F♭ in the autograph was engraved in the printed edition before being changed to F♮ in the plates, as can be deduced from marks at this point in the original edition.[31] With the Fifth Symphony Beethoven was even later with his final revisions, and they missed the first impression of the first edition altogether, only being incorporated in subsequent printings.[32] The same sort of thing may have happened with some of his works published by Steiner in Vienna. Beethoven was a frequent visitor to Steiner's shop, and when looking through newly published works he sometimes spotted errors which were then put right at a subsequent print run; it is possible that he also occasionally made improvements as well as corrections at this stage.[33] Other special cases worth mentioning here are the Second Piano Concerto, for which Beethoven's final thoughts came too late to be incorporated into the printed edition (see Chapter 17), and the Fourth Piano Concerto, of which he gave a performance with a more decorated piano part than the one in the already published edition but never arranged for publication of this later version.[34]

Problems sometimes arise where he made last-minute alterations after copies had been made of an autograph score—particularly if copies were being sent to two different publishers simultaneously. Sometimes the two copies do not agree with each other and with the autograph, thus creating formidable problems for modern editors trying to establish the correct version. In fact in some cases it is doubtful whether one can refer to a final, correct verion as such. Two works which have proved particularly intractable in this respect are the Violin Concerto and the last piano sonata (Op. 111);[35] in both works Beethoven's final intentions are at times somewhat ambiguous, and the practicalities of his situation prevented him from realizing all his intentions within the confines of a single manuscript.

[30] A-935, A-939, A-940.   [31] Cooper, 'Waldstein', p. 189.
[32] Brandenburg, 'Fifth Symphony', p. 148.   [33] See Tyson, 'Steiner'.
[34] N-II, pp. 74–8, and Badura-Skoda, 'Klavierkonzert'.
[35] See e.g. Tyson, 'Violin', and Timbrell, 'Op. 111'.

Once a work had been published he normally allowed it to stand unchanged, but he often expressed dissatisfaction with his earlier works[36] and evidently saw numerous faults in some of them. Commentators today sometimes wonder why he did not amend his early piano works to take account of the enlarged compass of later pianos; the reason seems to be that he saw many other faults besides the awkward figuration that had sometimes resulted from a restricted compass, and had he begun revising, the whole operation would have taken some considerable time and would really have necessitated a complete new edition of all his works. He did indeed often toy with the idea of producing just such a revised complete edition. The first mention of it appeared as early as 22 October 1803, when he stated: 'I shall soon make full announcement of a collection of my works to be made under my supervision and after a severe revision.'[37] The project was alluded to in numerous subsequent letters to publishers, and towards the end of his life he became very eager to carry it out, but nothing ever came of it.

Nevertheless there were two ways in which he did return to certain works long after publication—not so much to amend them as to add more precise indications of his intentions: cadenzas for concertos, and metronome marks. In his early years Beethoven expected performers to improvise their own cadenzas, but later on he sometimes wrote cadenzas out for particular players —mainly Archduke Rudolph. About 1809 he wrote cadenzas for all his first four piano concertos and the piano version of the Violin Concerto; in fact three alternative cadenzas are known for both the First Piano Concerto and the first movement of the Fourth. Each was composed after the relevant concerto had been published, but none of the cadenzas themselves were printed during his lifetime.[38]

The metronome, or rather its predecessor, the chronometer, was invented by Maelzel in about 1812. Up till then Beethoven's efforts to overcome the problem of indicating speeds were unsatisfactory, as can be seen in a letter of 17 July 1812 concerning the Mass in C: 'At the beginning of the Gloria I have altered C to ₵ time signature, thus altering the tempo; and that is the way the time was indicated at first. A bad performance at which the tempo was too fast induced me to do this [i.e. to make the initial change to C]. Well, as I had not seen the Mass for a long time, this point struck me at once and I saw that unfortunately a thing like that has to be left to chance . . .'.[39] The invention of the metronome meant that tempo no longer had to be 'left to chance', and an announcement was published on 13 October 1813: 'Herr Beethoven looks upon this invention as a welcome means with which to secure the performance of his brilliant compositions in all places in the tempos conceived by him, which to his regret have so often been misunderstood.'[40] Eventually he published metronome marks for many of his

---

[36] See e.g. TF, p. 871.
[37] TF, p. 339.
[38] KH, pp. 34–150, *passim*.
[39] A-375.
[40] TF, p. 544.

earlier works, including the first eight symphonies.[41] Some of his later works were also published complete with metronome marks, especially during the period 1817–19, but the marks never became an integral part of his creative process like dynamic and tempo marks; thus they do not appear in his sketches and were often added as a kind of afterthought. The score of the Ninth Symphony was sent to the publishers (after several delays) in January 1825 still without metronome marks, which were not sent until nearly two years later (13 October 1826),[42] by which time the symphony was already in print. Deciding the precise figures seems to have been a slow and rather mechanical activity—especially as Beethoven had such an abhorrence of figures in general—and he does not seem to have regarded it as part of the main creative process, even though he had a rough idea of what speeds he wanted.

It is clear from the sorts of compositional activity outlined in the present chapter that Beethoven habitually paid great attention to detail in his compositions, and would frequently notice possible improvements in places where a lesser composer would have been more than satisfied already. He was in no hurry to rush works into print, even during periods when he badly needed the extra income, and he would only publish works when he was fully satisfied with them. Although once they were published they were left unchanged, this does not mean that he remained satisfied with them for long. As well as his own statements of plans for a revised edition, several contemporaries report him in later life expressing dissatisfaction with his earlier works—particularly the Septet.[43] Works that are today so often regarded as perfect masterpieces were apparently considered by Beethoven to be full of imperfections and in need of sometimes severe revision; these revisions failed to be carried out only because he was too preoccupied with other matters.

---

[41] N-I, pp. 126–37; N-II, pp. 519–21; see also Stadlen, 'Metronome', for a more general discussion of Beethoven's metronome marks, which are not always fully reliable.

[42] A-1345, A-1535.   [43] TF, pp. 620, 684, 871.

III

STAGES IN THE
CREATIVE PROCESS

12

First Conceptions:
Piano Sonata in D Minor, Op. 31 No. 2

IN this part of the book we shall explore in detail a variety of compositional problems that were liable to confront Beethoven in the course of
composing individual works. Such a study cannot effectively be made with
just a single work, since not all works presented the same problems. In most
cases, too, not all the sketches survive, and some compositional problems do
not show up clearly in the extant sketches for a particular work, while others
seem very conspicuous. For example, the great wealth of sketches for the late
quartets impedes any overall view of a work's evolution, but it facilitates a
study of the various aspects of a particular question such as the number of
movements Beethoven was planning for the work. Conversely in the early
sketches one can sometimes trace the overall growth of a complete work
relatively easily, even though detailed study of the creation of individual
features is impossible because of insufficient sketches. Thus by careful selection of sketches from a number of different works, it is possible to put
together a picture of the pattern of evolution of Beethoven's compositions
in general which is fuller and more wide-ranging than any that could emerge
from just a single work.

Accordingly we shall examine sketches for six different works. These are:
the Second Piano Concerto (*c.* 1787–1801), the Piano Sonata in D minor, Op.
31 No. 2 (1802), the *Egmont* Overture (1810), *Meeresstille und glückliche Fahrt*
(1813–15), the late bagatelles—principally Op. 119 (1822)—and the String
Quartet in B flat Op. 130 (1825). They will not be discussed in chronological
order, however. In each case a particular problem from a different phase of
the creative process will provide a focus, ranging from the very earliest
conception of a work to its final assembly in score. The six chapters will
therefore be arranged so that they reflect the growth of composition from the
earliest to the latest stages of their evolution, while at the same time revealing
something of the range of compositional problems that was likely to
confront Beethoven at different periods of his life and in different types of
work.

We shall begin by examining the very first ideas for a work, and how those
ideas might be modified without being destroyed (Op. 31 No. 2). Chapter 13
investigates what happens when Beethoven approaches the later movements
of a work (Op. 130) without any clear idea of their nature; we are therefore

still concerned with initial conceptions, in a situation where Beethoven has a choice of several very different possibilities as to how to continue. Chapter 14 (on 'Meeresstille') shows him mapping out a complete movement and gradually filling in the details, expanding and intensifying them melodically and harmonically; it also shows how the composition of vocal music presents special problems not found in instrumental music. Chapter 15 focuses on the problem of the joins between the various sections of a movement (*Egmont* Overture); these joins could only be tidied up once the main sections had been extensively drafted. Next we shall investigate a group of pieces that were sketched in some detail before being abandoned, only to be taken up again many years later and polished up for publication (Bagatelles Op. 119 Nos. 1–6). And finally we shall consider the situation where a work was completed but was still unsatisfactory, and was gradually revised over a period of several years before eventually being published (Second Piano Concerto). It will become clear from these individual studies that Beethoven always adhered to the broad pattern of compositional methods described in the preceding chapters, but that the details within this pattern varied enormously, with each work presenting new problems and challenges peculiar to itself.

Like so many of Beethoven's works, the three piano sonatas of Op. 31 were apparently written in response to a specific request—in this case from the publisher Hans Georg Nägeli of Zürich for material for his series *Répertoire des clavecinistes*.[1] The request probably reached Beethoven about the end of May 1802, and he set to work on the sonatas fairly promptly, completing the first two (in G major and D minor) during the summer and the third (in E flat) slightly later. Even before he received the request, however, he had as usual been noting down in his sketchbook ideas for possible future works, so that when he started on the set he already had some material available for development. Thus Nägeli's request, like many similar ones, can be regarded as a stimulus to Beethoven to work out sonata ideas that he already had in mind to develop, rather than the very first idea for a new work.

The sketchbook in use during the first half of 1802 was the 'Kessler' (SV 263). Although most of the sketches for Op. 31 No. 2 were made after the book was finished and were written on loose leaves now lost, the earliest ones can be found in the sketchbook; and the book is an unusually complete record of Beethoven's sketching during this period, for all its ninety-six folios still survive intact, and there is no evidence that any significant amount of sketching was being done elsewhere at the same time: for example, the violin sonatas Op. 30, which occupy the central portion of the sketchbook (fos. 37–81), have not been located in any sketch sources outside 'Kessler'.[2]

---

[1] Brandenburg ed., *Kessler*, introduction, p. 16; JTW, p. 126.

[2] Kramer, 'Op. 30', pp. 25–6. For complete transcription and fac. of 'Kessler', see Brandenburg ed., *Kessler*.

All Beethoven's earliest ideas for the D minor Sonata are therefore likely to have been jotted down here if they were jotted down at all. Chief amongst these initial ideas are the following, listed in the order in which they now appear in the sketchbook:

1. fo. 3ʳ staves 5–16: ideas for three movements, two in A minor and one in A major, probably intended for a sonata in A minor;
2. fo. 65ᵛ staves 3–16: an extended plan for the first movement, transcribed in full by Gustav Nottebohm;[3]
3. fo. 66ʳ staves 3–14: a series of concept sketches for keyboard movements in B flat major, D major, and D minor;
4. fo. 68ʳ staves 3–4: an eight-bar fragment of a keyboard piece in E flat that contains figuration resembling the finale of Op. 31 No. 2;
5. fo. 89ᵛ staves 9–16: some ideas probably intended for a sonata in C;
6. fo. 90ᵛ staves 3–16: an extended plan for a D minor sonata movement, with a coda in 6/8 metre;
7. fo. 91ᵛ staves 5–6: a four-bar fragment in 3/4 beginning in C major;
8. fo. 95ʳ stave 15 – fo. 95ᵛ stave 13: an extended sketch for the exposition of a movement in A minor labelled 'Sonata 2da';
9. fo. 96ᵛ staves 1–4: a deleted sketch intended for part of the C major slow movement of Op. 31 No. 1.

The first of these consists of a sixteen-bar sketch (fo. 3ʳ staves 5–8) for a Presto in A minor, an Allegro in the same key (staves 9–12, 15–16), and a concept in A major probably intended for a slow movement (staves 13–14). Overall the synopsis sketch has little connection with Op. 31 No. 2 except that it is for a multi-movement piano work (i.e. presumably a sonata) in a minor key. But the main theme of the Allegro (Ex. 12.1) contains an idea that was to resurface several times in various keys and guises during the sketchbook before emerging in the finale of Op. 31 No. 2. The essence of the idea is a theme beginning with a series of repeated notes (usually the tonic) on strong beats, each preceded by some kind of anacrusis, and usually with some arpeggiated accompaniment; but the details vary with each appearance. Its next appearance (Ex. 12.2: fo. 68ʳ staves 3–4) is as a curious eight-bar theme in E flat, complete with pedal markings, repeats, and even some fingering.

Ex. 12.1 SV 263, fo. 3ʳ

---

[3] Nottebohm, *Skizzenbuch*, pp. 27–8.

Ex. 12.2 SV 263, fo. 68ʳ

The metre is now 3/4 (in Op. 31 No. 2 it is notated as 3/8), and the shape of the anacrusis is identical to that in the finale of the sonata.

At this stage Beethoven was working intensively on the violin sonatas Op. 30, but these were nearly finished by 22 April 1802, for on that day his brother Carl offered them to Breitkopf & Härtel.[4] Once they were out of the way Beethoven turned his attention to his next major project—the two sets of piano variations Opp. 34 and 35, which appear in the 'Kessler' Sketchbook from fo. 82ᵛ onwards (Op. 30 was finished on fo. 81ʳ). But before he had made much progress with these the offer from Nägeli arrived, and he laid aside the variations to work on the sonatas Op. 31. Whether he did this as soon as the offer arrived (about the end of May) or whether he waited until the price had been agreed, about two months later, is uncertain, but his change in direction is very evident in the sketchbook from fo. 89ᵛ onwards. On the lower part of this page are several sketches apparently for a piano sonata in C major, while on the opposite page (fo. 90ʳ) are more ideas for piano pieces—in A major, E flat major, another idea in C major, and an Andante movement in E minor. Thus up to this point there was simply a variety of preliminary ideas, with C major seeming the most likely key for the first sonata in the set.

As was seen earlier (Chapter 9), when planning such a set of three sonatas Beethoven was customarily guided by certain principles for creating maximum contrast between them; one of these principles was that of the three works one should be in a minor key and that there should be at least one flat key and one sharp key in the set. Thus if the first sonata was to be in C major it would rule out A minor for the minor-key one; and so instead of developing the A minor ideas sketched on fo. 3ʳ, Beethoven turned to D minor on fo. 90ᵛ. The top two staves of the page consist of a concept sketch for the Variations Op. 34 that was probably entered earlier, but the rest of it consists of a fairly detailed synopsis sketch for the whole of the first movement of a sonata in D minor (Ex. 12.3). The sketch shows the main

[4] JTW, p. 126. This offer was thought until recently to have referred to Op. 31; cf. KH, p. 81.

Ex. 12.3 SV 263, fo. 90^v

|staves 3 – 4|

|5 – 6|

m.g. |7 – 8|

erster Theil in B

etc

Schlu|ss|

2da parte colla repetizione e la prima senza |9 – 10|

in a moll [sic]

etc

Ex. 12.3 (Cont.)

corner-stones of the movement—principal themes, key centres, and so on
—but it omits the transitional material.

  The movement itself, though in a very unusual form, is closely related to
the first movement of Op. 31 No. 2 in many ways. It begins with a
'Mannheim rocket' motif accompanied by a repeated dominant internal
pedal; it continues with a descending quaver pattern leading on to a
dominant chord, and an answering phrase completes the theme. What
Beethoven intended next is uncertain, but a possible continuation would be
the opening figure transferred to the left-hand part. This possibility must
certainly have occurred to him at some stage, for in this form the passage
would be very similar to bars 21–2 of the final version of Op. 31 No. 2: in

these bars the six-note arpeggio motif of Ex. 12.3 has simply been reduced to its first four notes, and the repeated dominant replaced by an oscillating triplet figure (Ex. 12.4).

The next part of the movement to be sketched was the second subject. Beethoven first decided the key, with the words 'erster Theil in B' indicating that the exposition was to end in B flat; then he squeezed in a theme in that key, labelled 'm.g.' (*mitte Gedanke*)—a term he often used to denote the second subject.[5] The idea of taking the exposition to B flat is interesting, for this would have been the earliest sonata exposition in which Beethoven closed in a key other than the dominant or relative major (although he had recently done so in the Quintet Op. 29). In the final version of this sonata the second subject is in the dominant, but the use of B flat major was transferred to the slow movement. And the idea of moving from D minor to B flat major within a sonata-form movement was resurrected some twenty years later in his next big D minor sonata-form movement—the first movement of the Ninth Symphony.

The exposition in the sketch on fo. 90[v] ends with repeated B flat chords, which are developed after the double bar into A minor, another key whose position was to be shifted in the final version, this time from development section to second subject. These repeated-chord figures anticipate, and indeed help to explain, a similar idea in the recapitulation of the final version (bars 159–68). In this final version the chords seem to have little relevance to the rest of the movement (unless it be to the repeated minims at the end of the exposition), but they can now be seen as a borrowing from this sketch, where, as in the final version, they lead into rapid arpeggios. An interesting feature of the left-hand accompaniment to the arpeggios in the sketch is its anticipation of a similar motif in the first subject of the *Egmont* Overture.

The beginning of the development section is marked '2da parte colla repetizione e la prima senza'. The term '2da parte' refers to the development and recapitulation together (without the coda), and the way the whole phrase is laid out suggests that Beethoven decided straight away that the second part should be repeated—a relatively unusual feature in his sonata-form movements and one not eventually used in Op. 31 No. 2—and then later made a note that the first part should be without repeat. This idea, although

Ex. 12.4 Op. 31 No. 2. i

---

[5] See e.g. fo. 3[r] stave 15 and fo. 74[v] stave 1 of the same sketchbook.

extremely unconventional, was indeed put into effect in his next minor-key sonata, the 'Appassionata' (Op. 57), in the finale of which only the second part is repeated.

The development section in the sketch leads to a half close in D minor. Then comes a remarkably bold stroke, at the point in the movement where Beethoven was customarily most daring—immediately before the recapitulation. A slow section in 3/4 time and marked 'dolce', beginning in D major, is inserted before the resumption of the Allegro. The new theme is based on the motif immediately preceding it, but it is unrelated to the rest of the movement; it acts as a much-needed breathing-space between the incessant forward motion of the previous music and the return of the allegro tempo (marked 'dopo l'allegro di nove'). This leads to the end of stave 12 on the page, and the remaining four staves are taken up with a sketch in 6/8 time. This is presumably intended for the coda of the movement since it is a transformation of the opening theme—a technique Beethoven employed in certain other codas (see, for example, the finale of the Third Piano Concerto). This transformed theme begins a 'closed' binary form that leads from D minor to F major in the first part and then back to D minor in the second; the presence of double bars implies that both parts would be repeated, although repeats are not marked. In the final version there is no such elaborate coda (the coda is instead one of Beethoven's shortest); but the idea of a closed binary form within a coda was later resurrected—once again in the finale of Op. 57. The theme itself, meanwhile, is close to that of the Bagatelle Op. 119 No. 5, the only sketch for which appears earlier in the 'Kessler' Sketchbook on fo. 59^r.

Taken as a whole, the sketch on fo. 90^r could be realized into a most impressive movement, and with comparatively little effort since so much detail is already present. It contains many novel features, which clearly point the way towards Beethoven's 'second period' and which in several cases were actually taken up in later works such as the 'Appassionata' Sonata, *Egmont*, and the Ninth Symphony. Yet the movement contains inherent weaknesses that could not easily be removed through Beethoven's ordinary sketching methods: the opening 'Mannheim rocket' is far too conventional, looking backwards to Op. 2 No. 1 and beyond, rather than forwards; the second subject is rather lightweight and would have difficulty sustaining melodic flow and rhythmic drive in the kind of movement Beethoven obviously had in mind; and the slow interruption in D major had to be made more relevant, somehow, to the rest of the movement. The obvious solutions to these problems only throw up further difficulties: if the slow section in the major is prepared by adding a similar slow passage at the beginning the key structure is upset, since a fast movement in D minor cannot begin with a slow, lyrical introduction in D major,[6] and anyway the slow passage would

---

[6] The 'Kreutzer' Sonata (Op. 47) is the exception that proves the rule: the slow introduction stays in the major for only four bars before moving to the tonic minor, and it does not return at the end of the development section.

still not relate to the fast sections; having a slow introduction would also destroy the element of surprise—the unexpected lyricism—that Beethoven desired at the start of the recapitulation; and rejecting the 'Mannheim rocket' opening completely would remove the whole starting-point of the movement he was trying to create.

Beethoven was clearly immediately aware of the difficulties, for he did not develop the movement through any further sketches on the remaining six leaves of the sketchbook. Instead, after making another brief piano sketch in C major on fo. 91^v staves 5–6 (again foreshadowing the finale of Op. 31 No. 2, at least in the rhythm and the left-hand figuration: see Ex. 12.5), he began detailed work on a different sonata—Op. 31 No. 1 in G major. These G major ideas, which borrow a motif originally sketched for string quartet a few pages earlier (fo. 88^r), are immediately subjected to detailed sketching such as is usually found only for works that were later completed. Hence it seems that Beethoven decided immediately that this was to be Sonata No. 1 of the set; and as the sketches incorporate a rhythm and character somewhat similar to those in the tentative C major sketches of fo. 89^v, it is clear that C major had now been abandoned as a possible key for one of the sonatas. Instead it was taken up the following year in his next piano sonata—the 'Waldstein'.

While working on Op. 31 No. 1, the sketches for which continue to the end of the sketchbook, Beethoven as usual looked ahead from time to time, noting down possible ideas for the other two sonatas in the set. With G major having replaced C as the key for the first sonata, A minor was once again available as a possible key for the second, and an extended sketch in this key appears on fo. 95^{r-v}, actually headed 'Sonata 2da'. The main theme (fo. 95^r staves 15–16: see Ex. 12.6) is yet another variant of the earlier A minor sonata sketch (fo. 3^r) that foreshadows the finale of Op. 31 No. 2: it now has the same shape of anacrusis as the final version of the theme, but in the sketch there is an additional appoggiatura on the strong beat and the metre is 6/8.

The key of the third sonata, E flat major, was fixed even before Beethoven had decided on the order of the three sonatas, as is evidenced by some sketches in that key on fos. 93^r and 95^v: both show affinities with Op. 31 No. 3, the former recalling a motif in the second movement and the latter the

Ex. 12.5 SV 263, fo. 91^v

Ex. 12.6 SV 263, fo. 95^r

Sonata 2da

metre and mood of the first movement, but both are labelled 'Sonata 2'.
Beethoven seems to have attached no special significance to the order of the
pieces in a set such as this; although there are exceptions (such as the quartets
Op. 18), the published order usually followed the order in which the pieces
were composed, and this is certainly true of Op. 31.

When Beethoven reached the end of the 'Kessler' Sketchbook it still
contained some blank spaces on certain pages. There were probably no
completely blank pages left by this time, but some were nearly blank: on fo.
85^r only one of the sixteen staves had been used, and on fos. 42^v–43^r only
three and four staves respectively had been used, leaving an opening with
twenty-five staves that are still blank today. Another large blank space was
on fos. 65^v–66^r: the top two staves of fo. 65^v had been filled with a piano
sketch in D (perhaps an idea for a finale for a triple concerto in D that he had
been sketching on fos. 38–42), and the top two on fo. 66^r contained an early
sketch for a replacement finale for Op. 30 No. 1 (a movement worked out
later in the book), but the rest of the opening was blank. When he had
originally reached this point in the book (i.e. fo. 65^r) he had already finished
sketching the first three movements of Op. 30 No. 2 and was about to begin
detailed work on the finale; for this purpose he preferred to begin on a
completely fresh opening, and so he turned over to fo. 66^v, leaving blank all
but the top two staves of fos. 65^v–66^r, which must have been filled earlier,
until the sketchbook had been completed. Once he had reached the end of
the book, however, he returned to this space and filled it with ideas for Op.
31 No. 2: on the left-hand page he wrote a synopsis sketch for the first
movement (Ex. 12.7), comparable in scope to the earlier D minor synopsis
sketch on fo. 90^v but now bearing a clear resemblance to the final version,
while on the right-hand page he noted down a series of ideas for later
movements.[7]

The first-movement sketch, once again headed 'Sonata 2da', was clearly
intended to supersede other possible 'second sonatas' in E flat major and A
minor sketched near the end of the book and mentioned above. Although it
gives the appearance of being a sudden inspiration—a kind of written-down
improvisation that formed his very first thoughts on the movement—careful

---

[7] Reasons why this must have been the order of events are given in Cooper, 'Op. 31 No.
2', on which the present chapter is based.

examination shows that it is simply a thorough reworking of the material of the synopsis sketch on fo. 90ᵛ. The latter, as noted earlier, had several inherent weaknesses that led to it being laid aside, but it was now revived in a different shape with the weaknesses eliminated. In fact the end-result, though familiar enough today, is a model of how to solve several conflicting compositional problems without compromising the essence of the original idea; and the main solutions to the problems are already present in Ex. 12.7, after which it would have been simply a matter of Beethoven sketching in the details in his normal way.

As can be seen in Ex. 12.7, the compositional problems posed earlier were solved as follows. The slow passage at the beginning of the recapitulation in the first sketch could be anticipated, but still appear unexpected, by introducing only a fragment of it at the opening; the problem of key structure could be solved, while keeping the major-key element, by using a dominant chord, A major, instead of the tonic, for the slow sections; and these could be related to the 'allegro' sections by transferring the 'Mannheim rocket' motif itself to them. This last change was surely Beethoven's master-stroke, for by it the theme becomes completely transfigured, now veiled by the sustaining pedal and beginning deep in the bass clef in the final version. The answering phrase, though showing the same descending contour as in the first sketch, is now more animated, with an idea foreshadowed by an isolated sketch from the tentative C major sonata on fo. 89ᵛ stave 15 (Ex. 12.8) and by a rejected idea from Op. 30 No. 2 (fo. 55ʳ stave 9: Ex. 12.9). Meanwhile the introduction of recitative into the recapitulation in the sketch was a highly original way of prolonging the slow passage with a logical continuation of the main four-note motif.

All these changes altered the dramatic balance of the movement, thereby forcing other changes. There was by this time a series of interruptions to the forward drive of the movement, and a lyrical, relatively static second subject in B flat would have resulted in too many such interruptions, as well as too many references to major keys. Thus it was necessary to scrap the original second subject, keeping the key of B flat for the slow movement, and to replace it with a non-distinctive, rather unlyrical motif in A minor in the same mood and character as the main part of the movement. In the final version the second subject can hardly be called a theme at all, and it is significant that Beethoven made no attempt to sketch a second subject on fo. 65ᵛ of the sketchbook. He simply noted 'A moll erster Theil' to indicate that the exposition would end in A minor, and he actually sketched a compressed version of the entire recapitulation without any sign of a second subject. The extended 6/8 coda, by now another unwanted interruption to the rhythmic drive of the movement, also disappeared, replaced by just a few bars of the tonic chord.

Thus the sketch on fo. 90ᵛ can be seen as the main source of the D minor sonata, and the one on fo. 65ᵛ as a replacement for it, in which all the

Ex. 12.7 SV 263, fo. 65ᵛ

Ex. 12.7 (Cont.)

compositional problems posed have been resolved. The basic character of the
movement is still the same, as is the shape of the first four notes of the main
theme; even the layout of the sketch, in the form of a synopsis of the
movement, is retained. But the details have been rearranged and the interruptions to the moto perpetuo redistributed, so that the revised version is almost
unrecognizable as the same piece. In fact the only passage that remained
unchanged for the second sketch was the end of the development, with its
repeated minim As and its implied I–V–I–V harmony—and even this
appears altered and at half-speed in the corresponding place in the final
version (bars 134–8: Ex. 12.10).

The ideas for later movements sketched on fo. 66ʳ are much less advanced
than those for the first movement on the opposite page, and at first sight they
look like just a miscellany of ideas for keyboard pieces, connected with no
particular work. But it must be remembered that when Beethoven began

Ex. 12.8 SV 263, fo. 89ᵛ

Ex. 12.9 SV 263, fo. 55ʳ

Ex. 12.10 Op. 31 No. 2. i

sketching a multi-movement work he would often, despite starting with the first movement, jot down ideas for later movements at a relatively early stage. Thus concept sketches for all the movements are frequently found before the detailed work on the first movement; presumably he felt it unwise to proceed too far with the opening movement until he had at least some idea of what was to follow. This approach can be seen, for example, in other parts of the 'Kessler' Sketchbook itself, in the sketches for Op. 30 No. 1 and Op. 31 No. 1.

When viewed in this light, the sketches on fo. 66ʳ make perfect sense, for not only are they all in keys that might appear in later movements of a D minor sonata (B flat major, D major, and D minor itself), but they also show other features suggesting later movements of this sonata. The first sketch (Ex. 12.11), in 3/4 time and B flat, has the words 'alla menuetto' beside it. But this is surely no minuet—least of all a fast Beethovenian one—for its opening theme, bounding unevenly up the keyboard, would sound distinctly comical, if not ludicrous, played in minuet time. The explanation for the words 'alla menuetto' lies in the fact that they are situated at the end of the

Ex. 12.11 SV 263, fo. 66ʳ

sketch: the B flat sketch is for a slow movement, which is to be immediately followed by a minuet. The connections between the sketch and the slow movement of Op. 31 No. 2 are in fact numerous: both begin with a B flat major arpeggio; both consist of dialogue between low and high pitches; in both cases the low pitches are essentially chordal while the high ones use conjunct melodic motion; and both have alternating tonic and dominant harmony.

Although this sketch was intended for the slow movement, it also shows a remarkably close relationship to the earlier first-movement sketch on fo. 90^v (Ex. 12.3): both sketches begin with a six-note arpeggio starting on the tonic, followed by a descending phrase that ends with an appoggiatura on to the leading-note in bar 4 (on fo. 66^v, bar 5 on fo. 90^v), so that the sketch on fo. 66^r could be described as a major-key variant of the other theme. The second phrase in Ex. 12.11 is almost identical to the beginning of the second subject (in the same key) of Ex. 12.3, indicating that Beethoven intended to transfer not only the key but also some of the thematic material from the second subject to the slow movement. Thus he planned from the outset to make the slow movement very closely related to the first movement in its opening melodic shape, and despite the changes later made to both, the close relationship remained. Out of over a hundred piano sonata movements, these are the only two that begin with an arpeggiando chord; another obvious relation between the opening themes in the two movements in the final version is the descent to an ornamented feminine cadence on the dominant at the end of the first sentence of each (first movement, bar 6; second movement, bar 8) —a relationship already foreshadowed in the sketches quoted above.

The remaining sketches on fo. 66^r seem from details of their layout to have been written down in the order in which they appear on the page, but they do not show the movements in the right order and were probably not written at a single sitting, since they are in varied styles of handwriting. Staves 6–7 represent the start of the minuet announced on stave 3; staves 8–9 show another idea for the Adagio; staves 10–11 contain two sketches in D minor presumably intended for the finale; and staves 12–14 contain yet further ideas for the Adagio, this time somewhat more developed than before.

The very short sketch on staves 8–9 is labelled 'adgo' and is in 3/4 time but otherwise shows no very close relationship to any other sketch or to the final version; but the other Adagio sketch, beginning on stave 12, is of much greater interest (Ex. 12.12). It too is in slow triple time, and although now notated in 6/8, with each bar corresponding to two of the final version, it shows considerable progress over the first sketch. The first two bars are already close to the first four of the final version, especially in the high-pitched answering motifs, now rising instead of falling. The second of these motifs uses the notes c′′′–d′′′–e♭′′′ (with a deleted a″ upbeat), as in bar 12 of the final version, rather than a″–b♭″–c′′′ as in bar 4; the latter can therefore be seen as a relatively late alteration to the version in bar 12, rather than the

Ex. 12.12 SV 263, fo. 66ʳ

Bars 3-4, stave 12,
earlier version:

latter being a variant of the former.

In the final version of the Adagio the opening section consists of two sentences: the first (bars 1–8) ends with a half close and the second (bars 9–17), which is a variant of the first, with a full close. In the sketch there is only one statement, with a full close, but this sort of expansion between sketch and final version is quite common and was probably intended from the start. The first cadence in the sketch therefore corresponds to bars 15–17 of the final version, and again there is a close similarity, though the sketch is rather more plain. In bar 5 of the sketch the dotted (or double-dotted) motif is transferred to the bass clef, as in bar 9 of the final version, but after this there is little relation between the two versions.

The sketch on stave 12 continues with parallel thirds in the bass clef, while on stave 13 there is some sort of alternative. Stave 14, however, does not quite join on to the end of stave 12 or 13, and so some transitional music must have been omitted. Stave 14 probably represents the second subject and is in G major. This is not as surprising as it might seem at first sight. Beethoven had just rejected the idea of going to the submediant in the first movement and might well reconsider it for the second; and his next piano sonata movement in B flat—the first movement of the 'Hammerklavier', Op. 106 —does go to G major for the second subject, as does the first movement of the 'Archduke' Trio, Op. 97.

No more sketches for this Adagio survive, but there is in the 'Kessler' Sketchbook one idea, intended for another work, that contains related material: this is the deleted sketch for part of the slow movement of Op. 31 No. 1, found at the top of fo. 96ᵛ (Ex. 12.13). The figuration of this is very reminiscent of that in bars 51–6 of the slow movement of Op. 31 No. 2, and it draws attention to the similarity between these two movements, both being in a very slow triple time and marked 'Adagio', with simple themes capable of much ornamentation and starting with two bars of tonic harmony

Ex. 12.13 SV 263, fo. 96^v

[etc.]

followed by two bars of dominant. When Beethoven deleted the sketch on fo. 96^v he must have felt that there was nothing wrong with the underlying idea, and so it became one of his many abandoned sketches that were taken up in another work (cf. Chapter 5).

The remaining sketches on fo. 66^r reveal that Beethoven initially envisaged Op. 31 No. 2 as a four-movement sonata, like the majority of his earlier piano sonatas (nine out of the fifteen before Op. 31). In this four-movement plan, the key scheme was to be similar to that of the recently completed C minor Violin Sonata, Op. 30 No. 2, with the slow movement in the submediant and the minuet in the opposite mode to the outer movements of the sonata. As in the first two movements, Beethoven initially intended the minuet to modulate to an unexpected key—this time the mediant minor (Ex. 12.14).

The finale sketches on fo. 66^r are much less well defined. In the first, Beethoven seems to be planning a fast 2/4 movement in a similar mood and time to the finale of Op. 57, and the actual melodic material is similar too: thus yet again the 'Appassionata' was to provide the realization of an idea originating in sketches for Op. 31 No. 2. The sketch on fo. 66^r stave 11 is even more undistinguished; it seems to be intended for the same movement but is in 2/2, with note values doubled and with the main motif of the other sketch in a kind of varied inversion. Clearly Beethoven had at this stage no fixed idea of what sort of finale the D minor Sonata was to have. Eventually, however, he was to build on the idea that had occurred to him sporadically throughout the 'Kessler' Sketchbook—the idea of repeated main notes each preceded by an anacrusis and with arpeggiated accompaniment. We have already seen four variants of the idea, the fourth of which was in A minor and actually headed 'Sonata 2da'; and the D major minuet quoted in Ex. 12.14 can be regarded as a fifth. The final solution saw a sixth version, now in D minor for the first time, in a movement that superseded both the minuet and the finale ideas on fo. 66^r.

According to Czerny, Beethoven originally extemporized the theme 'as he once saw a horseman gallop by his window';[8] and in another place Czerny elaborates: 'During the summer of 1803 [actually 1802] he was staying in the

---

[8] Czerny, *Performance*, p. 54.

Ex. 12.14 SV 263, fo. 66^r

country in Heiligenstadt near Vienna. One day he happened to see a rider galloping past his window. The regular rhythm of the hoof-beats gave him the idea for the theme of the finale of his Sonata in D minor.'[9] Such anecdotes are notoriously unreliable, and the accuracy of this one is certainly called into question by the evidence of the sketches. Did the rider pass by before any of the relevant sketches, in which case it was before Beethoven moved to Heiligenstadt? Or were there six riders, one for each variant of the theme? Or did the rider just happen to go past as Beethoven decided to use the theme for the finale of the sonata? At all events it is clear that the movement should not be regarded simply as a musical representation of a man on horseback.

Sketch study can throw light not only on quaint anecdotes but on analytical and interpretative matters too, by providing hints about Beethoven's understanding of the music. One example in the sonata is the very first chord, which is not just a chord played arpeggiando but a transfigured arpeggio theme: consequently it should surely be played sufficiently slowly to be heard as such, with extra weight (i.e. prolongation) given to the first note of the

---

[9] Ibid., p. 12.

arpeggio, just as it was in the initial sketch for the start of the movement (fo. 90ᵛ). The same applies to the start of the second movement, which was also originally a six-note arpeggio theme with a relatively long first note, and which should in performance be made to match the start of the first movement.

Another detail on which the sketches throw light is the problem of what constitute the themes of the first movement. The second subject seems not to have been regarded by Beethoven as very important, for it is completely ignored in the sketch on fo. 65ᵛ; analysts who have denied that the movement has a proper second subject are not far from the truth. The question of whether the first subject occurs at bar 1 or bar 21 has also been much discussed,[10] and the sketches provide an interesting answer. Bar 21 contains the original first subject as found in the first sketch (fo. 90ᵛ), but this theme disappears in the second sketch, supplanted by a new, albeit related, first subject. Performers wishing to penetrate to the heart of the music by revealing something of the creative process behind it would be justified in emphasizing bar 21 at its first appearance as being the original first subject, but passing through it relatively lightly and swiftly in the repeat of the exposition, treating this part of the movement as a mere transitional passage as it is in the second sketch. Such a seemingly eccentric interpretation would not only help the listener to approach the music from an angle similar to that of the composer; it would also highlight the structural ambiguity of bar 21. Indeed a few pianists already tend towards such an interpretation, even without having studied the sketches.

Thus the sketches for Op. 31 No. 2, despite their very limited number, do suggest surprisingly many new insights into the music. One conspicuous feature about them is Beethoven's method of transferring ideas, whether of melody, rhythm, figuration, form, or key scheme, from rejected sketches for one work to the finished product of another. The sonata seems to be related in this way to about half a dozen of his other works, and such interrelationships, as was seen in Chapter 5, are actually quite a common feature of his sketching in general. The sketches also show how the sonata originated in a haze of different ideas which gradually came together in Beethoven's mind into a coherent whole. They show what features of the sonata were present from the beginning, how these elements were in some cases radically transformed, and what features were introduced only later; and they demonstrate how the initial sketches can be among the most significant for a work as a whole, whereas later sketches tend to be more concerned with working out relatively minor details.

[10] See e.g. Wehnert, 'Zum positionellen', pp. 335–41.

13

Planning the Later Movements:
String Quartet in B flat, Op. 130

As was seen in Chapter 12, when Beethoven was working on the first movement of the D minor Piano Sonata he had very little idea about what the later movements were going to be, and he was even uncertain how many there would be. Such uncertainty was by no means uncommon, and often while working on an earlier movement he would jot down possible ideas for later ones without being at all sure which of these ideas, if any, would be taken up. (There was, of course, a standard pattern for multi-movement instrumental works, so that he would normally expect to write a slow middle movement, a fast finale, and possibly a minuet or scherzo, but within this pattern there was enormous scope, and there was also always the possibility of breaking away from the pattern altogether.) Thus he was liable to finish the main sketching for one movement while still faced with the problem of what sort of movement should follow.

A place where this problem was for a while particularly acute was his work on the middle of the Quartet Op. 130, in which he made a great many sketches after those for the second movement before deciding what should follow it—how many movements and in what keys. The quartet was composed in the second half of 1825; as it is such a late work a large number of sketches survive, allowing his vacillations over the nature of the later movements to be seen in great detail. He had begun the quartet by sketching a first movement in sonata form and then a scherzo-like Presto in the tonic minor—all very traditional in design, if not exactly conventional in its realization. Next he was faced with the problem of what sorts of movement, and how many, were needed to complete the quartet. The main conditions were that the overall structure should be well balanced, that each movement should contrast well with the previous one (which meant that the third movement would have to be slow), and that there should be in his solution some element of novelty by which his art would be advanced (his devotion to the advancement of his art was always an important consideration, especially in his late works). Several possibilities emerged. Should he, as in the Quartet in E flat Op. 127, retain the old four-movement form, or would it be better, as in the newly completed Op. 132 in A minor, to experiment with five or even more movements? If there were to be more than four movements, of what kinds should they be, and in what keys? And what sort of finale would round off the work most effectively? At this stage of the work he was at a kind of crossroads, with several options open; but it was an unmarked crossroads, where nobody had ventured before, and so he had to rely on his own sense of direction in order to proceed. The eventual result —an Andante in D flat, a Danza tedesca in G, a Cavatina in E flat, and finally the *Grosse Fuge* (later replaced by a different finale)—emerged only after he had pondered long and hard about what should follow on from the Presto in B flat minor.

The manuscript where Beethoven's difficulties about the overall structure of the quartet show up most clearly is a pocket-sketchbook, the 'Egerton' (SV 189), a source which Nottebohm missed but which has been described briefly by both Joseph Kerman and Robert Winter.[1] It consists of sixteen folios (eight full-size folios folded by Beethoven down the centre in his customary way to create a pocket-sized book of pages of half the normal width), with twelve staves per page. It is one of a large number of sources of sketches for Op. 130, and four other sources are particularly close to it:

1. The 'Moscow' Sketchbook (SV 342). This pocket-sketchbook dates from slightly earlier than 'Egerton', being concerned mainly with the previous quartet (Op. 132) and the first movement of Op. 130.

2. The final (fifth or sixth) fascicle of SV 26, a composite manuscript in West Berlin consisting of a collection of several pocket-sketchbooks for the late quartets.[2] This sketchbook was used directly after 'Egerton'.

3. The 'de Roda' Sketchbook (SV 104).[3] This was the standard-size sketchbook in use at the same time as all three pocket-sketchbooks mentioned above; the section contemporary with 'Egerton' is approximately fos. 22–31, but it gives fewer insights into the structural problems Beethoven was encountering in the quartet, since the evolution of the work seems much faster here, with far more gaps.

4. A collection of sketches in Vienna (SV 282). Most of these are fairly advanced score sketches for the first and third movements of Op. 130, but a few pages (pp. 17–18, 59–60, and 67–8—the latter originally a pocket bifolio) are roughly contemporary with 'Egerton'.

A close examination of 'Egerton' is necessary first in a consideration of the structural plans for the later movements of Op. 130, and a summary of its contents is given in Table 1. As can be seen, late sketches for the first two movements occupy most of the early pages, but increasingly towards the end of the sketchbook Beethoven turned his attention towards what should

---

[1] Kerman, 'British Museum', pp. 78–85; JTW, pp. 424–5.

[2] Described briefly in N-II, pp. 1–6, and JTW, pp. 426–9; more fully in Klein, *Autographe*, pp. 40–4. Schmidt (SV) regards this sketchbook as no. 6 in the MS, but Klein, counting the first two parts together, calls it no. 5. All are agreed that it is the earliest of the six parts. Here it will be referred to as SV 26/6.

[3] Detailed description in de Roda, 'Quaderno'; see also JTW, pp. 306–12.

TABLE 1. *Contents of the 'Egerton' Sketchbook*

Fos	Content
1^r–2^r	i; ii; concept sketch in E♭ (3/8)
2^v–3^v	i
4^r	Concept sketches in G m/G (6/8) and C♯ m/D♭ (4/4)
4^v–5^r	i; ii; concept sketch in E♭ (3/8)
5^v	i; iii in G
6^{r-v}	Several concept sketches, the last in D♭ with *minore* in C♯ m
7^{r-v}	Finale sketch (2/4); further sketches in D♭/C♯ m
7^v–8^r	i; ii; sketches in D♭, in 3/8 ('adagio') and 9/8 (cf. Op. 130/v)
8^v–9^r	ii; concept sketch in D (2/2); sketches for the 9/8 movement (v) in D♭
9^v–10^r	ii; v (D♭, 9/8); plan for remainder of Op. 130; concept sketch in D (3/8); sketch for canon 'Odyssey'[a]
10^v–11^r	Concept sketch in D (2/4); v (D♭, 9/8); finale sketch (2/4)
11^v–12^r	v (D♭, 9/8); sketches in D (2/4 or 4/4); Op. 132[b]
12^v–13^r	Finale sketch (3/4); v (D♭, now 9/4)
13^v–14^r	v (D♭ and transposed to D, 9/4); two concepts in G and two in G♭
14^v–15^r	v (D♭ and D, 9/4)
15^v–16^v	v (D♭, 9/4 and 3/2)

[a] See Kerman, 'British Museum', p. 84.   [b] Quoted ibid., p. 81.

follow, with the most prominent and persistent idea being to have as third movement some form of what eventually became the Cavatina.

Altogether the 'Egerton' Sketchbook is very limited in scope and was probably in use for only a few weeks at most—in late July and early August 1825.[4] On fo. 1^r appears a draft for part of the second movement, more or less coinciding with the final version; yet by the end of the book the third movement is stil barely started, despite numerous different ideas for it. Thus the sketchbook is concerned mainly with the single problem of what to use for the third movement, while it also provides a glimpse of how Beethoven had reached different stages of work on the first two movements and contains a few ideas for a finale. Op. 132 was virtually finished at this time, and Beethoven was probably in the process of writing out or amending the autograph score; but this might throw up unforeseen difficulties that required further sketching, and indeed there are a few passages, at a late stage of evolution, being touched up on fo. 12^r.[5] At the same time the first movement of Op. 130 was almost ready to be written out, but it still had quite a number of doubtful passages which needed further sketching. Accordingly some of the sketches in SV 189, particularly near the beginning of the

[4] JTW, p. 425.

[5] Quoted in Kerman, 'British Museum', p. 81. The autograph score was completed (though possibly not in its final form) before 10 Aug. 1825 (see A-1409 and A-1410).

manuscript (fos 1^r–3^v), are concerned with these trouble-spots. Most of these first-movement sketches are on two staves, implying that the ideas and proportions were more or less fixed but the layout and texture still had to be confirmed. These sketches are quite short, usually not more than about half a dozen bars, and they often do not coincide exactly with the final version, but generally they are sufficiently close that they can be matched up against individual bars of it.[6] The sketches for the Presto occupy relatively little space, prove highly significant in Beethoven's next quartet (Op. 131), but as yet movement, as well as being much shorter. They are found principally on fos. 1^r, 4^v, and 8^v–9^v. Although the individual sketches for this movement are mostly not much longer than those for the first movement here, they have more of the character of ordinary continuity drafts, since they are relatively long in proportion to the size of the whole movement and are concerned mainly with the shape of whole phrases or sections of the movement, rather than individual bars or motifs.

In addition to these well-developed sketches for the first two movements, there are in 'Egerton' a large number of concept sketches containing a variety of different ideas. Perhaps not all were intended as possible themes for the later movements of the quartet, but it is hard to see what other work they might have been intended for. A few of them were even copied into the 'de Roda' Sketchbook or on to the score-sketch leaves in SV 282, and these two sources themselves both contain further concept sketches for possible third movements. Almost at the beginning of 'Egerton', with several features of the first two movements still not settled, Beethoven was already beginning to look forward to what might come next and he wrote a short concept sketch in E flat in 3/8 at the top of fo. 2^r (Ex. 13.1). Since it is at the top of the page it may be no more significant than hundreds of other concept sketches that appear at the tops of other sketch leaves elsewhere; but the key chosen is interesting in view of later developments in the middle movements of Op. 130. About the same time he noted down in 'de Roda' (fo. 22^r) a plan to write an 'Adagio in E [flat] con sordino', also in 3/8 though with a different theme from Ex. 13.1, and added: 'the first part into C minor, without repeat'.

Meanwhile in a different place (SV 282) he wrote down a quite different idea for a possible third movement—a series of slow, arpeggiated chords in C sharp minor followed by a recitative-like passage (Ex. 13.2), and leading via some more arpeggiated chords to a lyrical, aria-like movement in D major and 9/8. This combination of C sharp minor and D major was of course to

Ex. 13.1 SV 189, fo. 2^r

[6] See e.g. Kerman, 'British Museum', p. 82.

Ex. 13.2 SV 282, p. 17

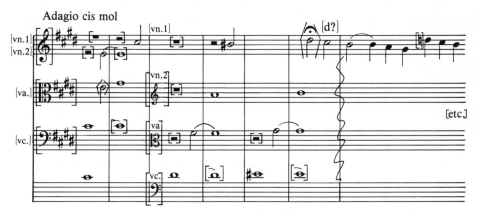

prove highly significant in Beethoven's next quartet (Op. 131), but as yet that had not been conceived, and the idea was instead being considered here for inclusion in Op. 130. Thus even at this early stage he had in mind the possible use of sharp keys to counterbalance the flat keys that prevailed elsewhere in Op. 130.

Returning to 'Egerton', Beethoven now began to consider in more detail on fo. 4ʳ what should follow the first two movements, even though he had still not quite finished sketching either of them. The first idea on the page is a movement in G minor in 6/8, followed by a section in G major (Ex. 13.3). The rest of the page is taken up with an alternative slow movement in C sharp minor and D flat major labelled 'oder adagio cis mo[ll] hernach des dur' (or adagio in C sharp minor then D flat major).[7] It has been suggested that this could be an early sketch for the Quartet Op. 131,[8] but the presence of the word 'oder' clearly marks it out as an alternative to the G minor/major sketch at the top of the page, and the surrounding pages make it almost certain that both sketches were drafted as possible slow movements for Op. 130. Of the two sketches it was the C sharp minor and D flat major one that Beethoven evidently considered more promising; it is much more extended,

Ex. 13.3 SV 189, fo. 4ʳ

---

[7] All quoted ibid., p. 84.
[8] See ibid., p. 85, and literature cited there.

and he copied it out virtually unaltered on pages 17–18 of SV 282, immediately below his earlier idea for a C sharp minor recitative and D major movement. It is interesting to note that the subsidiary keys of the two sketches on fo 4ʳ of 'Egerton', G major and D flat major, were both eventually used for the middle movements of Op. 130, unlike the main keys of the two sketches.

On the next two pages (fos. 4ᵛ–5ʳ), amongst further sketches for the first two movements, is an extended draft of nearly thirty bars in E flat major and 3/8 (Ex. 13.4)—the same key and metre as Ex. 13.1 but with different figuration. It shows a long, flowing, lyrical melody with something of the same character as the Cavatina that eventually emerged as the fifth movement, but the melodic shape is quite different. This melody was considered sufficiently important to Beethoven for him to copy it into the 'de Roda' Sketchbook (fo. 24ᵛ),[9] and it seems to be a possible realization of his earlier plan to write an Adagio modulating into C minor, since the melody twice veers into that key. The next page of 'Egerton' (fo. 5ᵛ) begins with yet another idea for a slow movement, and although it is in G major the theme is almost identical to the one used in D flat in the eventual third movement. This theme, too, was copied on to fo. 24ᵛ of 'de Roda', still in G major, but a few pages later (fo. 28ʳ) it reappears in G flat before eventually settling down in D flat on fo. 32ᵛ.[10]

This theme made no further appearance in the 'Egerton' Sketchbook, however; instead Beethoven tried still further ideas for the slow movement on the following pages. Some of these ideas are not very clearly defined, but on the sixth stave of fo. 6ʳ is a distinctive new theme (Ex. 13.5), in 3/8 like the earlier E flat sketches but in D flat. This sketch is fairly extended (about twenty bars), continuing on to the next page, where the D flat melody is answered by nine bars of a *minore* section in C sharp minor—a reversal of the key scheme planned in an earlier sketch. Ex. 13.5 can be considered to contain the germ of the fifth movement—the Cavatina—and most of the subsequent sketches in 'Egerton' can be seen to build on the ideas presented here. The key of D flat is retained in them while the melodic material is

Ex. 13.4 SV 189, fo. 4ᵛ

---

[9] See de Roda, 'Quaderno', p. 748, where it is wrongly given in G minor, with the first note D instead of E.

[10] See ibid., pp. 606–7.

Ex. 13.5 SV 189, fo 6ʳ

gradually modified and extended until the melody begins to resemble that of the final version; it is therefore possible to consider this sketch as being for the Cavatina, and the melody does foreshadow something of the lyrical quality of this movement, even though there are no very close melodic similarities. The triple metre is also significant, although it was to be changed from the 3/8 of this sketch to the 3/4 of the Cavatina by a rather roundabout method: as the melodic shape evolved, the time signature was altered to 9/8, 9/4, 3/2, and eventually 3/4.

Up to this point (fo. 6ᵛ) Beethoven had sketched a number of possible ideas for a slow movement, making use of three keys in particular—G major, E flat major, and D flat major. The sketches seem to imply that he was considering the three keys as alternatives for the slow movement, but they do not exclude the possibility that he was considering using all three keys in three different movements, as was eventually done in the final version. In the rest of the sketchbook, however, it is the triple-time sketches in D flat that predominate, with other ideas making only sporadic appearances. Although these triple-time ideas eventually evolved into the Cavatina, it must be remembered that Beethoven habitually sketched movements of a work in the right order, except in a few well-defined cases; accordingly, the presence of substantial numbers of sketches related to the Cavatina but of no further sketches related to the actual third movement (the Andante in D flat) clearly indicates that Beethoven at this stage intended the Cavatina (or at least something like it, but in D flat) as the third movement. It will be best, therefore, first to examine the development of Cavatina sketches in this sketchbook (and 'de Roda'), then to look at other possible ideas for middle movements, then to consider briefly how the Cavatina was removed to fifth place in the quartet, and finally to discuss the question of the finale, which even in the 'Egerton' Sketchbook was already occupying some of Beethoven's attention.

On fo. 7ʳ all the sketches for a planned slow movement are in D flat major or C sharp minor, and all but the first are in 3/8. The metre of the first is unclear (probably 2/4) but the melodic shape includes the important pattern ray'–fah–me, which was to emerge in bar 6 of the Cavatina. The sketches on the lower part of the page (staves 5, 8–12) make much use of an anapaestic

Ex. 13.6 SV 189, fo. 7ʳ

rhythm, as in Ex. 13.6. This rhythm also appears in a sketch on fo. 25ᵛ of 'de
Roda',[11] and so these two sketches are presumably more or less contemporary, since in later sketches this rhythm disappears. An extension of these
ideas, still with the anapaestic rhythm, appears overleaf on fo. 7ᵛ of 'Egerton',
while on the opposite page (fo. 8ʳ staves 4–5) a fresh start is made, as is clear
from the appearance of a key signature and the word 'adagio' (Ex. 13.7). This
adagio seems to foreshadow the slow movement of Op. 135, also in D flat
but in 6/8, at least as much as it does the Cavatina, none of whose characteristic melodic shapes is present here.

After most of this opening had been filled up with the sketches mentioned
and some for the first two movements, Beethoven made yet another fresh
start, still in D flat but now in 9/8. It would appear that initially he did not
intend to make an extended draft but just a brief concept, for it is squeezed
in on the bottom two staves of fo. 7ᵛ. As he extended this idea, however, he
had to resort to using smaller and smaller gaps on the opening, until he had
eventually written five separate fragments, related by a series of cross-
references using the numbers 10, 60, 70, and 80. When these fragments are
joined together an extended melody of over fifteen bars emerges; a few spots
(chiefly at the joins between the fragments) are not entirely clear and there
are a few alterations, but the result is something like Ex. 13.8. This sketch
is significantly closer to the final version of the Cavatina than any previous
one. The first four bars evidently function as a kind of introduction to the
main theme, which begins at bar 5 and has two particularly notable melodic
elements: the fifth and seventh bars closely match the head of the main theme
of the final version (bars 2 and 4); and the ray′–fah–me pattern of an earlier
sketch has been expanded so that now eight consecutive notes (indicated in
Ex. 13.8 by the editorial bracket) have the same pattern as the final version
(bars 5–7), even though the rhythm is somewhat different.

The next significant development in the composition of the movement

Ex. 13.7 SV 189, fo. 8ʳ

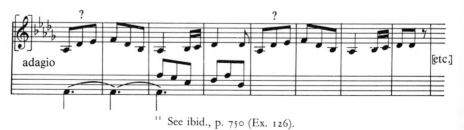

adagio   [etc.]

---

[11] See ibid., p. 750 (Ex. 126).

Ex. 13.8 SV 189, fo 7^v staves 11–12, fo. 8^r stave 12, fo. 7^v staves 9–10, fo. 8^r stave 3, fo. 7^v stave 8

appears on the first stave of fo. 9^v, where the five-note figure from the fifth bar of Ex. 13.8 is developed in isolation (Ex. 13.9), highlighting its importance in the overall melodic line. It continues to be developed as an isolated motif further down the page and at the top of the next, only occasionally being extended into a longer melodic phrase. Further odd fragments for the movement appear on fo. 11, but there is nothing very substantial until fos. 12^v–13^r, where the 9/8 notation is replaced by notation in 9/4 (although the omission of many of the dots from dotted minims sometimes gives the impression of 3/2). Among the sketches on these two pages, one (fo. 13^r staves 3–8) begins with seven bars similar to the opening of Ex. 13. 8 (though now in 9/4), but the continuation is different; and the phrase with the falling sixth, so prominent in Ex. 13.8, has temporarily disappeared again.

Further sketches in the rest of the book show the movement being worked on with increasing intensity, with less and less other material intervening, but progress remained painfully slow. On fo. 13^v there is a suggestion that binary

Ex. 13.9 SV 189, fo. 9^v

Ex. 13.10 SV 189, fo. 14^r

rhythm might after all be used ('oder 2/4tel takt'), and another that the theme
of the second section of the movement should be in G flat. On fo. 14^r
Beethoven tried the movement in D major (Ex. 13.10), still without any firm
idea of how to continue the opening theme and treating the five-note motif
of Ex. 13.9 as an isolated gesture. On the following pages it is not always
clear whether the key is D or D flat, though occasionally an accidental
indicates one or the other, and gradually D flat reasserts itself. Not until fo.
16^r is the initial rising sixth of the final theme encountered, and this is
significantly in 3/2 (Ex. 13.11). Most of the remaining sketches in the book
are in 9/4, but right at the end (fo. 16^v staves 9–12) 3/2 is firmly asserted in
two separate sketches.

   When he had finished the 'Egerton' Sketchbook Beethoven continued
with further work on the same movement, using loose leaves (SV 282, pp.
59–60 and 67–8) and the 'de Roda' Sketchbook (fos. 28^v–31^r). By now nearly
all the sketches were in D flat and 3/2 (though a few are in D major or 9/4
on fo. 30^r of 'de Roda'), and more of the main theme was being worked out;
but there was still a long way to go with the shape of the movement as a
whole, and there were still plans for a trio section in G flat (SV 282, p. 59).

   Although the intensity of sketching on this movement indicates that
Beethoven planned it at this stage as the third in the quartet, the intermittent
appearance of other material in the latter pages of 'Egerton' and the corresponding part of 'de Roda' suggests either that he still had doubts about the
movement or that he was considering a work in more than four movements,
with an extra movement probably in a sharp key as a constrast to the
emphasis on flat subsidiary keys (B flat minor, D flat major) in the rest of the
work. Some suggestions for sharp keys had already occurred in concept
sketches in G major and C sharp minor and in the D major sketches for the
Cavatina; two further D major concept sketches, both in duple metre, can be
found in 'Egerton' (fos. 8^v, 10^v), while two G major sketches appear at the
top of fo. 14^r, the first in 9/8 and the second in 6/4, showing that this key

Ex. 13.11 SV 189, fo. 16^r

was still very much in Beethoven's mind and suggesting that he may have been looking ahead to a fourth movement, even though at this stage he had not decided what this should be. A similar picture emerges from the corresponding pages of 'de Roda', where there are several ideas quite different form the emerging Cavatina movement—for example two themes for Adagio movements in D major or B minor.[12]

At this stage there are few indications of how all these various ideas were intended to fit into the overall structure of the quartet, but one or two sketches provide clues. An early idea for the structure appears on fo. 22ʳ of 'de Roda': after an Adagio in E flat was to come a 2/4 Presto in B flat (labelled 'nach dem Adagio'), followed by a 6/8 movement labelled 'leztes' (last). Far more significant, however, is a very brief synopsis sketch in 'Egerton', fo. 10ʳ (Ex. 13.12). The first two bars indicate some slow, arpeggiated pause chords similar to those in Ex. 13.2 and imply that Beethoven was still thinking of including a short recitative-like section, with held chords, followed by an aria-like movement ('arioso') in 2/4, presumably instead of the D flat Cavatina that was still at this point only an embryo. The phrase 'dann Fin', which follows, is particularly important for determining the planned structure of the work, for it indicates that Beethoven planned only five movements at that stage (or four if the recitative and arioso are counted as a single movement), rather than six. Meanwhile in 'de Roda' there is a sketch which shows similar slow, arpeggiated chords being followed by the 9/4 version of the D flat Cavatina instead of an 'arioso 2/4'.[13]

Hence there were altogether at least a dozen different ideas, in several keys, for the third movement of the quartet by the time Beethoven reached the end of the 'Egerton' Sketchbook, and his uncertainties about which was the way forward are reflected in his unusually slow progress during this period. Although at the beginning of 'Egerton' he was already fairly well advanced with the second movement and starting to look beyond it, the only real progress he had made on later movements by the end of the sketchbook was in developing something of the melodic shape and character of the Cavatina. Even this was still in the wrong key, with the wrong time signature, in the wrong position in the work (third instead of fifth movement), and with the

Ex. 13.12 SV 189, fo. 10ʳ

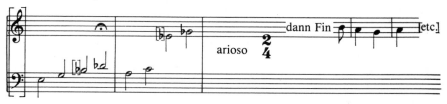

---

[12] Ibid., pp. 750–1 (Exx. 127–8). The former of these was definitely intended as a possible third movement, for it is labelled 'Zum 3ten Stk'.

[13] Ibid., p. 613.

movement as a whole not properly under way—there are no extended continuity drafts for it in the sketchbook.

In order to find out how these rather tentative ideas evolved into the final version it is necessary to turn to the Berlin pocket-sketchbook (SV 26/6) and the corresponding pages of 'de Roda' (approximately fos. 32–8). At the beginning of the Berlin manuscript there are still a few sketches in D flat for the Cavatina, now in 3/2 but with some sections using crotchet triplets to create a 9/4 effect. Almost immediately, however, Beethoven, perhaps receiving fresh inspiration from the sight of a new sketchbook, set aside work on this movement and plunged into intensive sketching for the Andante that became the third movement of the quartet. Right from the start the key is clearly D flat, not G or G flat as it had been when the theme appeared earlier. Almost all the sketching on fos. 1^v–8^r of SV 26/6 is devoted to this Andante, and a similar degree of intensity is apparent on fos. 32^r–34^r of 'de Roda', with numerous alterations and corrections as the movement took shape. Judging by the number of sketches, it is therefore clear that Beethoven spent far longer deciding what sort of movement to have as the third in the quartet than he did in drafting the entire movement itself, and that intensive work on it came to an end with a continuity draft for the latter part on fos. 7^v–8^r of the Berlin sketchbook, leading to the final bar of the movement on the first stave of fo. 8^v.

This work was immediately followed not by sketches for the fourth or fifth movement but by a series of sketches for the finale, which occupy the rest of fo. 8^v and the whole of fo. 9. The clear implication is that Beethoven was still thinking of the quartet as a four-movement work in the conventional pattern. By this time, however, he had two recent quartet movements that had been partially developed but remained unfinished: one was the D flat movement that became the Cavatina; the other was the one that became the Danz tedesca. The latter had originally been sketched in A major as a possible fourth movement for the A minor Quartet, Op. 132,[14] but had been replaced there by the Alla marcia we know today. Thus the possibility existed for Beethoven to resurrect both of these movements in Op. 130 to form a six-movement work. The key of A major had never been considered as a subsidiary key in Op. 130 and would anyway have been quite inappropriate; hence his initial idea was to transpose the Danza tedesca from A to B flat (SV 26/6, fo. 10^r) to reinforce the tonic key of the whole work. In this sketch he specifically noted that it was to be followed by a 'short Adagio' before the finale. It would appear that at this stage, however, he still considered a six-movement structure as only a possibility, for the following pages are devoted exclusively to the finale; but on fo 14^r the Danza tedesca reappears, now at last firmly in G major, with its subsidiary section in C. On the next page the Cavatina appears in E flat for the first time, and after slight

---

[14] N-I, p. 53. Nottebohm's source is SV 17/7; sketches for the movement in A major are also in SV 331, alongside work on Op. 132. iii (see Winter, 'Symphonie', p. 547).

vacillation the time signature of 3/4 was finally established. The six-movement structure of the work had at last fallen into place, and after a few further pages of sketching for the fourth and fifth movements the only major problem remaining was the finale.

The pages which reveal the emergence of the six-movement structure (fos. 10–14) can be dated almost exactly. Beethoven told his nephew in a letter dated 24 August (1825) that the quartet was to have six movements;[15] this was obviously very recent information since he had seen Karl only three days earlier and had also written to him on the 22nd without mentioning the length of the quartet.[16] These sketch leaves were therefore filled between 22 and 24 August 1825. He added in his letter of 24 August that the quartet as a whole would be 'quite finished in ten or, at most, twelve days',[17] and so he clearly did not anticipate that the finale would present any major difficulties.

But it did. Beethoven had again been confronted with a kind of unmarked crossroads, with a large number of turnings to explore, and the problem was finally solved only after a second attempt at the finale a year later (indeed some would argue that it was never solved). It is well known that when the quartet was first performed in March 1826 the *Grosse Fuge* was the finale, and that Beethoven later replaced this with a new finale, publishing the *Grosse Fuge* as a separate opus. It is less well known that the *Grosse Fuge* was by no means Beethoven's first idea for the finale, and that he had composed a large part of the quartet before the earliest sketches were made for the *Grosse Fuge*, which happened about the time when he first considered introducing the *Danza tedesca* to the quartet. Interspersed with sketches for the earlier movements are ideas for over a dozen possible finales for the work, all quite different and none resembling the themes of either the *Grosse Fuge* or the replacement finale.[18]

Probably the first finale sketch is the one on fo. 14^r of 'de Roda'.[19] Labelled 'leztes Stück des Quartett in B' (last movement of the quartet in B flat), it begins with a light-hearted 6/8 motif, although there is apparently to be a fugal section later on. Another early finale sketch appears in the 'Moscow' Sketchbook,[20] and as Beethoven progressed with the earlier movements finale sketches began to appear with increasing frequency. Excluding the sketch on fo. 14^r and the *Grosse Fuge* itself, there are six more finale ideas in 'de Roda',[21] all headed 'Finale' or 'leztes', plus a probable seventh on fo. 40^r.[22]

---

[15] A-1416.   [16] A-1414.

[17] A-1416; in a letter to Karl Holz written the same day, he was even more optimistic, hoping to finish the quartet by the end of the month, i.e. within eight days.

[18] A similar situation arose in Beethoven's work on the next quartet, Op. 131: he wrote nearly 20 possible finale themes in just one sketchbook (see Winter, *Op. 131*, p. 367).

[19] Quoted in de Roda, 'Quaderno', p. 757, Ex. 134.

[20] Kerman, 'British Museum', p. 84.

[21] De Roda, 'Quaderno', Exx. 135, 136, 137, 81, and 138; the latter contains two alternative finale concepts, while Ex. 137 quotes only the 2/4 Presto preceding the movement labelled 'leztes'.   [22] Ibid., p. 759, Ex. 139.

All have a somewhat light-hearted character, and one (fo. 32ʳ) is actually labelled 'humoristisch'. Four further finale concepts appear in 'Egerton' (fo. 7ʳ stave 1, fo. 10ʳ stave 5, fo. 11ʳ stave 9, and fo. 12ᵛ stave 1).[23] Again, none of them seems to have a very serious, weighty character; the single possible exception is the one sketched on fo. 10ʳ in conjunction with Ex. 13.12. Here the finale theme (Ex. 13.13) makes use, perhaps coincidentally, of the first phrase of the chorale melody 'Vom Himmel hoch', but the light 6/8 counter-melody seems to militate against a movement with the grandeur of the *Grosse Fuge*. Thus altogether in these three sketchbooks Beethoven had drafted no fewer than twelve possible finale themes; there may by this time have been others, too, either unlabelled, unidentified, or simply lost. A thirteenth finale sketch appears on fo. 3ᵛ staves 1–5 of the Berlin sketchbook, in the middle of work on the third movement. This sketch is slightly more substantial than most of the previous ones: there are two alternative opening themes (Ex. 13.14), one using quavers and the other using lively dotted rhythms; on the third stave are running semiquavers, and on the fourth and fifth is a motif in G flat major, a key actually retained in the middle section of the *Grosse Fuge* and one already used for the second subject of the first movement.

The thirteen finale sketches so far mentioned have a variety of metres and melodic figurations, but virtually nothing of their contents found its way into the *Grosse Fuge*. The first sketch from which one can trace a continuous line of descent to the latter appears a little further on in the Berlin sketchbook (fo. 8ᵛ), immediately after the last sketches for the third movement. It is a *perpetuum mobile* theme in running semiquavers (Ex. 13.15); the large natural sign at the beginning is simply a shorthand way of cancelling three of the five flats from the third movement, which had been sketched continuously for several pages before this. The same theme appears in a modified but still

Ex. 13.13 SV 189, fo. 10ʳ

Ex. 13.14 SV 26/6, fo. 3ᵛ

---

[23] Not just two, as stated in Kerman, 'British Museum', p. 84.

Ex. 13.15 SV 26/6, fo. 8ᵛ

recognizable form in bars 160–4 of the *Grosse Fuge,* where it is then developed in G flat as a countersubject to the main fugue theme. In the
sketchbook, however, the fugue theme had still not appeared at this point.
On the following page the theme of Ex. 13.15 reappears, slightly modified
and specifically headed 'anfang' (start), and it is immediately followed by
further sketches in which the theme of the *Grosse Fuge* appears in the
sketchbook for the first time.[24] This fugue theme was not entirely new,
however. Beethoven had earlier sketched a longer version of it (eighteen
notes) in E flat as a possible theme for the finale of the Quartet Op. 127 (SV
28/2, fo. 27ʳ);[25] part of it had then been transferred for use as the opening
theme of the Quartet Op. 132. Now, it seems, having started to work on the
finale of Op. 130, and with a main theme already sketched, he 'leafed through
an earlier sketchbook'[26] to find a continuation or subsidiary theme. First he
transposed the E flat version of the theme to B flat and wrote it out in the
bass clef in SV 28/2 on the opposite page to the E flat sketch. Then he wrote
out a revised version of just eight notes (instead of eighteen) in B flat, still
in the bass clef, and introduced it to the finale of Op. 130 in the sketches on
fo. 9ʳ of the Berlin sketchbook.[27] In view of later developments to the *Grosse
Fuge* it is quite astonishing that the fugue theme was introduced here not as
the opening theme of the movement (which was at this stage the semiquaver
theme labelled 'anfang') or even as a fugue theme at all, but as a subsidiary
motif, tucked away in the cello part with a countermelody above it. Once
introduced into the movement, however, the motif kept growing gradually
until it had taken over as the main theme, swamped the entire movement, and
even overshadowed the rest of the quartet too. Thus however great the
Grosse Fuge was to become, the movement clearly started out with quite
modest dimensions. Further sketches on the next page of the Berlin sketchbook (fo. 9ᵛ) emphasize this, for they include one for a 'M. gedank' (second
subject)—a playful little motif conventionally set in F major (Ex. 13.16).
    It was on the following page that Beethoven sketched the Danza tedesca

[24] Fac. of this page in Stadlen, 'Possibilities', p. 114.   [25] Fac., ibid., p. 113.
[26] Ibid.
[27] Stadlen (ibid.) has made a strong case for this being the correct order of events, which
was unclear to Nottebohm (N-II, pp. 550–1).

Ex. 13.16 SV 26/6, fo. 9ᵛ

M. gedank

in B flat with an indication that a short Adagio was to follow (see above), but after this the proposed finale took over for the next seven pages of the sketchbook. These finale sketches include two (fo. 10ᵛ staves 1–2, 6) in which the semiquaver theme appears in modified form simultaneously with the theme of the *Grosse Fuge*,[28] and also, more importantly, one which shows Beethoven's decision to place the fugue theme at the head of the movement and to write a fugue (fo. 11ᵛ staves 3–5):[29] the fugue theme appears beside the words 'All[egr]o' and 'Finale' (implying the beginning of the movement), and the theme then appears in the dominant beside the word 'Fug'.

One of the most surprising features about these pages of the sketchbook is the order in which the sketches for the last three movements appear. As suggested above, it seems that when Beethoven finished the main sketches for the third movement (fo. 8ᵛ stave 1) and was still planning a four-movement work, he had not completely rejected the possibility of a longer one. After working on the finale for a few pages (fos. 8ᵛ–9ᵛ) he began to sense that more movements might be necessary, depending on the size of the finale, and so he wrote a brief concept sketch for the Danza tedesca and following Adagio (fo. 10ʳ stave 2), to be used if necessary. After further work on the finale (fos. 10ʳ–13ᵛ) and the decision to write a fugue on the eight-note theme, it became clear that the finale would be very substantial and would require the extra movements beforehand to balance it out. Hence the two 'optional' movements were inserted and sketched in detail (fos. 14ʳ–17ʳ). After this he returned to the *Grosse Fuge*, which itself needed much further sketching before being completed in December 1825.[30]

Beethoven began to write the substitute finale in the autumn of the following year, after Op. 131 and most of Op. 135 had been composed. This time he apparently did not have so many false starts as the first time, but again he did not find the opening theme immediately. One rejected idea, actually labelled as the finale of this quartet, is quoted by Nottebohm, and occurs amongst sketches for the middle two movements of the Quartet Op. 135.[31] Two other concept sketches that come from the same sketchbook (SV 219) are shown in Ex. 13.17. Although both are in triple metre and neither is labelled as being for Op. 130, they were clearly planned as ideas for the

---

[28] The first is quoted in N-II, p. 5 (second ex.).

[29] Quoted ibid. (third ex.).   [30] See JTW, p. 315.

[31] N-II, p. 524. Nottebohm has silently suppressed bars 3–6 of Beethoven's sketch, which is in SV 219, fo. 9a.

Ex. 13.17

a SV 219, fo. 8d

b SV 219, fo. 2d

substitute finale—in particular, the motif in the first bar of the Presto sketch and that in the last two bars of the 3/2 sketch both contain ideas close to the opening theme of the new finale.

Why did Beethoven write a new finale? After steadfastly resisting pressure from friends and performers to make even slight alterations to the finale of the Ninth Symphony,[32] why was he prepared to make a much more substantial alteration to the quartet, affecting its entire shape and proportions, as a result of pressure from Karl Holz? Numerous hypotheses have been put forward, and endless speculation is possible; but although the sketches provide no firm answer they can at least add some substance to any new speculations. It is clear that when he was composing the first three movements of the quartet, the sort of finale he had in mind was not unlike the substitute finale—in character if not in theme. A few of the themes sketched even have the dactylic rhythm found in the new finale. There was certainly no intention of writing a mammoth fugue at that stage. When he did evolve the eight-note theme, he still regarded it only as a subsidiary motif

[32] Details in TF, p. 907.

at first, although he soon realized that the movement was developing into something more substantial, necessitating the insertion of the two previously 'optional' movements before the finale. Even at this stage, however, he seems to have had little conception of the scale of the movement as a whole, as is confirmed by his forecast of 24 August 1825 that the quartet would be completed within twelve days. But as he explored the theme itself he began to see more and more possibilities in it, and the movement gradually began to grow in size. Thus it was the theme itself—not the rest of the quartet —that demanded a big movement. The eight-note theme had already shown its strength by first joining and then displacing the original semiquaver theme, and it now became increasingly clear that, in order to do justice to it, a very large movement was demanded.

As we have seen, when Beethoven improvised at the piano it was not unknown for him to become somewhat 'carried away' and to develop a theme at great length during a single sitting. Similarly, the sketches suggest that his compositions often tended to grow beyond their originally planned sizes in the course of his work. This is what seems to have happened here in the *Grosse Fuge*, so that by the time he had finished he had created a massive movement of 741 bars. Larger-scale considerations of the balance of the quartet as a whole had been competing against the internal considerations of what was demanded by the musical material of the fugue, and the latter had won the day. Hence although Beethoven was justly proud of the fugue as a mighty work of art, he must have had certain doubts about it as a finale for Op. 130, despite its tonal and other links with the rest of the quartet; and he evidently remained uneasy that this finale had turned out so different from what he had anticipated while occupied with the earlier movements, as well as being so disproportionate to them. It then needed only the catalysing influence of Karl Holz, who was by that time Beethoven's closest associate, plus a financial inducement from the publisher Matthias Artaria, to persuade him to compose a new finale, so that the *Grosse Fuge* could be detached and published separately. The new finale was made sufficiently substantial to balance the extra middle movements—it is actually quite a long movement —but sufficiently light not to overwhelm them. Which of the two finales is a better movement, or a better conclusion to Op. 130, is a matter on which critics will no doubt continue to disagree. But now that the *Grosse Fuge* can be seen as something of an intrusion into the quartet, rather than the germ from which the work sprang, Beethoven's decision to replace it with a different movement, more in line with the others and with the finale he had intended while writing them, must seem entirely justified.

14

Musical Structure and Vivid Pictorialism: 'Meeresstille', Op. 112

WHEN planning a movement for an instrumental work, Beethoven often decided at an early stage to use a standard form such as sonata or rondo form, and so once he had decided on the nature of the main themes there were no major structural problems to face. If the movement was to have a more irregular form, this too was often determined at an early stage—usually with the aid of a synopsis sketch. In certain vocal works, however, the form was determined largely by the shape and content of the text. In such cases any elements of form other than those present in the text could be clarified only gradually, during the sketching. Hence successive drafts for such a work would not only refine and amplify details, as in an instrumental work, but also show substantial progress in the overall form of the movement, as well as evolving details to highlight the meaning of individual words.

A good example of such a work is 'Meeresstille', the first of a pair of Goethe poems set by Beethoven in 1813–15 as a two-movement chorus, *Meeresstille und glückliche Fahrt* (Calm Sea and Prosperous Voyage). The nine surviving continuity drafts for the first movement show the usual features of successive drafts, as in instrumental works, plus the additional problems of Beethoven's efforts to create a satisfactory musical structure while portraying individual words as vividly as possible. The sketches also show other interesting features associated particularly with vocal music, such as the problem of choosing the right key and metre to suit the text. An examination of these sketches is of special interest since they have not been discussed by Nottebohm (who mentions only two brief sketches for the second movement) or any other writers.

As has been seen, many of Beethoven's vocal works were written because of some deep personal significance in the subject-matter, or else because of some specific occasion or commission—and sometimes for both reasons. *Meeresstille und glückliche Fahrt*, for four-part choir and full orchestra, could therefore almost be regarded as exceptional in being composed for neither of these reasons. The main reason why it was written was stated by Beethoven in a letter to Goethe, who had published the text in 1796[1] and to whom the

[1] Frimmel, *Handbuch*, i. 400.

work was eventually dedicated: 'By reason of their contrasting moods these two poems seemed to me very suitable for the expression of this contrast in music.'[2] In other words, he simply liked the poetry and thought it eminently suitable for a musical setting. From a study of the two poems it is easy to see why.

Tiefe Stille herrscht im Wasser,	Deep calm reigns in the water,
Ohne Regung ruht das Meer,	Motionless lies the sea,
Und bekümmert sieht der Schiffer	And anxiously the sailor sees
Glatte Fläche rings umher.	Glassy plains all around.
Keine Luft von keiner Seite!	No breath of air from any side!
Todesstille fürchterlich!	Awful deathly stillness!
In der ungeheuern Weite	In the monstrous expanse
Reget keine Welle sich.	Not a ripple stirs.
Die Nebel zerreissen,	The mists are torn apart,
Der Himmel ist helle,	The sky is clear,
Und Aeolus löset	And Aeolus loosens
Das ängstliche Band.	The anxious bond.
Es säuseln die Winde	The winds whisper,
Es rührt sich der Schiffer.	The sailor takes action.
Geschwinde! Geschwinde!	Quick! Quick!
Es theilt sich die Welle,	The waves part,
Es naht sich die Ferne;	The distance draws near;
Schon seh' ich das Land.	Already I see the land.

The main attraction was the contrast of moods—the contrast between stillness and movement; but there are several other differences between the two poems which add to their interest for a composer. The falling rhythm of the trochaic metre in 'Meeresstille' creates a static effect directly opposed to the forward motion produced by the upbeat rhythm of 'Glückliche Fahrt'; and the metres themselves imply a change from duple to triple time—from 4/4 to 6/8. The two poems also highlight two opposing ways in which a composer can set a text to music: either he can set it in the manner of the madrigalists, with individual words illustrated so vividly that the form of the whole depends on the sum of the various sections; or he can set it to express the overall mood of the text and determine the form musically, disregarding any opportunities for individual word-painting. Most vocal works lie somewhere between these two extremes, but certain textual features can suggest one or other approach. For example, a text with few words, and therefore much repetition, gives little scope for word-painting, and once the overall mood is set the compositional procedures depend largely on musical considerations; on the other hand, if there are a large number of words the composer is much more likely to use a madrigalian approach. Similarly if there is vivid imagery and several contrasting ideas the same approach will

[2] A-1136.

suggest itself, whereas if the text lacks easily portrayable ideas or if all the ideas contain similar imagery the composer will have to rely more on musical means to create an overall shape.

Meeresstille und glückliche Fahrt illustrates both these points. Although the two poems are actually of virtually equal length (sixty and fifty-eight syllables respectively), in any musical setting the first poem would have to be sung much slower because of the subject-matter, and it is therefore effectively much longer. Consequently in this movement there could be much more emphasis on individual words, whereas in the second movement there would have to be much textual repetition and therefore less necessity for detailed word-painting. The first poem also contains plenty of imagery suitable for musical illustration: deep calm, lack of motion, anxiety, smooth plains, no breath of air, awful stillness, and monstrous expanse. The second contains relatively few: whispering winds, an active sailor, speed, and forward motion. The latter ideas are all closely related, leaving little scope for vivid word-painting.

Thus the musical style of each part is more or less predetermined by the poetry, and Beethoven was quite prepared to accept this from the start. In the first part he planned to illustrate each idea as vividly as possible, whereas in the second he decided to capture the mood of the whole text at once. This meant gradual stirrings at the beginning of the second movement as the wind arose, after which there was to be continuous motion through to the end, with no exaggerated word-painting to disrupt the flow of the music. The chief compositional problems therefore lay in the detailed pictorialism of the first movement, plus the contrasting effect of the start of the second; after this, constructing the rest of the second movement was just a matter of compositional technique, posing no special problems. Hence the most significant sketches are those for the first movement, which also contains the most striking and forward-looking ideas in the work. It was here that Beethoven faced most directly the problems of vivid pictorialism.

A likely date for the start of Beethoven's work on *Meeresstille und glückliche Fahrt* can be fixed with unusual accuracy: 3 March 1813. This, at least, is the date written by him at the head of the bifolio containing the earliest known sketches for the work, at the beginning of a now dismembered sketchbook (SV 252, fo. 1ʳ; other parts of the sketchbook are SV 138, 383, and 242).[3] This seems a surprisingly early date if Op. 112 was not completed until 1815, but all the paper in the sketchbook dates from 1812–13, and all the datable entries are from 1813 or early 1814.[4] In particular, an extensive group of early

---

[3] JTW, p. 237. A suggested reconstruction of the sketchbook has been made (see ibid., p. 238).

[4] Ibid., p. 237. They include early sketches for the revival of *Fidelio* (early 1814), remarks about the copying of the Seventh and Eighth symphonies (the former was performed on 8 Dec. 1813), and remarks about ear-trumpets, probably dating from the time of Beethoven's close association with their inventor Maelzel in 1813.

sketches for 'An die Hoffnung' (Op. 94) later in the sketchbook (SV 383, fo. 3ᵛ) were probably made by about November 1813,⁵ and so although Beethoven could conceivably have filled the sketchbook in a very irregular way, the balance of probabilities strongly suggests that almost all the sketches for 'Meeresstille' were made before then. 'Glückliche Fahrt', however, was apparently held over unfinished for more than a year before being completed on pages that are now lost.⁶ A few of the sketches in the *Meeresstille* Sketchbook may therefore have been entered at this later period, that is, early in 1815.

Beethoven's inscription 'On 3rd March 1813' could possibly have been made as a memorandum for some past or future event; but in all likelihood it was made on that day, probably as a pen trial, since it was evidently written with a rather thick quill, and underneath appear—significantly in pencil—the words 'Raben Federn' (crow-quills: a reference to an implement used for fine writing). The music sketched beneath on fo. 1ʳ of SV 252 consists mainly of unused concepts, but both sides of fo. 2 are taken up almost exclusively with work on Op. 112, and there are also one or two brief concepts for it on fo. 1ʳ. The earliest possible date for the start of work on Op. 112 therefore appears to be 3 March 1813; although it may have been begun up to half a year later, the traditionally accepted date of late 1814 clearly seems to be wrong.

Such an early date for the initial ideas for Op. 112 actually seems quite likely when biographical factors are considered. Beethoven had known and loved Goethe's works since his youth,⁷ and between 1790 an 1810 he set a number of his texts, culminating in the *Egmont* music of 1810. At that time the two artists had still not met, but they did so in July 1812 in Teplitz, and for a while they were in daily contact.⁸ During this period Beethoven was working on the Eighth Symphony, and immediately after this he wrote the Violin Sonata Op. 96 for Pierre Rode, who arrived in Vienna that December and who eventually performed the work on 29 December 1812.⁹ Once these works were out of the way it would have been natural for Beethoven to set about writing a sizeable work purely out of admiration for Goethe, and by March 1813 he had evidently found a suitable text. The early sketches must then have been held over while he wrote a number of other works of immediate need, such as *Wellingtons Sieg*, the cantata *Der glorreiche Augenblick*, and the revision of *Fidelio*. After these, he returned to *Meeresstille und glückliche Fahrt*, which was apparently completed in July 1815 and received its first performance on 25 December that year.¹⁰

All four constituent parts of the dismembered sketchbook contain substantial sketches for 'Meeresstille', but the order in which the four fragments

---

⁵ See N-II, pp. 119–121.

⁶ Two brief sketches, quoted in N-II, pp. 309 and 317, survive from about Dec. 1814 and June 1815; neither matches any sketches in the *Meeresstille* Sketchbook.

⁷ Cf. A-1136.   ⁸ A-379.   ⁹ TF, p. 545.   ¹⁰ KH, p. 322.

were filled is not entirely straightforward. SV 252 contains the earliest sketches for the work, but Beethoven began using SV 138 before SV 252 was finished, and so there is a draft that begins on SV 252, fo. 2^v, but continues on SV 138, fo. 2^r. The eight folios in SV 138 seem to have been filled by and large in the right order and to have been followed by the sketches in SV 383, a manuscript containing three folios (almost all the sketches for Op. 112 are on fo. 1). SV 242 also consists of three folios (a bifolio and a single leaf),[11] with a continuity draft for the latter part of the first movement and into the start of the second (fos. 2^v–1^r). But in some ways this draft is less advanced than that in SV 383, even though bibliographically SV 242 is the fourth and last fragment of the sketchbook; the draft may therefore have been sketched before that in SV 383, perhaps before SV 242 was added to the end of the sketchbook.

Like the sketches for so many of Beethoven's works, those for Op. 112 fall into two main types—continuity drafts of usually more than fifty bars, and shorter concepts, fragments, and alternatives of rarely more than a dozen bars. The sketches of intermediate length are usually found to join up with others to form longer drafts. In the continuity drafts, all or almost all of the text of the first poem is always represented (though Beethoven often misses out most of the words themselves), whereas the shorter fragments usually contain only about one line of text. Altogether there are nine continuity drafts for the first movement, and some of them continue into the second. This is about the number that might be expected for a work of this period. Their location and the approximate bars they represent are shown in Table 1. They are interspersed with short sketches too numerous to list individually, most of which are for the first movement; but there are some sketches, and even a few longer drafts, for the second movement, particularly towards the end of SV 138. Continuity Draft (CD) 6 in its latest form comes very close to the final version at the beginning, and CD8 matches the latter as far as bar 42 almost exactly; but Beethoven would have needed to make a few more sketches for the second half of the first movement. These sketches, like the autograph score, do not survive.

Beethoven encountered four main problems in the course of composing the movement: choosing the most appropriate key for the text; choosing a suitable metre to fit the words and also capture their mood; giving the movement some musical shape beyond a bald statement of each line of text; and illustrating each idea as vividly as possible by means of appropriate melody and harmony. In their most basic form these four problems—of key, time, form, and motif—occur in all Beethoven's works, but here each one had its own particular difficulty.

The problem of key shows itself particularly acutely in Op. 112. Most of the early sketches are in D, but one (SV 252, fo. 1^r stave 10) is clearly in E

---

[11] It is not entirely clear whether the loose leaf counts as fo. 2 or fo. 3. For present purposes it is regarded as fo. 3, as it is in all but one of the references in JTW, pp. 235–40.

TABLE 1. Continuity Drafts for 'Meeresstille'

Draft	Location (no. in SV: fo./staves)	Approx. no. of bars	Approx. bar nos. of corresponding passage in final version
CD1	SV 252: 2^r/11–12, 2^v/1–2	27	1–42 ⌣ 74–76 83–85
CD2	SV 252: 2^v/9–12; SV 138: 2^r/1–4	59	3–42 ⌣ 52–73
CD3	SV 138: 2^r/6–10, 2^v/1–4	54 + 9	3–42 ⌣ 52–87
CD4	SV 138: 2^r/5, 2^v/5–8, 10–12, 3^r/4–8	57 + 30	3–42 ⌣ 52–121
CD5	SV 138: 4^r/5, 6, 9, 7, 12–13	58	3–50 ⌣ 73
CD6	SV 138: 5^r/1–9	53 + 20	1–30 ⌣ 39–51 74–121
CD7	SV 138: 5^v/1–12, 6^r/2–6, 6^v/1–12, 7^r/1–4	79 + 83	3–73 ⌣ 74–end
CD8	SV 383: 1^r/5–14, 1^v/1–14	96	1–73
CD9	SV 242: 2^v/1–12, 1^r/1–8	48 + 22	52–73 ⌣ 74–95
Final version		73 + 164	1–237

Note: The curved line ⌣ indicates that the music is continuous in the sketch even if the bars indicated are not consecutive in the final version. Since the sketches often include extra bars not in the final version or omit bars that are there, the number of bars in a sketch does not normally correspond to the total number of bars represented in the final version. Where a sketch continues into the second part of the work, the number of bars drafted for each movement is expressed in the form x + y.

flat, and in another E flat was almost certainly intended (see Ex. 14.2*b*). Among the early D major sketches for the first movement is the remark 'leztes in B dur' (SV 252, fo. 2^r stave 10), indicating that Beethoven planned to have the second movement in B flat major. This plan can be seen being put into effect in some of the sketches in SV 138, for although he consistently omits the key signature, B flat major is the only key that makes sense in some of them (e.g. SV 138, fo. 3^r staves 4–5: see Ex. 14.1). On the other hand, these B flat sketches are preceded by some showing the second movement in D major (SV 138, fo. 1), although the theme is very far from the final version. A second movement in B flat is clearly intended in CD3, CD4, and even as late as CD6, by which stage the beginning of the first movement is almost as in the final version. But in CD7 both movements are put into E flat, a key which had already been rejected once. From this point to the end of SV 138, that is, in fos. 5^v–8^v, all the sketches for both movements appear to be in E flat. In CD8, however, the first movement is back in D major (the second is omitted), and CD9 shows the second movement in the same key as well.

Beethoven's final decision to use D major is represented by the remark 'le meilleur' written in ink at the top of CD6. It seems that after finishing SV 138 he reassessed his first seven drafts for the first movement, and that it was at this stage that he decided on D major and on the version in CD6. This draft, which like CD7 had been written in pencil, was then inked in (with minor amendments), and an improved and extended version was written out again as CD8, whereas CD7 was crossed out in ink. Thus after vacillating between D and E flat in the initial stages he settled on the former, with B flat for the second movement. Then he reverted to E flat, and since B major would be a most peculiar choice for the second movement (it was a key he rarely used), he placed this in E flat too. Only after a further extended trial with both sections in E flat did he transpose everything back to D major.

It was certainly unusual for Beethoven to progress so far with a work, right up to the point of having nearly finished drafting the first movement, while still being uncertain what key to choose. D major, the key of such energetic works as the Second Symphony, may have seemed in some way too

Ex. 14.1 SV 138, fo. 3^r

bright for the static opening section of Op. 112. Nevertheless there were precedents for using this key for a slow, profound movement, in such works as the Largo of the Piano Sonata Op. 2 No. 2 and the Andante of the 'Archduke' Trio. Another factor favouring D major was the compass of the flute: the highest note available on this instrument was a''', and Beethoven planned to use this note on the word 'Weite' (see below), as well as in the second movement; the lack of a bb''' meant that the effect would be lost if the work were in E flat major.

The question of the time signature was almost as problematical as that of the key signature. It was bound to be heavily dependent on the metre of the poems, and the obvious solution would be duple time for the first movement and quick triple or compound duple for the second; but Beethoven was not one to adopt the obvious until less orthodox alternatives had been tried. Hence among the earliest sketches for the first movement several metres are found. Altogether in SV 252 and SV 138 fo. 1ʳ are thirteen attempts at the opening phrase (see Ex. 14.2 *a–m*), many of which are in 3/4, and the whole of CD1 is written in 3/2. The thirteen attempts show some differences in melodic contour but their main differences lie in their rhythms. Beethoven was apparently trying the text in a number of rhythms to see which was the most effective, and nearly all of these sketches are rhythmically distinctive. It is also notable that none matches the final version; even among the later sketches the only ones in which the opening phrase exactly matches the rhythm of the final version are CD6 ('le meilleur') and CD8, and even these did so only after modification.

The metre of the second movement depended to a certain extent on that chosen for the first: in order to maximize the contrast between the two it was desirable to have one in duple time and the other in triple or compound time. Thus in the early sketches, when the first movement was being drafted in 3/2 (CD1), the second was sketched in duple time, as in Ex. 14.3, which already contains the idea of rising quavers eventually used in the orchestral introduction to the second movement. At one point (SV 138, fo. 1ᵛ staves 1–6) there is even an extended draft in duple metre for the second movement, lasting some thirty bars. Beethoven eventually fixed on 6/8 for the second movement at about the same time as he decided on 2/2 for the first movement: by the time of CD3 all the sketches for both movements are using the 'right' metre.

The musical structure of the first movement was determined largely by a close imitation of each line of the text in turn, in the manner of a madrigal. This procedure, if unmodified, however, would result simply in a through-composed movement, and Beethoven wanted to give it added musical shape by some kind of repeat or recapitulation; this would be particularly advantageous as it could help the movement to end where it began and thereby increase its sense of motionlessness. In the final version the main text (bars 1–34) is followed by a repeat of the last two lines (bars 35–42), development of the last line (bars 43–50), recapitulation of the first two lines (bars 52–9),

Ex. 14.2

a SV 252, fo. 2ʳ stave 4

[Tiefe . . .]

b SV 252, fo. 2ʳ stave 4

Tiefe   Stille   herrscht im Wasser

c SV 252, fo. 2ʳ stave 5

Tiefe[. . .]

d SV 252, fo. 2ʳ stave 7

[Tie-fe . . .]

e SV 252, fo. 2ʳ stave 7

[Tiefe . . .]

f SV 252, fo. 2ʳ stave 8

[etc.]

Tiefe[. . .]

g SV 252, fo. 2ʳ stave 11 (=CD1)

[etc.]

[Tiefe . . .]

h SV 252, fo. 2ᵛ stave 4

[etc.]

[Tiefe . . .]

Ex. 14.2 (Cont)

i SV 252, fo. 2ᵛ stave 6

|Tiefe . . .|

j SV 252, fo. 2ᵛ stave 9 (= CD2)

Tiefe   Stille |. . .|

k SV 138, fo. 1ʳ stave 1

Tiefe   Stille   herrscht

l SV 138, fo. 1ʳ stave 4

tiefe[. . .]

m SV 138, fo. 1ʳ stave 6

Tiefe   Stille   herrscht im Wasser

and a coda based on the text of line 2 (bars 59–73); but Beethoven reached this form only after experimenting with other forms using either less or more textual repetition.

The nine continuity drafts show this feature clearly. In CD1 the only repetition is of lines 7–8: this was a feature planned from the start, and it is found in all the drafts except CD6, where nevertheless it was probably still

Ex. 14.3 SV 138, fo. 1ʳ

die Nebel   zerreiss[en]   der Himel   ist   Helle   [und] A-olus

löset   das   ängstliche   Band

intended. In CD2–CD4 the opening two lines return at the end but there is no development of line 8 beforehand, and the coda consists of no more than a few tonic and dominant chords, as in Ex. 14.4 (CD2). In CD5–CD6 there is no recapitulation, but instead there is a short development of the material used for line 8, corresponding to bars 43–50, to conclude the section. The following draft (CD7) is structurally the closest to the final version: only here do we find both the development of line 8 and the recapitulation of lines 1–2; here, too, the coda is much more extended than before—in fact the recapitulation and coda, here consisting of twenty-five or twenty-six bars (Ex. 14.5), are together slightly longer even than the final version of twenty-two bars. In CD8 the reprise is longer still, with practically the whole poem repeated, so that at first sight the reprise looks like an additional draft for the main section, as it does also in CD9, where only the reprise is sketched. A summary of the changing form of 'Meeresstille' can be seen in Table 2.

In Beethoven's instrumental works expansion very often occurs between successive drafts, but it tends to be as a result of each section becoming larger while the overall proportions do not alter radically. Here, however, the expansion has occurred by more and more material being added at the end. The duration of the main text remains more or less constant throughout the first eight drafts, but whereas initially it occupied most of the movement, by CD7 it occupies less than half of it: an extension has been added after the repeat of lines 7–8, a recapitulation has been introduced, and this has itself been extended into a coda of about twenty-five bars, so that the main text occupies about thirty-eight bars while the additional repetitions and developments occupy about forty-two. If such proportions were to be retained there was therefore room for a complete varied restatement of the main material instead of just a series of repetitions and developments of part of it. Thus in the supplementary sketches after CD7 Beethoven drafted an idea for a reprise of lines 5–8 of the text, and in CD8 and CD9 he tried out a more or less complete restatement of the text, before abandoning the idea and returning to the structure of CD7 in the final version. (The sketches of CD8 seem to indicate that the complete restatement was abandoned because an extended coda would still have been necessary at the end to emphasize the overall mood, and to have both restatement and extended coda would have pro-

Ex. 14.4 SV 138, fo. 2ʳ

Ex. 14.5 SV 138, fos. 5ᵛ–6ʳ

longed the movement too much).

In addition to structural alterations, Beethoven as usual made numerous melodic changes between the different drafts. These were partly to improve the rhythmic flow of the words and partly to create more interesting melodic lines; but the prime purpose in this case was to intensify the pictorialism of the music, to bring out every nuance of the text. The final version shows how magnificently he succeeded. Right at the start the deep stillness is reflected by the very static first chord, which lasts four and a half bars (almost thirteen seconds)—an astonishing length in such a short piece. The word 'herrscht' is appropriately set slightly higher than the neighbouring notes. The second line is almost entirely on one note; the word 'bekümmert' introduces the first

TABLE 2. The Changing Form of 'Meeresstille'

Draft	Main text (bars 1–34)	Repeat of lines 7–8 (bars 35–42)	Development of line 8 (bars 43–50)	Reprise of lines 1–2 (bars 52–73)	Reprise of more text
CD1	✓	—	—	—	—
CD2	✓	✓	—	✓	—
CD3	✓	✓	—	✓	—
CD4	✓	✓	—	✓	—
CD5	✓	✓	✓	—	—
CD6	✓	—	✓	—	—
CD7	✓	✓	✓	✓	—
CD8	✓	✓	—	✓	✓
CD9	—	—	—	✓	✓

chromatic element; the smooth plains are again given a very flat melodic line; the lack of wind is reflected by the silences between the syllables of 'Keine Luft'; 'fürchterlich' is set to an unexpected B flat major chord. And by far the most striking piece of pictorialism in the whole work—in fact almost in Beethoven's entire output—occurs at the word 'Weite', where a closely spaced chord that implies resolution inwards is suddenly followed by a chord of extremely wide spacing, which threatens to resolve to an even wider chord (Ex. 14.6). All these devices may seem obvious enough with hindsight, but few of them were present in anything like their final form in the early stages of Beethoven's sketching.

The two-bar orchestral chord that forms the introduction is omitted from most of the main drafts, but it was sketched at an early stage (SV 138, fo. 1^r stave 2) and was probably intended even in sketches where it was omitted. There is no indication in the sketches about the unusual spacing of the first chord, with its doubled third and lack of a fifth, which considerably enhance the word 'Tiefe'; but this is the sort of problem that Beethoven usually worked out in his head or else in the autograph score. The static first chord is not held out to its full length (four and a half bars) in any of the sketches except the revision to CD6, and even here the notation is slightly ambiguous. Similarly the word 'herrscht' is given varying degrees of prominence in the early sketches (see Ex. 14.2), sometimes being on a relatively high note but often not; even in CD6 and CD8 there was doubt about its pitch, for both drafts originally differed from the final version, with the word 'herrscht' on an E rather than G. In the second line the original idea was to repeat the melodic shape of the first, but by CD3–CD4 Beethoven had already reached more or less the final version apart from the rhythm. In CD3 the treble is sketched, and in CD4 the bass is for these bars, so that the two can be fitted together as in Ex. 14.7.

The chromatic chord on 'bekümmert' in the third line is visible only in CD7, but some sort of chromaticism had been planned much earlier, for in CD2 there is a G minor chord (Ex. 14.8), indicating that Beethoven felt that some tonal instability was the most appropriate way of illustrating the

Ex. 14.6 Op. 112. i

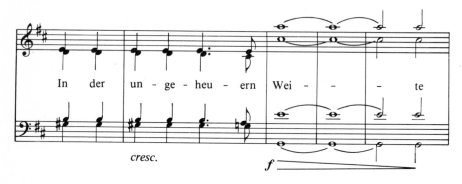

Ex. 14.7 SV 138, fo. 2ʳ

oh - ne Re - gung ruht das Meer

Ex. 14.8 SV 252, fo. 2ᵛ

und be - küm - mert

anxiety expressed in the text. The fourth line invariably shows a certain flatness of melodic shape, but the key to be chosen for the cadence long remained uncertain. Beethoven did not keep returning to these bars as he did to some others, which suggests that he did not regard the problem of the cadence as a major one; yet practically every time the cadence appears in a sketch it is different. Since only the melody line is sketched it is in some cases hard to tell what key the cadence is in, but in ten different sketches of these bars there are as many different endings and almost as many different cadences implied: each of the five keys closest to the tonic is represented, as well as (apparently) a half close in the tonic itself; the only thing that Beethoven clearly wanted to avoid was a perfect cadence in the tonic. The subdominant is found only in CD2, CD6, CD8, and a short sketch at the foot of SV 138, fo. 2ʳ, where a plagal cadence is implied. This key, however, seems with hindsight to be an obvious choice: not only does the subdominant represent the very antithesis of forward motion, making it particularly appropriate here, but Beethoven was being increasingly draw to experimenting with subdominant relationships at that period. The use of it here, therefore, is one of a number of progressive features in the movement.

In setting lines 5 and 6 of the text, like the cadence at the end of line 4, Beethoven came very close to the final version as early as CD2, where the melody already contains such features as the F natural on 'fürchterlich', and the main difference is that the line is not interrupted by crotchet rests as it was later. In the remaining drafts, however, instead of making the few modifications necessary he experimented with several quite different ideas in which the only common feature was the presence of some chromaticism (occasionally just implied) on 'fürchterlich'. Again the ideas of CD2 were

Ex. 14.9 SV 138, fo. 5ᵛ

[To - des - sti - lle   fürch - ter - lich]

finally restored in CD6, which is very close to the final version of lines 5–6 (bars 19–26), while CD7 contains further experiments which were not eventually adopted (Ex. 14.9).

Despite some interesting features in the sketches for lines 1–6 of the poem, it is in line 7 that the most remarkable sketching occurs. This is, as mentioned earlier, the most striking passage in the final version of the work (see Ex. 14.6) and it was probably this line more than any other that induced Beethoven to set the two poems in the first place. It was certainly the one to which he gave by far the most attention during his sketching, for there are no fewer than thirty-seven sketches (a few of which are themselves altered slightly) for this one passage (Ex. 14.10*A–Kk*). The first of these are found amongst the very earliest sketches for the work, and Beethoven then kept returning to the same passage during the course of sketching the rest of the movement. Even when the movement was more or less finished, sketches for this phrase were still being made, and none of them matches the final version. Thirty-seven is probably not the largest number of sketches he ever made for a single passage, but it is unusually large, and by far the biggest for any passage in Op. 112; the passage sketched next most often is, as one might expect, the first phrase, yet this appears little more than half as many times. Amongst other works, one frequently cited for its large number of sketches is the song 'Sehnsucht' (WoO 146),[12] composed only a few months after Op. 112, but here the main theme is sketched only about twenty-four times; and the layout of these sketches suggests 'not long and tedious labour, but the rapid tumbling out of ideas, one after another',[13] whereas with 'ungeheuern Weite' in Op. 112 there was a much more long-lasting problem which Beethoven kept returning to between sketches for the rest of the work.

The thirty-seven sketches shown in Ex. 14.10 are worth considering in more detail. Some are early concepts for inclusion in a future main draft, while others are squeezed in at the foot of a page as variants. Apart from those that form part of the nine main drafts, nearly all focus on just the single line of text, though a few carry on into the next line. All are concerned with extreme word-painting, and Beethoven's main concern seems to have been to ensure that the melodic line was sufficiently wide-ranging to capture the idea of enormous distance and expanse. Thus all the sketches display a wide compass, and most have at least one very large leap of more than an octave:

---

[12] See N-II, pp. 332–3, and Lockwood, 'Sehnsucht'.
[13] Lockwood, 'Sehnsucht', pp. 113–4.

Ex. 14.10

a SV 252, fo. 2ʳ stave 3

[In   der   un - ge - heu - ern   Wei - te]

b SV 252, fo. 2ʳ stave 6

c SV 252, fo. 2ʳ stave 8

in   der   un   -   ge - heu - ern   Wei - te   [re - get]

d SV 252, fo. 2ᵛ stave 1 (= CD1)

in   der

e SV 138, fo. 1ʳ stave 5

un - ge-heu-ern   Wei - te

f SV 138, fo. 1ʳ stave 5

ungeheuern _____ Wei - te

Ex. 14.10 (Cont)

g SV 138, fo. 1ʳ stave 13

In   der un - ge - heu - ern Wei - te

h SV 138, fo. 1ᵛ stave 10

[etc.]

i SV 252, fo. 2ᵛ stave 11

un - ge - heu - ern Wei - te

j SV 252, fo. 2ᵛ stave 12

in   der un - ge - heu - ern   Wei - te

k SV 138, fo. 2ʳ stave 1 (= CD2)

[etc.]

In   der un - ge - heu - ern Wei - te   re – get

l SV 138, fo. 2ʳ staves 8–9

[etc.]

re – get

Ex. 14.10 (Cont)

m SV 138, fo. 2^r staves 8, 10; 2^v stave 1 (= CD3)

In der un - ge - heu - ern Wei - te   re - get kei - ne

We - lle [sich]   In der un - ge - heu - ern Wei - te   re   -   get

n SV 138, fo. 2^r stave 11

o SV 138, fo. 2^r stave 12

p SV 138, fo. 2^r stave 12

in der un - ge - heu - ern Wei - te   [re-   get]

q SV 138, fo. 2^r stave 13

r SV 138, fo. 2^r staves 13–14

Ex. 14.10 (Cont)

s SV 138, fo. 2ᵛ staves 7–8 (= CD4)

In   der   re - get   [etc.]

t SV 138, fo. 2ᵛ staves 8, 10 (= CD4)

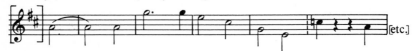

[etc.]

u SV 138, fo. 3ᵛ staves 11–12

v SV 138, fo. 4ʳ staves 1–2

In   der   un - ge- heu - ern │Wei - te │   re-get   [etc.]

w SV 138, fo. 4ʳ staves 9–10

[etc.]

x SV 138, fo. 4ʳ staves 10–11

in   der   ungeheu   [-ern   Wei - te   re-get]

y SV 138, fo. 4ʳ staves 7–8 (= CD5)

In   der   un   ge- heu - ern │Wei - te │ re - get   [etc.]

oder

Ex. 14.10 (Cont)

z SV 138, fo. 4ʳ stave 8

Aa SV 138, fo. 4ᵛ staves 4–7, 2

re - get [etc.]

Bb SV 138, fo. 4ᵛ staves 6–8

[etc.]

Cc SV 138, fo. 5ʳ stave 4 (= CD6)

In   der   un - ge-heu-ern   Wei - te [re-get]

Dd SV 138, fo. 5ʳ stave 14

[In   der   un-   ge- heu-ern Wei - te   re-get]

Ex. 14.10 (Cont)

Ee SV 138, fo. 5ᵛ staves 7–8 (= CD7)

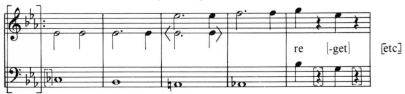

re   [-get]   [etc.]

Ff SV 138, fo. 5ᵛ staves 6 , 13, 14

[In   der un- In   der   un - ge-

heu - ern Wei - te]

Gg SV 138, fo. 6ʳ stave 10

in

Hh SV 138, fo. 8ʳ staves 1–6

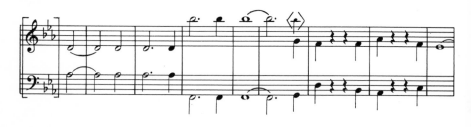

Ex. 14.10 (Cont)

Ii SV 383, fo. 1ʳ staves 8–14 (= CD8)

Jj SV 383, fo. 1ᵛ staves 5–8

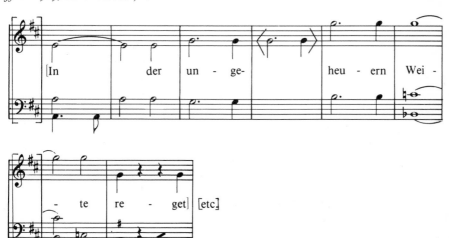

Ex. 14.10 (Cont)

Kk SV 242, fo. 2ᵛ staves 3–7 (= CD9)

some have an upward leap, some a downward one, and some have one in each direction. In most cases the leap is shown in the treble part but in a few it is shown in the bass or even both treble and bass. The size of the leap varies considerably, and in several sketches at least one leap is filled in by some sort of arpeggio (Ex. 14.10*F, H, N, P, S, T, V, Y*), although this idea disappears in the later sketches. Rising leaps include one of a minor tenth in seven sketches (*M, Q, Z, Aa, Bb, Dd, Kk*), an eleventh in five (*B, J, K, Cc, Ii* —in all but sketch *B* on the same notes as in the final version), a diminished twelfth in two (*I, O*), and a massive minor thirteenth in three (*Ff, Gg, Hb*). Among falling leaps an octave is the most common, as in the final version, but Beethoven also experimented with major and minor tenths (*M, P, Q, Dd, Hb*), an unnerving diminished tenth (*A, C, D*), an eleventh (*Y*), a diminished twelfth (*F, Z*), a perfect twelfth (*W*), and a minor thirteenth (*B*); here most of the strange intervals come in the early sketches. These huge leaps provide a foretaste of similar ones, also for expressive purposes, in the *Missa solemnis*, at such places as 'Deus Pater omnipotens' and 'descendit de coelis', and of a leap of two whole octaves contemplated in a sketch for 'Et resurrexit'.[14]

The idea of great distance could equally be expressed harmonically, as is dramatically illustrated in Ex. 14.10*R*, the shortest of these sketches and yet one of the most telling. This is a very odd sketch, and it appears to belong to a fairly early stage of work (unless it was a late addition to the page); but it contains the kernel of the final version—the highest and lowest notes of the chord eventually used for the word 'Weite'. In some of the other sketches

[14] SV 154, fo. 30ʳ; cf. Schmidt-Görg, 'Missa', p. 17, and Schmidt-Görg ed., *Diabelli*, i. 85.

on two staves the widest chord is preceded by a much closer chord, so that the texture expands either gradually (V) or suddenly (Aa), or else suddenly in the treble but gradually in the bass (Ee). Sketch S also shows an expanding texture and is actually almost the same as sketch V, but in it the treble and bass parts are compressed on to a single stave, creating a rather confusing impression.

One of Beethoven's main problems with the phrase 'ungeheuern Weite' was to decide which syllable or syllables should be highlighted the most, and the sketches show many different possibilities (they often omit the text but it has been added editorially in Ex. 14.10 where the underlay is not obvious). The problem originated with Goethe's text, which subtly conveys several layers and shades of meaning at once. The word 'ungeheuern' conveys not only impressions of great size but also overtones of something abnormal and almost supernatural, somewhat like the English word 'monstrous'. The word 'Weite' similarly suggests both distance and great breadth—a kind of 'far and wide' image. Thus the musical phrase had to contain not just high notes but low ones as well, preferably with very little in between. Although this could normally be done on the word 'ungeheuern', something had to be kept in reserve for 'Weite'. One possibility was to have some strange chromaticism on 'ungeheuern', followed by a large leap on 'Weite', as in sketches C and D; several other sketches also suggest chromaticism and strange intervals as well as large ones (A, I, Y, Bb).

Practically every syllable in turn was tried as the top note of the phrase, although the fact that they were not tried in any particular order and that anyway the sketches were not directly consecutive suggests that Beethoven was not simply going through all the possibilities rigorously. The syllable 'un-' appears at the peak of the phrase only once (N), and this is anyway a bass sketch; 'unge-' forms the peak once too (T), but generally it is later syllables that form the climax. In several sketches the peak is on '-heuern' (A, B, C, D, G, Q, U) or even just '-ern' (D (second time) and P); '-ern Wei-' is tried once (F), while 'Wei-' is tried several times (E, L, O, W, X, Y (first version) and Z); 'Weite' is tried in only four (J, K, Bb, Ii (first time)) apart from the final version, whereas the unlikely syllable '-te' is tried six times (H, I, S, V, Y (second version), Dd), and even 're-' is used once (Ee).

In a few sketches, mostly later ones, Beethoven prolongs the climax by using several syllables for the highest note: '-heuern Wei-' (M, Aa, Hh, Kk), '-heuern Weite' (Gg, Ii (second time), Jj), or 'ungeheuern Wei-' (Cc, Ff). The few possibilities not tried, such as '-ge-', '-heu-', and combinations of various syllables, were not necessarily discounted completely—the fact that they were not sketched does not mean they were not contemplated. The only thing Beethoven seems deliberately to have avoided is two peaks of equal height on non-consecutive syllables: in the few sketches where there are two distinct peaks (*I* and *W*) they are of different pitch, the second slightly higher than the first.

The idea of vast expanse being expressed rhythmically as well as by melody and harmony seems to have occurred to Beethoven only at a relatively late stage. In the early sketches there are no very long notes, but rhythmic expansion starts appearing from sketch *X* onwards. Here he merely uses larger note values, but in *Aa* he consciously prolongs the high note, making several alterations nearly all of which are concerned with the length of the high As. In sketch *Bb* the prolongation is mainly by contrapuntal means, but in *Cc* and in *Ff* onwards the top note itself is simply extended, with no implied movement in the lower parts. In most of these sketches the prolongation of the climax is achieved by having more syllables on the highest note rather than just one very long note. Even where a long note is used Beethoven seems not always to have had the courage of his convictions, for it is sometimes shortened again, as in *Aa*, where a seven-beat note is reduced to three beats, and *Cc*, where again a whole bar is cancelled, reducing the duration of 'Wei-' from nine crotchets to five. Only in one sketch (*Ii*, first time) is there a ten-beat note on the single syllable 'Wei-', as in the final version.

By the time Beethoven had drafted CD7 he had mapped out the eventual structure of 'Meeresstille', and his temporary satisfaction with the movement at that stage is marked by a turn to 'Glückliche Fahrt' for the next few pages (i.e. from SV 138, fo. 6ʳ, to the upper staves of SV 383, fo. 1ʳ), where there are only occasional references to 'Meeresstille'. He then returned to this movement in CD8 (and CD9), where he fixed the key for both movements and tidied up various details of the word-setting. Any further sketching after this would have been mere refinement of what is already present in the existing sketches, and their main significance can now be summarized.

Beethoven's initial problem was to find the key and metre most appropriate for the text, and in the case of the key the problem remained for an unusually long time. The structure of 'Meeresstille', and especially its rounding off before the lead-in to 'Glückliche Fahrt', also remained an intractable problem, since there was no pre-existing model such as sonata form to follow; the form therefore had to emerge gradually, and the amount of repetition, development, and reprise was not established until very late. The nine drafts cannot be seen as simply reflecting a steady process of modification and refinement from a crude and primitive first idea to a polished and elegant structure that approximates to the final version. Instead CD2 must be seen as containing much of the essence of the final version, and as a big advance on CD1. Further progress was then made through Beethoven producing a number of radical alternatives which could suggest new ideas to be incorporated into the overall plan or could equally confirm that in many places the earlier plan was indeed the best. CD6 incorporates some of these alternatives while restoring several ideas that had been abandoned in CD3–CD5, including the G major cadence and the melodic shape of lines 5–6. CD7 provides several further alternatives that were not taken up (including the key of E flat), but although it was cancelled in ink it is the only draft to match the final version in form. Meanwhile CD8 is melodically closest to the final version (at least until the reprise), while CD9 proved to be a dead end. Beethoven seems therefore to have been treating whole drafts in the way he had at an earlier date treated short variant sketches: several were places side by side in quick succession as alternatives before he reviewed them all and selected the best one, but ideas from the others were then incorporated into it. Such erratic progress was very common in his sketching, and serves as a reminder that the order in which the sketches were written down does not necessarily correspond exactly to the closeness with which they resemble the finished product, even though this is generally the case.

Questions of declamation and word-painting were not insignificant, but in most parts of the movement they do not seem to have given much trouble. In the phrase 'ungeheuern Weite', however, extreme word-painting was called for; Beethoven felt compelled to stretch towards unprecedented means of musical expression, and the numerous sketches for the phrase are evidence of his great determination to break new ground.

15

The Problem of the Joins:
Egmont Overture

BEETHOVEN'S overture and incidental music to Goethe's play *Egmont* were written as a result of a commission, in the autumn of 1809, from the Viennese Court Theatre. The music was not completed until the following June, with the overture as usual apparently being finished last. The subject of the play concerns Egmont's struggle against tyranny and foreign domination and his anticipation of ultimate victory—a subject particularly dear to Beethoven and also one of considerable topical interest in Vienna as a result of the French occupation of the city in 1809.

Composing a dramatic overture such as this immediately presents a problem: should the composer try to embody the whole of the drama in the overture or should he regard it just as a curtain-raiser to the first scene (in this case a shooting contest) without any suggestion of the drama that follows later on? Beethoven had himself tried both types of overture in those written for *Leonore*; in the first two *Leonore* overtures, now numbered 2 and 3, he had tried to embody the whole of the drama, including the climactic moment heralding the arrival of Don Fernando, whereas in the third (No. 1, composed in 1807) there is only a hint of what is to come.[1] The disadvantage of the first method is that after such a dramatic overture the opera, or at least the first part of it, can seem something of an anticlimax or even redundant: once the overture has been heard the opera is hardly needed since the overture has provided such a good summary. This disadvantage does not apply to the same extent to an overture to a spoken drama like *Egmont*, however; the music after the overture here is only incidental to the play, and there is therefore no danger that it will simply repeat the overture. In fact the overture is the one place where the whole dramatic substance can be portrayed musically.

Thus on this occasion Beethoven decided immediately to write an overture which summed up some of the main elements of the play. The play ends with a short 'Siegessymphonie' (Victory symphony) celebrating the ultimate victory of freedom over oppression, and so he decided to make the overture,

---

[1] The correct order of the three *Leonore* overtures was for a long while uncertain, but it has now been established fairly conclusively that 'No. 1' was actually written third, in 1807 (see Tyson, 'First Leonore').

too, end with the same music. The 'Siegessymphonie' was therefore not composed as a separate number before he started work on the overture but was conceived as one section it, to be detached and performed again with minor modifications at the end of the play. The rest of the overture was conceived as a slow introduction and sonata-form allegro, making three sections in all.

Beethoven had decided on this much at a very early stage in the conception of the work, when the other movements had apparently not been fully sketched and when even the key of the overture had not been established. This is clear from a sketch-bifolio now in Hanover (SV 328), which quite possibly contains the very first sketches for the overture and certainly the earliest ones extant.[2] The first page of the bifolio has a note that the overture will be 'perhaps in C minor' ('Vieleicht in C moll') and shows a main theme consisting of a descending phrase in the bass clef in C or G minor (Ex. 15.1), not unlike the main theme of the final version, despite the differences in key and metre. The final section of the overture was at this stage planned in C major, and here the themes are even closer to part of the final version (Ex. 15.2). The word 'victoria' appears amongst these sketches, confirming that as well as being intended for the final section of the overture they were to be used in the 'Siegessymphonie', which was to be roughly the same as the end of the overture. Nothing corresponding to the first section of the overture is found amongst the sketches in the Hanover bifolio, but there is on the second page an extended draft of about fifty-five bars in 9/8 in C minor, ending in C major;[3] it seems likely that this was an early attempt at a slow section for the overture, especially as it does not correspond to any other part of the *Egmont* music, although it does contain some ideas akin to the final version of No. 7 ('Klärchens Tod') and could therefore have been intended for this number instead.

Once Beethoven had decided that the overture should have three strongly

Ex. 15.1 SV 328, fo. 1ʳ

Ex. 15.2 SV 328, fo. 1ʳ

[2] See Fecker, 'Hannover', and Fecker, *Egmont*, pp. 107–9.
[3] Fac. and transcription in Fecker, 'Hannover', pp. 370–1.

contrasting sections, one of his biggest problems was to join them together convincingly. The difficulty lay not in making the sections interrelate, which was ingeniously achieved by motivic means (note especially a falling fourth motif that occurs in the Introduction before returning both speeded up and in slower note values in the Allegro in bars 25–8 and 36–42 and finally in inversion at the beginning of the Coda). Instead the problem lay in joining the sections in the smoothest possible way, to make them seem to grow out of each other. The problem of such joins occurs, of course, in all works of any length, but it is even more acute here than usual. The solution to the problem is today so familiar that it is hard to imagine just how great a problem it could be; an examination of the sketches, however, most of which belong to a fairly late stage in the evolution of the overture, highlights some of the difficulties.

Apart from the Hanover bifolio already mentioned, the main extant sketches for the overture are on two pairs of bifolios now in Vienna (SV 272 and 273: Gesellschaft der Musikfreunde, A42 and A43 respectively). Neither was discussed by Nottebohm but they have recently been described in detail, complete with facsimiles, by Adolf Fecker,[4] although his account gives little idea of Beethoven's overall progress on the movement. The two bifolios in A42 form a gathering, with the pages today numbered 1–8, and all the sketches are in ink apart from some later alterations and additions in pencil, chiefly on page 8. The bifolios in A43, however, are now ungathered, with one numbered as pages 1–4 and the other as pages 5–8. But matching ink-blots indicate that the bifolios originally formed a gathering like A42: the pages should correctly be in the order 7/8, 3/4, 1/2, 5/6, and they were also for a time used in the order 1/2, 5/6, 7/8, 3/4 (see Fig. 1).[5] Some of the sketches are in ink, some in pencil, and some in pencil that has been inked in.

Altogether in the two manuscripts there are three continuity drafts (which will be referred to as CD1–3), each of which covers practically the whole movement. There is also an additional draft for the Coda (CD1a), falling chronologically between CD1 and CD2, while CD3 lacks the Coda. The beginning of CD1 is in pencil, but the rest of the draft is in ink and was probably made at a later stage. CD2 was originally drafted in pencil, but the draft has been inked in and extended by the addition of a Coda sketch. CD3 is in ink but has occasional pencil alterations. Hence the three main drafts actually represent at least six phases of compositional activity. The location of the drafts and other sketches in the two manuscripts is summarized in Table 1.

For a work of this date and complexity one would expect Beethoven to have made at least five or six main drafts before writing the autograph score, and so it is likely that there are at least two or three missing, as well as several

[4] Fecker, *Egmont*, pp. 107–76 and plates XXIV–XXXVIII.
[5] See Cooper, 'Egmont', for a fuller explanation.

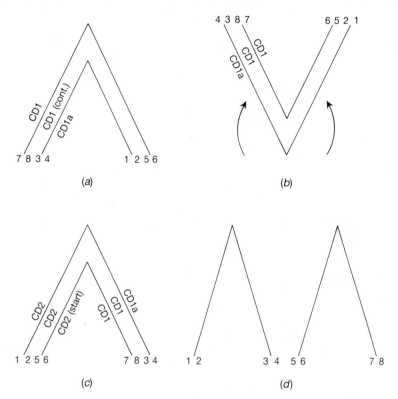

FIG. 1. Changing make-up of Vienna, GdM, A43: (*a*) probable original make-up, during drafting of CD1 and CD1a; (*b*) A43 folded inside out along the arrows so that p. 6 is opposite p. 7; (*c*) the same rotated through 180° to show p. 1 at the front: ink offsets from p. 2 to p. 5 and from p. 6 to p. 7 confirm that this was the correct order at one time; (*d*) present order, with the inner bifolio placed after the outer one.

shorter drafts and variants. This theory is supported by the fact that CD1 is already quite well developed in its general outline, implying that earlier drafts are missing. On the other hand, CD2 shows little further progress, and even CD3 is still different from the final version in many places, especially in the Introduction and development section, and does not include a proper Coda at all, so was therefore probably not the final draft from which most of the autograph score was made. Despite the missing material, however, the surviving sketches throw much light on the problems of the joins. Whereas in the early sketches Beethoven would have been concerned with establishing the main ideas of the overture, and in the final sketches (also missing) he would have been working mainly on refinement of detail, the sketches in A42 and A43 come from precisely the stage when the joins were causing the biggest problems.

TABLE 1. *Summary of Contents of A42 and A43*

MS	Page	Contents
A43	7	CD1 (Introduction and exposition), plus variants for exposition
	8	CD1 continued (exposition to end of codetta after recapitulation), plus variants for this section
	3	CD1 (Coda), plus variants for Coda and preceding codetta
	4	CD1a (Coda), plus variants for Coda
	1	CD2 (recapitulation to Coda), plus Coda variants
	2	CD2 (Coda, unfinished)
	5	CD2 (exposition, bar 59, to recapitulation)
	6	CD2 (Introduction and exposition, to bar 59), plus variants mainly for Coda
A42	1	CD3 (Introduction and exposition), plus variants
	2	CD3 continued (exposition to recapitulation), plus variants
	3	CD3 continued (recapitulation), plus variants
	4	CD3 continued (end of recapitulation and codetta), plus variants and discontinuous Coda sketches
	5	discontinuous Coda sketches
	6	blank
	7	discontinuous Coda sketches
	8	discontinuous Coda sketches, plus variants for Introduction and exposition

All three continuity drafts show the shape of the overture firmly established as a slow Introduction and a sonata-form Allegro, both in F minor, followed by a coda in F major—a scheme already foreshadowed in the Hanover bifolio. With the three sections so sharply contrasting, one might have expected Beethoven to draft each one complete before going on to the next one; but this might have made the problems of joining the sections together even more formidable. Instead he viewed the movement as a complete unit, so that all three sections were evolving simultaneously throughout the extant sketches. He tended to work on each section in turn as a separate problem, as is indicated by such features as changes in writing implement and spatial separation between the sections; but he kept alternating between the sections without spending very long on any one at a time. Thus his procedure was liable to result in each section being more advanced at a given moment than the links in between, and this is indeed what happened. In addition the main Allegro section tended to be more advanced than either of the outer sections.

The main thematic ideas of the overture are already present in CD1, although some of them—particularly the second subject—still had to be modified; many of the main subsidiary keys are also established, including the use of D flat major, rather than the more orthodox F minor (or possibly F major), for the recapitulation of the second subject. By this stage the principal problem remaining was therefore already that of the joins, including both the links between the three main sections and also, to a lesser extent, the joins within each of the sections. The locations of the joins in the final version are illustrated by a brief analysis of the form, which is summarized in Fig. 2. The slow Introduction is in two sections, the first (bars 1–14) alternating heavy string chords and soft woodwind phrases, while the second (bars 15–24) makes much use of a four-note descending motif. The Allegro is in a very regular sonata form. The first group of themes is introduced by a four-bar anacrusis (bars 25–8) and includes three main motifs (1A, 1B, 1C —see Ex. 15.3*a–c*)—the first a descending arpeggio on the cellos (bars 28–36), the second a descending four-note scale played three times (bars 36–42), and the third a four-note rhythmic figure repeated numerous times over a long dominant pedal (bars 58–66); theme 1A is then restated by the full orchestra (bars 58–66). The transition to the relative major follows (bars 66–81), and the second subject consists of a speeded-up variant of the first theme of the slow Introduction, plus a little excursion into A major. The closing theme in the exposition consists of long rising scales followed by some heavy chords (bars 104–116). The development section is based mainly on 1A, and the retransition uses the anacrusis from bars 25–8, so that it leads almost imperceptibly into the recapitulation at bar 159. The first group of themes, including the anacrusis, returns exactly as in the exposition (bars 159–200), then the second motif (1B) appears again and the transition is modified to take the music into D flat major; the second subject and closing

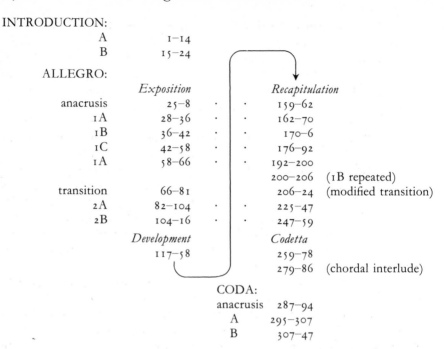

INTRODUCTION:
A   1–14
B   15–24

ALLEGRO:

Exposition   *Recapitulation*

anacrusis   25–8   ·   ·   159–62
1A   28–36   ·   ·   162–70
1B   36–42   ·   ·   170–6
1C   42–58   ·   ·   176–92
1A   58–66   ·   ·   192–200
200–206   (1B repeated)

transition   66–81   206–24   (modified transition)
2A   82–104   ·   ·   225–47
2B   104–16   ·   ·   247–59

Development   *Codetta*
117–58   259–78
279–86   (chordal interlude)

CODA:
anacrusis   287–94
A   295–307
B   307–47

FIG. 2. Form of the *Egmont* Overture

theme return almost exactly as in the exposition, and the Allegro closes with
a codetta that turns the music from D flat major back to the tonic and
concludes with four slow chords. the F major Coda, like the exposition,
begins with a kind of anacrusis; then come two main sections, the second
(from bar 307) based initially on a chromatic eight-note ostinato. Thus the
principal joins are from the Introduction to the Allegro and from the latter
to the Coda; subsidiary joins occur at the transition to the second subject, the
beginning of the development section, the retransition to the recapitulation,

Ex. 15.3 Op. 84

and the transition within the recapitulation itself. Internal joins occur in the middle of the Introduction, between the three motifs in the first group, between the second subject and the closing theme, and in the middle of the Coda.

In the first main join the four-note descending scale which appears repeatedly in the Introduction was planned to continue at the beginning of the Allegro, and the problem was to effect a smooth transition. At the end of the Introduction in CD1, Beethoven had already prepared many of the features found in the final version: the horns, actually labelled 'Corni' in the sketch, are in octaves on C; the descending figure appears on various degrees of the scale in turn as four quavers and a crotchet; and then in the bass clef on the notes C–Bb–Ab–G, it is slowed down to four crotchets and a minim (Ex. 15.4). The remainder of this part of the draft is difficult to decipher as it has been concealed by a later ink layer, but the continuation appears to show another bar of crotchets (this time an octave higher but with the remark that the cellos are to play in octaves with the first violins) and then three bars of statements of the four-note motif in quavers leading to the first subject (Ex. 15.5).

Thus in this sketch the link between the Introduction and the Allegro is already very close to the final version, in which the descending figure again appears on various degrees of the scale in quavers, then in the bass clef, then in crotchets, and finally in rapid repetitions in 3/4 time leading to the first subject. The underlying idea was therefore already firmly established as early as CD1, and the details are so close that one might have expected one further sketch to be sufficient. But achieving the best effect from a series of statements of a commonplace motif such as this four-note descending scale could be quite an arduous task, precisely because there is so little to choose between the various possible variants; and there is also the problem that the desire for

Ex. 15.4 SV 273, p. 7

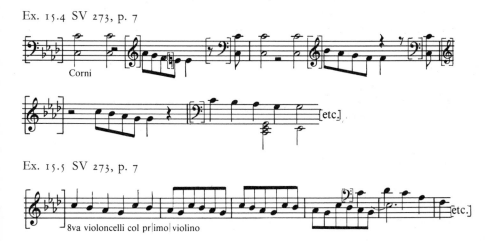

Ex. 15.5 SV 273, p. 7

continuity and the desire for appropriate proportions between phrases sometimes suggest different solutions, which somehow have to be reconciled. Hence this little passage was sketched several more times before the final version was ready to be written out.

The next sketch for the link occurs in CD2, a draft that originated as a pencil sketch for the first dozen bars or so of the slow Introduction (A43, p. 6 staves 3–5). Beethoven later inked in and extended this sketch to the end of the stave (stave 5) and then by means of the customary 'Vi=de' sign he continued it by superimposing the ensuing bars on the corresponding part of CD1 (p. 7 staves 5–6). The lack of spatial continuity has resulted here in a slight discontinuity of thought, for the two bars on either side of the 'Vi=de' do not quite join up; and there is also some notational uncertainty in that some of the bars have an irregular number of beats (see Ex. 15.6). But the main changes from CD1 seem to be that the phrase in the bass clef is now in quavers instead of crotchets and the bar of six crotchets in the treble clef now runs into a second, similar bar before the quavers resume at the implied change of time signature. Noteworthy is the fact that the descending figures still have no upbeat as they do in later versions (though such upbeats were sometimes omitted from sketches even when they were intended) and also that the bars of crotchets in 3/2 run straight into the 3/4 quaver bars whereas in the final version there is a brief rest in between. Beethoven's intention at this stage to effect a gradual transition is confirmed by the appearance of 'strg' (stringendo), indicating a gradual speeding up from the slower tempo to the Allegro during the repetition of the four-note figure.

In CD3 the join is still not clearly made, and the problem is compounded by the fact that the quavers in the Introduction are notated as semiquavers, leaving once again a certain amount of ambiguity as to speed and rhythm. The anacrusis to the main theme—in the final version just four bars long and with only five occurrences of the four-note descending figure—is here six bars, and is it still does not end up on a C on the right beat of the bar it has been extended in pencil to seven bars (Ex. 15.7). This is unduly long,

Ex. 15.6 SV 273, pp. 6–7

Ex. 15.7 SV 272, p. 1

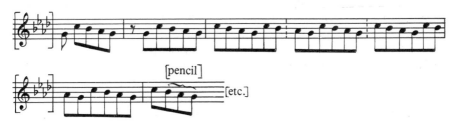

particularly in such a tightly knit movement, and Beethoven's dissatisfaction is shown by the presence of two alternative versions for this passage, one at the foot of the page (A42, p. 1 staves 13 and 16), where the anacrusis is significantly shorter (Ex. 15.8), and the other a brief sketch overleaf, where the motif is slowed down to a series of alternating minims and crotchets (Ex. 15.9). Part of the trouble was that the four-note figure was bound to create a cross-rhythm in triple time; it therefore needed twice the normal amount of concentration and attention for the composer to be able to synchronize the two rhythms properly and to create a length of anacrusis that suited both rhythms.

Once the third main draft of the overture (CD3) had been completed, Beethoven returned to certain special difficulties (A42, pp. 5–8), and although most of these sketches concern the Coda, some were, perhaps inevitably, devoted to this difficult link at the end of the Introduction (A42, p. 8). Here there are yet more versions of the four-note figure, with one passage (p. 8 staves 12–13) close to the final version and the pencil additions (p. 8 staves 13–14) even closer, but they still do not quite match it. In particular there is still no clear break between the Introduction and the Allegro as there is in the final version, and Beethoven still seems to have been envisaging a gradual transition from a slow tempo to a quick one, as is clear from the reappearance of the word 'stringendo' (abbreviated) in two of the sketches. Thus the exact shape of the link and the material immediately

Ex. 15.8 SV 272, p. 1

Ex. 15.9 SV 272, p. 2

preceding it were left indeterminate until a very late stage of evolution of the overture; almost all the ingredients of the final version can be found amongst the sketches, but not in the right combination.

The second main join, from the F minor codetta to the F major Coda, proved an even bigger problem. This was partly because it was a much more unusual one—no other minor-key sonata-form movement by Beethoven has a coda in the major—and also because the Coda had to function as an independent movement (the 'Siegessymphonie' at the end of the incidental music) as well as being a suffix to the overture. The link in fact posed three separate problems, each of which comes to the fore in different sketches: how to conclude the Allegro; how to lead up to the main theme of the Coda; and whether there should be anything between the end of the Allegro and the lead-up to the Coda theme. In the final version there appears to be nothing in the score between the 3/4 section and the Coda, but the last eight bars of the 3/4 section actually function as an independent interlude: although they are notated in 3/4 they are preceded by a pause and contain four slow chords, so that any metrical relationship to the preceding bars is destroyed. Aurally the effect is therefore of a slow 4/4 bar inserted between the Allegro and the Coda, and in performance today the passage is rarely played at the speed notated. None of the sketches resembles the final version of this interlude, but as will be seen, a number of them show a quite different idea for an interlude—a return of the slow Introduction in 3/2.

One of the most remarkable features about the sketches for the join is the paucity of those showing both the end of the F minor section and the beginning of the Coda. It is as though Beethoven had a certain hesitancy or apprehension about making sketches for the join itself until the last possible moment, even though he was prepared to make sketches for what came either side of the double bar. He may also have felt that the two parts were virtually separate movements, each with its own problems, and that there was therefore no more necessity to sketch both in succession than there was to sketch the join between two independent movements of a sonata or symphony, something which he did not normally do unless there was a connecting link between them. The location of the sketches for this crucial part of the overture is shown in Table 2. As can be seen, although there are several sketches for the end of the Allegro, several for the interlude, and several for what eventually became an eight-bar anacrusis to the main Coda theme, there is only one sketch which runs from F minor material into the Coda without a break.

In the first draft (CD1) the F minor section concludes with a rest and pause (A43, p. 8 stave 13) and then resumes at the top of the next page (p. 3 stave 1) with the Coda (Ex. 15.10), with no sign of either an interlude or any kind of dominant preparation or anacrusis to the Coda theme (which is itself very different from that of the final version). Whether these two sections of the

TABLE 2. *Location of Sketches for the F minor—F major Link*

MS	page/stave	End of 3/4 section (bars 267–78)	Interlude (bars 279–86)	Anacrusis in 4/4 section (bars 287–94)
A43	8/12–13 (CD1)	√	–	–
	8/14 ('oder')	√	–	–
	3/11	√	√	√
	3/12	–	–	√
	3/13	–	–	√
	6/(1 and) 16	–	–	√
	1/7–10 (CD2)	√	–	√
A42	4/2–4 (CD3)	√	√	–
	4/5	√	–	–
	4/6a	√	√	–
	4/6b	–	√	–
	4/10–11	–	√	–
	4/12–13	–	–	√
	5/15–16	–	–	√
	8/1	–	√(?)	–
	8/5	–	√	–

Ex. 15.10 SV 273, pp. 8, 3

overture were intended to be consecutive as in Ex. 15.10 is uncertain, though
there is no evidence to suggest that Beethoven at this stage planned anything
more between them.

A variant sketch on page 3 stave 11, however, is of considerably more
significance (Ex. 15.11). This is the only sketch that runs through from F
minor music into the Coda, and it therefore helps to confirm how the various
more fragmentary sketches should fit together. (It poses slight problems of
transcription, for the clef intended at the beginning is unclear—probably
treble and bass clefs were intended simultaneously in the first bar—and the

Ex. 15.11 SV 273, p. 3

figured bass in bar 7 makes no real sense;[6] moreover there is no corresponding mark to match the 'N 1000' at the end, though the continuation may be overleaf (p. 4 stave 1) in the next draft, i.e. CD1a.)[7] The layout of the sketch shows quite unmistakably that Beethoven planned here to insert a reminiscence of the slow Introduction, in the manner of the 'Pathétique' Sonata, before proceeding with the Coda. The sketch begins at about the end of the recapitulation, with the music still in D flat; it is then worked round to F minor by means of an augmented sixth, followed by a dramatic general pause which was to re-emerge in the final version. The rhythm and metre of the Introduction, but not the melodic ideas, then return for just four bars before the Coda bursts in with dactylic rhythms similar to those that had been labelled 'victoria' in the Hanover bifolio. There is still no dominant preparation at the beginning of the Coda, but the theme does at least begin here with one bar on the dominant; and the first eight bars do function as a kind of anacrusis, for the full orchestra enters only at the ninth bar of the Coda (marked 'orchest'), with the first eight bars presumably intended just for trumpets. The Coda theme is still not really established, but the A–G–F–G motif in the sixth to eighth bars of this part of the sketch anticipates the final version of the theme.

Two other sketches on the same page, both probably written slightly before the one just discussed although positioned lower down, show further work on the beginning of the Coda. The first (stave 12) is actually cued into CD1 by means of a large cross and the remark 'Zu 1 Mal', and it shows four bars to be placed at the end of the CD1 Coda sketch (Ex. 15.12). The two slow chords in octaves clearly contain the seeds of the interlude (bars 279–86)

---

[6] In Fecker, *Egmont*, p. 169, the figures are transcribed as $\frac{6}{4}$, which makes better sense although it is clearly not what Beethoven wrote.   [7] Ibid., p.171.

Ex. 15.12 SV 273, p. 3

of the final version, even though the chords are here in 4/4, that is, after the double bar instead of before it. (This reinforces what was said earlier about this interlude being in 3/4 only notationally, and that it could equally easily have been notated in binary metre as in this sketch.) The other sketch on this page intended for the beginning of the Coda (stave 13) is fairly similar to the corresponding place in Ex. 15.11 and needs no separate discussion. Similarly the two sketches on page 6 (staves 1 and 16) show little progress on the join except that the Coda theme itself is slightly more developed.

The next sketch for the join between the Allegro and the Coda occurs as part of CD2 (A43, p. 1). Beethoven was still very uncertain how to connect the two sections: the draft, after continuing uninterrupted right through from the exposition of the Allegro, suddenly contains an uncomfortable gap of two and a half staves between the end of the recapitulation and the beginning of the Coda, to allow space for the linking passage to be filled in later. (Such gaps were often used to represent unsketched bars, though in the end the space here was filled with more Coda sketches.) The original pencil version of CD2 in fact peters out altogether at the end of the recapitulation, still in D flat, but in the ink revision it is extended by eight bars, with the last four marked 'pp' and presumably representing just the start of the link (Ex. 15.13); the long middle C at the end of Ex. 15.13 suggests the beginning of a return to F minor, but it was surely not intended to conclude the 3/4 section, for earlier sketches had already indicated that the link was to be much more substantial than this one, which would be very inadequate on its own. The big gap that follows between this sketch and the beginning of the Coda is a further indication that Beethoven still planned an extended link at this point.

At the beginning of the Coda in CD2 there is a new idea (Ex. 15.14) which shows a major advance on previous attempts and clearly foreshadows the final version. Over an implied dominant pedal there is a gradually rising phrase that builds up to a climax on an a''' for the main theme. This anacrusis to the Coda theme is so successful because it provides a much more gradual change from minor to major, and from the old mood to the new mood of freedom (expressed by very high notes) and victory. The only real defect in

Ex. 15.13 SV 273, p. 1

Ex. 15.14 SV 273, p. 1

this extended anacrusis is its proportions. As usual, being the first sketch, it is somewhat shorter than the final version, and it needed extending. As first drafted it consisted of nine and half bars in 2/2 time; this was soon expanded to ten and a half bars by lengthening the fifth bar to form two bars (see the upper notes in this bar, in Ex. 15.14). Obviously an odd half-bar could not be retained, and by the time Beethoven had ironed out this and other unevennesses in the phrase lengths the result was sixteen bars; this was, however, notated as eight bars of 4/4 time in the final version, with the note values halved.

The next sketches for the join between the Allegro and the Coda occur in connection with CD3. This draft, like the pencil version of CD2, breaks off shortly before the Coda (A42, p. 4), and concludes with the connecting sign 'Vi=No 1000' (stave 5); this could well be intended to connect to the 'N 000' placed at the head of the Coda in CD2. Assuming this is so, we can deduce that Beethoven was provisionally satisfied with his previous Coda draft when writing CD3, and simply ended the latter with a cross-reference to the previous draft. His main concern at the end of CD3, then, was to draft a satisfactory ending to the Allegro, and there are about five separate variants for this passage on A42, page 4 (some of them run into each other, making it difficult to establish exactly how many there are).

Prominent in almost all of them is the return of the 3/2 metre from the Introduction. This had already been tried in a previous sketch (Ex. 15.11) and now it was extended and developed before eventually being discarded. In the main draft (Ex. 15.15) the four-note figure already used at the end of the Introduction is reintroduced. Such commonplace motifs as these scale fragments are of course particularly often used in links and transitional passages, where prominent thematic ideas are generally less suitable; but here the motif has the advantage of being both a commonplace idea and an integral part of the thematic material of the overture. Another way of extending the 3/2 link was simply to continue the main theme from the

Ex. 15.15 SV 272, p. 4

sempre piano

Ex. 15.16 SV 272, p. 4

Introduction a little further and prolong the cadence (Ex. 15.16). Yet another possibility was to reintroduce not just the main 3/2 theme but the answering woodwind phrases as well, possibly extending them into the four-note figure to demonstrate their close relationship to it (Ex. 15.17).

After all these alternatives the final version of the interlude is surprisingly different (Ex. 15.18), but unfortunately no further sketches survive to show how Beethoven arrived at it. Thus the sketches for the second main join as a whole show a considerable diversity of ideas and reveal some of the problems he encountered when drafting this part of the movement; but at the end of the latest surviving sketches the final version of the join was still some way off. The four-chord interlude had not been conceived, although there was a clear desire for a slow interlude of some sort; and the anacrusis at the beginning of the Coda still needed refining. The join as a whole must

Ex. 15.17 SV 272, p. 4

Ex. 15.18 Op. 84

therefore have emerged only as Beethoven worked on the Coda itself. Nevertheless one can now see roughly how he approached this join: first he worked out the style of the Coda and some of its main motifs; then he introduced the idea of bringing back a reminiscence of the slow Introduction immediately before the Coda; then he drafted the extended anacrusis to the Coda theme; and finally at a very late stage he abandoned the idea of a reprise of the Introduction, substituting the version we known today. The order of events is therefore not quite what might have been expected, but it does have a certain sense and logic to it: the middle part of the join could not be fixed until he had a clear idea what was on either side of it, and so it is perhaps inevitable that the slow chords were among the last material to be conceived.

The subsidiary and internal joins in the overture are on the whole less complicated than the two main ones, but a few features are worthy of comment. The retransition sketches are, for once, relatively unremarkable, and the most notable of the subsidiary joins is the preparation for the second subject, for which the sketches show a number of possible approaches. In CD1 the transition leads to a lengthy preparation on the dominant of F minor before a rapid modulation to A flat major for the second subject (Ex. 15.19). The suddenness of this modulation was perhaps already apparent to Beethoven by the time he reached the recapitulation in the same draft, for here there are about five bars of dominant-seventh harmony in D flat as preparation for the second subject in this key, and the whole effect is consequently much smoother. In CD2 the transition was improved by being pruned down: instead of eleven bars based around a C chord as before, there are now only eight; and the rapid modulation into A flat is excised to give a direct juxtaposition of the dominant of F minor and the second subject in A flat—a much more dramatic effect (Ex. 15.20).[8] Only in CD3 do we find an E flat preparation for the second subject, as in the final version. This third draft has two alternatives, one in the main draft (Ex. 15.21*a*) and one in a 'Vi=de' (Ex. 15.21*b*); both show a preparation based on an implied E♭ pedal similar to the final version, with the differences lying mainly in the surface

Ex. 15.19 SV 273, p. 7

[8] In the corresponding recapitulation sketch (A43, pp. 5 and 1), the music is similar at this point, with the second subject again appearing in A flat but this time being restated in D flat.

Ex. 15.20 SV 273, p. 5

Ex. 15.21 SV 272, p. 2

a

b

detail. Thus the harmonic and tonal scheme was as usual established before the precise melodic shape, since a satisfactory underlying scheme of chord progressions was always of prime importance in such transitional material. Surprisingly, however, in this case the earlier melodic shape—that of the main draft—was carried through to the final version rather than the 'Vi=de' revision.

Internal joins within a theme group tend to create different problems from the joins between sections, as is well illustrated in the first subject group in the overture. As stated earlier, the group contains three motifs (see Ex. 15.3), each of which is a self-contained unit. Only the third one (1C), the recurring rhythmic pattern, has any elasticity; the first two have fixed lengths of eight and two bars respectively. The three themes can therefore be repeated or alternated in almost any combination without creating serious problems of continuity. Beethoven tried a few of the possibilities in the three surviving drafts, and the combinations used in these and in the final version are shown in Table 3. As can be seen, each draft provided two opportunities for

TABLE 3. *Structure of First Subject in Sketches and Final Version*

Draft	Exposition						Recapitulation					
CD1	1A	1B × 2	1C	1A	1B × 2	1C	1A	1B × 2	1C	1A	1B × 2	1C
CD2	1A	1B × 2	1C	1A	1C	1B × 2	1A	1B × 2	1C	1A	1B × 3	1C
CD3	1A	1B × 2	1C	1A	(1B × 2)ᵃ	1C	1A	1B × 2	1C	1A	1B × 3	1B × 1
Final	1A	1B × 3	1C	1A	1C		1A	1B × 3	1C	1A	1B × 3	

ᵃInserted.

experiment—the exposition and the recapitulation—and in no version are the two quite identical.

Some further comments need to be made about Table 3. The transition after the first subject group is normally based on motif 1C, and the point where the transition begins cannot be fixed unequivocally; thus where 1C is the last motif in the first group it simply merges into the transition, and this cannot be indicated here. The very short motif 1B was particularly susceptible to repetition and transplant because of its brevity and self-sufficiency, and it really needs repetition to acquire sufficient weight. Therefore in the earlier sketches it is always stated twice; but in the recapitulation in CD2 the second pair of statements is followed by a third after two intervening bars that use the rhythm of 1C. In the same place in the recapitulation in CD3, the three statements are consecutive, anticipating the final version, but in the corresponding place in the exposition the motif was initially omitted altogether in CD3; two statements of it were then squeezed in (A42, p. 1 stave 11), with another statement added on the stave immediately below, implying that three statements were now intended here as well. But the idea of having three statements of 1B on each of its appearances was clearly only a very late change. Table 3 also illustrates the primitive form of the first subject in CD1: in the exposition the three parts of the subject are just repeated *en bloc*, while in the recapitulation the repetition is simply omitted. CD2 has a more complex plan but reveals a degree of uncertainty about where 1B should occur, and the solution adopted in this draft seems a little illogical. In CD3 the insertions display a continuing uncertainty over 1B but this time the draft, with or without the inserted bars, is less irregular. And in the final version, which is only slightly different in structure, the second group of statements of 1B in the recapitulation represents an ingenious way of hinting that the transition is about to diverge from that of the exposition; hence it combines elements of surprise and logicality, characteristic of Beethoven at his best.

The links and transitions in music of the late Classical period were evidently among the most difficult passages to compose, and they are often the least satisfactory parts of movements by lesser composers. This is not true of Beethoven's music, mainly because he devoted so much time and energy to these passages during sketching, but even so his joins are rarely the most striking parts of a movement. Nor are they intended to be. Their function is to highlight the main thematic material and provide smooth continuity without drawing attention to themselves. Listeners are rarely struck at first by the effectiveness of the joins in the *Egmont* Overture when the movement contains so much other powerful music, and these inconspicuous joins well illustrate the art of concealing art. They had to be composed at a relatively late stage so that Beethoven would know what he was joining together, and they had to be based largely on commonplace motifs such as scale figures, albeit derived from thematic elements in the overture. Yet thanks to

Beethoven's intensive sketching of these passages they contribute much to the strong sense of continuity and unity that pervades the overture despite its disparate elements. The sketches show many of the problems liable to be encountered in transitional material in general: the question of length and proportion when moving gradually from a slow tempo to a quick one (as in the first main join); the question of what material should be used at the second main join; and the question of a suitable modulation before the second subject. Meanwhile the first subject illustrates the other main problem of continuity—that of arranging a series of elements and any repetitions of them in the best order, even though there were no links as such to be composed.

16

A Creation in Three Phases:
The Late Bagatelles

THE two late sets of bagatelles—Op. 119 (eleven pieces) and Op. 126 (six pieces)—raise a number of questions about Beethoven's creative process. Why did he, during a period when he was working on the *Missa solemnis* and the Diabelli Variations and had other large-scale compositions in mind such as another Mass and an opera, bother with such relatively trivial pieces? How much trouble did he take in composing them? And how far is each set a unified whole rather than a collection of oddments? The answer to the first two questions is best provided by a detailed look at the origins of the pieces. The traditional answer to the third question is that Op. 119 is a heterogeneous collection while Op. 126 is a unified cycle, but this view is somewhat misleading, as will be seen. Before the two published sets of bagatelles are examined, however, it will be necessary to consider some other bagatelles that Beethoven did not publish, for it is clear from his correspondence and his sketches that the seventeen pieces were not the only bagatelles he considered publishing during the 1820s. In particular he seems at one time to have assembled a group of at least twelve bagatelles, most of which were not published until long after his death.

Of the late bagatelles that were published, the first five to appear were Op. 119 Nos. 7–11; these were first sketched in 1820 (SV 11, pp. 76–9), and the autograph score is dated 1 January 1821.[1] They were intended specifically for a *Wiener Pianoforteschule* being prepared by Friedrich Starke, and were eventually published in it in June 1821. About a year later, in response to a request from the publisher Peters of Leipzig for symphonies, quartets, trios, songs, and piano solos 'among which there might be small pieces',[2] Beethoven offered him an unspecified number of bagatelles on 5 June 1822.[3] He repeated the offer on 6 July, naming his price (8 ducats apiece), mentioning that some of them were rather long and that they could be published separately or together and adding optimistically that Peters 'could have them immediately'.[4] He would have been in no position to offer Peters the five bagatelles already published by Starke; and the main sketches for Op. 126 were not

---

[1] KH, p. 344. See the thematic index of pieces at the end of this chapter.
[2] TF, p. 788.   [3] A-1079.   [4] A-1085.

drafted until early 1824 (in SV 280, pp. 14–24).[5] It might therefore be assumed that the pieces referred to in the two letters were Op. 119 Nos. 1–6. There must have been others too, however, for after offering Peters 'four of the bagatelles' on 3 August 1822,[6] Beethoven stated in a later letter to him (22 November): 'I could send you several more bagatelles than the four we decided on, for there are nine or ten more of them.'[7]

Thus there appear to have been about thirteen or fourteen bagatelles more or less ready at the time, in addition to Op. 119 Nos. 7–11 (already published) and Op. 126 (still unsketched). These other bagatelles, however, were not newly composed. During the course of his life Beethoven had at various times drafted a number of short piano pieces that had for one reason or another not been published (often they had been left not quite finished). Now in 1822, as a result of Peters's request, he began to search through his old papers hunting for manuscripts containing likely-looking bagatelles, and those that he found he placed in a portfolio. The cover for this portfolio still survives (in SV 222) and consists of a rather worn bifolio of manuscript paper, blank apart from the one word 'Bagatellen' on the front. Inside this cover he placed the loose leaves and bifolios containing possible bagatelles, and each piece was allotted a number, written at its head. In some cases these numbers were altered, which indicates that Beethoven did not simply add successive numbers as he placed the manuscripts in his portfolio but was actually trying to arrange the bagatelles into a definite order. Thus one of the pieces (WoO 56) was first marked 'No 3' and later 'No 5';[8] another (Hess 69) has 'No 9' in ink at the top and 'No 3' in pencil (probably added later) in the right-hand margin.[9] Another bifolio in the collection (SV 88) contains (in addition to a draft of 'Flohlied', Op. 75 No. 3) about twenty very densely packed, miscellaneous notations, none of which were published in Beethoven's lifetime. One in A major (WoO 81) has the title 'Allemande' and is headed 'No 6' but has another deleted number (probably 'No 7') in the right-hand margin. Four others are headed 'No 7' (previously a different number), 'No 8', 'N 9' (perhaps altered from another number), and 'No 11' (altered from '10'). Although only one of these five (WoO 81) was a more or less complete piece, the other four are sufficiently substantial to have been able to form the basis of bagatelles.[10] A further manuscript in the collection is a single leaf (SV 223) containing, amongst other material, drafts for Op. 119 Nos. 2 and 4, the former unnumbered and the latter headed 'No 3'.

Altogether in the collection there are therefore two numbered 9 and three numbered 3, none of these numbers being deleted although some were apparently superseded. Yet Op. 119 No. 2 has no number, and certain

[5] See Brandenburg ed., *Op. 126*, for facs. of the sketches, autograph score, and 1st edn. of these bagatelles, with commentary.

[6] A-1092.   [7] A-1106.   [8] Paris, Bibliothèque Nationale, Ms 29.

[9] Ibid., Ms 82 (= SV 234).

[10] For fac. and transcription of the bifolio, see Schmitz, *Unbekannte*.

TABLE 1. *Bagatelle Numberings*

No.	Work	Key
1	Untraced: possibly a lost draft for Op. 119 No. 1	(G m)
2	Untraced: possible a lost draft for Op. 119 No. 3	(D)
3	Op. 119 No. 4 (SV 223) and Hess 69 (SV 234)	A, C m
4	Untraced: possibly a draft for Op. 119 No. 5	C m
5	WoO 56 (Paris Ms 29)	C
6	Allemande, WoO 81 (SV 88, fo. 1^r stave 1)	A
7	Piece in D♭ (SV 88, fo. 2^v stave 5)	D♭
8	Piece in G (SV 88, fo. 2^v stave 1)	G
9	Piece in A (SV 88, fo. 2^v stave 11)	A
10	WoO 52 (Bonn, Beethoven-Archiv, SBH 581)	C m
11	'Rondo' in A (SV 88, fo. 1^v stave 15)	A
12	'Für Elise', WoO 59 (SV 90)	A m

numbers have not been traced at all, indicating that some manuscripts from the portfolio are now lost. Once the deleted and superseded numbers are discounted, the final list of numbered bagatelles as far as is known reads as in Table 1.

Beethoven's search for possible bagatelles during the summer and autumn of 1822 was clearly very extensive, for the pieces he considered for publication at that time had originated much earlier, on a wide variety of different occasions and for different purposes. Their compositional history is best illustrated in the form of a calendar, as follows.

c. 1793. The bifolio (SV 88) containing the pieces later numbered 6, 7, 8, 9, and 11 appears to have been filled soon after Beethoven's arrival in Vienna.[11] He seems to have used it as a repository for interesting ideas that he had improvised at the piano; for if he followed the advice he gave to Archduke Rudolph to jot down ideas in the form of sketches while sitting at the piano,[12] one would expect the result to resemble what is in this manuscript—a jumble of longer and shorter drafts in various keys, some extending to almost complete pieces but others considing only of a few chords. The ideas might then be taken up in some form in a later work (cf. Exx. 8.2 and 8.3).

c. 1794. The drafts for Op. 119 Nos. 2 and 4 were probably made about this time.[13] Their original function is unclear but may have been the same as that of the drafts in SV 88 described above.

c. 1795. In addition to the autograph score of WoO 52 (SBH 581), sketches for this are found in SV 31, fo. 24^r, adjacent to sketches for the C minor Piano Sonata Op. 10 No. 1, suggesting that WoO 52 was initially intended for that sonata as a scherzo and trio.[14]

[11] Johnson, *Fischhof*, i. 88. [12] A-1203 (the relevant portion is quoted in Ch. 1 above).
[13] For date see Johnson, *Fischhof*, i. 371. [14] Ibid., pp. 422–5.

c. 1795–6. The draft for Hess 69 may possibly have been intended for another sonata movement.[15]

c. 1796–7?. No sketches survive for Op. 119 No. 1, but an early date can be presumed on stylistic grounds. A possible origin is as an abandoned middle movement for one of the sonatas Op. 49—more likely No. 2 (1796)—with which it seems to share a certain stylistic affinity. In this context it would create a structure similar to that used about the same time for Op. 10 No. 2 and Op. 14 No. 1: two fast movements in the major flanking a triple-time Allegretto in the tonic minor and in minuet-and-trio form.

c. 1798. A revised version of WoO 52, in 6/8 instead of 3/4, is found in SBH 581, fo. 3, on paper dating from about 1798, adjacent to the original version on fos. 1–2.[16]

Early 1802. A sketch for Op. 119 No. 5 appears in SV 263 ('Kessler' Sketchbook), fo. 59ʳ, amongst sketches for the first two movements of the Violin Sonata Op. 30 No. 2, also in C minor. The sketch was probably an early idea for a possible finale for the sonata.

Summer 1802. A sketch for Op. 119 No. 3 appears in SV 343 ('Wielhorsky' Sketchbook), page 24. The piece may have been conceived for possible use in one of Beethoven's collections of dances for aristocratic balls.

Late 1803. In addition to the autograph score for WoO 56, sketches for this piece appear in SV 60, pages 145–7, immediately after some for the finale of the 'Waldstein' Sonata (in the same key); hence the piece may have been planned as a possible minuet and trio for the sonata.

1808 or 1810. The now missing autograph score for 'Für Elise' is dated '27 April' but the year is unspecified, although it must have been 1808 or 1810.[17] As well as the incomplete preliminary draft for the piece in SV 90, a short sketch definitely dating from 1808 survives in SV 64, page 149. The heading on the lost score, 'For Elise on 27 April as a memento from L. v. Bthvn', indicates that the piece was written as a present for one 'Elise', usually identified as Therese Malfatti.[18]

Apart from Op. 119 No. 6, which we shall come to later, we therefore know of fourteen pieces that Beethoven considered for publication as bagatelles in 1822—the first five in Op. 119 and the nine numbered 3 and 5–12 in Table 1. This concurs extremely well with his remark to Peters (22 November 1822) that in addition to the four bagatelles decided on he had 'nine or ten more', and it suggests that of the material in the portfolio in November 1822 the only parts now unaccounted for are drafts that presumably existed at one time for Op. 119 Nos. 1, 3, and 5.

Once Beethoven had assembled the bagatelles in the portfolio his problem

[15] For date, see ibid., p. 141.   [16] Ibid., pp. 422–5.   [17] See Cooper, 'Für Elise'.
[18] KH, p. 505. In German poetry 'Elise' was a standard name for a beloved; thus Beethoven might well have used it to denote Therese Malfatti.

was to make a suitable selection for publication. Although at one stage he promised to have a set ready for Peters by 15 August 1822,[19] there were delays, partly because of slight ill health, partly because of other commitments (notably the composition of music for *Die Weihe des Hauses*, which occupied him for virtually the whole of September), but more significantly because the bagatelles themselves were not quite in a publishable state. As Beethoven himself said in a letter of 13 September (with characteristic understatement): 'Here and there something has to be added.'[20]

Since he was apparently already making such additions in September 1822, fully two months before he made his final selection of bagatelles, we should expect to find alterations and additions in both the pieces of Op. 119 and those eventually left unpublished, and indeed nearly all of the fourteen pieces show evidence of having been revised, presumably in 1822. In Op. 119 No. 2 the rather ethereal coda, the higher register of which links up so well with that of the start of No. 3, is clearly a late addition: not only does it make use of higher notes than were available when the piece was first drafted but there is also a short sketch for it, in later ink, written at the foot of the page containing the main draft. Op. 119 No. 3 also strays well outside the compass available when it was composed, using a d'''', a note not available to Beethoven until about 1808; the trio section and coda, too, are not in the original sketch and may well be additions from 1822.[21]

The draft of Op. 119 No. 4 contains several amendments and additions, partly in ink of a darker colour than the original, partly in pencil, and partly in pencil that has been inked over in the darker ink. The very style of this sketching—that characteristic mixture of pencil and ink—is found almost exclusively in sketches from Beethoven's later years, and the musical style of some of the revisions also suggests late Beethoven. In bar 9 first- and second-time bars have been created, with short linking motifs added, instead of just a plain repeat. The lower parts in bars 6–7 are also a late addition to a previously unharmonized melody (Ex. 16.1), and two features in this example stand out as very characteristic of Beethoven's late style—the tying of the harmony across the barline and the eventual resolution of the dominant-seventh chord on to a second inversion rather than a root position of D major. In Op. 119 No. 5 the coda is also presumably a late addition because of its keyboard compass and because it is absent from the original sketch.

Op. 119 no. 1 poses more of a problem since no early source material survives; certain passages, however, do seem to suggest that they are late revisions in an otherwise early piece. The first- and second-time bars at the repeat signs contain rather irregular left-hand links of a style and type not normally found in Beethoven's early works but common in his later ones as he strove for greater continuity and unity (Ex. 16.2). The retransition from

---

[19] A-1092.   [20] A-1100.

[21] It is significant that in some marches that Beethoven was selling to Peters at the same time, he specifically mentioned having added trio sections; see A-1100.

Ex. 16.1 Op. 119 No. 4

Ex. 16.2 Op. 119 No. 1

E flat major to G minor (bars 32–6) similarly increases the sense of continuity and contains some harmonically rough passing-notes of a sort found mainly in his late works. In the coda the subdominant orientation with an internal G pedal, so skilfully preparing for the start of Op. 119 No. 2, which is in the subdominant itself and complete with G pedal (Ex. 16.3), is probably also the result of a late revision made as Beethoven was trying to put together a coherent set. Not only do the passages suggested contain elements typical of his later style but they are also in precisely the places where one might expect revisions in the light of the known additions to Op. 119 Nos. 2–5, namely first- and second-time bars, links, and the coda.

Most of the unpublished bagatelles contain revisions similar to those outlined above. Among the pieces in SV 88, the Allemande (WoO 81) has several revisions, with the result that two different versions can be distinguished—the original one of about 1793 and a revised one that presumably dates from 1822.[22] The revisions are confined mainly to bars 9–12, where the

Ex. 16.3 Op. 119 Nos. 1–2

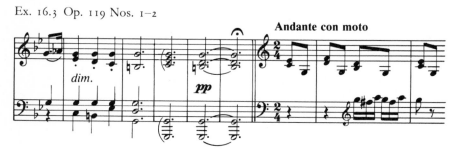

[22] The earlier version is published in Schmitz, *Unbekannte*, and the later one in the *Gesamtausgabe*; see KH, p. 535.

melodic figuration has been made less conventional, and bars 8 and 16, where first- and second-time bars have once again been created with added links, just as in Op. 119 No. 4. The D flat major piece ('No 7') on fo. 2ᵛ of the same manuscript has a revised ending squeezed in at the foot of fo. 1ʳ, and the use of very low notes down to low CC indicates that this ending must be of late date rather than contemporary with the rest of the piece.

Piece 'No 8' in G also has a revision at the foot of fo. 1ʳ of the same manuscript. This fragment is on a supplementary stave below the sixteen ruled staves, and it is unclear how it fits into the rest of the piece, but the form of treble clef used is later than that found in the main part of the manuscript,[23] and so this revision too must be of late date. The so-called Rondo in A (actually in ternary form) headed 'No 11', found on staves 15–16 of fo. 1ᵛ of the same manuscript, has a short link inserted in the rests between the two main sections of the piece, and it also has a coda added on staves 13–14. In this coda we again find the harmony tied across the barline (as in Op. 119 No. 4), suggesting once again a late date. It seems likely, therefore, that all the revisions outlined above to the pieces in this manuscript were made at about the same time, in 1822.

The same is true of four out of the five remaining bagatelles (the one headed 'N 9' does not appear to show any definitely late revisions). In each of WoO 52, WoO 56, Hess 69, and 'Für Elise' the sketching style (in rather scrappy pencil), the musical style, or both, indicate that revisions were made in Beethoven's later years, and the handwriting of the revisions in Hess 69, utilizing his latest form of system brace, also confirms that these revisions were made long after the original draft. In the case of WoO 52 the situation is rather complex because Beethoven had already revised it once, in about 1798, and changed the notation from 3/4 to 6/8, halving the note values. In his final revision he restored the 3/4 time signature and made a few other alterations. The layout of the final version seems to indicate that it was written after the heading 'No 10', which would confirm that this version dates from around 1822.[24]

In WoO 56 there are several alterations in what looks like the original ink, plus a number in pencil which have been inked over in different ink. Only the latter probably date from 1822, and among them two changes seem particularly striking. The first occurs, as in other pieces, at repeat bars (bars 24 and 36), where the phrase shown in Ex. 16.4*a* was altered in pencil, providing an irregular cadence very characteristic of late Beethoven (Ex. 16.4*b*); this was then inked in as Ex. 16.4*c*. The second occurs in the coda (bars 47–8), where the rhythm is altered so that instead of the harmony changing with the beat (Ex. 16.5*a*) it is carried across the barline and changed a beat

---

[23] It is Beethoven's latest form of treble clef, used from the late 1790s onwards; for a discussion of his treble clefs see Johnson, *Fischhof*, i. 29–30.

[24] Ibid., p. 425.

Ex. 16.4 WoO 56

Ex. 16.5 WoO 56

later (Ex. 16.5*b*). Again this is a type of change we have met more than once
before.

   With Hess 69 Beethoven had a major problem. The bifolio containing the
piece has the first seventy-three bars on the first leaf and the last nineteen bars
on the second, but the two sections do not join up: he had lost a page
containing the middle portion and so was left with something that could not
be published as it stood. Thus in 1822 he had to recompose the missing part,
and there are drafts and sketches for it (partly in pencil and partly in ink)
occupying virtually all the remaining space in the manuscript. These drafts
and sketches fit together to fill the gap exactly; a reconstruction of the piece
has been published by Willy Hess.[25] The main draft, however, contains very
few pencil alterations, and so Beethoven must have been reasonably satisfied
with it.

   The revisions to 'Für Elise' are very interesting, particularly as the piece
is so well known. The score from which Beethoven was working was, like
that of Hess 69, incomplete, for it had been only a rough draft and he had
given away the fair copy to 'Elise'. So unless he could remember the piece
he would have been unable to reconstruct it precisely from his draft, and
indeed he did not attempt to. Instead he altered it freely to produce a revised
version of the piece. The original draft is in ink and contains very few
alterations; in its final state it corresponded closely to the autograph score
presented to Elise, which is the version familiar today. On top of this ink

[25] Hess ed., *SGA*, ix. 19–22.

layer are numerous pencil markings, presumably dating from 1822, which alter the music from a version corresponding to the autograph to a different reading. The discovery amongst Beethoven's manuscripts of early drafts of well-known works is not unusual, but to find a version that is later than the one we are familiar with, and therefore (at least in Beethoven's mind) an improvement on it, is much more remarkable. Although the notation is not quite sufficiently complete to enable a definite reconstruction of the revised version, most of the details are clear enough. The revisions include the addition of links in first- and second-time bars (as in several of the bagatelles discussed earlier), slight changes in texture, a reorganization of the structure, and the addition of an 'una corda' marking for the final statement of the main theme.[26]

Thus Beethoven's main concern in revising all these pieces was to increase continuity within them. The problem of the joins, so evident in the *Egmont* overture, re-emerged in these bagatelles, most of which fall into several separate sections. In his earlier years he had been content to leave rests or held notes at the ends of sections, but by the 1820s he clearly felt that these resulted in a rather disjointed effect, and so at practically every junction he added some kind of link to propel the music forward either to the next section or to a repeat of the one just ended. His other revisions were concerned mostly with making rhythms more subtle where they were previously too four-square and extending pieces by adding a coda or other extra material.

In most cases these revisions affect just the internal features of individual bagatelles; but the addition at the end of Op. 119 No. 2 and the putative one at the end of Op. 119 No. 1 indicate that Beethoven's aim of increasing continuity spread beyond the limits of single bagatelles to the creation of satisfactory continuity between one bagatelle and the next. His desire to produce a coherent series of pieces rather than a random collection of oddments is already evident from the way he kept renumbering the bagatelles in an attempt to create a greater sense of continuity and overall structure. But this desire is also evident from a closer examination of Op. 119 Nos. 1–6. Op. 119 has long been regarded as a heterogeneous collection of pieces rather than a unified cycle, in contrast to Op. 126; many writers have taken up the view, first expressed by Nottebohm, that Op. 119 is 'a collection of pieces internally and externally not belonging together, and dating from various times'.[27] This view must now be modified.

Since Op. 119 Nos. 7–11 were written as a single group from the start, the only pieces that could be described as 'not belonging together' are Nos. 1–6; but their stylistic diversity must not be allowed to hide a number of unifying elements in the group. Now that we are more aware of the wide range of bagatelles available to Beethoven when he made his selection for Op. 119

[26] See Cooper, 'Für Elise', for details.
[27] N-II, p. 206. Echoes of this view are found e.g. in Cone, 'Bagatelles'.

Nos. 1–6 we are in a much better position to appreciate these unifying elements. He finally made his selection of bagatelles from his portfolio towards the end of 1822, choosing five (Op. 119 Nos. 1–5) written much earlier but newly revised and one (Op. 119 No. 6) of much more recent date (see below). He had clearly not made his selection when he wrote to Peters on 22 November, yet the autograph score of Nos. 1–6 is dated 'November 1822'.[28] The manuscript would therefore appear to have been written out during the last eight days of that month.

The pieces were clearly not chosen randomly, for in some cases arguably better ones (such as 'Für Elise') were omitted for the sake of balance of the whole. Nor is their order random, either, nor simply chronological as Nottebohm maintained (the dates he attributed to Nos. 2 and 4 are several years too late).[29] Several internal features create a sense of unity, continuity, and cohesion in the group of six pieces. They begin and end with the same tonic (whereas Op. 126 begins in G and ends in E flat) and the keys of the first two, G minor and C major, are neatly balanced by those of the last two, C minor and G major. To compensate for the flat keys the middle two pieces are in sharp keys—D and A. The moods of the pieces are also strongly contrasted, the first five being alternately fast and slow and No. 6 rounding off the pattern by having a slow introduction to a fast movement. The joins between the movements, too, are carefully planned. The subdominant orientation at the end of No. 1, with the G pedal, prepares for No. 2, as noted earlier (see Ex. 16.3). The high register at the end of No. 2 is taken up at the start of No. 3 even though there is an abrupt shift of key, which is designed to increase the feeling of contrast that the fast movement is intended to make. The slow No. 4 follows on naturally in the dominant of No. 3, while No. 5 is deliberately set as a complete contrast, with the change of mood heightened by the contrast of C minor after A major. At the end of the sketch for No. 4 Beethoven actually wrote 'Attacca la seguente Bagatelle', an indication that he was thinking of the two pieces as parts of a single unit. Finally, after No. 5 in C minor, No. 6 begins on a C to provide a smooth transition to G major. Thus each piece that begins slowly leads on smoothly from the previous one, while the fast pieces, Nos. 3 and 5, contrast sharply with those preceding them; this is particularly true of No. 5, the most impassioned of the set.

The key scheme, though less obvious than the major-third relationship that connects the pieces in Op. 126, adds further to the unity and balance of the set, while the placing of a piece of much more recent date at the end of the group provides a fitting climax in terms of increased sophistication and subtlety as well as greater length. The time signatures are also very skilfully arranged: the first five are all different—3/4, 2/4, 3/8, 4/4, and 6/8 respectively—while No. 6 provides a summing up by using three different time

[28] KH, p. 344.   [29] N-II, p. 146.

signatures (3/4, 2/4, and 6/8) representing each of the three main types—triple, duple, and compound time.

This internal evidence of unity in Op. 119 Nos. 1–6 is confirmed by a remark by Beethoven in a letter to Peters of 20 December 1822: 'As to the bagatelles, there are now exactly six of them, and you only want four. I am reluctant to make this division, for indeed I have treated them as belonging together. But if you insist on taking only the four, well then I must make a different arrangement.'[30] These comments clearly imply that he had spent some time working on the pieces in order to make them belong together; and not only the succession of the pieces but also the overall structure of the group was evidently important to him, for he was not prepared to send Peters just the first four. The pieces had been formed into a self-contained cycle with a definite beginning and end, and if any other arrangement were to be made the order would have to be thought out all over again.

The unity of Op. 119 Nos. 1–6 becomes even clearer when they are compared to the set of twelve numbered bagatelles in the portfolio. Although Beethoven obviously made some effort to produce a satisfactory arrangement of these, as is evidenced by the amount of renumbering, there are several inherent barriers preventing the close cohesion and balance found in Op. 119. Too many of the twelve pieces are in either C minor or A major; in some cases there is neither smooth continuity nor dramatic contrast between successive numbers; and the lengths are very uneven. The durations of the first six pieces in Op. 119 are remarkably consistent, but in the unpublished pieces there is much greater variation: some are very short while others are rather long—particularly WoO 52, which is an extended scherzo and trio.

Beethoven's efforts to achieve a sense of unity in Op. 119 Nos. 1–6 can also be seen from a closer examination of No. 6. As noted earlier, this piece is of much more recent date than the other bagatelles. The rough draft for it appears on two folios (SV 210 and 247) each of which also contains sketches for the *Missa solemnis*. These sketches are from a very late stage in the evolution of the Mass, probably after Beethoven had begun writing the autograph score. In SV 210 he tried several alternatives for 'judicare vivos' from the Credo, all very similar to the final version;[31] in SV 247 he sketched bars 358–9 of the Gloria and altered the sketch so that it now coincides exactly with the final version. A date of 1822, when he was putting the finishing touches to the Mass, therefore seems most likely for both the Mass sketches and the bagatelle draft.

A more precise date for the latter, however, can be surmised from internal evidence. It would appear that the piece was written specifically as a conclu-

---

[30] A-1111.

[31] Quoted in N-II, p. 155. They are probably contemporary with some similar sketches from about Oct. 1822 in SV 14, pp. 120–1.

sion to the bagatelle cycle after he had tried all possible combinations of the existing pieces in his portfolio and found that no arrangement of them would make a satisfactory set. It is not too difficult to find a suitable first piece from a group of existing bagatelles, nor to find some contrasting middle ones; but to find one which somehow sums up the whole set and contains hints of the opening piece would be almost impossible in any group of pre-existing unrelated pieces, and so he was really forced to write a new bagatelle. How well it fulfils its function has already been hinted at. The bagatelle continues the sense of key contrast that had characterized the first five pieces in the cycle by being in a new key—G major—but it recalls No. 1 by having the same keynote. Its internal contrasts—a mixture of fast and slow, with three different time signatures—summarize those of the rest of the cycle. It also contains some subtle motivic references to the main theme of No. 1. Beethoven had already employed a similar device in his song cycle of 1816, where the theme of the final song is subtly related to that of the first,[32] but there the opening theme is recalled at the end, making the relationship more conspicuous. In the bagatelle cycle there is no recall of No. 1 at the end, but the connection between Nos. 1 and 6 is still unmistakable, and the fact that such a device had been used elsewhere confirms that the resemblance is no accident. First the upbeat dotted rhythm of No. 1 is reused, again in 3/4, in the opening bar of No. 6; then the main theme of No. 6 has approximately the same outline as that of No. 1—a brief rise and longer descent beginning on d″ (see Ex. 16.6). In the middle sections of the two bagatelles the resemblance is slightly less close, but the two are still sufficiently similar to suggest that the relationship is deliberate and not just fortuitous (see Ex. 16.7). Thus No. 6 provides the perfect counterbalance to No. 1, contributing much to the overall unity that Beethoven had managed to create out of the diversity of the original drafts; and it possesses so many features essential to its function of unifying and concluding the bagatelle cycle that it clearly must have been written specially for this purpose. It was therefore probably composed during the last eight days of November 1822, immediately before the autograph score was written out.

　　The unity of the cycle has been overlooked by writers largely because of the way in which the music was first published. The cycle was eventually

Ex. 16.6 Op. 119 Nos. 1 and 6

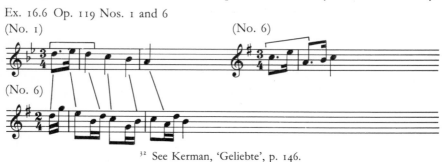

[32] See Kerman, 'Geliebte', p. 146.

Ex. 16.7 Op. 119 Nos. 1 and 6

(No. 1)

(No. 6)

dispatched to Peters on 8 February 1823.[33] As was his custom, Beethoven tried at about the same time to dispose of the pieces to an English publisher; his music often appeared in two editions, one English and one Continental, for each of which he received a fee, but it was not normally possible to sell works to two different Continental publishers because they tended to compete for the same market.[34] Hence he sent a copy of Op. 119 Nos. 1–6 to Ferdinand Ries in London on 25 February 1823, asking him to 'dispose of them as favourably as you can'.[35] And as Op. 119 Nos. 7–11 had not at that time appeared in an English edition he enclosed a copy of these too. Ries sold the eleven pieces to Clementi & Co. and they were published in England later that year.[36]

Peters, however, returned the six bagatelles he had been sent, along with a covering letter dated 4 March 1823, saying in effect that the pieces were not of the type he was expecting, that he wanted better works from Beethoven, and that they were so uncharacteristic of the composer that if they were published many people would suspect Peters of having made a fraudulent attribution.[37] The six bagatelles eventually appeared on the Continent in an edition by Moritz Schlesinger of Paris pirated from Clementi's, and later in another pirated edition by Sauer & Leidesdorf of Vienna.[38] Both publishers naturally included all eleven of the pieces that Clementi had printed.

Beethoven tended to regard his Continental editions as the official ones, and had editions published in England simply to provide extra income; for example, with the 'Hammerklavier' Sonata he was quite happy for movements to be omitted or interchanged in the English edition[39] since the Continental one would indicate his full artistic intentions. In the case of Op. 119, however, the planned Continental edition that would have contained an independent set of six bagatelles never materialized. Thus the structure of Op. 119 Nos. 1–6 became obscured by the addition of Nos. 7–11, resulting in a very odd number of pieces in a variety of styles with no obvious overall plan. It is therefore hardly surprising that later musicians have tended to

[33] A-1137.
[34] See A-1012 for Beethoven's explanation of this system of dual publication.
[35] A-1143.   [36] See Tyson, 'Op. 119'.
[37] The relevant part of the letter is quoted in Brandenburg ed., *Op. 126*, ii. 47–8.
[38] Tyson, 'Op. 119'.   [39] A-939.

conclude that Op. 119 consists of a collection of unrelated works, and Nottebohm's information that some of the pieces were of early origin merely strengthened this impression. It is now clear, however, that Op. 119 consists of a carefully arranged, thoughtfully planned cycle of six pieces followed by a second group of five, and they are best heard—and played—in this way rather than as a group of eleven or as a mixed bag from which to make a random selection.

Once Op. 119 had found a publisher Beethoven laid aside his portfolio of bagatelles for nearly a year while he concentrated on finishing the Diabelli Variations and then devoting himself to the composition of the Ninth Symphony. The latter was more or less finished by about February 1824, and after this he once again turned back to bagatelles. The immediate reason for doing so was apparently that he was in debt to his brother Johann. Op. 119 Nos. 1–6 were to have been used as part payment for the debt, and so when the sale to Peters fell through, Beethoven seems to have felt obliged to give his brother a replacement set instead.[40] This time, however, instead of trying to polish up those he already had he decided to compose an entirely new set. Perhaps his experience with Op. 119, where No. 6 seems to have cost him no more effort than any of the first five even though it was newly written, and also the obvious difficulties he would face in trying to create a coherent set from the very varied bagatelles that still remained, persuaded him that it would be better and quicker to compose a new set rather than continuing to try and touch up existing ones. (He may have remembered his problems of 1814 during the revision of *Fidelio*, when he told Treitschke: 'I cannot work as quickly as if I were composing a new work.'[41]) Composing new bagatelles would have several incidental advantages too. They would provide a welcome change from the enormous effort involved in the Ninth Symphony; they would provide an opportunity for experiment in a context where 'not too much was at stake';[42] and they would give him a chance to show that he could still excel in small forms just as much as in large ones.

He may also have considered that his artistic aims in Op. 119 Nos. 1–6 were not fully realized because he was working with old material of various dates, or that these aims had been foiled because of the unfortunate way in which the cycle had appeared in print; in this case Op. 126 could be regarded as an attempt to do the same as in Op. 119 Nos. 1–6 but better. At all events the cycles do have much in common: both consist of six pieces, and the time signatures in Op. 126 are almost identical to those in Op. 119 Nos 1–6: 3/4, 2/4, 3/8, 2/2 (4/4 in Op. 119), 6/8, and a mixture of duple and triple metre in the final bagatelle.

The earliest evidence that Beethoven was planning the new set of bagatelles comes in a letter of 25 February 1824 to the publisher Heinrich Probst, offering '6 bagatelles for piano solo which, however, are longer than the ones

---

[40] See Brandenburg ed., *Op. 126*, ii. 48–50.
[41] A-479.   [42] Cone, 'Bagatelles', p. 85.

I previously published'.[43] This could refer to six more of the unpublished bagatelles in the portfolio (or even conceivably to Op. 119 Nos. 1–6, if news of Moritz Schlesinger's edition had not yet reached Beethoven), but it more probably refers to a planned new set. Nevertheless most of the sketches for Op. 126 appear to date from May and June 1824.[44] They indicate that from the start Beethoven had the firm intention of writing what he called in the sketchbook a 'Ciclus von Kleinigkeiten' (cycle of bagatelles);[45] he rapidly sketched the whole of the set and eventually produced the final autograph score, several pages of which are replacements for earlier discarded pages. These discarded pages were once again placed in his portfolio of bagatelle drafts.[46] The set was accepted first by Probst and then by Schott, the latter of whom finally published the work in 1825.[47]

The creative process underlying the late bagatelles, and in particular the composition of Op. 119 Nos. 1–6, can therefore be divided into three phases. The pieces had initially been conceived for a variety of purposes—written-down improvisations or ideas for possible future use (the pieces in SV 88), ideas for ballroom dances (possibly WoO 81 and Op. 119 No. 3), discarded sonata movements (WoO 52 and possibly WoO 56, Op. 119 No. 1, and Op. 119 No. 5) and as a personal gift to a friend ('Für Elise'). They would have remained unpublished but for a pressing financial need that Beethoven felt in the early 1820s.[48] To try and ease the crisis he started selling as many old works as possible, and with some (e.g. the three overtures Opp. 113, 115, 117) the ploy was quite successful. Peters's request for short piano pieces provided another opportunity to earn some much-needed cash quickly, for Beethoven knew he had several suitable pieces amongst his papers, and this was the incentive for him to gather together for publication as many bagatelles as he could. It seems that initially he though he could publish a substantial collection of them fairly quickly, and he rapidly went through them numbering them. But when he came to the third phase, that is, producing a publishable version of them, artistic requirements took over and demanded that, even if the pieces were only trifles, they must be of the highest quality. Thus additions to individual pieces had to be made and a suitable selection had to be found to give some sense of overall cohesion and balance. He soon found that much more work was needed on them than he had anticipated, both individually and for the sake of the set as a whole, before they could

---

[43] A-1266.

[44] Brandenburg ed., *Op. 126*, ii. 51.

[45] N-II, p. 196. Fac. in Brandenburg ed., *Op. 126*, i. 52.

[46] For the relationship of the discarded pages to the autograph, see Brandenburg ed., *Op. 126*, ii. 65–6. At least three discarded bifolios were placed in the portfolio: see Cooper, 'Portfolio', on which much of the present chapter is based.

[47] KH, pp. 381–2.

[48] See e.g. A-1143 (25 Feb. 1823): 'The winter and several factors have again reduced my resources; and it is not easy to have to live almost entirely by my pen.'

be published. After spending some time revising most of the pieces and struggling to find a suitable group to form a coherent cycle he eventually realized that no satisfactory grouping could be made without him composing at least one new piece, Op. 119 No. 6, and that the best arrangement was to precede this with only five of the original group of twelve or more. When he returned to his bagatelles a year later he decided that it would be better and quicker to compose an entirely new set, somewhat along the lines of the previous one, rather than continue persevering with the existing ones.

His decision to write new pieces for Op. 126 seems to mark the final abandonment of plans to publish the remaining unpublished bagatelles, for after 1824 he made no further offers of bagatelles to publishers. One reason was the difficulty of planning coherent groups for the pieces he had ready: it took considerable time to plan a set, and the right material had to be available in the first place. Moreover by the time Op. 126 was printed he had only two years to live, and so although he may still have intended to publish the remaining bagatelles he simply ran out of time. His attention, too, had been diverted elsewhere—to string quartets, which he no doubt found a much more rewarding medium and for which there was now a ready demand.

But the portfolio of bagatelles was never entirely forgotten by Beethoven, for it still contained useful musical material that might be salvaged somehow. Thus when he came to write the trio section of the second movement of the A minor Quartet, Op. 132, in 1825 he incorporated virtually the whole of the first part of the A major bagatelle labelled 'Allemande' (WoO 81), though with the structure completely altered and the rhythm astonishingly shifted by a beat. This provides further evidence that he had abandoned the pieces as bagatelles and was hoping to use the music some other way. And finally, on the very last page of sketches that he ever wrote (SV 27 part 2, fo. 6^v), according to Schindler only ten or twelve days before his death, Beethoven entered a C minor sketch marked 'presto' which incorporates the very striking opening motif of WoO 52, another of the bagatelles still unpublished.[49] Was he thinking of resurrecting his bagatelles again, or was the entry just a half-forgotten memory that resurfaced as he lay sick and dying? The most likely explanation is that he was thinking of incorporating the motif into the quintet in C (WoO 62) that he was working on at the time; but we shall never know for certain.

[49] The sketch is transcribed in N-II, p. 523, though Nottebohm does not relate it to WoO 52.

THEMATIC INDEX OF PIECES DISCUSSED

Op. 119 No. 1

Op. 119 No. 2

Op. 119 No. 3

Op. 119 No. 4

Op. 119 No. 5

Op. 119 No. 6

Op. 119 No. 7

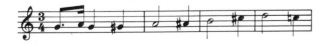

Op. 119 No. 8

Op. 119 No. 9

Op. 119 No. 10

Op. 119 No. 11

Op. 126 No. 1

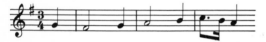

Op. 126 No. 2

Op. 126 No. 3

Op. 126 No. 4

Op. 126 No. 5

Op. 126 No. 6

WoO 52

WoO 56

WoO 59

WoO 81

Hess 69

'No 7'

'No 8'

'No 9'

'No 11'

17

A Long-Running Revision:
Second Piano Concerto

It is easy to imagine that by the time Beethoven progressed from preliminary sketches to drafting an autograph score his main compositional problems were solved and that little further composing activity remained. With some works this was undoubtedly so, but with others he continued to make changes—even quite major changes involving the replacement of whole sections or movements—right up to and occasionally beyond the time of publication. A well-known example is *Fidelio*. But a work with an even longer period of gestation and even more versions (not all extant) is the Second Piano Concerto, Op. 19, with a period of about twenty years between the probable date of the first autograph score (the late 1780s) and the date of the last phase of composition (1809). The main reason for the long delay between its composition and the date of publication (December 1801) was that the concerto, like his other early piano concertos, was written for his own use as a performer. In this situation it was better that the concertos remained unpublished so that rival pianists would not be able to use them, and so he deliberately held them back, as he explained in a letter of 22 April 1801: 'Musical policy demands that one should keep one's finest concertos to oneself for a time.'[1] As a result of this policy, each time he turned to the Second Piano Concerto during the period before publication he was liable to notice defects, and so parts of the work were continually being revised.

The source material reflecting these revisions is very fragmentary and incomplete, and the exact details of many of the revisions will probably never be known; but the picture has become a great deal clearer in recent years thanks to the work of Joseph Kerman, Hans-Werner Küthen, Geoffrey Block, and particularly Douglas Johnson,[2] in which several misapprehensions found in earlier literature have been corrected. Johnson was the first to distinguish and classify all the different paper types of all the surviving early sources of the concerto (both sketches and autograph fragments); the resultant chronology he has proposed is completely convincing except in a few minor details. Nevertheless there are still additional observations to be made

---

[1] A-48.

[2] Kerman ed., *Miscellany*, ii. 45–58, 279–80; Küthen, 'Op. 19' and *Klavierkonzerte I*; Block, 'Gray Areas'; Johnson, *Fischhof*, i. 364–85, ii. 71–93. Kerman and Johnson have between them published transcriptions of all known sketches for the work.

TABLE 1. *Early Sources for the Second Piano Concerto and Rondo (WoO 6)*

Approximate date	1st movement	2nd movement	3rd movement	Paper type
1787			SV 185, fo. 75^{v}: theme later used in WoO 6 (middle)	Bonn II-B
1787	SV 31, fo. 15: score fragment (devel.?)			Bonn II-A
1790	SV 214, fo. 2^{v}: score sketch (devel.)			Bonn II-C
Late 1793	SV 185, fo. 89: score fragment (retrans.) plus sketches		Vienna, GdM, A3: WoO 6, autograph score	I-A16
Late 1793	SV 185, fo. 46^{f}: cadenza sketches			I-A16
Early 1794	SV 95: score fragment (devel.)			I-C16
First half of 1794	SV 223: cadenza sketches			I-F12
Late 1794	SV 185, fo. 148^{v}: short sketch (devel.)	SV 185, fo. 148^{v}: draft for most of movement	SV 185, fos. 147–8: short sketches and longer drafts	I-E16
Late 1794/ early 1795		SV 185, fo. 134: short section		I-I12

Late 1794/early 1795			SV 185, fo. 97: extended draft	I-C16
Spring 1795		SV 185, fo. 127r: draft for Adagio in D		I-K16
1795	SV 185, fo. 45r: cadenza sketches			I-C16
1795	SV 185, fo. 55v: probable cadenza sketch			I-C16
Mid-1796		SV 31, fo. 16v: short note about bassoon part		II-C15
1798		SV 185, fo. 64v: two brief sketches	SV 185, fos. 64–5: extensive sketches and complete draft	III-G18
October 1798		SV 45, fo. 21r: short sketches	SV 45, fo. 21v: short sketch	III-H16
October 1798	SV 45, fos. 19r–20v: extensive sketches		Berlin, SPK, aut. 13: autograph score (piano part incomplete)	III-I16

about some of the material and certain areas where differences of opinion are possible.

Before we trace the chronological development of the concerto, some preliminary remarks about the early sources are necessary. Although no autograph score survives from before 1798, it is virtually certain that at least one—and probably more than one—existed at one time. A remarkably large number of pre-1798 sources are not single-line sketches but full-score fragments (strong evidence that a full score existed), although these are of several different types and functions. One source in particular calls for initial comment. This is the autograph score of a Rondo in B flat for piano and orchestra (WoO 6) of 1793.[3] Scholars have long believed this to be an early finale for the Concerto Op. 19, and although there is still no proof the evidence is very strong: the movement is in the right key and form, with exactly the same scoring as the concerto; the manuscript gives every indication that it was originally not a separate work but part of a longer one, for the first page is not a proper title-page but just bears the word 'Rondo' (written across some largely empty bars) without the name of the composer; and the earliest sketches for the present finale of Op. 19 are from a later date than the WoO 6 autograph. A list of all the early sources for the concerto (and the rondo) up to and including the autograph score of 1798 is shown in Table 1.[4]

The earliest two sources for the concerto appear to date from between 1786 and 1790—perhaps about 1787. One (SV 185, fo. 75) contains an extended sketch for what looks like a movement in E flat, but the theme was eventually used for the middle section of WoO 6, with very little modification. The early origin of this sketch does not constitute firm evidence that Beethoven was writing the concerto at the time, for he not infrequently borrowed thematic material from sketches made much earlier. The other leaf, from the 'Fischhof' Miscellany (SV 31, fo. 15), however, gives a clear indication that he was already writing out an autograph score of the concerto at this stage. Both sides of the page are laid out as a full score, with all ten staves linked by a system-brace on the recto (the left-hand edge of the verso is missing), and with the bottom two staves on both sides containing a fully written-out piano part; the upper staves, however, were left blank and later used for unrelated sketches. It seems that the leaf was to have been part of a full score, that the piano part of the score was entered first, and that before the other instruments were added Beethoven rejected the leaf for some reason. The passage appears to have been part of the development section, for it passes from F major through F minor towards C minor (Ex. 17.1), a progression that would be unusual outside a development at this date. It is unrelated to any part of the final version of the development, and so

---

[3] This is in Vienna, GdM, A3; its date was established by Johnson (*Fischhof*, i. 368).

[4] The dates and paper types are based mainly on Johnson, *Fischhof*, i. 364–79; see also Küthen, *Klavierkonzerte I*, p. 33.

Ex. 17.1 SV 31, fo. 15ᵛ

Beethoven may have substituted something more like the final version almost immediately. Doubtless he retained the discarded leaf because it had so much blank space that could be (and later was) used for other sketches, whereas the score to which it presumably was to have belonged would have been discarded when it was superseded by a revised score.

The next source chronologically is also a score fragment (SV 214, fo. 2ᵛ), which probably dates from 1790.[5] But unlike the 'Fischhof' leaf, SV 214 is clearly not a rejected fragment from a complete score, for two reasons: most of the instruments are specified at the beginning of the page, which would not be necessary if it had continued from a previous page; and the fragment is on the verso of the second leaf of a bifolio (the other three sides are filled with other material). It is almost inconceivable that Beethoven would proceed from another leaf to a page in this position in the middle of writing out a score. This fragment, then, can best be described as a score sketch, in which the string parts are largely left blank and there are gaps in the piano part—features that indicate it is not an addition or replacement for part of an existing score but merely the rough draft for such a replacement.

When Beethoven left Bonn in 1792 he presumably took with him his score of the concerto, but a year later he wrote out a new one. This is evident not only from the score of WoO 6 but also from a four-bar score fragment from the first movement (bars 282–5), which is written on the same type of paper. This fragment (SV 185 fo. 89ʳ), like the one from around 1787 in SV 31, was apparently rejected while it was being written out, since much of the leaf was left blank. But unlike in the earlier fragment, where the piano part was being

[5] Johnson, *Fischhof*, i. 366.

entered before the other instruments, in this one all the instruments were entered more or less simultaneously, so that four bars were fully scored before Beethoven broke off near the beginning of the fifth bar, leaving the rest of the leaf blank (the space was later used for cadenza sketches and other jottings, all in a similar ink to the score fragment and hence perhaps written soon afterwards). The four-bar fragment, which represents the last three bars of the retransition and the first of the recapitulation, are somewhat lacking in subtlety (Ex. 17.2), and Beethoven probably abandoned them for something more sophisticated and closer to the final version (shown in Ex. 17.3), although unfortunately there are no other sketches for this passage with which to make comparison.

The score of WoO 6 is written in brown ink (apparently different from the

Ex. 17.2 Score reduced from SV 185, fo. 89ʳ

Ex. 17.3 Op. 19.i, bars 282–5

previous source) and much of it is free of alterations, indicating that it could
have been copied from an earlier version, as suggested above. But in certain
places there are minor revisions of texture, and there are also a few larger
changes. These include the excision of eight complete bars between bars 200
and 201 and the substitution of bars 242–54 for the outline of an earlier
version.[6] Thus the score is not simply a fair copy of one previously worked

---

[6] Details of this and other major revisions are given in Hess ed., *SGA*, iii. 73–5.

on, but itself contains compositional changes made either while it was being written out or shortly afterwards.

Yet another leaf associated with the putative 1793 score is SV 95. Johnson groups this with sources from 1794–5, but he observes that neither the paper type nor the handwriting point to 1794 rather than 1793,[7] while 1795 seems much less likely. Once again the music, which corresponds to bars 248–68 of the final version except for being two bars shorter, is in full score. But unlike the earlier score fragments, which were either score sketches or rejects from a draft score, this one is fully filled out for all the parts (except for the left-hand piano part); this feature, together with a characteristic cross-reference sign ($\emptyset$) at the beginning of the fragment, indicates that it is a late addition intended to replace part of an existing score. Not surprisingly, the leaf is a different paper type from the autograph of WoO 6 and the rejected retransition fragment, since it must post-date them. It was probably filled not long after the main score had been completed (i.e. at the end of 1793 or early in 1794) and then handed to a copyist, along with the main score, for the preparation of orchestral parts for a performance. The copyist would not have needed to write out the piano part since this would have been played by Beethoven from the score (or from memory), and this is one reason why the left-hand part was omitted in the score fragment; also, by this time Beethoven was evidently acquiring the habit of not fully writing out the piano parts of his concertos—a habit very obvious by the time of the score of 1798. There is also evidence that the Rondo WoO 6 was prepared for performance about the same time, for at one point it contains an instruction for a copyist preparing parts.

No record survives of any such performance of the concerto in 1794, but several aristocrats maintained private orchestras in Vienna for at least part of the year,[8] and so it seems highly probable that Beethoven played this concerto at one or more private performances at that time. One would not expect any record of such a performance to survive. Additional evidence that one or more performances took place about this time appears in SV 185 fo. 46ᵛ and SV 223, which probably date from late 1793 and the first half of 1794 respectively;[9] both leaves, like SV 185 fo. 89, contain sketches for a cadenza for the first movement—sketches Beethoven would have been unlikely to make unless a performance were imminent.

The next group of sources consists of sketches that probably date from late 1794 and/or early 1795. There seems to be a clear chronological gap between this group and the earlier sources, and the group reflects a new phase in the long-running sequence of revisions of the concerto. In the phase of 1793–4 Beethoven had been preparing a full score, so that orchestral parts could be made, and sketching ideas for cadenzas to be used in a performance. Now, perhaps as a result of dissatisfaction with certain passages in performance, he returned to the work for a fundamental overhaul.

---

[7] Johnson, *Fischhof*, i. 368–9.   [8] TF, p. 155.   [9] Johnson, *Fischhof*, i, 367, 371.

Four sources reflect this new phase of major revision—all in the 'Kafka' Miscellany (SV 185, fos. 147–8, 134, 97, and 127). Of these, fos. 147–8 are clearly earlier than fos. 134 and 97 on internal evidence, and earlier than fo. 127 on the grounds of handwriting. It is not impossible that fos. 147–8 are even earlier than the score fragment in SV 95; but most scholars have concluded that the 'Kafka' bifolio is later, and a detailed analysis of the two sources strongly supports this view. The only first-movement sketch on these two folios (fo. 148ᵛ staves 14–15) is for bars 258–68, and therefore by chance covers exactly the same passage as part of the score fragment in SV 95, enabling a close comparison to be made. The strongest evidence that fo. 148 is of later origin occurs in the last four bars of each passage; these are shown in Ex. 17.4, along with the corresponding bars in the final version (bars 265–8). Although the chord sequence in SV 95 is the same as in the final version, motivically it is very weak: the figuration is purely decorative, with no reference to the theme that was being developed in the previous bars, and it is extremely repetitive. The 'Kafka' sketch is much stronger, for the first two bars continue the development of the motif used in the previous bars, and then the last two bars contain some different figuration to provide variety. It is difficult to imagine Beethoven progressing from this version to the very bland one in SV 95, even though the latter is harmonically closer to the final version. It would seem that in his attempt to improve the figuration of SV 95 he weakened the harmonic scheme when he drafted the 'Kafka' sketch, bringing in the dominant chord too soon, but that in the final version he was able to combine the original harmonic scheme with the 'Kafka' figuration in the first two bars and some still more elaborate figuration in the last two.

Apart from this one passage the group of sources from late 1794 to early 1795 is concerned entirely with the last two movements. No earlier sources are known for either movement and so it is possible not only that was the finale a replacement for WoO 6 but also that the Adagio was a replacement for an earlier slow movement. If there was an earlier slow movement it could even have been based on the same material as the 'Andante' section of WoO 6: as noted earlier, the sketch for this section gives the appearance of being for an independent movement, and several of Beethoven's other finales incorporate a quotation from the preceding movement (e.g. the Fifth and Ninth symphonies, the Quartet Op. 18 No. 6, and the piano sonatas Op. 27 No. 1 and Op. 110).

The first sketch for the Adagio (SV 185 fo. 148ᵛ) is a continuity draft covering the whole movement except for the first section and the closing twenty-three bars; it corresponds roughly to bars 18–69, although it is slightly shorter and very different from the final version. Thus either he was drafting a new movement and the sketches for the beginning are now lost, or the movement was already in existence but was so unsatisfactory that only the opening section was retained, with the middle part being completely

Ex. 17.4

a SV 95, fo. 1ᵛ (piano and viola parts only)

b SV 185, fo. 148ᵛ

c Op. 19.i, bars 265–8 (piano right-hand and viola parts only)

redrafted. Either way the sketch must represent a major advance on what had earlier been the slow movement. Further work on the Adagio appears on fo. 134 of SV 185, which contains a number of sketches for various parts of the movement. Many are for transitional passages—in particular the retransition (cf. bars 31–6)—while some are for the coda, including one labelled as the cadenza (cf. bars 74 ff.). The presence of so many transitional and coda sketches suggests that this was a fairly late stage of sketching and that at the time Beethoven considered his work on the rest of the movement to be nearly finished; indeed one of the retransition sketches (stave 7) does come fairly close to the final version, but the remaining sketches indicate that he still had a long way to go.

Whether or not the E flat Adagio was new in 1794–5, Beethoven certainly did contemplate an entirely new slow movement at this date, for there is an

Adagio in D, labelled as being for the B flat Concerto, in SV 185 (fo. 127ʳ). It is an outline of a complete movement, with a considerable amount of detail including harmony on two staves and certain indications of instrumentation. It appears to date from after the above-mentioned sketches for the E flat movement, which suggests that the latter was still nowhere near satisfactory in Beethoven's mind. Nevertheless it was the E flat Adagio, not the D major one, that was incorporated into the concerto about this time (if it had not been there already). It certainly belonged firmly in the concerto by the time of his tour to Prague and Berlin in 1796, for there is a brief reference to it in a sketch on paper dating from the tour. But it is significant that the sketch is not very close to anything in the final version of the concerto.

The finale sketches from 1794–5 are very extensive for a work of such an early date, and they cover all sections of the movement except the one containing the main theme, which like the Adagio had presumably been sketched elsewhere (or perhaps even composed at the piano without any written sketches). The earliest sketches show that the movement was already clearly in sonata-rondo form, like WoO 6, and there are several continuity drafts; these include one for the whole of the first episode—transition to the dominant, second group in that key, and modulation back to the tonic (fo. 148ʳ)—one for most of the middle episode (fo. 147ʳ), one for most of the third episode (fo. 147ᵛ), and one for most of the coda (fo. 147ᵛ). The original idea for the second subject (Ex. 17.5) was soon replaced by an idea much closer to the final version (see Exx. 17.6 and 17.7). The middle episode was initially sketched in D minor and G minor but without the syncopated arpeggio theme eventually used. This theme was introduced in the next phase of sketching (SV 185, fo. 97), but in B flat minor; only later did Beethoven conceive the idea of having this theme first in G minor and then in B flat minor. The coda sketches show that even at this early stage he had decided to bring in the main theme in a remote key (G major)—a device which, as

Ex. 17.5 SV 185, fo. 148ʳ

Ex. 17.6 SV 185, fo. 148ʳ

Ex. 17.7 Op. 19. iii

Johnson has noted,[10] is very characteristic of Beethoven's works of 1795. The sketches for the new finale have no obvious connections with WoO 6 apart from similarity of key, metre, instrumentation, and overall form. As in other cases where one movement was designed to replace another (e.g. the finale of Op. 30 No. 1, the middle movement of the 'Waldstein' Sonata, and the finale of the Quartet Op. 130), Beethoven preferred to make a fresh start with completely new material rather than reuse motifs from the original movement.

The extensive sketches made for the last two movements around the beginning of 1795 suggest that a performance of the concerto may have been planned at the time, and an obvious possibility for such a performance is a concert which took place on 29 March 1795 and which is known to have included a Beethoven concerto. Whether this concerto was Op. 19 rather than that in C major (Op. 15), however, is a matter of considerable controversy. The same applies to the only other known performance of a Beethoven concerto that year—at a public concert on 18 December. An important but equivocal piece of evidence is provided by Beethoven's friend Franz Wegeler, who was in Vienna from late 1794 until after Beethoven had left for Prague and Berlin in January 1796[11] and who reports having been present at the first rehearsals of the C major Concerto, the finale of which he says was written only two days before the performance.[12] He provides certain circumstantial details about four copyists being handed the score a page at a time and the piano at the rehearsal being a semitone flat, which add weight to his account; moreover, he is a generally reliable witness, and the main sketches for Op. 15 do indeed date from 1795.[13] This concerto must therefore have been performed at one or possibly both of the two public concerts. Johnson suggests Op. 19 was performed in March;[14] this would mean that Op. 15 must have been performed in December, and Johnson points to two cadenza sketches for this work (SV 185, fos. 57 and 72) that seem clearly to have been made late in 1795.[15]

There are certain weaknesses in his argument, however. There is no clear agglomeration of sketches for Op. 19 from early 1795, and the nine sources he lists from around this date were probably made over a two-year period from 1794 to 1796; they use six different paper types (see Table 1 above), and the only type used more than once (I-C16) is one that was used by Beethoven over a particularly long period.[16] Johnson points out that sketches for the finale of Op. 15 are found on the same leaf (SV 110) as some for the Quintet Op. 4, and that Op. 4 was published about the same time as Op. 2 and Op.

---

[10] Johnson, 'Decisive', p. 25.   [11] Johnson, *Fischhof*, i. 352.
[12] TF, p. 174; Wegeler and Ries, *Beethoven*, p. 38.
[13] Johnson, *Fischhof*, i. 353–4. Evidence which at one time seemed to contradict Wegeler has evaporated in recent years.
[14] Ibid., i. 378.   [15] Ibid., i. 354–5.   [16] Ibid., i. 98.

3, in about March 1796;[17] yet evidence suggests that Op. 2 and Op. 3 were composed early in 1795,[18] and so it would be more logical to assume that Op. 4 (and hence Op. 15) was being sketched about the time of the March concert that year rather than the December concert, which was anyway uncomfortably close to the date of Beethoven's departure for Prague and the date of publication. Moreover the leaf containing the sketches for Op. 4 and Op. 15 is the same paper type as thirty-seven other known leaves used by Beethoven, all of which apparently date from 1794 or early 1795.[19] And most significantly, Küthen has pointed out that two contemporary references to the March concert describe the concerto played as being 'new' and 'entirely new';[20] this would not be an accurate description of Op. 19, despite the revisions, and assuming it was played in private in 1794 some members of the audience in March 1795 would surely have recognized it, whereas the concerto Op. 15 would indeed have been entirely new. By contrast the concerto at the December concert was not announced as new, even though some Haydn symphonies played at the same concert were advertised as 'not yet heard here'.[21] Thus it seems that Op. 15 was probably the concerto played at the March concert. The few later sketches for it that appear to date from late 1795 (such as the cadenza sketches mentioned above) may indicate that the same concerto was also performed at the December concert; but on the other hand, there are also two cadenza sketches for Op. 19 from 1795 (SV 185, fos. 45 and 55), suggesting that this work was probably performed either at the December concert or at some unrecorded private performance that year.

Apart from the brief Adagio sketched mentioned earlier there are no known sketches for Op. 19 from 1796–7, but in 1798 Beethoven returned to the work for still more revisions, culminating in a new autograph score by the end of the year. Two sketch sources date from this period, the earlier being a bifolio in the 'Kafka' Miscellany (SV 185, fos. 64–5) and the later being in Beethoven's first sketchbook, Grasnick 1 (SV 45, fos. 19ʳ–21ᵛ), and dating from late 1798. The 'Kafka' bifolio contains two very short sketches that are probably for the Adagio (they are in the right key and metre), plus one or two (fo. 64ʳ, staves 1–4) possibly for the first movement—they are in B flat and 4/4 time, but Kerman does not connect them with the concerto and there is no thematic relationship. The finale sketches on the bifolio, however, are very extensive and include three long continuity drafts, one of which covers virtually the whole movement. Most of the sketches are quite close to the final version, and Beethoven would probably not have needed any further continuity drafts before writing out the new autograph score (there is only one short finale sketch in SV 45). But rather surprisingly the main theme, which in the sketches of 1795 had begun in the same way as the final version, is rhythmically altered in the sketches of 1798 (see Ex. 10.29). The sketches in Grasnick 1, unlike those in the 'Kafka' bifolio, appear to

[17] Ibid., i. 354, 498.   [18] Ibid., i. 138, 318.   [19] Ibid., i. 118.
[20] Küthen, *Klavierkonzerte I*, p. 5.   [21] Ibid.

be in the same ink as the autograph score,[22] and were therefore probably made very shortly before the score was written out. Since the concerto was apparently performed by Beethoven in Prague in October 1798,[23] and the score was used at some stage for the preparation of orchestral parts by a copyist with handwriting that is probably not Viennese,[24] it seems very likely that both the Grasnick sketches and the autograph score were written in Prague that month. This group of sketches is mainly concerned with a part of the work that had received virtually no attention in the earlier sketches that survive—the tutti and solo expositions in the first movement. There is also some intensive sketching for a nine-bar passage (bars 61–9) in the Adagio—bars that evidently gave a great deal of trouble—but there are hardly any sketches for the finale or the second half of the first movement (except the cadenza).

The first-movement sketches consist mainly of two long continuity drafts, the earlier (fo. 19ᵛ) leading from bar 24 to the end of the solo exposition (bar 198) and the second (fo. 20ʳ) leading from bar 1 to early in the development section (bar 239). In both cases there are occasional gaps in the drafts—blank bars, blank spaces, or the familiar 'etc'—in places where Beethoven intended to retain his earlier version, and in two places in the second draft this intention is expressed verbally: 'bleibt wie es war' (stays as it was). The earlier draft is fairly similar to the final version, and all the main themes have already reached their final form except for the occasional difference in decoration. But there are still some notable differences between the draft and the autograph score, particularly in the orchestral exposition, which in the draft is considerably longer and includes two important themes that in the final version are reserved for the solo exposition (bars 90 and 128). The second draft is much closer to the final version: the first forty-two bars correspond exactly, and only in a few places is the final version significantly different from both the draft and the variant sketches that appear on nearby staves. Most of the differences occur, as happens so often, in linking passages. This, then, was surely the draft that Beethoven used when writing out the first part of the autograph score; for the second half of the movement he may have retained the development section from his earlier score or drafted a new one on pages now lost, while the recapitulation would not have needed a separate draft as it is based almost entirely on the first part of the orchestral exposition and the second group in the solo exposition.

In its original state in 1798 the autograph score contained relatively few alterations. This was no doubt because it was based on an earlier score, so that the problems of texture and orchestration had largely been solved already; also the score may have been completed in a hurry to meet a performance deadline, thus limiting the time available for revisions. The most substantial alterations at this stage occurred in the finale—particularly

[22] Ibid., p. 32.   [24] Ibid., p. 28.
[23] Ibid., p. 33.

the final four bars, where a revised version (in the original ink) was pasted in over an earlier one. Throughout the work most of the piano part was not filled in but just left as blank staves (the same happened with the Third Piano Concerto a few years later). Beethoven would then have rehearsed and conducted the concerto from the piano, using this incomplete score and playing his own part largely from memory, perhaps adding a few improvised embellishments or variants in places.

Although the concerto was now ready for publication, Beethoven still held it back for a while—presumably for the reasons of 'musical policy' mentioned earlier, in order that any performances he gave would have a bigger impact. Eventually, however, he offered it to Hoffmeister & Kühnel of Leipzig in a letter dated 15 December 1800,[25] and they published it a year later. Since the concerto was published in parts without a full score, the now lost orchestral parts that had been used in Beethoven's Prague performance were probably reused as the engraver's copy for the edition. Engravers of orchestral music in parts preferred to work from manuscript parts rather than directly from a full score where possible, and there seems to have been no reason why Beethoven should have gone to the trouble and expense of arranging for a fresh set of parts (or a score) to be copied specially for Hoffmeister & Kühnel.[26] There remained, however, the question of the piano part, which up till 1801 had never been fully written out and existed only in Beethoven's head. In April that year he finally found time to write it out (the manuscript is now in the Beethoven-Archiv, Bonn, SBH 524); and since Hoffmeister was complaining about Beethoven's slowness in sending the concerto, the composer, to avoid further delay, sent this manuscript to Hoffmeister, as he said, 'in my own not very legible handwriting' rather than having it written out neatly by a copyist.[27] Alterations within this manuscript, and differences between it and the piano staves in the full score, indicate that only at this stage did the piano part reach its published form.

In normal circumstances the version of the concerto sent to the printers would effectively have marked the end of the compositional process for the work (revisions at the proof stage were theoretically possible, but Beethoven apparently did not always have a chance to see any proofs if a work was being engraved outside Vienna as in this case; and once a work was published he hardly ever returned to it for further revisions). Op. 19, however, is once again an exception. Round about the time the concerto was sent to Hoffmeister & Kühnel, Beethoven went through the autograph score of the first movement making substantial revisions in several places, using a distinctive grey ink very different from the reddish-brown ink of the main part of the score, although none of these revisions were included in the printed version.

---

[25] A-41.

[26] Block's claim ('Gray Areas', p. 112) that the full score was a *Stichvorlage* (engraver's copy) for Hoffmeister's edition is untenable.

[27] A-27. The letter implies that the rest of the material is not in Beethoven's hand.

Whether they were made before the piano part in SBH 524 was written out, as is stated by Küthen and Block without any supporting evidence, or after, as might seem more likely since the piano part does not incorporate them, is uncertain. It is also unclear whether the last two movements lack grey-ink revisions because Beethoven did not finish going through the concerto or because these two movements, being much less complex than the first and of more recent date, no longer needed any further alterations. The grey-ink revisions have been discussed briefly by Johnson and in more detail by Block and Küthen,[28] but nowhere is there a full explanation of them or even a complete list. Altogether there are grey-ink revisions or annotations in eighteen separate parts of the first movement, as listed in Table 2.

A full account of the seventeen revisions (not counting the one in bar 198 cancelled by smudging—one of Beethoven's commonest methods of making an immediate cancellation while the ink was still wet) would be out of place here; but it will be noted that they are of many different types and illustrate once again Beethoven's concern for every aspect of each of his compositions. Large-scale design was the problem at bars 91–106 (the start of the solo entry) and the corresponding passage at the beginning of the development (bars 214–22), and also at bar 63. In each case there are cancelled bars, and a replacement would have had to be written out on separate sheets (if this was in fact done, these sheets have been lost). We can only guess what the replacements might have been, but the sketches in SV 45 provided a possible answer. The first solo theme (Ex. 17.8) would most likely have been replaced at bar 91 by a solo statement of the first orchestral theme (a common procedure in eighteenth-century concertos, and one that appears amongst the sketches), and bar 214 would probably have been similar. This would have meant the first solo theme being removed completely from the concerto, since it does not appear anywhere else; but Beethoven may have considered the movement rather too diffuse and motivically heterogeneous with so many themes, so that removing the one which was least integral (in that it is neither developed nor recapitulated) would make the movement more unified motiv-

Ex. 17.8 Op. 19. i

---

[28] Johnson, *Fischhof*, i. 374–5, 381–2; Block, 'Gray Areas', pp. 111–22; Küthen, 'Op. 19', pp. 287–92, and *Klavierkonzerte I*, pp. 28–34.

TABLE 2. *Grey-ink Revisions in the Autograph of the Second Piano Concerto*

Bars	Revision
19	Cello/bass motif altered slightly
41–2	Modulation to Db major better prepared
43–50	Viola quaver figuration replaced by semibreves
63	'Vi=' beside Violin 1, but with no '=de' or replacement text
75–80	Cello/bass figuration altered slightly
81–4	These bars cancelled
91–106	These bars cancelled
128	a' added to Violin 1
136–7	String parts cancelled
167–73	Piano part extensively reworked
184–97	Piano part recomposed as 12 bars (strings in bars 194–7 cancelled)
198	'Vi=' beside Violin 1, with '=de' plus one bar in margin (smudged out)
204–5	Cello/bass altered as in bars 75–6
214–22	These bars cancelled, with 'Vi=' at the beginning but no '=de' (cf. corresponding passage in bars 91–6)
230–1	Altered to match revision in bars 41–2
330–6	Piano part, originally blank in the score, inserted in grey ink, with bars 335–6 slightly different from published version
351–8	Altered to match approximately revisions in bars 167–73
368–83	Piano part recomposed as 12 bars to match the revision of bars 184–97

ically. On the other hand, two additional statements of the main theme might have tended to monotony, and so this theme was removed from the orchestral exposition at bar 63 (where there is a grey 'Vi='), to be replaced by other material—probably the second subject, as in some of the sketches.

Bars 81–4 have a similar cancellation sign, but here no replacement is necessary since the music can proceed perfectly satisfactorily from bar 80 to bar 85 with only slight adjustments of the part-writing. These four bars are thus completely redundant, as is confirmed by the fact that they do not reappear in the corresponding place in the middle ritornello (i.e. between bars 207 and 208). The only other places where the length of the movement was altered are bars 184–97 and the corresponding passage in the recapitulation (bars 268–83). Each of these passages consists of a kind of mini-cadenza of piano figuration based around a prolonged 6-4 chord, but they seem disproportionately long and rather lacking in momentum in the middle; they also do not correspond properly with each other, for in the exposition the passage is fourteen bars long while in the recapitulation it is sixteen bars. So Beethoven reduced both of them to a more satisfactory length of twelve bars and made them correspond more closely to each other.

Two of Beethoven's main concerns at this stage seem therefore to have been to make the movement more concise and to make it more unified motivically; but he was also concerned with smaller details, and his other alterations deal with matters of texture, figuration, chord spacing, and harmonic progression, often resulting in greater clarity. For example, the

Ex. 17.9

a Op. 19. i, bars 75–6, published version (string parts only)

b Op. 19. i, bars 75–6 as amended in autograph score, fo. 6ʳ (string parts only)

rather confused sound of a suspension and its resolution being sounded simultaneously in bars 75–6 (Ex. 17.9*a*) is simplified by removing the suspension (Ex. 17.9*b*). In bars 43–50 an oscillating figure in the viola part is replaced by plain semibreves; similar revisions occur in the version made in 1801 of his Quartet Op. 18 No. 1, where almost all the oscillating accompaniments found in the version of 1799 are removed since they are too pianistic.[29] Meanwhile in bars 41–2 the rather bald change of key to D flat major (see Ex. 17.10*a*) was replaced by a more imaginative modulation heralded by a mysterious G flat (Ex. 17.10*b*).

Ex. 17.10

a Op. 19.i, bars 37–44, published version (string parts only)

b Op. 19. i, bars 37–44 as amended in autograph score, fo. 3ᵛ (string parts only)

[29] See Levy, *Choices*, esp. pp. 64 and 66.

Why did Beethoven omit all these improvements from the published score? As we have seen, in other situations he occasionally had second thoughts about individual revisions in his sketches, so that sometimes a later sketch was discarded and an earlier one restored; but in general his later ideas were improvements, and his latest sketches were more often than not retained in the final version. Hence in the case of Op. 19, where he made revisions in the autograph in seventeen separate places, it is inconceivable that he would on aesthetic grounds eventually have preferred his earlier ideas at all seventeen points, particularly as some of the revisions are such obvious improvements. Some reason other than an artistic one must therefore be found for the rejection of these revisions. The cause seems to have been pressure of time. After offering Hoffmeister the concerto and three other works in a letter of 15 December 1800, to which Hoffmeister responded positively shortly afterwards, Beethoven wrote again about 15 January 1801 stating his prices for the works.[30] Hoffmeister presumably replied promptly to this and could therefore have expected to receive the works sometime during February. Yet nothing had arrived by the end of March, and Hoffmeister felt obliged to write to Beethoven again complaining about the delay. Beethoven immediately felt under pressure to produce something, as is indicated by the fact that he did not arrange for the piano part of the concerto to be written out by a copyist. His revision of the first movement in grey ink must have been under way by this time, but to complete it would have taken quite a while. Even if one assumes that the last two movements needed no revisions and that the replacement passages for bars 63 ff., 91–106, and 214–22 were already fully written out in score, it would probably still have taken him several days to go through each of the eleven orchestral parts that were to be sent to Hoffmeister, making revisions and additions in a dozen or more places in each part. It must have seemed better to Beethoven to send off the concerto as it stood, having already excused himself by saying it was not one of his best works and was being sold at half-price, rather than give himself an additional task when he was already very busy and when Hoffmeister was becoming impatient.

The implications of this conclusion are highly significant. Here, for once, Beethoven had to compromise his artistic goals in one work in order to satisfy a customer and leave himself with more time for new and better compositions. More important, the version that was published and is the one now always performed was not the final one conceived nor the best one, but more on the level of an intermediate draft as far as the first movement is concerned. It would therefore be desirable to restore some of the amendments that had to be rejected in 1801. Not all of them could be restored, since no replacements survive for the three cancelled passages, and so any suggested reconstruction of these would contain a large element of conjecture. But

---

[30] A-41 and A-44.

the remaining fourteen amendments could all be restored either exactly as they stand (in six cases) or with some minor editorial adjustment or amplification (in eight cases).

The one part of the concerto still not written out in 1801 was the cadenza. In performance this had always been improvised by Beethoven, although he often wrote down some of the ideas beforehand, as various cadenza sketches from the 1790s indicate. After he had abandoned his career as a virtuoso pianist on account of his deafness, however, there was likely to be a demand from other pianists for a cadenza from him, especially at a time when cadenzas were gradually being more frequently provided by composers in general. Eventually in about 1809 he provided a cadenza—not just for Op. 19 but for each of his first four piano concertos and the piano arrangement of the Violin Concerto. The cadenza for Op. 19,[31] like its companions, was apparently written for his pupil and patron Archduke Rudolph, and the autograph score is so clear that Rudolph would have been able to play from it direct. It is not based on any of the cadenza sketches of the 1790s but is entirely new and in a more advanced style than the rest of the concerto. Beethoven must have made sketches for it and possibly a rough draft, or *Urschrift*, before writing out the neat version, or *Reinschrift*, which contains only about three minor alterations of substance in the whole of the seventy-nine bars; this preliminary material, however, has not been located.

It is impossible to say how many version of Op. 19 existed during the course of Beethoven's life, since the work was for a long period being subjected to minor revisions almost every time that Beethoven looked at it. But one cannot, without blurring important differences between the stages of revision, reduce the number to less than seven: the Bonn version of around 1787; the early Vienna score of around 1793; the revisions (including a new finale and probably a new Adagio) of 1794–5; the score of 1798 based partly on sketches in SV 45; the grey-ink version that had to be abandoned but which would have been the final version of the orchestral parts; the version with the newly written-out and revised piano part published in 1801; and the version with the cadenza of 1809 in a more advanced style. The concerto thus provides an excellent illustration of how Beethoven's creative process did not stop once he had written out a full score: his fertile mind was continually seeking, and was continually able to find, improvements to a work, and it was only lack of time that eventually persuaded him to call a halt and move on to his next project.

[31] Autograph score in Bonn, Beethoven-Archiv, SBH 525; fac. in Hess ed., *Cadenzas*.

Bibliography

A. Gesamtausgabe (Complete Edition)

Ludwig van Beethovens Werke: Vollständige kritisch durchgesehene überall berechtigte Ausgabe, i–xxv, Leipzig, 1862–5, 1888. (See also Hess ed., *SGA*, below.)

B. Facsimile Editions of Autograph Scores

Violin Sonata in G, Op. 30 No. 3, ed. Alan Tyson, London, 1980.
Piano Sonata in C, Op. 53 ('Waldstein'), ed. Dagmar Weise, Bonn, 1954.
Piano Sonata in F minor, Op. 57 ('Appassionata'), Paris, *c.*1926.
String Quartet in F, Op. 59 No. 1, ed. Alan Tyson, London, 1980.
String Quartet in E minor, Op. 59 No. 2, ed. Alan Tyson, London, 1980.
Violin Concerto in D, Op. 61, ed. Franz Grasberger, Graz, 1979.
Cello Sonata in A, Op. 69 (first movement), ed. Lewis Lockwood, New York, 1970.
Violin Sonata in G, Op. 96, Munich, 1976.
Missa solemnis, Op. 123 (Kyrie only), ed. Wilhelm Virneisel, Tutzing, 1965.
Bagatelles, Op. 126, ed. Sieghard Brandenburg (see Brandenburg ed., *Op. 126*, below).
'Sehnsucht', WoO 134, ed. Paul Mies, Bonn, 1970.
Cadenzas, ed. Willy Hess (see Hess ed., *Cadenzas*, below).

C. Other Literature

Works cited are referred to first by their short titles.
Otto E. Albrecht, 'Beethoven Autographs in the United States', in Dorfmüller, *Beiträge*, pp. 1–11.
Anderson, *Letters*
 Emily Anderson, ed. and tr., *The Letters of Beethoven*, 3 vols., London, 1961.
Arnold and Fortune, *Companion*
 Denis Arnold and Nigel Fortune, *The Beethoven Companion*, London, 1971.
Badura-Skoda, 'Klavierkonzert'
 Paul Badura-Skoda, 'Eine wichtige Quelle zu Beethovens 4. Klavierkonzert', *ÖMz*, xiii (1958), 418–26.
Eva Badura-Skoda, 'Performance Conventions in Beethoven's Early Works', in Winter and Carr, *Detroit*, 52–76.
Bahle, *Schaffensprozess*
 Julius Bahle, *Der musikalische Schaffensprozess*, Konstanz, 1947.
Eveline Bartlitz, *Die Beethoven-Sammlung in der Musikabteilung der Deutschen Staatsbibliothek*, Berlin, [1970].
Beck and Herre, 'Schindler'
 Dagmar Beck and Grita Herre, 'Anton Schindlers fingierten Eintragungen in den

Konversationshefte', in *Zu Beethoven*, ed. Harry Goldschmidt, Berlin, 1979, pp. 11–89.

Biba, 'Concert Life'
Otto Biba, 'Concert Life in Beethoven's Vienna', in Winter and Carr, *Detroit*, pp. 77–93.

Block, 'Gray Areas'
Geoffrey Block, 'Some Gray Areas in the Evolution of Beethoven's Piano Concerto in B flat major, Op. 19', in Lockwood and Benjamin, *Essays*, pp. 108–26.

Sieghard Brandenburg, 'Beethovens "Erste Entwürfe" zu Variationenzyklen', in Dahlhaus, *Bonn*, pp. 108–11.

—— 'Beethovens Skizzen zum zweiten Satz der 7. Symphonie Op. 92', in Dahlhaus, *Bonn*, pp. 355–7.

—— 'Bemerkungen zu Beethovens Op. 96', *BeJ*, ix (1973–7), 11–25.

Brandenburg, 'Dankgesang'
—— 'The Historical Background to the "Heiliger Dankgesang" in Beethoven's A-minor Quartet Op. 132', *BS*, iii, Cambridge, 1982, pp. 161–91.

—— 'Die Beethoven-Autographen Johann Nepomuk Kafkas: ein Beitrag zur Geschichte des Sammelns von Musikhandschriften', in *Divertimento für Hermann J. Abs*, ed. Martin Staehelin, Bonn, 1981, pp. 89–133.

—— 'Die Quellen zur Entstehungsgeschichte von Beethovens Streichquartett Es-dur Op. 127', *BeJ*, x (1978–81), 221–76.

Brandenburg, 'Fifth Symphony'
—— 'Once Again: On the Question of the Repeat of the Scherzo and Trio in Beethoven's Fifth Symphony', in Lockwood and Benjamin, *Essays*, pp. 146–98.

Brandenburg ed., *Kessler*
—— ed., *Ludwig van Beethoven: Kesslersches Skizzenbuch*, 2 vols. (fac. and transcription), Bonn, 1976–8.

Brandenburg, 'Op. 18 No. 2'
—— 'The First Version of Beethoven's G major Quartet, Op. 18 No. 2', *ML*, lviii (1977), 127–52.

Brandenburg, 'Op. 125'
—— 'Die Skizzen zur Neunten Symphonie', in *Zu Beethoven*, ii, ed. Harry Goldschmidt, Berlin, 1984, pp. 88–129.

Brandenburg ed., *Op. 126*
—— ed., *Ludwig van Beethoven, Sechs Bagatellen für Klavier Op. 126* (fac. of sketches, autograph score, and original edn., with commentary), 2 vols., Bonn, 1984.

Brandenburg, 'Petter'
—— 'Ein Skizzenbuch Beethovens aus dem Jahre 1812: Zur Chronologie des Petterschen Skizzenbuches', in *Zu Beethoven*, ed. Harry Goldschmidt, Berlin, 1979, pp. 117–48.

—— 'The Autograph of Beethoven's Quartet in A minor, Opus 132: The Structure of the Manuscript and its Relevance for the Study of the Genesis of the Work', in Wolff, *Quartets*, pp. 278–300.

—— 'Über die Bedeutung der Skizzen Beethovens', in Goldschmidt, *Bericht*, pp. 39–51 (plus 'Diskussion', pp. 52–66).

—— 'Zur Textgeschichte von Beethovens Violinsonate Opus 47', in *Musik—Edition—Interpretation*, ed. Martin Bente, Munich, 1980, pp. 111–24.

Brandenburg and Loos, *Kammermusik*

—— and Helmut Loos, eds., *Beiträge zu Beethovens Kammermusik: Symposion Bonn 1984*, Munich, 1987.

—— and Martin Staehelin, 'Die "erste Fassung" von Beethovens Righini-Variationen', in *Festschrift Albi Rosenthal*, ed. Rudolf Elvers, Tutzing, 1984, pp. 43–66.

Michael E. Broyles, 'Beethoven's Sonata Op. 14 No. 1—Originally for Strings?', *JAMS* xxiii (1970), 405–19.

Cone, 'Bagatelles'
Edward Cone, 'Beethoven's Experiments in Composition: the Late Bagatelles', *BS*, ii, London, 1977, pp. 84–105.

Cooke, 'Unity'
Deryck Cooke, 'The Unity of Beethoven's Late Quartets', *MR*, xxiii (1962), 30–49.

Cooper, 'Egmont'
Barry Cooper, 'New Light on the Sketches for the Egmont Overture', in *Beethoven Studies*, ed. William Kinderman, University of Nebraska Press (forthcoming).

Cooper, 'Für Elise'
—— 'Beethoven's Revisions to *Für Elise*', *MT*, cxxv (1984), 561–3.

Cooper, 'Op. 31 No. 2'
—— 'The Origins of Beethoven's D minor Sonata Op. 31 No. 2', *ML*, lxii (1981), 261–80.

Cooper, 'Oratorio'
—— 'Beethovens' Oratorio and the Heiligenstadt Testament', *BeJ*, xi (forthcoming).

Cooper, 'Portfolio'
—— 'Beethoven's Portfolio of Bagatelles', *JRMA*, cxii (1987), 208–28.

Cooper, 'Tenth Symphony'
—— 'Newly Identified Sketches for Beethoven's Tenth Symphony', *ML*, lxvi (1985), 9–18.

Cooper, 'Waldstein'
—— 'The Evolution of the First Movement of Beethoven's "Waldstein" Sonata', *ML*, lviii (1977), 170–91.

Coren, 'Op. 28'
Daniel Coren, 'Structural Relations between Op. 28 and Op. 36', *BS*, ii, London, 1977, pp. 66–83.

Czerny, *Performance*
Carl Czerny, *On the Proper Performance of all Beethoven's Works for the Piano*, ed. Paul Badura-Skoda, Vienna, 1970.

Czesla, 'Skizzen'
Werner Czesla, 'Skizzen als Instrument der Quellenkritik', in Dahlhaus, *Bonn*, pp. 101–4.

Dahlhaus, *Bonn*
Carl Dahlhaus *et al*, eds., *Bericht über den Internationalen Musikwissenschaftlichen Kongress Bonn 1970*, Kassel, 1971.

Dahlhaus, 'Malinconia'
Carl Dahlhaus, 'La Malinconia', in *Ludwig van Beethoven*, ed. Ludwig Finscher (Wege der Forschung, cdxxviii), Darmstadt, 1983, pp. 200–11.

de la Motte, 'Scherzando'
Diether de la Motte, '"Scherzando"—für wen?', in Goldschmidt, *Bericht*, pp. 130–7.

de Roda, 'Quaderno'
 Cecile de Roda, 'Un quaderno di autografi di Beethoven del 1825', *Rivista musicale italiana*, xii (1905), 63–108, 592–622, 734–67.
Dorfmüller, *Beiträge*
 Kurt Dorfmüller, *Beiträge zur Beethoven-Bibliographie*, Munich, 1979.
William Drabkin, 'Some Relationships between the Autographs of Beethoven's Sonata in C minor, Opus 111', *Current Musicology*, xiii (1972), 38–47.
—— 'The Sketches for Beethoven's Piano Sonata in C minor, Opus 111', Ph.D. diss., Princeton University, 1977.
—— 'Beethoven's Sketches and the Thematic Process', *PRMA*, cv (1978–9), 25–36.
Fecker, *Egmont*
 Adolf Fecker, *Die Entstehung von Beethovens Musik zu Goethes Trauerspiel Egmont. Eine Abhandlung über die Skizzen* (Hamburger Beiträge zur Musikwissenschaft, xviii), Hamburg, 1978.
Fecker, 'Hannover'
 —— 'Die Beethoven-Handschriften des Kestner-Museums in Hannover', *ÖMz*, xxvi (1971), 366–79, 639–41.
Nathan L. Fishman, 'Das Skizzenbuch Beethovens aus dem Jahren 1802–03 aus der Familienarchiv Wielhorsky und die ersten Skizzen zur "Eroica"', in Dahlhaus, *Bonn*, pp. 104–7.
Fishman, 'Wielhorsky'
 —— 'Das Moskauer Skizzenbuch Beethovens aus dem Archiv von M. J. Wielhorsky', in Dorfmüller, *Beiträge*, pp. 61–7.
Fishman ed., *Wielhorsky*
 —— ed., *Kniga eskizov Beethovena za 1802–1803 gody*, 3 vols. ('Wielhorsky' Sketchbook: fac., transcription, and commentary), Moscow, 1962.
Allen Forte, *The Compositional Matrix*, New York, 1961.
Frimmel, *Handbuch*
 Theodor Frimmel, *Beethoven-Handbuch*, 2 vols., Leipzig, 1926.
Goldschmidt, *Bericht*
 Harry Goldschmidt, Karl-Heinz Köhler, and Konrad Niemann, eds., *Bericht über den Internationalen Beethoven-Kongress 20. bis 23. März 1977 in Berlin*, Leipzig, 1978.
Goldschmidt, *Unsterbliche*
 Harry Goldschmidt, *Um die unsterbliche Geliebte: ein Bestandsaufnahme*, Leipzig, 1977.
Gossett, 'Marzelline'
 Philip Gossett, 'The Arias of Marzelline: Beethoven as a Composer of Opera', *BeJ*, x (1978–81), 141–83.
Gossett, 'Sixth Symphony'
 —— 'Beethoven's Sixth Symphony: Sketches for the Fist Movement', *JAMS*, xxvii (1974), 248–84.
Graf, *Beethoven*
 Max Graf, *From Beethoven to Shostakovich: The Psychology of the Composing Process*, New York, 1947.
Peter Gülke, *Zur Neuausgabe der Sinfonie Nr. 5 von Ludwig van Beethoven: Werk und Edition*, Leipzig, 1978.
Hanson, 'Incomes'
 Alice M. Hanson, 'Incomes and Outgoings in the Vienna of Beethoven and

Schubert', *ML*, lxiv (1983), 173–82.

Erich Hertzmann, 'The Newly Discovered Autograph of Beethoven's Rondo a capriccio, Op. 129', *MQ*, xxxii (1946), 171–95.

Hess ed., *Cadenzas*

    Willy Hess, ed., *Ludwig van Beethoven, Sämtliche Kadenzen: The Complete Cadenzas* (fac. edn.), Zurich, 1979.

Hess ed., *SGA*

—— ed., *Ludwig van Beethoven, Supplement zur Gesamtausgabe*, 14 vols., Wiesbaden, 1959–71.

Hess, *Verzeichnis*

—— *Verzeichnis der nicht in der Gesamtausgabe veröffentlichten Werke Ludwig van Beethovens*, Wiesbaden, 1957.

Standley Howell, 'Beethoven's Maelzel Canon: Another Schindler Forgery?', *MT*, cxx (1979), 987–90.

Kathryn John, 'Das Allegretto-Thema in Op. 93, auf seine Skizzen befragt', in *Zu Beethoven*, ii, ed. Harry Goldschmidt, Berlin, 1984, pp. 172–84.

Douglas Johnson, 'Beethoven's Scholars and Beethoven's Sketches', *NCM* ii (1978–9), 3–17 (see also ibid., pp. 270–9).

—— 'Beethoven's Sketches for the Scherzo of the Quartet Op. 18 No. 6', *JAMS*, xxiii (1970), 385–404.

Johnson, 'Decisive'

—— '1794–95: Decisive Years in Beethoven's Early Development', *BS*, iii, Cambridge, 1982, pp. 1–28.

Johnson, *Fischhof*

—— *Beethoven's Early Sketches in the 'Fischhof Miscellany': Berlin Autograph 28*, 2 vols., Ann Arbor, 1980.

—— 'Music for Prague and Berlin: Beethoven's Concert Tour of 1796', in Winter and Carr, *Detroit* pp. 24–40.

—— 'The Artaria Collection of Beethoven Manuscripts: A New Source', *BS*, i, London, 1974, pp. 174–236.

—— and Alan Tyson, 'Reconstructing Beethoven's Sketchbooks', *JAMS*, xxv (1972), 137–56.

Oswald Jonas, 'Bemerkungen zu Beethovens Op. 96', *AcM*, xxxvii (1965), 87–9.

—— 'An Unknown Sketch by Beethoven', *MQ*, xxvi (1940), 186–91.

JTW

    Douglas Johnson, Alan Tyson, and Robert Winter, *The Beethoven Sketchbooks: History, Reconstruction, Inventory* ed. Douglas Johnson, Oxford, 1985.

Kerman, 'British Museum'

    Joseph Kerman, 'Beethoven's Sketchbooks in the British Museum', *PRMA*, xciii (1966–7), 77–96.

Kerman, 'Early'

—— 'Beethoven's Early Sketches', *MQ*, lvi (1970), 515–38 (reprinted in Lang, *Creative* pp. 13–36).

Kerman, 'Geliebte'

—— 'An die ferne Geliebte', *BS* i, London, 1974, 123–57.

Kerman ed., *Miscellany*

—— ed., *Ludwig van Beethoven: Autograph Miscellany from circa 1786 to 1799*, 2 vols. (fac. and transcription), London, 1970.

KH

Georg Kinsky (completed by Hans Halm), *Das Werk Beethovens*, Munich, 1955.

Kinderman, *Diabelli*

William Kinderman, *Beethoven's 'Diabelli' Variations*, Oxford, 1987.

Kirkendale, '*Missa*'

Warren Kirkendale, 'New Roads to Old Ideas in Beethoven's *Missa solemnis*', *MQ*, lvi (1970), 665–701 (repr. in Lang, *Creative*, pp. 163–99).

Klein, *Autographe*

Hans-Günter Klein, *Ludwig van Beethoven: Autographe und Abschriften* (Staatsbibliothek Preussischer Kulturbesitz: Kataloge der Musikabteilung, ed. Rudolf Elvers, I/2), Berlin, 1975.

Klimowitzki, 'Autograph'

Abraham Klimowitzki, 'Autograph und Schaffensprozess: Zur Erkenntnis der Kompositionstechnik Beethovens', in *Zu Beethoven*, ed. Harry Goldschmidt, Berlin, 1979, pp. 149–66.

Knapp, 'Mass in C'

J. Merrill Knapp, 'Beethoven's Mass in C major, Op. 86', in Lockwood and Benjamin, *Essays*, pp. 199–216.

Koch, *Versuch*

Heinrich Christoph Koch, *Versuch einer Anleitung zur Composition,* 3 vols., Rudolstadt, 1782, repr. Hildesheim, 1969.

Shin-Augustinus Kojima, 'Die Solovioline-Fassungen und -Varianten von Beethovens Violinkonzert Op. 61—ihre Entstehung und Bedeutung', *BeJ*, viii (1971–2), 97–145.

Richarch Kramer, 'Ambiguities in *La Malinconia*: What the Sketches Say', *BS*, iii, Cambridge, 1982, pp. 29–46.

Kramer, 'Concertante'

—— 'An Unfinished Concertante of 1802', *BS*, ii, London, 1977, pp. 33–65.

—— '"Das Organische der Fuge": On the Autograph of Beethoven's Quartet in F major, Opus 59 No. 1', in Wolff, *Quartets*, pp. 223–65.

Kramer, 'Graun'

—— 'Beethoven and Carl Heinrich Graun', *BS*, i, London, 1974, pp. 18–44.

—— 'Notes to Beethoven's Education', *JAMS*, xxviii (1975), 72–101.

Kramer, 'Op. 30'

—— 'The Sketches for Beethoven's Violin Sonatas, Op. 30', Ph. D. diss., Princeton University, 1974.

Klaus Kropfinger, 'Das gespaltene Werk—Beethovens Streichquartett Op. 130/133', in Brandenburg and Loos, *Kammermusik*, pp. 296–335.

Küthen, *Klavierkonzerte I*

Hans-Werner Küthen, *Klavierkonzerte I: Kritischer Bericht* (Beethoven Werke, III/2), Munich, 1984.

Küthen, 'Op. 19'

—— 'Probleme der Chronologie in die Skizzen und Autographe zu Beethovens Klavierkonzert Op. 19', *BeJ*, ix (1973–77), 263–92.

Küthen, 'Wellington'

—— 'Neue Aspekte zur Entstehung von *Wellingtons Sieg*', *BeJ*, viii (1971–2), 73–92.

Christa Landon and Alexander Weinmann, 'Beethovens Sonate Op. 111: Eigenhändiges Korrekturexemplar der Wiener Ausgabe von Cappi & Diabelli. Eine neu ausgefundene Quelle', *FAM*, xxvi (1979), 281–94.

Lang, *Creative*

Paul Henry Lang, ed., *The Creative World of Beethoven,* New York, 1971 (reprint of *MQ*, lvi (1970), 515–793, here numbered as pp. 13–291).

Lester, '*Missa*'

Joel Lester, 'Revisions in the Autograph of the *Missa solemnis Kyrie*', *JAMS*, xxiii (1970), 420–38.

Levy, *Choices*

Janet Levy, *Beethoven's Compositional Choices: The Two Versions of Opus 18, No. 1, First Movement*, Philadelphia, 1982.

Lewis Lockwood, 'Beethoven and the Problem of Closure: Some Examples from the Middle-period Chamber Music', in Brandenburg and Loos, Kammermusik, pp. 254–72.

Lockwood, 'Definition'

—— 'On Beethoven's Sketches and Autographs: Some Problems of Definition and Interpretation', *AcM*, xlii (1970), 32–47.

Lockwood, 'Earliest'

—— 'Beethoven's Earliest Sketches for the *Eroica* Symphony', *MQ*, lxvii (1981), 457–78.

—— '"Eroica" Perspectives: Strategy and Design in the First Movement', *BS*, iii, Cambridge, 1982, pp. 85–105.

Lockwood, 'Op. 69'

—— 'The Autograph of the First Movement of Beethoven's Sonata for Violoncello and Pianoforte, Opus 69', *The Music Forum*, ii (1970), 1–109.

Lockwood, '*Sehnsucht*'

—— 'Beethoven's Sketches for *Sehnsucht* (WoO 146)', *BS*, i, London, 1974, pp. 97–122.

Lockwood, 'Unfinished'

—— 'Beethoven's Unfinished Piano Conceto of 1815: Sources and Problems', *MQ*, lvi (1970), 624–46 (repr. in Lang, *Creative*, pp. 122–44).

Lockwood and Benjamin, *Essays*

—— and Phyllis Benjamin, eds., *Beethoven Essays: Studies in Honor of Elliot Forbes*, Cambridge, Mass., 1984.

Lutes, 'Re-uses'

Leilani Kathryn Lutes, 'Beethoven's Re-uses of his own Compositions, 1782–1826', Ph.D. diss., University of Southern California, 1975.

Alfred Mann, 'Beethoven's Contrapuntal Studies with Haydn', *MQ*, lvi (1970), 711–26 (repr. in Lang, *Creative*, pp. 209–24).

Nicholas Marston, 'Schenker and Forte Reconsidered: Beethoven's Sketches for the Piano sonata in E, Op. 109', *NCM*, x (1986–7), 24–42.

William Meredith, 'Beethoven's Creativity', *The Beethoven Newsletter*, i (1986), 25–8, 37–44; ii (1987), 1, 8–12.

—— 'The Origins of Beethoven's Op. 109', *MT*, cxxvi (1985), 713–6.

—— 'The Sources for Beethoven's Piano Sonata in E major, Opus 109', Ph.D. diss., University of North Carolina at Chapel Hill, 1985.

Paul Mies, 'Ein Menuett von L. van Beethoven für Streichquartett', *BeJ*, v (1961–4), 85–6.

Mies, *Sketches*
—— *Beethoven's Sketches*, London, 1929.
Mikulicz ed., *Notierungsbuch*
Karl Lothar Mikulicz, ed., *Ein Notierungsbuch von Beethoven aus dem Besitze der Preussischen Staatsbibliothek zu Berlin*, Leipzig, 1927 (repr. Hildesheim and New York, 1972).
Ludwig Misch, *Neue Beethoven-Studien und andere Theme*, Munich and Duisburg, 1967.
Arnold Münster, *Studien zu Beethovens Diabelli-Variationen*, Munich, 1982.
N-I
Gustav Nottebohm, *Beethoveniana*, Leipzig, 1872 (repr. New York, 1970).
N-II
—— *Zweite Beethoveniana*, Leipzig, 1887 (repr. New York, 1970).
N-1803
—— *Ein Skizzenbuch von Beethoven aus dem Jahre 1803*, Leipzig, 1880 (repr. New York, 1970).
—— *Beethoven's Studien*, Leipzig and Winterthur, 1873.
Nottebohm, *Skizzenbuch*
—— *Ein Skizzenbuch von Beethoven*, Leipzig, 1865 (repr. New York, 1970).
Emil Platen, 'Eine Frühfassung zum ersten Satz des Streichquartetts Op. 131 von Beethoven', *BeJ*, x (1978–81), 277–304.
Réti, *Sonatas*
Rudolph Réti, *Thematic Patterns in Sonatas of Beethoven*, London, 1965.
Christopher Reynolds, 'Ends and Means in the Second Finale to Beethoven's Op. 30, No. 1', in Lockwood and Benjamin, *Essays*, pp. 127–45.
Reynolds, 'Op. 35'
—— 'Beethoven's Sketches for the Variations in E flat, Op. 35', *BS*, iii, Cambridge, 1982, pp. 47–84.
Benito V. Rivera, 'Rhythmic Organisation in Beethoven's Seventh Symphony: A Study of Cancelled Measures in the Autograph', *NCM*, vi (1982–3), 241–51.
Romain Rolland, *Beethoven the Creator*, tr. Ernest Newman, 2nd edn., New York, 1964.
Rosen, *Classical*
Charles Rosen, *The Classical Style: Haydn, Mozart, Beethoven*, London, 1971.
Schindler/MacArdle, *Beethoven*
Felix Anton Schindler, *Beethoven as I Knew him*, tr. Constance S. Jolly, ed. Donald MacArdle, London, 1966.
Schmidt, SBH
Hans Schmidt, 'Die Beethovenhandschriften des Beethovenhauses in Bonn', *BeJ*, vii (1969–70), pp. vii–xxiv, 1–443.
Schmidt, SV
—— 'Verzeichnis der Skizzen Beethovens', *BeJ*, vi (1965–8), 7–128.
Schmidt-Görg ed., *Diabelli*
Joseph Schmidt-Görg, ed., *Ein Skizzenbuch zu den Diabelli-Variationen und zur Missa solemnis*, 2 vols. (transcription and fac. of SV 154), Bonn, 1968–72.
—— 'Die Wasserzeichen in Beethovens Notenpapieren', in Dorfmüller, *Beiträge*, pp. 167–95.
Schmidt-Görg, 'Missa'
—— 'Missa solemnis. Beethoven in seinem Werk', in Dahlhaus, *Bonn*, pp. 13–25.

Schmidt-Görg ed., *Missa solemnis i*
—— ed., *Drei Skizzenbücher zur Missa solemnis: i. Ein Skizzenbuch aus den Jahren 1819–20*, 2 vols. (transcription and fac.), Bonn, 1952–68.
Schmidt-Görg ed., *Missa solemnis ii*
—— ed., *Drei Skizzenbücher zur Missa solemnis: ii. Ein Skizzenbuch zum Credo*, 2 vols. (fac. and transcription), Bonn, 1968–70.
Schmidt-Görg ed., *Missa solemnis iii*
—— ed., *Drei Skizzenbücher zur Missa solemnis: iii. Ein Skizzenbuch zum Benedictus und zum Agnus Dei*, 2 vols. (fac. and transcription), Bonn, 1968–70.
Schmitz, *Unbekannte*
Arnold Schmitz, *Beethoven: Unbekannte Skizzen und Entwürfe* (Veröffentlichungen des Beethovenhauses in Bonn, iii), Bonn, 1924.
Manfred Schuler, 'Zwei unbekannte "Fidelio"-Partiturabschriften aus dem Jahre 1814', *Archiv für Musikwissenschaft*, xxxix (1982), 151–67.
Boris Schwarz, 'A little-known Beethoven Sketch in Moscow', *MQ*, lvi (1970), 539–50 (repr. in Lang, *Creative*, pp. 37–48).
—— 'Beethoveniana in Soviet Russia', *MQ*, xlvii (1961), 4–21.
—— 'More Beethoveniana in Soviet Russia', *MQ*, xlix (1963), 143–9.
John S. Shedlock, 'Beethoven's Sketch Books', *MT*, xxxiii (1892), 331–4, 394–7, 461–5, 523–5, 589–92, 649–52, 717; xxxiv (1893), 14–16, 530–2; xxxv (1894), 13–16, 449–52, 596–600; l (1909), 712–4.
Solomon *Beethoven*
Maynard Solomon, *Beethoven*, New York, 1977.
—— 'Beethoven and Schiller', in Winter and Carr, *Detroit*, pp. 162–75.
—— 'Beethoven's Ninth Symphony: A Search for Order', *NCM*, x (1986–7), 3–23.
Solomon, 'Faith'
—— 'Beethoven: the Quest for Faith', *BeJ*, x (1978–81), 101–19.
Solomon, 'Invention'
—— 'On Beethoven's Creative Process: a Two-part Invention', *ML*, lxi (1980), 272–83.
Solomon, 'Periods'
—— 'The Creative Periods of Beethoven', *MR*, xxxiv (1973), 30–8.
Solomon, 'Tagebuch'
—— 'Beethoven's Tagebuch of 1812–1818', *BS*, iii, Cambridge, 1982, pp. 193–288.
Stadlen, 'Metronome'
Peter Stadlen, 'Beethoven and the Metronome', *Soundings*, ix (1982), 38–73.
Stadlen, 'Possibilities'
—— 'Possibilities of an Aesthetic Evaluation of Beethoven's Sketches', in Dahlhaus, *Bonn*, pp. 111–17.
Staehelin, 'Quintet'
Martin Staehelin, 'Another Approach to Beethoven's Last Quartet Oeuvre: The Unfinished String Quintet of 1826/27', in Wolff, *Quartets*, pp. 302–23.
TDR
Alexander Wheelock Thayer (rev. Hermann Deiters and Hugo Riemann), *Ludwig van Beethovens Leben*, 5 vols., Leipzig, 1907–23.
TF
Elliot Forbes, ed., *Thayer's Life of Beethoven*, 2nd edn., Princeton, 1967.

Timbrell, 'Op. 111'
Charles Timbrell, 'Notes on the Sources of Beethoven's Op. 111', *ML*, lviii (1977), 204–15.
Alan Tyson, 'A Reconstruction of the Pastoral Symphony Sketchbook (Add. 31766)', *BS*, i, London, 1974, pp. 67–96.
—— 'Beethoven's Home-made Sketchbook of 1807–1808', *BeJ*, x (1978–81), 185–200.
—— ed., *Beethoven Studies*, i, London, 1974; ii, London, 1977; iii, Cambridge, 1982.
Tyson, '*Christus*'
—— 'The 1803 Version of Beethoven's *Christus am Oelberge*', *MQ*, lvi (1970), 551–84 (repr. in Lang, *Creative*, pp. 49–82).
Tyson, 'Copyists'
—— 'Notes on Five of Beethoven's Copyists', *JAMS*, xxiii (1970), 439–71.
—— 'Das Leonoreskizzenbuch (Mendelssohn 15): Probleme der Rekonstruction und Chronologie', *BeJ*, ix (1973–7), 469–500.
Tyson, 'First Leonore'
—— 'The Problem of Beethoven's "First" Leonore Overture', *JAMS*, xxviii (1975), 292–334.
Tyson, 'Heroic'
—— 'Beethoven's Heroic Phase', *MT*, cx (1969), 139–41.
Tyson, 'Op. 70 No. 1'
—— 'Stages in the Composition of Beethoven's Piano Trio Op. 70, No. 1', *PRMA*, xcvii (1970–1), 1–19.
Tyson, 'Op. 104'
—— 'The Authors of the Op. 104 String Quintet', *BS*, i, London, 1974, pp. 158–73.
Tyson, 'Op. 119'
—— 'The First Edition of Beethoven's Op. 119 Bagatelles', *MQ*, xlix (1963), 331–8.
Tyson, 'Razumovsky'
—— 'The "Razumovsky" Quartets: Some Aspects of the Sources', *BS*, iii, Cambridge, 1982, 107–40.
Tyson, 'Steiner'
—— 'Beethoven in Steiner's Shop', *MR*, xxiii (1962), 119–27.
—— *The Authentic English Editions of Beethoven*, London, 1963.
Tyson, 'Violin'
—— 'The Textual Problems of Beethoven's Violin Concerto', *MQ*, liii (1967), 482–502.
—— 'Yet another "Leonore" Overture?', *ML*, lviii (1977), 192–204.
Max Unger, *Eine Schweizer Beethovensammlung: Katalog*, Zurich, 1939.
Unger, *Handschrift*
—— *Beethovens Handschrift* (Veröffentlichungen des Beethovenhauses in Bonn, iv), Bonn, 1926.
Unger, 'Workshop'
—— 'From Beethoven's Workshop', *MQ*, xxiv (1938), 323–40.
Wilhelm Virneisel, 'Aus Beethovens Skizzenbuch zum Streichquintett Op. 29', *Zeitschrift für Musik*, cxiii (1952), 142–6.
—— ed., *Beethoven: Ein Skizzenbuch zu Streichquartetten aus Op. 18, SV 46*, 2 vols. (fac.

and transcription), Bonn, 1972–4.

—— 'Zu Beethovens Skizzen und Entwürfen', in *Studien zur Musikgeschichte des Rheinlandes: Festschrift zum 80. Geburtstag von Ludwig Schiedermair,* Cologne, 1956, pp. 150–4.

Rachel Wade, 'Beethoven's Eroica Sketchbook', *FAM,* xxiv (1977), 254–89.

James Webster, 'Traditional Elements in Beethoven's Middle-Period String Quartets', in Winter and Carr, *Detroit,* pp. 94–133.

Wegeler and Ries, *Beethoven*
Franz Wegeler and Ferdinand Ries, *Remembering Beethoven* (tr. Frederick Noonan from *Biographische Notizen über Ludwig van Beethoven,* 1838–45), London, 1988.

Wehnert, 'Zum positionellen'
Martin Wehnert, 'Zum positionellen Aspekt des Thematischen bei Beethoven', in Goldschmidt, *Bericht,* pp. 335–41.

Dagmar Weise, ed., *Beethoven: Ein Skizzenbuch zur Chorphantasie op. 80 und zu anderen Werken* (transcription of SV 47), Bonn, 1957.

—— ed., *Beethoven: Ein Skizzenbuch zur Pastoralsymphonie Op. 68 und zu den Trios Op. 70, 1 und 2* (transcription of SV 188), Bonn, 1961.

—— 'Zum Faksimiledruck von Beethovens Waldsteinsonate', *BeJ,* ii (1955–6), 102–11.

Westphal, *Einfall*
Kurt Westphal, *Vom Einfall zur Symphonie: Einblick in Beethovens Schaffensweise,* Berlin, 1965.

Winter, 'Ode'
Robert Winter, 'The Sketches for the "Ode to Joy"', in Winter and Carr, *Detroit,* pp. 176–214.

Winter, *Op. 131*
—— *Compositional Origins of Beethoven's String Quartet in C sharp minor, Op. 131,* Ann Arbor, 1982.

Winter, 'Plans'
—— 'Plans for the Structure of the String Quartet in C sharp minor, Op. 131', *BS,* ii, London, 1977, pp. 106–37.

—— 'Reconstructing Riddles: The Sources for Beethoven's *Missa solemnis*', in Lockwood and Benjamin, *Essays,* pp. 217–50.

Winter, 'Symphonie'
—— 'Noch einmal: Wo sind Beethovens Skizzen zur zehnten Symphonie?', *BeJ,* ix (1973–7), 531–52.

Winter and Carr, *Detroit*
—— and Bruce Carr, eds., *Beethoven, Performers, and Critics: The International Beethoven Congress Detroit 1977,* Detroit, 1980.

Wolff, *Quartets*
Christoph Wolff, ed., *The String Quartets of Haydn, Mozart, and Beethoven: Studies of the Autograph Manuscripts,* (Isham Library Papers, iii), Cambridge, Mass., 1980.

INDEX OF SKETCH SOURCES

Sketchbooks with commonly used names are listed first, with a cross-reference to their SV number; all the sources are then listed by their SV number.

Berlin, Deutsche Staatsbibliothek (DSB) and Staatsbibliothek Preussischer Kulturbesitz Musikabteilung (SPK); Kraków, Biblioteka Jagiellońska (BJ)

Bonn, Beethoven-Archiv

INDEX OF WORKS

GENERAL INDEX